Alan Burt

The Remarkable Life of
Victoria Drummond
Marine Engineer

The Remarkable Life of

Victoria Drummond

Marine Engineer

Cherry Drummond

Cherry Drummond
14t October 1994

The Institute of Marine Engineers

Published by The Institute of Marine Engineers
The Memorial Building
76 Mark Lane
London
EC3R 7JN

First published 14th October 1994

© 1994 The Institute of Marine Engineers

ISBN 0-907206-54-9

A catalogue record for this publication is available from the British Library

Printed in the United Kingdom by Burgess Science Press

Contents

Chapter One

Scottish Sundays

When I was a very little girl I was blissfully happy. A daisy chain was as valuable to me as the jewelled pendant my godmother had given me at my christening. But inside me I always had a feeling of being different from my sisters because my godmother was Queen Victoria.

As I grew older I entered the kingdom of imagination. All my early games were imaginary and my dolls and pets accompanied me into this world of fantasy. The white kitten was a fairy and when tactfully persuaded would wear a gold paper crown when asleep in the sun.

We had Andrew Lang's fairy books illustrated in colour and a big dolls' house made by Mr Tyrie, the local carpenter. Mummy painted and decorated it and filled the rooms with miniature furniture which she made for us. I can see our dolls' house now, its façade painted in warm stone tones, a skilfully traced pink climbing rose sketched in oil paint covering the three storey frontage. It contained five rooms and a veranda, and was built close to the sea, the nursery carpet.

This carpet was a greenish blue Brussels and had come from the house my great-grandfather, Admiral Sir Adam Drummond, rented in Brussels in the 1820s. It was very worn in places, but the white threads became foam breaking on the reefs where ships were wrecked. Fortunately the coast guard was near: the kitten became a white horse pulling the cardboard lifeboat which put to sea to assist a sailing boat in danger of shipwreck on the nursery table legs. There was a village built along the sea shore, constructed of cardboard shoe boxes and a lot of imagination. The only real building, so to speak, was a school, an imposing structure with its steep roof curving beneath the eaves and high set windows. It was made of white wood and the walls were built of wooden pieces notched at the ends so that they fitted perfectly together. The whole packed neatly into a flat wooden box. This house was made in Russia, for ships often came to Dundee from Russia with cases of brightly coloured wooden toys. Years later when I was in Siberian Russia, I realised that the roof was so steep to let the snow slide off and the windows were built high in the walls to be above the snow level.

In those happy, sunny days life was only measured by Sunday and the start of a new week. On Saturday all toys had to be put neatly away in the toy cupboard and the fairy books put back on the nursery bookshelf. Only Sunday books could be looked at till Monday morning.

I shall never forget as a child waking up to the quiet of a Scottish Sunday morning—no sound of grass being scythed or the busy plying of hone on blades being sharpened, no sound from the distant high road, not even the rumble of cart wheels; only perhaps a dog barking far away, or near at hand the noise of pigeons' wings as they flew to and from the big dovecote in the stable yard or cooed on the roof and the rattle of tin milk pails being put in the dairy after 7 o'clock milking. This was Sunday morning and only work of necessity could be done today.

Before breakfast we repeated verses we had learned in the week and, when old enough, the Collect for the day. After breakfast we were allowed to play with a Noah's Ark. Sunday was the only day we might play with it and it was the only toy we might play with on Sunday. One Sunday we lined up the animals two by two going into the ark and the next Sunday we lined them up coming out. There is really not much more one can do with a Noah's Ark except the departure of the raven or the return of the dove. We used to tie a bit of cotton to the dove to assist its flight to the ark with a green jasmine leaf we had picked from the great white jasmine which grew outside the dining room window and scented the whole house.

Noah's Ark animals gave one a very dim idea of the real size of animals. I remember Billy Cecil, a cousin who was at Eton, coming home for Christmas holidays when we were staying at Didlington, my mother's old home in Norfolk, with a cage done up in brown paper. What an excitement when the paper was removed from the cage on the nursery table and I saw a cream coloured animal with bright pink eyes and a long tail. The length of his tail did not register with me, but I was told his name was Ivory and he liked bread and milk.

Next morning I said, "I saw Ivory the polar bear last night."

Polar bear! My idea of the relative size of polar bears derived from Noah's Ark animals and I was bitterly disappointed when told Ivory was a white rat!

After we had played with the Noah's Ark and put it away, we drove to church in the pony trap, sometimes the Church of Scotland in Errol, sometimes the Episcopal Church in Glencarse. In summer I wore a white picot frock, a large leghorn straw hat, a red coral necklace, white socks and bronze shoes. I was three when I first went to church. The old-fashioned pews were so high it was not possible to see out, but as I grew I could see over the edge of the book board by standing on a footstool. From there I could see the brilliantly coloured glass of the large west window designed by my grandfather, Captain John Murray Drummond, and the pulpit and the minister, Dr Graham, in his black gown with white bands and coloured hood. I could see the red velvet cushion made from an evening dress of my great-grandmother, Lady Charlotte Drummond, whose godfather was King George III and whose godmother was Queen Charlotte. There were red tassels hanging down from the cushion on which the great Bible was placed by the minister's man, who preceded the minister from the vestry carrying the Bible, then stood aside till the minister had mounted the pulpit stairs when he solemnly shut the door; we knew that Dr Graham had been shut into the pulpit for a very long time—an hour and 40 minutes at least. The pews were high and straight backed and it was not possible to lean back because of one's leghorn hat in summer and one's white beaver hat in winter.

In those days there was no organ and the starting note was given to the choir by the preceptor's tuning fork. I always listened for this "ting". The other noise which we didn't have to listen for because it was so loud, was when the two metal collection plates were emptied of their load of pennies and half-pennies and the total amount of the collection was poured out. As children we used to call it the Great Crash!

Mummy gave us a sweetie to suck quietly during the sermon and Papa handed us a book illustrated with steel engravings of the Masters. As a boy he had been allowed to look at this book during the very long discourses of Principal Caird or Dean Stanley. At the end of the sermon and last prayer the whole congregation stood motionless for the blessing, but the moment the minister's hand dropped, there was a great helter-skelter dash out, made more surprising by the dead silence during the sermon. One could hear a pin fall in the sermon or the prayers, but now this sudden rush, the noise of feet on the wooden gallery floor and steps, the banging of every pew door made a din so terrific and appalling, as the whole church emptied itself within seconds into the open air and the sound of the last tackety boot descending the stone gallery stairs died away.

We were not allowed to join in this sudden stampede or dash out with the throng, much as we would have loved to do, but instead remained quietly till the noise had abated and the exodus was over.

Provost Smythe, a cousin who conducted the service one Sunday, said to Mummy, "How can you account for this terribly noisy departure of the congregation?"

But no one could and nothing could stop it.

The view was lovely from the church door. To the north the distant Sidlaw hills with the Roman camp; to the east the Tay flowing away to

Dundee and the sea; to the south the hills of Fife, Norman Law and the Lomonds; and to the west the county town of Perth. Papa and Mummy talked to various friends while we looked at the stone recumbent figure from the tomb of a Crusader lying with his feet crossed. Fragments of their conversation floated to us...

"It's good weather for the hay..."

"Aye, Captain, but the neeps need rain." The answer was never hopeful, always qualifying.

On Sundays before lunch we had catechism. It always seemed strange to me that potatoes could not be peeled on Sunday but that one could take baked potatoes out of their jackets. I remember the bowl of cold water in which peeled potatoes floated in the scullery on Saturday night and the bowl with all the diced vegetables, carrots, turnips and green peas ready for the Sunday hodge potch the next day.

After lunch we had afternoon prayers before we were old enough to attend afternoon Sunday School. Prayers consisted of the whole of evensong without hymns—it seemed immensely long—and the white muslin curtains fluttered in the warm afternoon breeze while the sunbeams danced through the open windows, calling us to come and dance with them among the sweet scented flowers of the old world garden.

But this was Sunday. We might not even run on Sunday but had to walk sedately and dancing was absolutely taboo. The only time we were allowed to run was in a traditional race from the front door to the old oak tree which stood on a green mound opposite. My father and his father before him had done the same as children. We received no prize, only the honour and glory of being the first to touch the oak.

My mind wandered and I thought of the strawberries in the garden and the chocolate we might each have when prayers were over. My sister Jean always read the first lesson, but I had to read the second lesson, so I stood up in my rosebud muslin frock which I wore on Sunday afternoons, my socks not so white and pristine as when I had started for church. If the lesson was a long one I used to cut bits out of it when I didn't think anyone would notice.

Once, when a clergyman great-uncle was staying, he said quietly to me afterwards, "Victoria, I never knew Saint Paul said so little."

"Of course, I never clip Saint Paul's shipwreck and the serpent," I said.

He smiled. He was awfully nice and never gave me away.

Prayers over and out into the garden, the hot summer air heavy with the scent of flowers and the drone of a multitude of bees working busily in the cream foam of blossom in the lime tree planted by my great-great-great-grandmother, Bethia Drummond, in the early 1700s. The seed had come from Holland where my ancestors went by sea from Dundee to attend the University of Leiden. The Dutch chest in which they took their books and clothes to Holland stood in the hall. Her daughter-in-law, Mrs Colin Drummond, measured this tree in the mid 18th century by putting her handkerchief round the stem. From the seed of this lime tree, Mummy grew a seedling which we also used to measure with our handkerchiefs.

On some Sundays instead of going to church in Errol we would drive to the Episcopal Church in Glencarse, a stone built village about 4 or 5 miles away. The Church was large without galleries and stood back from the road surrounded by grass. The cane chairs with space between the rows were far more luxurious than the narrow straight backed pews of the established church, but even with this comfort the three psalms seemed a long time to stand and the litany an equally long time to kneel.

But there were advantages. I could see out through the wide open door in summer, away over the quiet road to the undisturbed railway station and beyond to the sleeping cattle in the fields. Sometimes a wasp or bee would fly in through the open door, buzz round the hats of the congregation, pick out the ones heavily trimmed with artificial flowers and after being disappointed in its search for honey would become angry and buzz out. Once a member of the congregation made an effort to open one of the windows wider to assist the exodus of the bees. The clergyman, who had just finished reading the second lesson, solemnly intoned, "Here endeth the Second Lesson. You will find the hooker in the porch."

The veiled advice was promptly followed and the window pulled down.

After the service was over it was always fun to meet our Drummond-Hay cousins whose home, Seggieden, was on the River Tay about 2 miles away. They had salmon fishing rights and would often arrange for us to come over and spend the day with them. They always gave us sweeties for the long drive home after church in the carriage.

It always seemed strange wearing shoes and socks on Sunday. Every other day of the week we ran barefooted during summer and our feet became so hard that we could run on the rough gravel paths without feeling the stones.

On Sunday afternoons we always walked round the large brick walled kitchen garden. The high walls had been built by my great-great-uncle, Robert Drummond, a captain in the East India Company. The bottom walls were lined with a heating device and hot air passed through pipes set in them to ripen the fruit early. He also built the large dovecote that stood in the centre of the cobbled expanse of the stable yard, octagonal in shape with a weathervane on top. The weathervane was a model of his ship, the *General Elliot*. Sometimes as a great treat we were allowed to crawl under the strawberry nets on the hot dry straw and eat some deliciously sweet fruit from under the dark green leaves, or wander in and out of the prickly gooseberry bushes nibbling on the hairy berries. There was an abundance of wall fruit—peaches, nectarines, apricots—and we might be given a taste of one cut with a dessert knife, but stoned fruits were supposed to be bad for children. Why I never knew. Could it have been grown-up propaganda?

When we were a little older, instead of afternoon prayers we went down to Sunday school, which was held at Shipbriggs where Thomas Hood, the poet, lived and described in his poem *The House Where I Was Born*. The Sunday school was held next to the curling bothy, which Mummy had done up for the purpose, having a cement floor laid and putting in wooden benches and pictures on the walls. About 50 or 60 children attended. My nanny, Nana Watt, was superintendent and there were four classes, the teachers giving up their Sunday afternoons to walk over and teach.

The Sunday school was under the auspices of the Church of Scotland and the minister used to visit it. In summer he would conduct an open air service on the green outside. There was an open fronted cart shed that could be retreated to if wet, but I can't remember it raining. The fine swing of the Paraphrases and the Old Hundredth were impressed on my mind as the clear voices of children and the deeper tones of farm workers soared over the still summer air scented with hay and wild flowers, while the swallows flew midway between earth and heaven.

When the children left Sunday school at fourteen each received a Bible in which Mummy had written three texts. The minister presented the Bibles and the yearly prizes of books, and then the Sunday school was closed for the worst two months of winter. The children of that little Sunday school scattered all over the world and I sometimes met them in my travels.

I remember once when my sister Jean and I were told to walk down to Sunday school we started in plenty of time, our hymn books in our hands. It was a lovely summer Sunday, but suddenly a midsummer madness possessed us and we thought we would spent a few minutes, just a very few minutes, at the ditch catching a minnow or two in a jam jar. We planned to leave the jar in the grass and pick it up on our way home from Sunday school, but the golden minutes slipped by as we climbed up and down the steep bank peering into the water in search of minnows. We were nearly hidden in the long grass and tangles of purple vetch, nearly hidden, but unfortunately not quite.

A voice called: "Hullo! What are you doing there?"

We looked up and saw Cousin Alice and Cousin Lucy Drummond-Hay bicycling to have tea with my Aunt Ayia at the Mains of Megginch.

We struggled out of the long grass, our white frocks with ominous green stains and our socks bespattered with mud. Our straw hats were smudged with mud where small hands had pushed them back from hot faces.

"We are going to Sunday school," we explained.

"And what time is Sunday school?" they asked.

"Three o'clock," we replied.

"Well," they said rather dryly, "it's ten minutes to four. You'd better hurry up."

We knew we could not appear like that even if we had not been so late, so we clutched our precious jar with the few minnows we had managed to catch and scattered for home up the long shady path smelling of honeysuckle, over the fields, through buttercups and waist high red sorrel.

Later, Nana said we couldn't be trusted, which was the most awful thing that could be said. Papa was in waiting on the Queen and Mummy was in London. My imagination ran riot and I even wondered if Papa might hear from our cousins and tell the Queen. Would she say she couldn't be godmother any more to a child who couldn't be trusted?

"Can one's godmother ever stop being godmother if one is naughty?" I asked Nana.

"Of course not. When you're older you'll understand more about it."

I felt reassured and almost happy and then Nana with her perception of the child's mind said, 'I don't want to hear any more about this afternoon. All you can do now is to show how good you can be and that you can be trusted.'

When we next met Aunt Ayia she said, "Choose a better time for catching minnows!"

We had dry bread for tea. I always pretended I liked dry bread as I had an idea that if it was thought I enjoyed it and didn't like cake I would be given cake, but this never worked.

Sunday evening always ended with hymns and everyone chose their favourite. Glasses of milk and a Bible story ended the day for us, though the grown-ups had evening prayers in the dining room where a green cloth was laid on the dining room table. The drawing room door would open and a voice call, "Prayers." Once, the usual formula of "Dinner is on the table" was substituted by mistake for "Prayers is on the table."

7

But I was in bed and asleep by then, tired out by a long Sunday.

Once when asked by a grown-up which day of the week I liked best, I replied promptly, "Monday."

"Why, dear?"

"Because it is the furthest day from Sunday," I replied.

Chapter Two
High Days and Holidays

When I was small I looked forward to the great events in life like hay making. I shall never forget looking out the window on a July morning and calling to the others, "The hay's being cut!"

This meant all the delights of the hayfield: helping with the hay; being buried in the hay and tea in the hay. We ran out to await our summons.

"If this drying wind and hot sun lasts, you can bring out your forks and turn it day after tomorrow," we were told.

To bring our forks and help turn it, the importance of it! Our forks were hazel sticks forked at the end, cut to our respective heights. When the moment arrived and the hay was ready to toss we were down in the hayfield, three little girls, complete with forks, in our brown holland pinafores and pink shell sunbonnets. The bonnets were made of pink cotton with light canes run through them to form a shell; gathered flaps hung down at the back of the neck. We always wore these in the summer till we were older when we wore hard straw hats with Guards ribbon. We worked with the grown-ups in a long line turning the hay and felt very important, though I don't think our work amounted to much. The bright red sorrel, the clover and white daisies lay drying in the sun. The long grasses were cut by "The Machine", as it was called, drawn by two farm horses. Once my small sister Frances found a baby rabbit in the hay and laboriously carried it to safety in another field. As she put it carefully down, it bit her finger before running off. Later as she had the bite tied up, she was told, "That is what you call ingratitude."

In Scotland the hay was built into "tramp coles" and left out in the field for some weeks. These coles were built round a wooden boss to a height of 10 or 12 feet. First the field was raked by a hay rake, also called "The Machine", drawn by a farm horse, and the hay brought near the boss. It was then raked into piles for forking to the cole, where the trampers walked round the wooden boss packing the hay firm. When the hay was built up a few feet from the ground I would beg to be lifted up to help tramp, too, round and round the boss I scrambled as the hay was forked up. It became very exciting as the hay mounted higher and higher and the distance to the ground grew more and more till it looked a very long way below.

"Hold on," I was told when the top of the cole was nearly reached, and then the dramatic moment of climbing down the ladder to the ground. I have been down many high ladders of 50 and 60 feet since then, but nothing has ever felt as high as the ladder in the hayfield.

From the ground I watched the skilled hands of a grown-up tramper finishing off the top of the cole into a neat round and then binding it with a rope of hay made on a wooden winder fed with handfuls of hay until a long supple rope formed. This construction was later supplemented by ropes weighted with stones to prevent the hay blowing away. For a treat I was allowed to climb on "The Machine" to help pull back the lever that released the hay.

Then it was tea time, buttered scones and milk never tasted so good as in the hayfield. As the shadows grew long, it was time for bed. So the glorious day ended with scratched hands and knees and hay seeds being combed from our hair.

When I looked out of the nursery window next morning I missed the silken meadow grass studded with wild flowers waving and rippling in the breeze. The grey-green hay packed into neat coles dotted over the shorn field looked as different as hard black seaweed strewn along a high water mark of some distant beach with no resemblance to the coloured waving weeds swaying with the salt tide. I almost felt an underlying sorrow that the hay was cut.

We always thought that summer began when the heavy rose rep curtains were taken down from the library and drawing room windows and put in the great chest for summer, strewn with camphor balls between the folds. They were replaced by fine white fairy-like muslin and we knew long summer months stretched before us; from the clear spring sun-shot hours when bright yellow celandines starred the young grass in the orchard and the pear trees showed their white blossom like snow, until the gold of the falling autumn leaves rivalled the yellow of the celandines of early spring and the apples hung red on the orchard trees.

After the hay came the fruit picking and when we were old enough not to squash the berries we were allowed to help. Every fine weekday the fruit picking was in full swing during the berry season. The currant leaves were like a green tent over our heads and through them the sun shone lighting up the red transparent clusters or opaque black fruit. The air was scented with the fragrant yellow musk that carpeted the ground under the bushes and which used to smell so sweet in our nursery window box. The black currants were picked singly so as not to be squashed and the red ones in bunches. During the long afternoons pushing our way through high raspberry leaves seeking rasps among the lower leaves and pulling the velvet fruit from the white hasps, we felt a great sense of achievement as our row of chip punnets lengthened along the box-edged path. When we had finished picking for the afternoon, all the chips were counted and everyone could see how much they had picked, rather like the Last Judgement. One of our little companions could pick quicker than a grown-up. For black currants, one punnet per quarter of an hour was 'good picking'. All the output was carried on wooden trays to the tool shed and packed in crates for dispatch by rail to Dundee, Perth or Glasgow.

Our greatest treat of the summer was Errol Games Day, called The Race Day by the grown-ups. Papa and Aunt Ayia could remember the race being held on the high road from the village to the main highway and as children they sat on the Megginch wall at the corner, which was called the Old Post, where the stage coach stopped to take passengers. In fact, we still have a panel from the last stage coach which passed along the dusty highway with its rumble of wheels, cracking of whips, blowing of horns, and jingle of harnesses.

The Games were held in a field close to the village, adjoining the Manse grounds, and when we were too small to withstand the crowds in the games field, the minister let us stand on a packing case on the Manse side of the hedge which afforded us a grandstand view. I remember once the porter at Errol Station was kidded up to enter his white Pomeranian in the whippet race and told he was sure to win. I can see that dog now, looking like a white snowball with a blue ribbon round his neck, doing its best to win, totally outclassed by the sleek whippets entered by the miners from Fife. He received a consolation prize for trying.

The Games Day was packed with events. The first excitement really began the night before when we completed our wild flower bunches. We always went in for variety as well as arrangement. We scoured the fields of the carse for ox-eyed daisies, bright red poppies, purple vetch and blue corncockles; we searched for the hill flowers, shaking grass orchises, knapweed, bluebells, sometimes a small piece of heather in early bloom, in the Sidlaws; and the river flowers which grew in profusion on the banks of the Tay, flat button bunches of orange tansy, toadflax and the tall stem crowned with fluffy cream flowers of Queen of the Meadow.

Every stage of the construction of a wild flower bouquet had to be done by the competitor, however small. But at last the strings were tied round, the stalks squeezed into a glass jam jar brimming with water and the sealed envelope with the competitor's name tied on. All were placed ready for the morning on the hall table, the coolest place, everyone said.

Hardly could we contain our excitement as we drove in the pony trap to the Village Hall. Would the poppy have opened in the night? Would the wild rose bud open at all? All was thrilling: the village band marching through the street opening the day's festivity, the crowds of people, the noise of heavy nailed boots on the wooden floor, the staging weighed down with every kind of exhibit, the smell of onions mingled with flowers, and the agonising moment when one anxiously looked to see if the envelope had been opened, whether a bright red, blue or yellow third ticket reposed on the top of the wild flower bouquet. If one had none, a kindly voice would say, "You'll do better next time, it's a wee bit flat," or "You have too many grasses," or "It's a wee bit loose," or "The poppies have fallen."

Sometimes I would hear comments like, "But look at that one with the corn daisies. Those flowers came with the grain and are not, they say, a British wild flower. They're disqualified you're no' that."

But perhaps a coloured ticket reposed amid the bouquet and then the joy of the day was boundless.

When the opening speech was over there was a babble of voices and Papa, Mummy and Aunt Ayia moved around talking to friends while we went home with Nana to have lunch and a rest before the afternoon. We walked up the footpath which zig-zagged the edge of the fields, by wood planks over ditches, under shady trees, through fields drenched with sunshine and the sweet smell of wild roses, spurred on by the music on the fairground, where I could see red and white striped awnings and the glitter of a merry-go-round.

How can I explain the excitement of standing in the fairground with the merry-go-round music playing all the popular tunes? One of the highlights was to ride on the dashing horses with flashing eyes and red nostrils. I held the reins perched on a scarlet, brass-studded saddle and pranced round at an incredible speed to the music of *A Bicycle Built for Two*.

There were coconut shies with heaps of bearded coconuts and rather worn balls to knock them down, brilliantly painted faces stuffed with straw so that the three wooden balls for a penny did not bounce back but knocked them backwards when hit squarely and the showman put them into place again with a lever. For one down a shiny monkey, for three a velvet flower sprinkled with silver glitters.

Perhaps the greatest excitement of all were the goldfish. Some could be got by a lucky penny draw, pieces of paper rolled up in a basket. Others could be got by knocking down pyramids of white wood blocks with balls. It was a great moment when a gleaming goldfish was handed over swimming around its glass jam jar.

Down the village street we went to the tiny grocer's shop, which had been there in my great-grandfather's time and before. I can still hear the creak of the door and the ring of the bell which hung behind it. For the treat of the year we were each given a paper bag and allowed to fill it with whatever sweets we fancied by Mrs Pearson, who as a little girl was sent with a message the day my father was born: 2nd March 1856. She asked to see the baby, but instead was given a piece of cake and told, "Another day."

After filling our bags with sweets, we went into Mrs Pearsons narrow dining room which overlooked the garden. On the white cloth-covered table stretching the length of the room was spread a special Race Day tea, home baked scones and cakes and jam. Frances would sometimes be given a sugar pig as well, of which she was particularly fond. As we all sat round the table the green reflections of the garden currant bushes danced on the white cloth. After tea, the Misses Pearson filled our goldfish jars with fresh water for the long walk home.

Then we would rest till it was quite late and afterwards walk down to the station and sit on the lodge gate and watch the race crowd go for the Games Special to Dundee. It was here that I saw the first car I had ever seen. It was painted green and black, and as it roared along in a cloud of dust and smoke, someone called from the signal box, "We soon won't want any trains!"

And finally home in the long light from the north, with the pink and white rose petals that had fallen on the road looking like little sweeties.

One summer we stayed in the Highlands at Ballyoukan, near Pitlochry, and Papa fished. The hillsides were yellow with broom and gorse, giving way to purple heather. It was fun to live in the white harled house covered in scarlet tropaeolum with views of distant blue hills. On the grass we used to count the slippery trout that Papa caught which we ate fried in oatmeal for breakfast.

Granny came to stay with us at Ballyoukan. She had her own pair of ponies and pony cart and took us for drives, which was fun. We had two rag dolls made by Cousin Alice and Cousin Edith Drummond-Hay called Eddie and Julia, and Granny made a blue frock for Julia and a red tie for Eddie. She sewed beautifully and I loved learning to sew although I still made a lot of "dog stitches", as Granny called the long uneven ones.

One day we were walking along the road and we saw a tandem bicycle and, as it was slowly pedalled up the hill, I ran out and sang as loud as I could all I could remember of the song *Daisy, Daisy*. Nana apologised and I was told I must never do such a thing again.

When I was very small we once celebrated 12th August by being allowed to stay up late and look out of the nursery window to see the bag laid out on the grass where the grouse were counted. I saw the tired pointer and setter being lifted out of the tea cart, and Papa patted them and gave them a biscuit before they were taken away to the kennels and fed. Cousin Jim and Cousin Harry Drummond-Hay, who had been out shooting too, waved to us, and Mummy brought us a big bunch of wild flowers and heather and told us how lovely it had been on the moor all day. She showed us her water colour sketches and gave us tiny grouse she had carved from gorse wood, painted and packed with heather in a matchbox, "A Brace on the 12th," written on the lid. Papa came up and hung a piece of stag's horn moss and white heather on the top of our cots after we were tucked up. The dining room table was arranged with heather and a smell of roast grouse came from the kitchen.

It was now autumn, the harvest was cut, the leaves were red and gold, and I was beginning to ask how many days to my birthday when we began to realise that people were talking a lot about a war. I wasn't very clear on the meaning of the word war, but supposed it meant the same as the Scottish word "waur" which meant something bad. I also thought that wars only happened long ago and not now. I knew the gleaming swords and arms that hung on the stairs had belonged to the red and blue coated ancestors whose oil pictures hung on the walls. Once, a Grenadier friend of Papa's, Captain Ellis, was staying for a few days partridge shooting. One afternoon as the rain came down he spent his time examining the swords that hung on the stairs.

I watched him with great interest and asked suddenly, "Are swords for killing people?"

He looked down rather distractedly to see where the child's voice came from. "Yes." he said kindly, "Like Jack the Giant Killer, and St George and the Dragon. You know giants and dragons have to be killed by brave men to make the world happier and safe for good people to live in."

When I was older I knew who all the swords had belonged to. There were small dirks, dress swords and a great two-handed crusader sword that had belonged to my ancestor Malcolm Drummond over 500 years ago. Its last battle had been fought for Mary Queen of Scots at Langside.

On 13th October an exciting wooden box came from Granny at Didlington and we guessed it must be a birthday cake, but it was not to be opened till the 14th. That day there was more talk than ever about war and the evening paper announced that the Boers had declared war on Britain. We were told that lots of cousins and friends who were soldiers would be going out in big troop ships with their horses to South Africa, landing at Cape Town. I traced on the map where the ships would go and where they would coal. Africa, shiny with varnish on our nursery screen, looked so very far away.

Soon the pink and white birthday cake with my name on it that I had cut and handed round so joyously was finished, and we were in the throes of Halloween festivities ducking for red apples, burning nuts in the bright wood fire, or partaking in the game of cutting slices from a flour shape topped by a lead bullet without unseating the bullet. In one of the slices was a silver sixpence with Queen Victoria's head on it. But even the discovery of the sixpence failed to rouse the grown-ups from their conversation about Ladysmith, Kimberley and Mafeking where our soldiers were shut in by the enemy and could not get out.

For quite a long time I used to say "The Anemone," as I thought it was the same name as the flowers. But it wasn't.

Chapter Three
Queen Victoria's Godchild - 1897-1901

As children we spent some of the winter months each year at Didlington, Mummy's old home in Norfolk, and also at my grandfather Lord Amherst's house in Grosvenor Square, London. It was very exciting when the boxes were packed. There were piles of our small starched clothes, white frocks for the evenings, white and holland pinafores, coloured sashes and hair ribbons to match—and only a very few precious dolls which might be packed. It got more and more exciting as the day of departure arrived, a dark winter night, often snowing, with last minute goodbyes to our beloved pets after which we all bundled into the landau with its pair of shining horses and drove to Errol Station, the reflection of the carriage candle lamps casting weird shadows on the tree trunks of the avenue.

We clambered into the darkness and were escorted to the waiting room where there was a roaring coal fire. Papa and Mummy talked to Mr Henderson, the stationmaster more snow was the opinion as the blue flames played in the fire and through the window the long fingers of the northern lights flickered and glimmered in the sky. Then with a roar the train rushed in and pulled up with a snort and shower of red sparks. We were lifted up the high step in the darkness and put into the reserved carriage. Last words were exchanged with Nana, the door was locked and, as the train moved out, Papa, Mummy and Mr Henderson waved from the platform till they were lost in darkness. We were off to London.

The seats were covered in dark blue cloth and an oil lamp glimmered from its glass guarded holder bolted to the roof. Two long, narrow tin foot warmers with handles at each end were the only form of heating. There were no corridors in the trains then. Beds were made up with rugs and wooden bars held together by webbing were stretched between the seats to make an extra bed for us little ones.

Then came the lights of Perth. We could see through the gaps of the window blinds that we were running into a large station. The carriage shunted and joined to the London Express. There were all sorts of strange sounds: a boy walked along the carriage roofs hooking out the old oil lamp and dropping in a newly cleaned, trimmed and filled one. With a terrific noise and banging of doors the tepid foot warmers were hauled out of each compartment of the train.

The ticket collector came to inspect our tickets and wished us a good journey, as did the Inspector with his shining silver buttons. The Guard told Nana that there was a lot of snow over Beattock and he would look us up at Carlisle to see that we were all right. Then the train glided from the platform with clouds of sparks and pink and black smoke rushing up to the immense glass roof.

We tried to keep awake to see the flames lighting the night sky from the iron foundry at Falkirk; then Nana pulled the green baize hood over the oil lamp and we slept through the jolts and stops and frozen snow beating on the windows till we woke at Carlisle. Lamps were checked and foot warmers changed. Lumps of frozen snow fell from the roof as the lamp boys traversed the whole length of the train. Nana made us hot milk on a spirit lamp and gave us sponge fingers, and there was tea and sandwiches too. The Guard said we were an hour late, but we may make it up, and then as the train glided from the platform the green baize hood was pulled over the lamp again making it look like a pale yellow moon. We slept till the grey winter dawn at Rugby when more tea was made and the Guard looked in to say we had made up the time.

As we drew into Euston, porters lined up on the platform the whole length of the train. Nana beckoned two porters, one for the carriage baggage and one for the van. As we walked up the train, there were piles of baggage and fevered travellers repeating: "Twenty in the carriage, fifteen in the van!" As we passed the huge engine, we called up our thanks to the engine driver and fireman who, with blackened faces, waved to us before we were swept into the waiting horse-drawn omnibus, with the baggage on top, and driven off through the cobbled streets of London, now awaking to the business of the day.

Shop men were taking down their shutters, boys calling out "Paper!", milkmen delivering milk with a rattle of cans heard above the noise of the wheels on the cobbles. There was, too ,a London smell in the air—a smell of smoke and soot and stables, and everything one touched was black. We drove to my grandfather's house, No 8, at the corner of Grosvenor Square and Brook Street.

Everything was different from home. We had strawberry jam for breakfast, electric lights instead of lamps and candles, and a bath with hot running water in which I sailed toy boats. At home we had a tin bath, cold water from the tap and hot boiled in a kettle. We were usually more or less alone with Nana in the large London house, which was often being springcleaned or under dust-sheets when we were there.

Mummy was the second youngest of seven sisters. Auntie Bee, the very youngest of all, had died when she was fourteen, long before I was born. But there were all the others. The eldest was Auntie May, who had married Lord William Cecil, an Equerry in the Royal Household. They had four boys who were often staying in the house on their way to or from boarding school. Auntie Sib, Auntie Flo, Auntie Maggie and Auntie Allie also came up and down to the London House. Papa was also an Equerry and later Groom-in-Waiting at Windsor and Osborne. When he was in waiting Mummy would come to London, too.

We used to play in the park nearly every morning and buy half-penny balloons from the balloon woman. She wore a bonnet, white apron and black shawl, and carried a brilliantly coloured collection of balloons tied by long strings to a stick. We also used to run and play with wooden hoops in Hyde Park. All the men who walked by wore black silk top hats and the ladies had leg-of-mutton sleeves and furs.

I remember that I was very interested in the begrimed seed balls hanging on the oriental plane trees or, as we called them, Balley trees. Of course we were very keen to see what they looked like close up and longed to have one in our hand, but we never found one on the ground, though we looked every time we went to the Park.

One day I said, "I will get one."

So I took a stick and threw it as hard as I could at one of the lower bunches of blackened seed balls. A whole bunch fell to the ground, but the stick had glanced off and hit an old gentleman who was walking by, squashing in the front of his black silk top hat.

He was furious I could see that as he turned to Nana and said with the utmost restraint, "Nurse, control your charge."

Nana replied, "I am very sorry, sir, it was an accident," and looked at me. I blurted out, "I am very sorry," but unfortunately added, "couldn't you wear it back to front?"

He gave me a scathing glance and strode away.

Nana said, "That you were sorry was quite enough; you should not have said anything more."

"But Nana," I argued, "what was he to do?" I knew he could not walk without a hat. I grabbed the black bunch of balls from the ground and in a minute my white gloves were black too.

Later Papa took me out to tea with cousins who lived near Berkeley Square. I sat on the edge of my chair, my feet not reaching the ground. What a noise grown-up people made. Then, to my horror, I heard someone say quite near me, "Poor Arthur was hit on the head with a stick by a dreadful child in the Park today. He might have been hurt. Hat ruined, had to be re-blocked...."

I missed the end, but went scarlet to the roots of my hair.

When we were driving back in a hansom, Papa said, "I suppose children do play in the Park, and even throw sticks," and laughed.

There were so many excitements in London: the fire engines rushing through the streets drawn by galloping white horses, gleaming red paint of the engine, shining brass helmets of the firemen and the loud clanging of the bell rather like a dinner bell; the boys dodging in and out of the traffic with short-handled shovels and brushes cleaning up with lightning speed the horses' droppings; and the crossing sweepers. They all had their own crossings rather like robins with their own territories. All pedestrians crossed by the crossings. They were swept and re-swept as the wheels and horses' hoofs covered them with mud. A hopeful cap lay on the pavement for half-pennies or pennies. The shoe blacks did a thriving trade.

"Give you a shine, sir! Give you a shine, miss!"

Then there were many country carrier carts. A small boy stood at the open back holding on to a swing rope that hung from the roof so that he could jump out at any minute to deliver a parcel. There were errand boys with parcels, telegraph boys with orange envelopes and the muffin man who came round the Square about three in the afternoon ringing a hand bell and carrying a flat wooden tray covered by a green cloth on his head. What we loved to see most was a Punch and Judy Show with clever little Toby, a bell round his neck.

We loved looking out of our nursery windows. The hansoms and four wheelers passed all day long, sometimes summoned by a sharp whistle from the steps of one of the houses on the Square. Carriages drove past with a coachman and footman on the box, wearing black fur capes in winter, their high hats with cockades, shining buttoned coats, knee breeches and high boots looking very smart, and the glittering harness and polished carriages reflecting the dull winter light as they passed. Then there was the flower seller with hyacinths at the corner of the street which cost 8 pence for a lovely pot.

Of course we could not see the buses as they were in Oxford Street, where we sometimes walked, although we wished that they came through the Square. They were different colours for different routes. They had an outside stair and passengers with umbrellas on top. The driver sat on the high box seat all muffled up with a rug over his knees as the bus progressed, stopping and starting at the various stops which the horses knew as well as the drivers. The noise of the traffic passing over the cobble stones was terrific.

There was a toy shop with windows full of toys where we could feast our eyes on such lovely china dolls with real curled hair and beautiful wax dolls with large blue eyes and pink cheeks, dressed in frilly frocks; brilliantly red, stiffly erect wooden soldiers in their forts; and sailing ships with starched sails and yellow decks. Dolls' house fitments cost a penny, small china dolls cost sixpence and we could get lovely toys for 3 pence or 4 pence.

Our greatest joy was when Papa took us to Covent Garden Market. One of my earliest recollections was of a seething crowd going in every direction shouting and calling; huge baskets were carried on heads and shoulders, overflowing with flowers and fruit. Banks of flowers, mountains of vegetables and great heaps of oranges, the air was pervaded with the strong smell of all three. On the outskirts of the market, white-aproned, black shawled and bonneted old ladies carried on a brisk trade in flowers and small plants. I remember Frances gazing enraptured at the velvety pansies whereupon an old lady gave her one and would accept nothing for it.

In those days there was a winding stair that led off the fruit market to a glass-roofed wonderland where yellow canaries sang, brilliant red and blue macaws screamed their loudest, monkeys chattered and goldfish swam. It was a very old building and the establishment had been carried on since Regency days. Papa talked to the proprietor, whom he knew, and we were allowed to gaze at all the wonders this large room contained till we were reluctantly taken away in a hansom, one on each side of Papa, to our grandfather's house.

On Sunday afternoons we were taken to the Abbey or to St Paul's to hear the anthems, or to the Tate or National Galleries where Mummy would show us the pictures, or we would go to the Zoo. As we drove through the streets I felt sad, for the dark blinds were down on every shop window and nothing would look bright or pretty again till Monday.

I can remember the choking yellow or black fogs that made my eyes and throat smart, but they were exciting too, with linkmen holding torches preceding the buses, flares on street corners and everything silent and muffled, covered in a great blanket. People came in saying, "We can't see our hand before our face. It is a peasouper."

Once we had a fog that lasted for three weeks and we couldn't go out at all, so we amused ourselves with our own games, sliding down the banisters and holding imaginary receptions based on scraps of grown-up conversations, pretending to receive guests at the top of the wide stairs, or holding a musical afternoon in the drawing room, turning on as many of the crystal chandeliers as we could to defy the choking fog.

Outside we could hear the melancholy voices of the paper boys calling round the Square. One could never hear it all, either the beginning or the end and always something sad: "All dead..." "All lost...", "Terrible murder...".

Then Nana took us down to Didlington, Daddans and Granny's home in Norfolk. We were met at the small country station by an omnibus with a pair of horses and many a friendly greeting. Did the horses remember us? We went to see as the baggage was piled on and then we were all bundled in and rumbled away into the darkness along the sandy flint and chalk roads, bordered by the high Scotch fir hedges"deal rows", as they are called in Norfolk. We drove for 9 miles through the darkness to Didlington with the carriage lamps casting reflections on the white chalk. Then at last we stumbled out of the darkness and, blinking like owls, were enveloped in a blaze of electric light as the doors were thrown open and we passed into the warmth of the house and were welcomed by our grandparents and aunties.

Didlington was a large Georgian red brick house with white facings. A magnolia grandiflora spread over the south wall facing the terrace lawn and the lake. To the west lay the deer park and the lime avenue, while to the east there ran a clear trout stream bordered by the flower garden, and to the north close by was the little flint church with its square ivy-covered tower. It was a house full of sunshine, music and laughter. There was always so much going on. Someone playing on a piano, or singing, or writing a book, or translating some manuscript from Sanskrit or Persian, or working in watercolours or oils. Daddans, as we always called my grandfather, spoke seven languages. Auntie Sib was fluent in six, including Russian and Flemish. My mother spoke French, German and Italian, as indeed did all the others.

But all the sisters were talented. Auntie May loved watercolour sketching and illustrating. She was also very fond of needlework and embroidery, and wrote a book about the birds of the Nile.

Auntie Sib wrote many short stories and articles and produced *Job* which was acted by the Norwich Players. She was also a sculptress.

Auntie Flo, whom we also called Auntie Fluff, was fond of dogs, importing the original breeding strain of Salukis to this country from Arabia. As children we loved playing with the dogs which I remember for their, their expressive eyes and coats the colour of desert sand. She invented the "electric hare" for exercising her hounds. Her other great interest was poultry breeding, and she won many prizes for this, as well as writing books on hens and organising an early egg marketing depot in Norfolk.

Auntie Maggie was very musical and played and sang, and like all of the sisters, she painted in watercolours.

Auntie Allie was very keen on gardening and wrote and illustrated many books on the subject, besides being Horticultural Correspondent for the Times for many years.

My mother also sketched beautifully and studied geology. No picnic was complete without her little hammer. She was also a keen graphologist and for many years used to earn money by doing it professionally. She published one book of great charm, *Orynthia and Flowers*, and also told fortunes by tea leaves.

The Amhersts were a Kent yeoman family, one of whom had married Mary Tyssen, the heiress of Hackney. The Tyssen ancestors were cloth merchants from Ushant Island, owning a ship called *The Golden Falcon*. They traded in England during the reign of James II and bought land in Hackney, North London, which was then country.

There were so many exciting things at Didlington. There were large stables since riding or driving were the only means of transport. The house was about 10 miles from Swaffham, 12 from Thetford and to some places one had to post. The yellow, sandy roads stretched away to the distance, bordered by wide strips of grass for riding. Here the gypsies, or Pharaohs as they were called in the Eastern counties, camped with their gaily painted caravans and tethered their grazing horses. The gypsy women used to smile from their caravan doors and we would wave, thinking their gold earrings, black hair and bright clothes were very exciting.

We loved the Home Farm with the red poll cows, white poultry and turkeys, ducks and geese. In those days all the workers wore smock frocks and cords, while the keepers wore grey wool suits with silver buttons. This material was woven specially at Otterburn in Northumberland.

Didlington was really an oasis in a desert so to speak: a centre of employment and training for miles around, as were all the great country houses then. Boys were apprenticed in the gardens, or became keepers or stable boys. Girls learnt in the laundry and in all departments of the house: the kitchen, the still room, and general house work, and then went on, fully trained, somewhere else, while others filled their places from the school. There were no health services then and my grandfather had an arrangement with the local doctor whereby he called each day and any-one who was not feeling well saw him, or messages were left for him to call at outlying houses on the property.

My grandfather was MP for Norfolk from 1880 to 1892 after which he was created Lord Amherst of Hackney. He loved pictures and books and spent hours in his library studying when not working in the Business Room. He talked to us about books and pictures just as if we had been grown-ups and used to show us exciting coloured plates in rare books, like *Audubon's Birds*, and sometimes blue beads, scarabs and bracelets from his large Egyptian collection. He did a lot of research work and my grand-mother later wrote a standard history of Ancient Egypt.

Daddans had a yacht called the *Daydream* and took his Master's certifi-cate so that he could take her to sea himself. Many trips were made in the yacht to Norway, the Continent and the Mediterranean. She was a very good sea boat and Mummy had loved sailing in her as a girl.

My grandfather was also a very keen shot and there were many big house parties during the shooting season. I can remember the Royal par-ties were a great thrill. The house was a blaze of light from the crystal chandeliers and the dining room table was the most lovely thing one could imagine. We used to slip downstairs to see the table after we were thought to be quietly in the nursery. I was thought rather small for this thrilling expedition which we had been thinking of and planning for all day, but I begged to come, too, and my cousins Tommy and Billy relented.

"You mustn't make any noise or we will be stopped doing it ever again," Tommy said.

They carried me part of the way and then firmly took my hand as we crept out of the nursery, down the stairs and into the huge dining room. I remember thinking I would never see anything as lovely again. It was like being in fairyland, with the red poinsettias, the stephanotis and green fern and little lights shining amongst the flowers, and great silver candelabra with shades to match the colour of the flowers, the whole length of the long table covered in snowy white damask and glittering silver. Then we slipped back to the nursery where Henny, youngest of the cousins, Frances and I went to bed, while my elder sister Jean, in a white frock holding a tray of buttonholes, and Jacky Cecil, who was a year older than her, carry-ing a white satin pincushion stuck with pins, descended to the drawing room and walked round the assembled guests handing out buttonholes and the accompanying pin before the grown-ups went in to dinner.

When a wet afternoon came we were allowed the great treat of making toffee on the nursery fire, and our greatest friend, the housekeeper, Mrs Ford, who had been kitchen maid to Talleyrand, sent up to us the correct quantities of butter and sugar. If it got singed we added lemon. As we were making the toffee, our cousins' nurse gave us a mild lecture on not being selfish and greedy.

"What is greedy?" I asked, as at that date there were quite a lot of words whose meaning I had not grasped.

She explained that it would be both selfish and greedy if we were to eat this toffee all ourselves. We should offer it to other people and eat our share last.

We poured the toffee on a buttered plate and cut it into squares and put it outside the nursery window to cool. When it was cold we offered it to Nana and to Nanny Cecil, but they both smiled and said "Later we would like some."

So there we were with a whole plate of toffee which we could not eat ourselves without being selfish and greedy.

Then a bright idea came. We would take it down and hand it to the grown-ups. They wouldn't be selfish or greedy and we could eat what was over. So when we were changed into our white evening frocks and our cousins into sailor suits to go downstairs, we quietly and unnoticed took the plate of toffee with us. The large house party were just finishing an informal tea after shooting, the ladies in tea gowns, the gentlemen in smoking jackets, sipping tea round the fire in the large room called the Museum. Gobelin tapestries hung from the walls and the chairs too were covered in tapestry. It was quite a distance to walk over the panelled oak floor to where the assembled company were seated.

We made our curtseys and bows as we always did, but instead of melting away quietly to a distant corner and looking at picture books on the floor, we solemnly handed the total output of our afternoon's work to the assembly. Everybody, including the Prince of Wales, took a piece and thanked us.

My grandmother said, "This was not on the programme," and everyone laughed.

Afterwards we were told "You should not have handed a piece of that sticky toffee to the Prince of Wales."

Mummy and Auntie Fluff said, "There are times for doing things, and times not. Perhaps this was rather a not time."

After dinner on the evenings when my grandmother sang, we would be roused and allowed to stand in our dressing gowns and slippers at the top of the stairs with all the staff who had crept in to hear her sing. She was a beautiful mezzo-soprano with a very large compass, and when her voice died away on the last note of *Ave Maria* people used to cry.

On the morning of the Prince's departure we were allowed to come to the hall with all the grown-ups to see the Prince drive away. We were told that when the Prince passed us we were to make curtsies and my cousins were to bow. When it came to my turn to make my curtsey, I felt my instructions could be improved upon. So I held out a very small hand and said, "Goodbye, sir," in a loud, clear voice.

The Prince bent down and took my outstretched hand, patting me on the head, and said to Papa, "A dear little girl."

But no one else thought I was and I was well and truly scolded.

At Christmas the school children sang carols as the men rang carol tunes on bells. These carolling sessions were known as "waits". Everyone talked about Lord Roberts and Kitchener and some people said that a century that comes in with a war goes out with a war.

We went to church on New Year's Day, the beginning of the new century, but everyone talked about our soldiers and the people still shut up in the three towns of South Africa and there were prayers for them in church. How long would they hold out?

I remember that Granny had a lathe and loved turning. She worked in wood and ivory and her work was of such a high standard that she was made a member of the Worshipful Company of Turners. Her lathe was in a room in the tower, and I used to creep up the stairs after her and was allowed to stay and watch provided I didn't touch anything. I loved watching her setting up a piece of wood or ivory for the lathe and then watching the long ribbons of wood or curls of ivory fly from her tool as the piece began to take shape. She let me brush up the shavings and chips when she had finished and bring her the oil can with which she would oil all the parts.

One day she said to Mummy, "That child has neat fingers. Some day I will teach her to turn. She might even make an engineer."

A year later on a cold grey morning in January I heard Nana talking in a low voice. "A wire has come. The Queen is dead."

Papa and Mummy went up to London and we were left at Didlington with Granny. Everyone was very sad and talked in whispers. We wore black sashes with our white frocks and black shoes instead of bronze, and I remember being lifted up to see the two wreaths on the table in the hall.

One was enormous, made of green laurel leaves and tied by a huge bow of purple satin ribbon. Every village in England sent one and they were hung on each lamp post along the funeral route in London. The other was a personal wreath. It was most beautiful, made of white arum lilies and stephanotis and freesia and many other white flowers grown in the glass houses in the garden. The whole wreath smelt so sweet.

Granny said, "You must remember this wreath sent to your godmother's funeral. The Country will never be the same again."

I remember the service in the old flint church, the birds flying in and out of the thick ivy on the square tower finding roosting places for the night, and pheasants crowing in the near distance, the sound carrying away over the frosty ground from the woods. I had a dark coat and a black beaver hat, and a black band on my arm. My sister Jean had the same, and my little sister Frances was held up to the nursery window; she had black shoulder bows on her white frock. The four Cecil boys had dark coats and black ties and black bands on their arms, and with the bell tolling we walked up the church path with Granny under the widespread oaks. The sun was setting pink behind the trees of the west.

I whispered, "The sunset isn't in mourning. Will the Queen be in Heaven now and much more happy than us?"

Someone said, "Hush."

It was very cold and gloomy in the little church, and as the pink flush faded from the sky all I saw through the windows was a dark winter's day, and everything in the church was black. The pulpit and pews were draped in black, the brass lectern was covered in black, the clergyman was in a black cassock and everyone was dressed in black. The Dead March was played on the hand blown organ and the ivy leaves against the windows were all covered in white hoar frost as the wind moved in the trees outside and a few snowflakes fell.

I didn't show how frightened I was, or how cold I felt as the solemn voice went on and on and the flickering candles made dark uncertain shadows and everyone cried into their handkerchiefs. I felt I must cry too, but I knew it would be a loud sobbing cry if I did, so I held the edge of the oak pew very tightly as I stood on a footstool, quivering with cold and fright.

Granny bent down and said, "Come, dear," and taking my small black gloved hand led me out and took me over to the house and into her warm boudoir all done up in pale blue silk. She gave me peppermint in hot water to drink and took off my black hat and gloves, and put a rug over me and let me lie on the sofa, while she mended the cover of my prayer book with paste, which in my efforts not to cry I had bent backwards and forwards till it cracked. Then she read a story about the Queen when she was a little girl, and when the others came in from the long, black service, frozen with cold, I was warm and happy and ready for nursery tea.

I felt so sad that I would never see the Queen now; it had been my great imaginary game that I would go and see her. I was always considered too small to be taken when she passed through Perth Station, very early in the morning, and Papa and Mummy had gone. But it had been arranged that she would see me and I was to be presented by my other godmother, Victoria Baillie, when the Queen came back to London from Osborne, but she never did return and my imaginary game was gone for ever.

Papa said that each godchild that was presented was given a lovely toy horse and cart, the horse covered in real skin so that one could groom it, and all the buckles on the harness actually undid. Cousin Victoria had one which she gave to her nephews, but when I was much older she gave me the gold and pearl cross that the Queen had given her.

I had always felt a strange feeling of connection with the Queen; I had always felt that she was part of my life. Every birthday and Christmas Papa would take out of the safe the lovely pendant she had given me at my christening and I was allowed to wear it. At the time, the Queen was the only person who had rejoiced at my birth. Everyone else had wanted a boy and were disappointed when I arrived. However, the Queen wired: *REJOICE AT BIRTH OF LITTLE DAUGHTER.*

Chapter Four
Edwardian Childhood - 1901-10

My Seggieden cousins Jim and Harry Drummond-Hay both went to fight in the Boer War. Cousin Jim was my godfather and I used to print letters to him. He wrote back the most marvellous letters illustrated with pen and ink sketches with lots of South African stamps on the envelopes.

On the way home from Didlington in February 1900 we heard of the Relief of Kimberley and saw all the flags and crowds of cheering people. Everyone waved flags in the streets and wore red, white and blue bows. We had bows pinned on our coats and lots of people were singing in the streets *Blue Bell* and *Soldiers of the Queen*.

About the end of February, when we had been home for some time, Ladysmith was relieved and we wore the tricolour bows on our frocks again. All the new puppies or kittens that we met were called Bobby or Kitchener or Kimberley. When Mafeking was relieved we were given Mafeking horns, which seemed about a foot long, made of curled up cardboard with a wooden mouthpiece and striped in red, white and blue. When blown they made a loud blaring noise. We were also given red, white and blue Mafeking sweets. Everyone talked of the great rejoicing everywhere and Mafeking night in London was so well celebrated that Mafeking became a word that people used for having an uproarious time.

That was the winter the Queen died and on our way home from Didlington to Megginch we stayed as usual in my grandparents' house in Grosvenor Square. Papa and Mummy came to Euston Station to see us travel home with Nana. The station was full of soldiers in khaki uniform who had just come off a troop ship from South African and were catching the train. Khaki was a new name for a new colour made to match the colours of the veldt, Papa told us, so they could not be seen so easily when they advanced.

As we were gazing at the khaki clad figures with boots and rifles marching past, we suddenly saw Cousin Harry. We rushed after him shouting his name in the greatest excitement and he recognised us even after such a very, very long time, as it seemed to us.

News of the troops coming home had gone before us and when we got to Perth there were crowds of people cheering and waving flags and there were more flags over the line .

Later, when more soldiers had returned, Papa and Mummy gave a reception and there was cake and wine and speeches. Everyone cheered and sang *God Save the King*, which seemed sad as they had sung *God Save the Queen* for so long. We still had black bands on our coats and straw hats and Mummy still wore black. Some of the soldiers had been under canvas so long that they forgot they were not out on the veldt and tipped the tea leaves from the bottom of their cups onto the carpet. Now the Bobby and Kitchener kittens and puppies were getting quite big and the new ones were called Khaki.

In June every year we went to stay at Elie in Fife, a children's paradise. Elie and Earlsferry adjoined, but Earlsferry, which was smaller, was a Royal Borough, while larger Elie was not. Mummy took a small house overlooking the bay, with its golden sands, and exciting rocks at low tide where brown sea palms and shiny green seaweed swayed with the ebbing tide. A curfew bell rang every night, but we were asleep by then and never heard it, nor saw the long beam of the Isle of May lighthouse.

On the day peace was declared and the Boer War was officially over, the town crier came up the main street ringing a bell and announcing a fancy dress parade of bicycles through the town that evening. The parade was to be headed by the band of the *Mars* boys from the old wooden *Mars* training ship. We were very excited and helped to put decorations on our house and the whole town was bright with flags. It was a lovely evening and we stood in great excitement to watch the fancy dress parade on bicycles. After the band of the *Mars* boys had passed playing rousing tunes, there were only three bicycles. We were very disappointed. Later, when it was quite dark, Papa woke us up and let off rockets from the garden which fell in showers of golden rain in the bay, reflecting the fireworks from the *Mars* boys opposite.

We saved some of the rockets for the Coronation and Mummy arranged strings of red, white and blue flags and a big ER which were all to be lit by night lights on the great day. When the baker's boy came with the bread he brought a shiny new King Edward penny and gave it to me.

Then we heard that King Edward was suddenly very ill and there would be no Coronation. Everyone was upset about the King being so ill, though no one could explain to me what appendicitis was. All the pencils and Coronation souvenirs with pictures of the King were taken from the shop windows and the flags were put away.

It wasn't until August that the Coronation was rearranged to take place. Once again we put up our strings of red, white and blue lights. There were Chinese lanterns hung on the trees of the back avenue and tables laid for supper under the weeping ash. Mr Macdonald, the gamekeeper, played the pipes and someone else played the fiddle and there was dancing after supper. Then Papa let off the rockets we had saved, we watched as they whizzed into the night with a breathtaking roar. Even though we stayed up til 1 o'clock, we could still hear the music playing outside when we were in bed.

With the accession of King Edward there was a change in many of the Household staff. Papa, who had been Groom-in-Waiting to Queen Victoria, was not re-appointed. This meant less money and a gradual decline of things at Megginch, but for us children the happy annual routines continued unchanged. In December we again travelled south to London after which we went to Didlington for a large family Christmas with my Amherst grandparents. The Cecil boys went back to boarding schools while we stayed at Didlington until April, later in the year returning to Elie for our seaside holiday.

I think it is difficult to appreciate now that people have cars and there are buses and aeroplanes, how very local everything was when I was a child. Church at Errol or Glencarse in the pony cart was a 2 or 3 mile excursion. Of course bicycles were a great emancipation, but for most journeys people went by train, in a pony cart, or on foot.

The first car I saw close up was a Panhard Levasseur in 1903. Cousin Henry Effingham arrived in it, complete with a chauffeur who was a racing driver. The car was white outside with red upholstered leather seats. When Cousin Henry drove her he wore a long grey wolf skin coat with the fur outside, a black cap with shining peak and large goggles with leather flaps at the side that tied behind his head. Attired like this he was a terrifying spectacle who caused small children to cry when they saw him, even grown-ups looked alarmed. Everyone said then that the motorcar went at a terrible pace. Horses used to shy and bolt and people had to cover their heads from the clouds of choking dust. The only mechanical terror on the roads up to the advent of the motorcar had been the slow-moving traction engine which was preceded by a man with a red flag.

All the passengers said their breath was taken away and they could not speak on arrival at their destination. There was no windscreen and they were driven at the top speed of 40 mph which seemed incredible. Cousin Henry said that the motorcar could not go slower or it would overheat.

I used to watch the chauffeur working on the Panhard in the stable yard. I learnt the various names and uses of the parts as the chauffeur unfolded the mysteries of the car to me. Sad to say, he was killed later while racing in France.

During the visit of the motorcar everyone who could tried to get a glimpse of her, tearing along in clouds of choking dust. Papa remarked, "You will see, the coming of the petrol engine will destroy the world."

The next year Cousin Henry returned with a CGV, and later with a Shallon, but by that time motorcars were becoming more common; when I was in London in 1904 I kept a count of the number I saw in a little notebook, there had been 325.

We had a great thrill on arrival at Didlington that year. We found a large shut car, dark blue, almost black. The cover looked like a square box that opened by pulling back two long catches which hooked over studs in the half of the roof that didn't open. The great excitement was that Daddans and Granny were going to drive across France in it. Our friend the head coachman had learnt to drive, and after tea in the library Daddans showed us maps of the routes they were to take.

We used to go driving in the pony cart to see people Granny knew and deliver messages from her. Sometimes we went to see an old lady whose son was a sailor. She offered us elder flower wine, though Nana would only allow us to have a biscuit, and showed us shell boxes and pictures brought back by her son from foreign parts.

"Where?" I would ask. "Which foreign parts?"

But she only smiled and showed us more pictures of palm trees, or pictures made of coloured shells, or bright green and red wooden beads, or dried and painted seaweed, or a whale's tooth, or a dried sun fish with its mouth wide open saying, "Ow." One day she gave me a shell he had brought back for me from foreign parts. Granny let me write "Thank you for the lovely shell" at the bottom of her Christmas letter which went in with her parcel of jerseys, socks and tobacco, but even she never knew from which foreign parts it came.

We loved the gardens and hot-houses, especially the orchard house where we picked up the prunings of the peach trees, and after being kept in water, the buds would open. The orange trees and the camellia trees were also covered in flowers. We wandered through the vinery with the bare knotted vines, the lovely spring houses a blaze of bulbs, or entered the tropics in the hottest house of all where banana and cocoa trees fruited. There was also a pond of Chinese and Japanese goldfish swimming in the warm water among the lotus leaves. This was where the Victoria water lily grew and flowered with its giant tray shaped leaves.

My brother John used to sail his model yacht, a cutter called the *Dryad* after one of Admiral Sir Adam Drummond's ships, on the lake. Once, when he was four, it got too far out to reach and he gaily started off to man one of the boats in the boathouse to retrieve it. As he was trying to untie the painter he was espied by one of the gardeners. Mummy was sketching and had noticed nothing.

When my grandparents were abroad we were left with Nana and Mrs Ford, the housekeeper. She wore a black silk dress and had a black velvet bow in her auburn hair and we loved going to the housekeeper's room where she sat making hook rugs. She usually wore her bunch of keys on a chain at her side and would sometimes take us into the store room next door. It was a very large room with shelf upon shelf from floor to ceiling. At the end there was a smaller room with lemons hanging in a net and a chair and table where she made up her monthly lists. Sometimes she gave us chocolates or sugared almonds or fondants. She had a special recipe for orange wine which she used to make for Talleyrand.

When Papa came we would fish in the river for chub by the old flour mill that had been mentioned in Domesday Book. The river was clear and deep with a gravel bottom and bright green river's hair, as we called the weed waving in the stream. In March the banks were spun gold with marsh marigolds. Sometimes the miller would look over the half door, white with floating meal, and inside the dark mill we could hear the clang of the machinery running. We knew him well and he used to talk about the old days and sometimes give us meal worm for bait.

But when we were alone with Mummy we fished in the lake for perch and roach and would eat our catch grilled with butter for breakfast. Our rods we got at the village shop for a shilling each. There was everything one could possibly wish for in that shop. The line and float were 9 pence, while the hooks were another 3 pence. There were little dolls with china heads for a penny, brightly coloured wool in shades from pink to scarlet for a farthing, a single bladed knife for sixpence or a two bladed one for a shilling.

I used to get pieces of soft wood at the saw mill near the Home Farm to cut little things with my knife for my brother John's railway. There I would peep round the corner of the door to see the clouds of sawdust and hear the screech of the bright circular saw as it sliced into the wood with its fangs. Then I loved to see the electric light engine; I suppose now it would be considered a museum piece. The engine house was near the courtyard and I was never allowed to go in unless the engine was stopped, and even then only under strict supervision. The hot oily smell and the black and white floor intrigued me. In the small workshop I was sometimes allowed to polish a nut or bolt with emery cloth and then see it put back in place. Once I drew a diagram in chalk on the board to show my idea of how the engine worked. Of course there were many corrections from the master-mind in charge, but he agreed the engine did work like that.

Then there was the fire engine which was a great excitement to us children, and we loved watching fire drill every Saturday morning. Once an inspector came and wanted to see someone come down the escape sheet and be caught in the sheet held at the bottom. My sister Frances and I begged that we might and he let us go. We were told exactly how we must go down the chute at the top window and to regulate our speed with our elbows, but of course we didn't, and arrived breathless and bouncing on the tightly held sheet at the bottom, before we knew where we were. Mummy came and said we were not to go down again.

It rather reminded me of a time at the London house when I was sent to rest after lunch in a top room. I climbed out of the window into the wide lead gutter and then on to the parapet and walked along. Somebody in the house opposite sent a footman over to say there was a small child walking on the parapet at the very top of the house. There was a general rush and heads popped out of the window.

"Come along, dear," Mummy said. She had gone to the next window. "Just do what I tell you. Don't walk back, just slide down from where you are and take my hand."

She held it out. I did exactly what she said and was inside the room again in a minute.

One of the many people who seemed to have collected in the room had said, "If you come in, I'll give you a box of chocolates." But I never got it.

Nana shut the window and said, "Now will you promise me that you will never do that again?" and I did. Of course it was a sheer drop to the street below, but I was only interested in seeing the top of the hansoms and the backs of the horses and people's heads below.

Another time I climbed up a tree at Didlington and the branch below me snapped so I couldn't get down till rescued by a ladder .

Mummy taught us how to handle a boat and a punt, on the lake. She taught us all the general boating rules: never change places, or stand up, how to bring the boat into the boathouse, or throw a rope over a mooring post, or take the boat through the lock. Mummy was a good oar and had pulled with the Oxford stroke. My grandfather had been at Oxford and on Boat Race Day would go in a hansom with a dark blue bow on the whip, while my father, who was Cambridge in principle, would choose one with a light blue bow.

Once I got into difficulties with the punt. The punt pole stuck in the mud and I stuck to the punt pole. There I was left clinging as the punt went on. Mummy laughed and called, "Hang on, and I will pick you up," and she guided the punt some yards out and I dropped in like a monkey off a stick.

Occasionally we drove to Swaffham or Thetford where we spent the whole day, as the horses had to be rested before driving back. We used to have lunch and tea and visit the old church at Swaffham with the carvings of the tinker and his dog. At Thetford we loved to climb the mound and see the pulp works where Thetford ware was made. Sometimes we went to tea with neighbours' children and played games in their gardens.

On Sundays the deerhound and dachshund would sit on the doorstep watching the church party set off for morning service and on their return they would find the dogs still there, but with sandy paws and noses and tired out. One morning there was no morning service so they went to another church a few miles away. The dogs saw them off as usual. On their return over the heath two sandy heads suddenly appeared from a clump of gorse bushes. Their expressions of dismay at seeing the church party were unforgettable.

My brother John was keen to catch trout in the swift flowing trout stream. This stream was protected from the herons by poles laid across with wire netting stretched over them. John, while fishing, slipped off one of these poles and fell under the wire netting into the stream. We rushed along the bank trying to grab him but were foiled by the wire netting. His Drummond kilt acted as a sail and he was swiftly whirled downstream. However, we were finally able to grab him from the small bridge just as he was drawn under it. He was pulled out soaking wet and protesting strongly that he had lost his rod.

We had lessons in the mornings with Mummy and Nana and on Saturday mornings we had to do our mending, but most afternoons were our own. At Megginch we each had our own flower garden, under two big horse chestnut trees behind the main garden. It had always been the children's garden, box bushes and rhododendrons surrounded it and the wood was behind. There were small round beds surrounded by stones and a summer house built of logs with a thatched roof, made for our great-grandmother, Lady Charlotte Drummond. We could do whatever we liked in our garden. Nothing really grow there because of the deep shade, however snowdrops, aconites and little blue scillas would all flower before the chestnut leaves unfolded. There was a big lime tree by the garden with the initials CD carved on the stem, cut by Charles Drummond, our great uncle. I spent a lot of time on the swing. I used to imagine looking up through the green sunlit lime leaves to the sky that it must be the same as looking up from the bottom of the sea with fathoms of clear green water above me. My great ambition was to swing high enough to swing right over the pole. One day I achieved this and found it not quite so pleasant as I had anticipated. My head hurt, my knees were grazed, and my pinafore was torn.

Later we were given a better garden between the eastern kitchen garden wall and a beech hedge which bordered an old path called Lover's Lane. Here we grew special yellow and mauve radishes and violets, which we would market in Dundee. As we actually earned money from our garden, we became more ambitious and grew sweet peas and cucumbers in a frame. We even exhibited and won prizes at the Dundee Flower Show.

When I was twelve I started making butter in a small old-fashioned churn of conical shape. I held the churn between my knees and beat the cream up and down by means of a long spindle, one end protruding through the lid, the other fixed to a wooden vane by which the cream was beaten to butter. I think it had been in the dairy for at least 50 years. Later I used the big barrel churn when large quantities of cream had been skimmed into the earthenware crocks from the basins on the stone shelves. The butter had to be washed clean in the stone sink before patting into pounds and then all the utensils had to be scalded with salted boiling water.

The dairy was a pleasant place with its blue and white tiles, cool stone floor, and sweet white jasmine that grew over the south wall. One door opened into a garden full of pink roses, the other into the courtyard where the stone cheese press stood, with which salt caboc cheeses were made. I also salted butter and filled many brown earthenware jars for winter. In thundery weather the butter would not come and the strong arm of a kind passer-by would often give a turn to the churn. Sometimes I would slip a silver sixpence into the churn to keep the witches away and make the butter form quicker.

My little sister Frances was busy with the poultry, setting eggs, rearing chicks and feeding hens. I remember she once thought she would take a short cut to collect the eggs by crawling through the hen hole in the poultry yard door. Halfway through, the large gander caught hold of her pink pinafore and every time she tried to crawl through he pulled her back

until someone rescued her. She loved the fluffy chicks and yellow duck-
lings and always said the hen smiled when she settled down on a whole
setting of eggs which Frances had neatly arranged in a straw nest. She
crossed various breeds to get the darkest brown eggs, for which she won
many prizes.

I won prizes for my butter too. I remember once while carrying a plate
with two pounds of show butter, I fell over a box in the dark of the kitchen
passages with disaster to the butter and the plate. However I went back to
the dairy, where there was luckily enough cream to make up a fresh lot. I
won first prize with it.

If there was a message for the blacksmith or carpenter I was the one who
volunteered to take it. The blacksmith's forge was about a mile away on
the main Perth-Dundee road at the Halfway House. I used to linger watching agricultural machinery being repaired or horses being shod. Sometimes I was allowed to blow the forge or watch the process of welding on
the anvil. I used to watch in the carpenter's shop next door, too window
frames or new cart wheels being made for a farm cart, or the hay bosses
for tramp coles being nailed together.

Down the back avenue there was the Post Office, and opposite this was
Morton's Engineering Works, a large stone building with steel hammers
working and shaping out pieces of metal. Once I was allowed to place a
penny under the hammer and the terrific pressure ironed it flat. I put it in
my treasure chest. Then I summoned up enough courage to ask Mr Morton,
"How can I learn to be an engineer and go to sea?"

"You will have to serve an apprenticeship," he said smiling. "Find a
shop with a vacancy and start at the beginning, and when you have served
your time, find a ship that will give you a berth as an engineer." He smiled
at me in my holland pinafore and pink sunbonnet and I don't think he
believed for a moment that I meant what I said.

On the other side of the railway was Doe's where agricultural machinery was assembled. Sometimes I was allowed inside the doors to inspect
more closely the threshing mills and the reapers and binders to see how
they worked.

There was a white Iceland pony, Hekla, who went in the trap and pulled
the lawn mower and the garden cart. She had been Mummy's pony. My
grandfather had been at Hull when a cargo ship came in from Iceland. On
her was a consignment of 20 Iceland ponies. My grandfather asked about
them and was told that they were to be sold for pit ponies. He was told

that once they went down the pits they would never come up again during their working lives. He bought all 20 of them and had them sent to Norfolk where he distributed them amongst his friends. Mummy was given Hekla for her own and she chose the only grey "the pick of the bunch", everyone said. When she married she brought him to Scotland and we took turns riding him.

Sometimes Mr Dalgetty, the horse dealer, would have a large consignment of Shetland ponies, about 300. They lived in one of the fields by the avenue until they were shipped to America or sold as pets. We used to slip down to the field to catch them with sugar and ride them bareback. Often we were pitched over their heads or kicked off, but we got very fond of them during the days when they were there. I chose a chestnut and Frances a black as our special ponies, and they came when they saw us. We called them "our" ponies.

One day when we went to the field with the sugar in our hands, it was empty. They had all gone.

"They've gone to America," Mr Dalgetty said, "but I'll be getting some more, perhaps next summer, and you can ride them."

But we felt unconsoled as we gazed at the empty field with the sugar sticky in our hands, and thought of the velvet noses and dark eyes of the two we loved best.

Mr Dalgetty was always our friend. I remember on one occasion when Frances and I went to Perth Cattle Show alone by train for the first time. We had many instructions as to where to meet Papa inside the show ground and we were given our return fares to Perth, and our show entrances, and told not to lean on the carriage doors. Off we walked to the station in our cream serge coats and skirts with our straw hats banded by Brigade ribbon, held by elastic under our chins.

At the station we solemnly bought our tickets, two half returns. The train came in and the stationmaster put us into a carriage with the minister and his wife, who were going through to Edinburgh, but kindly helped us out at Princes Street Station in Perth. We were almost swept from our feet by the exodus of the show crowds.

The way to the show led through the fairground. Of course we succumbed, and very soon had lost all our entrance money. We stood dejected and unhappy beside the show turnstile through which we had to pass to meet Papa inside. Panic seized us. What would happen if we were not at the rendezvous? Suddenly we were saved by an angel from heaven in the form of Mr Dalgetty.

"So what's the trouble?" he asked.

We threw ourselves on his mercy and explained.

"You shouldn't gamble," he remarked, and paid for us to go through. "Now be off with you," he brushed aside our thanks, "you don't want to keep the Captain waiting."

Struggling through the cattle and horses we arrived scarlet and out of breath at the rendezvous tent 2 minutes before Papa.

"You found your way all right," he remarked.

"Yes," we gasped, and trotted happily round with him talking to old friends, looking at hill ponies and Highland cattle, heather honey and goats. Finally we left before the ring broke and walked back to the station through the fair, where Papa casually knocked down a couple of rows of heads for us and won us the knife and fluffy dog we had so coveted earlier in the day. Suddenly we came face to face with our deliverer, and Papa stopped to talk to him.

Mr Dalgetty nodded to us and said with a twinkle, "You found your way all right then? Quite old campaigners, Captain."

Papa laughed.

Mr Stewart, the farmer at the Kingdom, was also our friend, and in late July would invite us down to pick a basket of delicious black May Duke cherries from a cherry tree that covered the sunny brick wall of the farmhouse.

In the autumn he would formally engage us to lift potatoes. My sister Jean and I, and later Frances and I, shared a piece, but the soil was very heavy clay and one could hardly move the potato basket. The machine used to come round the drills turning up the potatoes and scattering the browned shaws from the first frost. It was all hurry-scurry to get our baskets filled and our piece cleared before the cart came round and the baskets were thrown up and emptied. If we were quick enough, we could sit on the upturned basket till the machine came down the next drill. It was a non-stop job and we carried on till the October sun slipped behind the trees in a round red ball and the damp mist began to rise from the ground. On the last evening we all lined up and were paid for our work. Later we were taken to Dundee and fitted out with winter boots, which we had paid for with our own money, and then given a lovely tea as a treat.

In the winter Papa did a great deal of curling and Mummy sometimes skated. We had skates too, and when the pond was bearing, we loved trying to copy the elegant figures they made on the ice. We also had a little toboggan which Papa had brought back from Canada when he was ADC to the Governor of Newfoundland in the '80s. Once my sister Frances and I took our sledge on the high road and tied it behind a van. At first it was lovely as we glided along, then the snow became bumpy and we found we could not untie the knot and the driver could not hear us calling because the wind was against us. Finally he whipped up his horse and we could hardly keep on the road. We were carried on and on until at last he stopped at Inchture about 3 miles away. Two breathless children came rushing up to him as he jumped off the van, but he kindly untied our sledge and hailed a passing van that was going towards Megginch. As he lifted us in he called, "Never tie a knot you can't undo."

The Crash, as my mother and aunts called it, happened in 1906, just after my grandparents' golden wedding. The agent who had been managing all their financial affairs had been gambling with their money on the Stock Exchange. He lost it all and, unable to face the people he had defrauded, committed suicide. His suicide was the first that my grandparents knew of it. From having been millionaires with money no object, everything had to be sold. My grandparents were ill with shock and anxiety and the three unmarried aunts, Auntie Sib, Auntie Maggie and Auntie Flo, took them out to Valescure.

The two elder married aunts, Auntie May Cecil and Auntie Allie Rockley, moved into Didlington to arrange the sale of the house, the property, the marvellous library, the pictures, the furniture and the collection of Egyptology. Mummy did not join them, whether because she was not asked or for reasons of her own we never knew, but afterwards there was a coolness, and we were always treated as poor relations. When my grandparents returned in the spring, all had been finished and arranged, and they were able to move straight into the dower house of Foulden Manor, which was all that remained of the once great property. Not long after this my grandfather died.

We were all very sad as we were extremely fond of him. It was the end of a lot of nice things: the heronry, the fishing, the lake, evenings looking at marvellous books in the library, the sheets of orange blossom and camellias in the winter, the flowering lotus in the tropical pools, the museum, Mrs Ford, the gamekeeper, the chef, Mrs Bell's village shop, poinsettias and stephanotis and princely parties, the house in Grosvenor Square. The whole solid background of my childhood vanished as if it had never been.

John went to boarding school at the New Beacon in Kent soon after. Mother and Father went abroad, and the next year in May 1910, King Edward died quite suddenly. All the flags were at half mast and we flew the Red Ensign at half mast at Megginch. Everyone said how sad it was and what a brilliant statesman we had been deprived of as the church bells were tolled. The bell at Kilspindie was tolled so loudly by hitting it with a hammer that it cracked.

We all went to the combined memorial service in Errol Church. It was Frances' birthday, 20th May, and a glorious day, very hot and summery, the oak trees bursting into yellow green leaves. We climbed the stone stairs to the Gallery and sat in the high pews in the church, and stood while the Dead March from *Saul* was played on the new organ, big enough for a cathedral. The whole gallery shook with the vibration and I had to put my hands over my ears the noise was so loud. The church was packed, but at the close of the service the huge congregation streamed out quietly without the noise and clatter of the usual stampede.

I remembered with sadness a fat old man with a beard who had taken sticky toffees out of politeness and smiled kindly at a very little girl who had spoken out of turn.

Chapter Five
Coming Out - 1910-14

In 1910 Papa bought a Panhard car—a French taxi. It was red with the body covered in yellow cane basket work. It had large brass head lamps and low seats covered in French grey cloth. Inside it held four grown-ups, two on the back and two on folding chair seats that pulled out. The driver sat on the outside. The top was black leather and would open back in the style of a taxi. It was very comfortable and the seats were very soft. The tyres were large and pneumatic and mounted on wooden-spoked wheels. The car made a big difference to our way of life.

So did bicycles. We would pack up a basket of cold boiled new potatoes, hard boiled eggs and off we would set with our fishing rods, up to the hill burns at Kilspindie and Pitroddie to fish for trout. John was the best fisherman, but we all caught quite a lot though they were only 4 or 5 ounces.

Now we too went out all day beating among the heather on the 12th, with the drone of a myriad bees and the blue hills only matched in colour by the bright blue butterflies that flitted about. The distant sapphire highland hills made a striking panorama: Schiehallion, Beinn-y-Ghlo, Ben Vrackie, Ben Venue. One could look right away to Aberdeenshire or to the hills of Argyll in the far west, and nearer at hand the Sow of Atholl and Birnam Hill, and close at hand Dunsinnan. One could imagine Birnam Wood walking to Dunsinnan over the flat strath between the famous hills. If one looked south the whole Carse of Gowrie was spread below with its golden harvest fields and orchards stretching away to Dundee and the sea with the Lomonds of Fife in the distance beyond the far bank of the Tay.

We used to plunge lemonade bottles into the cold pools of brown peat water that tinkled away beneath grasses and bunches of heather, a natural refrigerator which would do its work before lunch. We would drop in the heather and watch the pointers working, suddenly standing poised, tail stiffly horizontal, front paw raised in a point, then slowly advancing till with a whir the covey of grouse rose. By lunch time our legs were scratched and our faces and hands blue with blaeberry stains and we were nearly as hot as the pointers and setters tied to the keeper's stick, their pink tongues so far out we thought they would never go back again. We knew they might have a piece of bread and butter each, but never a cheese sandwich because this would spoil their nose. Mummy used to sketch and sometimes Papa brought her a bunch of white bell heather, twice as lucky as the ordinary white. At the end of the afternoon's walk we would all meet at the spring by the alder trees above Evelick where the water was the coldest and clearest for miles, then back we would go in the tea cart with bunches of heather to decorate the house, the pointers asleep at our feet.

We also loved the river, and when the salmon nets were taken off at Seggieden we delighted in spending a day fishing there with our Drummond-Hay cousins. We used to troll for brown trout, sea trout and sometimes net a grilse. It was lovely on the river during the late August and September days, the water quietly slipping past the tarred sides of the coble. The feathery topped reeds had tints of gold as we glided past the mud flats with bright patches of Michaelmas daisies and yellow tansy. Suddenly the line would run out, backwards and forwards dashed our invisible fish, till a dripping landing net deposited the flapping sea trout at the bottom of the boat.

When the river was low we would go fishing for pearls, gazing through glass bottomed tins and bringing up mussels from the mud with a forked stick. Occasionally our catch produced a brown pearl or sometimes a very small white one, but we were always spurred on by the thought that the pearls in the crown jewels of Scotland were Scottish.

Now that we were older we did fewer lessons and learnt housework: how to sweep and polish, turn out a room, care for furniture, polish silver and how to cook. There was also the laundry work of washing and bleaching, starching and ironing. Mummy said whatever one learnt one must learn from the foundation. We were also more responsible for the fruit picking, and very hard work it was among the small fruit, the strawberries and raspberries, black currants and red currants in July, and later in the orchards, working among the plums, apples and pears.

We also went in for competitions. Frances won painting competitions and I made models. I saw an advertisement in *Little Folks* for an international toy competition and I made a model of an Indian camp, about 18 by 12 inches in size, complete with wigwam, birch bark canoe, Indians, papooses, pond, trees and dogs. I kept it in a box and spent every spare minute working on it. I started making it in January and finished and despatched it the next August. Anything I thought not good enough I would make over again. At last I remember looking at it and thinking, "I can't do any more to it." I made a wooden box to pack it in, sent it off and heard no more. Each day I went to look for the post, but I heard nothing. At last, one dark day in November, a letter and a packet came to me. I had won first prize, a medal and a silver watch.

After that there was no holding me. Any competition I heard of I would enter. Much later I entered a model toy in a show in the Albert Hall where thirty thousand dolls and toys were on view. It was opened by the Lord Mayor of London. I made a lighthouse, painted red and white, a beam cast by an electric light on top. It stood on rocks washed by white crested waves. The lighthouse was about 18 inches high and the rocks and sea below 14 inches square. I won second prize.

The next year I made a model of The House that Jack Built. The rat, the malt, the cow with the crumpled horn, everything in the house I thought out and made. Sunflowers and hollyhocks grew round the door. I tried hard to get the character of the various figures and fit each piece of wood neatly in the building of the house. I won a special prize for it.

Our biggest disappointment was the great cocoa competition. We had to collect labels from tins of unsweetened cocoa. No one liked it very much, although we kept forcing ourselves to drink more and more to get enough labels. If we sent in enough with a suitable verse praising the cocoa we would receive a jewelled casket of chocolates. When the casket arrived, it was a small, embossed and painted tin and only contained one layer of unsweetened chocolates wrapped in a great deal of paper scraps.

When John returned from school one holiday he was bubbling over with excitement at seeing the plane in which Bleriot crossed the Channel displayed in Selfridges. Everyone was inclined to think that flying was an interesting but passing experiment that would never be of any real practical use, but John made endless little cardboard planes driven by elastic which he flew over the fountain.

Another great innovation was to cycle on the high road without a hat. "Have you joined the Hatless Brigade?" I was asked one day when I arrived hatless and breathless with a message at the Station. The Hatless Brigade were a small number of people who thought hats unnecessary. Most people would rather have thought of flying the Channel in an aeroplane than of going shopping in Dundee without a hat.

1911 was Coronation Year and Jean, who had been presented the year before, went down to London to see the Procession with my parents. John was given a seat in the House of Lords stand and came up for the day from prep school with his cousin Robert Cecil. Frances and I were very envious of Jean and the two boys, but to make up Nana took us to see the decorations in Edinburgh during the King and Queen's visit.

My parents always gave a School Treat and Garden Party in the summer. It was held in June after the thinning of the neeps and before the cutting of the hay so that all the farmers could lend corn carts and men for a day to transport the children down. As the corn carts, loaded with cheering and singing children, left the village en route for Megginch $2^1/_2$ miles away we could hear the musical Scottish voices carried on the still summer air. We were thrilled when we saw the first cart turn into the avenue among the wild dog roses, the sun glinting on the brass studded collars of the horses decorated in coloured wool and tassels, their manes plaited with ribbon. The children had mugs tied with string round their necks and they sat on each side of the path in a long line while grace was said by the minister and trays of sausage rolls and bridies were handed out and milk poured into outstretched mugs. And then there were the races. I shall never forget winning first prize in the boys' obstacle race when I was eight. What a triumph that was and how cross everyone had been at the state of my hair, dress and knees.

For the Coronation Year even more people were invited to the garden party. All the children were given Coronation Medals and mugs and Papa let off fireworks in the evening. We could see two bonfires alight on hills which seemed to burn until dawn. That year we spent Christmas at home as there was no Didlington. We had a huge Christmas tree in the hall lit by candles and there was a Christmas party in the house for the Sunday school children.

In the cold winter of 1912 I cut out all the pictures I could find in the papers and made a little model of the *Titanic*, the great new liner that was to sail in the spring. She was to be the fastest liner in service on the Transatlantic run. We were all speculating how long her maiden voyage would be, but no one ever imagined that she would be at sea for such a short time; she went down on 14th April. The news came as a great shock and I put my little model away in a cupboard.

I was eighteen this year and on my birthday we had a small dance at Megginch. Miss Scott in Errol made my first evening dress. It was a long pale blue dress covered with filmy white lace and made from the court train of Cousin Katie Smythe. There were pale blue shoes to match. We danced in the dining room to the strains of the pipes and violin, the soft lighting from lamps and candles shining on the portraits of my ancestors who seemed to smile down on us, or catching the sheen of the dresses or the swing of the kilts. There were candles in pink shades lighting the home-made buffet, sparkling on the silver and the best china. Jean had already been to lots of dances. She wore a white dress embroidered with pink rosebuds and pink satin shoes to match. Frances, who was only fifteen, wore a short evening frock. It was all such a success that Papa said I should be presented the next year.

"Oh no," said Mummy, "she is too young."

Papa quoted from Mistral, the Provençal poet:

"Gay lizard, enjoy the sun;

The hour passes too quickly.

Tomorrow it may rain perhaps."

And so it was agreed that I would be presented in the early spring.

We started south on 5th February, Jean's birthday, catching the early train at Errol Station. We left nothing behind except Mummy's fur coat. There were lunch baskets bought at Stirling, where the fields were flooded, and tea baskets at Crewe. When we got to Euston, Papa went to stay at his club and Mummy, Jean and I to Cousin Seschie in Hill Street. It was a little different from my grandparents' great house in Grosvenor Square where there was always room for everyone, but Cousin Seschie was enormously kind to us and gave us pineapple for dinner.

The day before the Presentation, people rang us up and we received lots of letters. It was all so exciting. Mummy took us in a taxi to the Junior Carlton Club to find Papa who took us to the market at Covent Garden. Later, I changed into my blue silk dress again and we went off for dinner at the Savoy, finishing with cherries and cream, and then went to see *The Headmaster* at the Playhouse.

Friday 7th February was the day of my Presentation. Cousin Henry took Mummy and Jean to the Tate Gallery and Papa and I went for a walk to a French book shop and to Gorringes, and finally to Peels where he was fitted for a pair of shoes.

My court dress was white satin with Spanish silk lace and bunches of snowdrops. When I was dressed, Jean did my hair and Mummy put on my feathers and veil. We had dinner at 7pm and an hour later started off in a motorcar with white linen on the seats and an electric light. Cousin Seschie's footman came with us.

We joined the long line of carriages and motorcars in the Mall, gradually moving up to Buckingham Palace through the pouring rain. At the entrance we went up a flight of red carpeted stairs and left our coats, then into a long passage with pictures and hothouse flowers banked in moss, and finally into a large room where we sat on white cane chairs. All was white and gold, mirrors and sparkling chandeliers. Through the door we saw the diplomats and members of the Household going to the Throne Room. After them we were allowed out two rows at a time. Then it was our turn, and as Mummy made her curtseys to the King and Queen, the King recognised her.

The King wore the scarlet uniform of Colonel-in-Chief of the Coldstream Guards, and the Queen wore a shimmering silver gown shot with pink and shining with emeralds and diamonds, and lace on her train. Behind the King and Queen were the Royal Circle. I gave up my card and heard my name called out: "Miss Victoria Alexandrina Drummond," but I wasn't a bit nervous. When I curtseyed, the King smiled at me, though I didn't expext it. It all went so quickly I could hardly believe it. So many people, and so much glitter of jewellery. Mummy seemed to know lots of people and she told me, "In the Royal Circle were the Princess of Battenberg, the Duchess of Albany, Princess Marie-Louise of Schleswig-Holstein, and Prince Arthur of Connaught standing just to the right of the King."

Afterwards we had a supper of soup and sandwiches, cakes and sweeties and plenty of lemonade. I put some sweets in my bag to take home for the others.

The rest of our week in London passed in a whirl of excitement and entertainment. We signed our names in the books at Buckingham Palace and at Marlborough House, we went to the Portrait Gallery and the Wallace Collection, to Gorringes and the Army and Navy Stores, and Cousin Henry took us to the pantomime of *Sleeping Beauty* at Drury Lane and to *Drake* at His Majesty's. On Sunday we went by train to Sevenoaks and took John out to lunch from the New Beacon, driving up the yellow sandy street to the Crown Hotel. After lunch I gave John the sweet I had saved for him from Buckingham Palace, a bit sticky by then, and we walked through the gardens at Knole.

At the end of our lovely week Mummy went to Foulden to stay with Granny and the aunts, while Papa, driving to Euston through the thickest of peasoupers, took us home on the train.

That summer John went to Eton and in June my parents were commanded to attend a Court Ball and to my great joy so was I. The snowdrops were taken off my presentation dress and white rosebuds sewn on. I had new satin shoes and new gloves. Mummy's dress was black and silver, trimmed with a new red rose from Paris. The State Ball was in honour of the President of France and everyone said it would be the most brilliant event of the season.

It was a lovely hot evening as we drove through the streets to the Ball. We passed flower sellers with baskets of roses, but a policeman told a footman to put the windows up as the suffragettes intended to throw ink on the ladies' dresses.

"That's the last thing we want," Mummy laughed, but we agreed that votes for women must come in the end. "It's a pity the suffragette movement have to do such silly things," said Mummy.

There was a Guard of Honour of the Coldstream Guards in the quadrangle, and the Bodyguard in their brilliant uniforms on duty in the palace. The ball opened with the royal quadrille, the King dancing with the Crown Princess of Sweden and the Queen with the Duke of Connaught to Strauss's *Opernball*. It was a wonderful spectacle; the sparkling jewels, shining dresses, glittering uniforms as the 22 couples went through the stately movements. A cousin invited me to dance and as we waltzed it was like gliding in a dream over a floor of glass.

One side of the supper room was banked with plants in green moss while on the other a long buffet glittered with shining silver and shaded lights. I was intrigued with the bows and trails of tricolour spun sugar ribbon as a compliment to France. Behind the food the gold plate was displayed. And through it all went the music from *Romeo and Juliet*, *Samson and Delilah*, *the Meistersingers*. Long after I had gone home the music ran in my head and I hummed the tunes from that enchanted evening.

Everything about the summer seemed golden, not least the weather. We did all the usual things, had our garden party for the children, went to Oban on the west coast which Papa preferred to Elie, went shopping on Fridays in Dundee with Nana, often went swimming in the Dundee swimming baths, picked fruit, made butter and helped to entertain a constant flow of visitors. Jean went abroad or on visits, so much of the work of entertainment fell on Frances and me.

I had heard of the Atholl Highlanders' Gathering at Blair and the dance there in September, so I broached the subject cunningly to Papa, professing ignorance. Finally he was driven into saying, "Fancy knowing so little about the home of your ancestors. You had better go up with your Aunt Maggie and see for yourself."

As this was exactly what I had been planning, I took care not to show too much enthusiasm in case he might change his mind. However, all was well, and on Friday 5th September, Aunt Maggie and I took the train from Errol and headed for Blair Atholl, where we arrived early that evening. We went to the Atholl Arms Hotel where we found an invitation for the

Ball and an invitation from Cousin Helen Murray to dine with them at 7.30pm.

My presentation dress was disguised this time with a Drummond tartan sash and I wore a sprig of Drummond holly on it and a wreath of holly leaves in my hair.

It was a beautiful night as we drove up to Blair. The castle looked very large shining out of the darkness, a light in nearly every window. As we stopped at the front door, footmen in kilts came out. When they opened the door of the drawing room, we walked into a blaze of electric light and a room filled with about 30 people.

Many of them were from the Atholl family. The Duke, huge, bearded and very frightening, said "How do you do?" Cousin Hamish came up and asked me to draw a card from a pack to see who I would go into dinner with. It was the two of clubs and Hamish said, "Bother, I'm out of it!" I had Mr Wallace, who was rather difficult to talk to, but we got on better when I learned he liked fishing.

The table was huge, covered with gold plate, yellow marguerites and smilax trails. There were ten courses for dinner and near the end the doors opened and seven pipers came in playing the *Marquis of Tullibardine*. They went three times round the table and then out of the door, where they played *Tummelside*. The noise was deafening.

After dinner we went into the drawing room which had a huge fire and where two kilted footmen handed round coffee. Cousin Kitty then took me and Auntie Maggie to tidy up in her room. We walked down passages and stairs for ages and then through a very long passage where the walls were hung with horns.

"I'm afraid it's a bit dark," Kitty said, "we're saving the lights as there is not much water in the dam."

After we had got our gloves buttoned we went all the way back to the drawing room. By this time a lot more people had arrived, I think they were shooting tenants. We were all introduced and then we went down to the ballroom in a long procession, arm in arm. I went down with Kitty's nephew, Mr Ramsay.

The ballroom was enormous, the walls hung with horns and swords and flags, and everything was brilliantly lit with electric light. There was a dais at one end where all the ladies sat. There was a tight row of Atholl Highlanders round the room and when the pipe band struck up the *Atholl Highland March* they all marched up and down the room. Their bonnets all had pieces of juniper stuck in them and they danced a foursome together. It was a very fine sight.

I danced most of the dances and when supper was served Hamish took me down. We had lobster pates and lemonade. Then we had to go back and I danced even more.

We said goodbye to the Duke, who was quite affable, and to Hamish, whom I found at the door. Auntie Maggie said she was afraid we were very late. "Not late for Blair," Hamish laughed. We went down the steps and into the carriage and next day we got the train home; it all felt like a wonderful dream.

Further excitement was in store that year, on 11th December Jean and I were invited by Cousin Helen to join her party for the Highland Ball in Edinburgh. We went by train with Nana. Presently Helen came in on the Highland train. She seemed very pleased to see Jean and me, and said we could all travel to Edinburgh together.

I had to say, "We are travelling third."

"Never mind," said Helen, "I will change and come with you." But of course we wouldn't let her.

When we got to Edinburgh we met up with Helen again and went into the Caledonian Hotel. Our rooms were on the third floor, looking out at the Castle. We lit the fire and I had a sleep while Nana and Jean went out shopping and then to tea with Nana's friend Mrs Cook.

I wore my white satin dress and tartan sash with holly in my hair, my pearl cross locket around my neck. Jean wore her blue satin dress and silver in her hair.

Hamish was waiting in the Coffee Room with the other men and he seemed very pleased to see Jean and me. It was lovely talking to Hamish; I felt as if I had known him always, we had the same sense of humour, and the same jokes. I said I remembered him coming to Megginch when I was four, and we talked about the pictures. He said I was just like the picture of Lady Charlotte, who had been a Murray with huge grey eyes and black hair. He said, "If your parents, brother and sisters are fair, where do you get your black hair from?"

I had to say, "I don't know."

After dinner we all went off in cabs to the Assembly Rooms where there were 850 people. The ballroom was brilliantly lit and decorated with ever-greens, deer heads and tartan.

Next day we went Christmas shopping and then we had to go home. Hamish asked if we were coming to the concert that night, but we said we couldn't as we hadn't got tickets. We were a little sad having to leave in the middle of it all, but it couldn't be helped and it had been so lovely.

We saw Hamish again the next spring when we stayed with my Oswald cousins at Dunnikier in Fife. One day Papa took me to Edinburgh where we met Hamish and he showed us all over the castle. He said, "I wouldn't take the others round the castle at the time of the Highland Ball since I was saving it up for you."

Mummy was making great plans for the next year. She intended to take Frances and me to Rome to stay with her friends the Giustiniani-Bandinis, so that we could learn Italian and study art. 1914 seemed to be full of promise.

In June Papa took me to Normandy. One day as I rushed on to the sands, I felt myself sinking into quicksand. A Frenchman in a brown suit wearing a straw hat pulled me out and luckily retrieved my shoe which had come off. All Papa said when I rejoined him on the cliffs was, "You look very wet", and he laid down his field glasses.

Normandy was lovely, little cobbled streets, green forests and fields of white marguerite daisies, stained glass windows in the Cathedral at Rouen, patisseries selling apple pastries, piles of sabots in shops, pink sunsets over the sea and long summer shadows.

When we returned home we heard of the assassination of the Archduke Franz Ferdinand at Sarajevo on 28th June. As we drove up the avenue on the way home, the field on the right opposite the railway line was high in growing corn.

Papa said, "That field has not been sown in wheat since I was a boy, and we stood on the road with our ponies as they ate the green wheat while waiting for news of the Franco-German War. I hope it does not mean war again."

But we did not pay much attention and everything went on much as usual. We were busy with the small fruit and the hay, the school picnic and thinking of the flower show in Errol on 29th July.

July 25th was a lovely hot day. I remember helping Mummy cut lavender in the garden, which she laid on a white sheet to be dried for lavender bags or to make twists for bazaars.

She said, "You will need a new dress before we go to Italy in October, and a new pair of shoes, too, as you can't cover those again. The pink silk lining of my court train might be very pretty. We will think about getting it made up."

On the day of the Errol Flower Show everyone was talking of a possible war. We won first prize for our sweet peas for the third time running and Jean won a first for her baking, but no one could talk of much except the war.

Everywhere was rumour and tension. Even Aunt Ayia's traditional birthday party on 31st July in the log house built for Lady Charlotte was overshadowed by the headlines in the evening paper:

GERMANY DECLARES WAR ON RUSSIA
STOCK EXCHANGES CLOSE
BANK RATE DOUBLES
BELGIUM AND HOLLAND MOBILIZE

By Sunday 2nd August, all the reserves were called up and the stillness of Sunday peace was broken by the rumble of trains passing through the night.

Tuesday 4th August 1914 was the sort of day when it was impossible to settle to anything. I think the air was so charged with everyone's anxious thoughts all over the country that it built up this terrific tension. Trains unscheduled and uncounted rumbled and thundered all that night along the railway line below the Park. By 5th August 1914 the headline of the morning paper was:

GREAT BRITAIN AND GERMANY AT WAR

I think we all knew it was the end of a golden age.

Chapter Six
War and Apprenticeship - 1914-18

On 5th August 1914, we drove down with Papa and Mummy to Errol Station to see off the reservists. Things happened so quickly. Anyone who was a reservist left his tools in the field and went. A boy had been hoeing weeds in the garden, and left his hoe where it fell when his mother came with the news that he had been called. Papa and Mummy gave them all cigarettes and they cheered and sang, calling from the departing train, "We will soon be back. It won't last long once we get there!" And everybody waved and gave them such a cheer as the train puffed out.

Later in the day an official asked Papa and Mummy how many wounded they could take if there was a big naval engagement. They said they could manage a hundred and they were told that if there were an emergency, equipment and nurses would be sent. Luckily there never was.

In the afternoon paper censorship was announced and notices were given that all private or experimental wireless sets had to be dismantled. On a more local note, Papa was made Chairman of the Errol Defence Committee. He sent us to fetch the evening paper from the Station and see if any more news had come through, so Frances and I dashed off on our bicycles. While we were waiting for the paper to come off the train we saw Mr Dalgetty, the horse dealer.

"Will you take a message to the Captain?" he said. "Tell him the government officials come this evening. They are going round requisitioning horses."

"Will they take Punchie and Hekla away?" we asked tremulously.

"Yes, if they want them."

I suppose we must have looked very sad, for he remarked kindly, "Don't worry, I shall be there."

We had hardly time to give Papa the message before they arrived and he went with the deputation to the stables. They were in a great hurry. Our hearts were in our mouths, but as they left we heard them say to Mr Dalgetty, "You're right, they are well preserved, but old horses are a liability."

So we breathed again. Mr Dalgetty smiled at us and we ran down to throw our arms round the horses' necks and give them sugar, telling them they weren't going to leave us after all.

In the early days of the war it was thought that invasion would be attempted almost within hours. Papa was hard at work with his meetings of the Defence Committee, which also had to cope with the arrival of the Belgian refugees. Mummy was called in here as she was bilingual in French and so was constantly required to translate. Nana went to the Red Cross Hospital in Perth two days a week to cut out material for shirts, she could cut out without wasting a scrap. We girls were organised into knitting sock tops for the Highland regiments. We all knitted at every available moment. Mummy also ran the local Soldiers and Sailors Help Society and the Families Association, which involved a great deal of visiting and writing, so both of us helped her. We also did a lot more garden work as the gardeners had all been called up.

"I would rather use a sword than a ploughshare," I said to Frances as I picked up Jimmy's hoe and attacked the weeds.

Twice a week, too, we picked through spaghnum moss in the rooms we had laid out for the Naval wounded. Sacks and sacks of it arrived from the Highland bogs, fluctuating in colour from pale shades of cream to green and pink. This moss had to be carefully picked over to remove bits of heather or leaves and the hard bud at the end of each strand. The cleaned soft moss was then made up in flat gauze bags ready for wound absorbent dressings; the supply of cotton wool or lint was already limited.

My Aunt Ayia, who was on a Defence Committee in Perth, had formed an organisation called the Perthshire Patriotic Barrow. This was a tea trolley run by voluntary helpers to provide tea and sandwiches to all troop trains which came through Perth. The trolley was more colloquially known as "The Barrow" and shifts of ladies met every train from five in the morning until midnight, bearing hot cups of tea and welcome sandwiches to all men in the forces who came thundering through Perth in the big troop trains. By the end of the war they had supplied over a million and a half cups of tea.

We also helped the war effort by providing fresh vegetables for ships. We dug some from our own garden and drove round in the donkey cart collecting from neighbouring gardens. Even the school children grew vegetables on their allotments. The vegetables were then despatched to Dundee by train where they were taken on board ships. By 1915, the Vegetable Products Committee, as it was called, had 549 branches across the country. Jean ran the Megginch branch.

So many of our friends were killed or wounded.

Reading the casualty lists in the papers every day was compulsive but dreadful. My cousin Billy Cecil was killed in 1915, so was James Stewart with whom I had danced at the Edinburgh Highland Ball and Logie Leggatt, who had been at Eton with my brother and had stayed with us in 1912. Mummy sent him food parcels and letters as she did to so many; William Murrie, Duncan Robertson and William Bannerman from Errol, who were all prisoners of war.

On 14th October 1915, I was 21. Mummy gave me a silver mounted umbrella, one pound, four packets of socks, three books on conjuring and a writing block. Papa gave me a paint box and two Parisian sparkly shoe buckles. Jean and Frances and John clubbed together with my parents to give me a silver blue fox fur boa and muff. Jean also gave me a book, and Frances a box of chocolates.

Papa said, "Now you are 21, you can choose your own career."

"I'm going to be a marine engineer," I said, but I don't think he took me seriously.

It was just over a year later that I made a start on my career. I went into Perth by train with my parents, and while they were shopping, I went for an interview to the Garage in South Street. They said I could have a week's trial, so I bought overalls ready to start on Monday. I caught the train home with Mummy and Papa.

"Well, how did you get on?"

"The first shop I tried has given me a week's trial," I said in great excitement, "and I have bought overalls to start on Monday."

So I started in the garage in Perth on Monday 18th October 1916.

My first job each morning was to sweep up the shop floor, brush down the bench and put the tools in order for the day's work. My other job was washing various parts of machinery in a large paraffin bath, scraping off the dirt and scraping out the oil and grease from gear boxes, carefully soaking and picking out any broken fragments from the black paraffin of the bath and placing them in a tin lid beside the cleaned part that I dragged over and lifted on to the bench.

I was always on the look out for metal grindings and the corresponding bright polished patches on the moving parts. When I had finished cleaning a job, the foreman, Mr Malcolm, would ask me, "What did you find?" And I was able to show him exactly and quickly any discoveries I had made.

The bath was situated at the back of the shop and by the end of the day's work the cement floor was awash with paraffin from the various dripping parts. This was strewed with sawdust to sweep down the rest of the shop and get rid of the oil. Each evening I was black.

At the end of the week, to my great delight I was asked to stay on as an apprentice and was told I would have an apprentice's pay. My first week's pay was kept back as "lying time", but at the end of the next week I arrived home proudly with my first pay packet of 3/- per week. I was also insured, the 6 pence stamp money deducted from my weekly pay. In those days the usual apprenticeship pay was 3 shillings a week for the first year, 6 shillings a week for the second year, 9 shillings for the third year, 12 shillings for the fourth year, and the last and fifth year improved to a journeyman's pay.

Everyone's apprenticeship days are much the same. One is always black, hungry and tired by the end of each day.

Usually I would bring a "piece" from home as I was too black to go out in the dinner hour, but sometimes I would clean up and take my sandwiches to the station and have a cup of coffee in the refreshment room with my Aunt Ayia. We could see the long troop trains crowded with khaki-clad soldiers. They would hang out of the windows as the train moved out, singing the songs of the moment. Sometimes a long silent hospital train wound through, displaying the Red Cross. This was always a very sad sigh. My Aunt Ayia was so proud of me in my dirty boiler suit, black finger nails and all.

"This is my niece Victoria," she would introduce me, "who is doing war work in a garage."

I was extremely lucky to be under as good a foreman as Mr Malcolm. He had served his time on the Clyde before going to sea where he rose to the rank of Chief Engineer. He had also worked in every branch of engineering in his time, and there was nothing he did not know about it.

"What you don't understand, ask," he would say, "and try and keep all your fingers. Remember always, a hand for yourself and a hand for your master."

Later on, in 1917, when another apprentice, Johnny Young, started, he was given the job of sweeping the shop floor and bench and washing the machines in the paraffin bath. I was promoted to assisting at the bench or dismantling various engines and handing the parts over to the new apprentice to wash and clean.

My work as an assistant at the bench mostly consisted of "holding the job" or "passing the tools". A good apprentice should watch all the time and know the next tool required, handing it smartly. Soon I was given jobs on various cars and agricultural machinery, and on completion of the job my work was tested by the foreman.

Some of Mr Malcolm's seafaring days had been spent in the Baltic and White Sea. I remember we had a very cold spell of weather and the temperature fell below zero, but when we apprentices shivered with the cold, lying on snow-sodden sacks in our cotton overalls and old jerseys under a lorry, the only comfort we got was, "Wait till you are frozen in Archangel with no heating on the ship."

My jobs were numerous and varied now, and three times a week in the evenings I took special instruction in maths and engineering subjects with Mr Martin of Dundee Technical College. Sometimes when I got home I would give Frances a hand by the light of an oil lantern to sort and grade apples, and pack the ten stone barrels, as it was often midnight before she could finish work for the day.

She had to stand on a box and hang over the barrel to reach the bottom, packing the apples round and round in layers, not too tight to bruise when packing, not too loose to bruise in transit, till the large barrels were full and ready to cover. She managed all the fruit for Papa, a big undertaking with two large orchards, also a big kitchen garden with only a few elderly men and young boys to assist her. So it entailed working from dawn to dusk, and a bit more. When the fruit was too wet to be picked, or it was too wet and dark to work outside, she would paint designs for window displays which she had been commissioned to do.

I continued to make butter at least once a week, even though it meant getting up very early in the morning before I started for work.

In 1917 Jean also took off to do war work. She went to an explosives factory at Gretna where she worked as Supervisor in the Acid Section, a very dangerous job where no hair pins could be worn nor anything metal, and the girls had to have their hair tied up in bath caps. The fumes of the acid were also very bad for the skin.

My bicycle played a large part in those days; I took it to Perth with me on the train in the morning, and delivered messages on it. In summer I often bicycled the 10 miles home instead of waiting at the station, as local trains were often delayed by hospital and troop trains.

In those war days at work it was very difficult to obtain spares and often I had to make sketches from reconstructed broken parts, occasionally for turning gear wheels. Mr Malcolm sent my sketches away for renewals to be cast, and on receipt of the castings I had to work out the pitch of the teeth for the current ratio, mark them off and cut them out by hand. The foreman taught me how to set the trimming of the valves on various cars, and once he stood at the shop door after I had reset the steam valves of a traction engine and watched me drive her in the street. I think it was one of those days when drink had got the better of him.

I tried to learn everything I could and worked on every kind of engine. By jumping in and out of cars when opportunity offered I soon learnt to crank them up and drive them. No self starters in those days. We always had a lot of bottom ends to re-metal and fit, also electrical repair work. In fact a bit of everything that came along. I learnt to braze, weld and case harden, also to turn, and I could set up my job on the lathe and turn in metal or wood. I could also use a hammer and chisel as a tradesman and not as if I were knocking in tacks, as the foreman said. He had many quick methods of doing jobs, and calculating weights and strength of tackle for a "lift" that were quite original and have often proved very helpful.

There were always minor accidents in engineering shops and I had my share. Once when I was holding a job that was being soldered a big lump of molten solder fell on my hand.

"Teach you to hold the job still," I was told, as the solder was dug out with the tang of a file and paraffin poured into the hole. Paraffin was a cure for everything, though there was a strong theory that tarry string bound round was better. These remedies were considered far superior to the first aid box.

Another time the large blow lamp blew up, but luckily no one was hurt since I grabbed the glass bottle of petrol from the bench as it became enveloped in flames.

Mr Malcolm remarked as he poured oil over my burnt fingers, "Someone might have lost an eye if that glass bottle had burst, too."

My worst accident was when I was working under a 10 ton lorry and it slipped off the jacks and came down on top of me. I was pinned underneath and Johnny could not lift her, so with great presence of mind ran into the street for help and through the strength of a kind passer-by the lorry was raised enough to pull me out with nothing worse than a broken collar bone and a couple of broken ribs.

"I think now you must have a holiday and a rest, Victoria," Mummy said firmly, and sent me to stay with my Granny and Auntie Flo in Foulden Manor. The train went past Gretna and I looked out to see if I could see Jean's explosives factory.

After spending some days in London, I went on to Foulden. Inside the house was filled with dark oak furniture and there was a huge grandfather clock. Outside there was a Dutch garden with a mirror pond in front of the brick house, with water lilies floating on the water, on either side a double row of pleached limes. There was a lavender hedge, a paved herb garden full of scented herbs and a hollow tree where there had once been a hornet's nest.

I spent most of my time at Foulden exploring the fens and swimming in a small stretch of water called Becket End. Granny was so pleased that I had learnt to turn, and we talked a lot on the subject comparing notes. In the evenings she liked music, and would sometimes still sing with her faultless voice. Sometimes, when the wind was in the right direction, we could hear the guns in France.

On the way back I stopped off at Gretna where I stayed with Jean at her Bungalow. She was now a supervisor in charge of 200 girls. One evening we went to a concert in the factory, and as I was returning on my bicycle a man pounced out from a ditch and tried to pull me off. Luckily Jean had gone on and I had just reached the crest of a hill, so I kicked him as hard as I could and hit his hand grasping the handlebars. He reeled back for a moment and I flew down the other side of the hill, leaving him running after me in the distance! Away I sped towards the safety of Jean's bungalow.

Back at the garage feeling fit again, there seemed more work than ever. Once Johnny and I had to tackle the overhaul of a most complicated continental car of a make we had never seen before. It was New Year and Mr Malcolm was having one of his more and more frequent bouts of drinking, so there was no supervision. By the time the repairs were completed there were a few bits and pieces we could not account for, so we put them at the bottom of the car's tool box and hoped for the best. Our minds were soon relieved as the owner said the car was easier to start and had never gone better, so we came to the conclusion that the bits and pieces had been superfluous.

Some jobs did not require much engineering skill. Once I was sent to a car stranded outside a pub. The owner had been trying to start the engine for many hours with the petrol turned off!

We always enjoyed trial runs and Mr Malcolm continually told us that we must tune our ears to the sound of the engine so that if we heard anything different we would know something was wrong and stop. "This applies to all engines," he said, "so remember that."

On stopping he would ask us, "What is wrong? Come on. You should know by the sound, and also what adjustments I am about to make. You are learning to be engineers, not fitters."

When he was sober, Mr Malcolm was very good company, and in the dinner hour we would sit round the fire in winter, or on the bench in

Her father

With her mother as a baby

Victoria, Frances and Jean

The children with Nana Watt

In the garden at Megginch

In her coming-out dress

*During her
apprenticeship*

*The Lilybank
Foundry*

In her deck uniform

Her beloved Second

SS Anchises

The first woman to hold a Board of Trade Certificate as a Marine Engineer

On board TSS Mulbera

With the crew of TSS Mulbera

Ashore in Colombo in 1928

With the de Booys in Holland

Her photograph of Hitler from a hotel room in Vienna

summer, while he told us stories of the Clyde engineering shops and of the sea, about Indian conjurors and the tricks they performed when they came on the ship in port, of sharks and whales he had seen or captured and of shipbuilding on the Clyde.

"If you want to be a marine engineer," he said, "you will have to train with a shipbuilding company."

"I am going to be a marine engineer,"I told him.

In winter it was very cold hanging about in the dark station waiting for a hospital or troop train to go through before the local train could leave, but once out at Errol Station, it was only a mile to cycle home. White hoar frost sparkled on bushes and trees in the moonlight, while on moonless nights the darkness seemed to close in about me. The oil lamp on my bicycle only showed a pale beam ahead. When the snow was deep I had to walk pushing my bicycle, wading through the ever deepening snow with snow flakes whirling all around me and beating on my face and back as the black branches of the trees overhead lashed by the force of a blizzard would beat together violently while the wind moved through them with a dreary howling note.

But after a wash, dry clothes and tea, I would get out my books and study for a couple of hours. Three times a week my friend Betty Henderson came to give me extra maths.

After two years at the garage the periods between Mr Malcolm's drinking bouts were becoming shorter. Johnny and I used to try and cover up for him as best we could but, inevitably he was discovered and the garage fired him.

I said to the owner, "Mr Malcolm is a very good engineer. He has taught me all I know. If he is fired, then I do not want to work here without him, so I would like to hand in my cards too."

I think I had known for some time that I had to move on.

Mummy got me an introduction to the Manager of the Caledon Ship Works in Dundee, and so I went of by train to Dundee. I left the West Station and crossed the cobbled street towards the quays. There was the smell of damp seaweed and seagulls were flying overhead, as I made my way to the tram stop. On arrival at the Caledon Yard Gate I showed my precious card of introduction and was sent to the office, where they were expecting me. I was hot and out of breath from running so far, but it was exactly 3.30 pm when I entered.

The Manager greeted me cheerily. "So you want to be a marine engineer and go to sea," he said. "Just sit down and tell me about it." The muffled noise of the yard even filtered through to this sanctum.

I explained as quickly as I could.

The Manager said, "Here where ships are built, we fit to $^1/_4$ inch. At Lilybank where engines and boilers are made, they fit to $^1/_{64}$ inch," and he laughed. "Where you should be is Lilybank. Your work there would give you plenty of opportunity to come down here on various jobs. Let me see. About 3,000 men are employed in the yard and foundry just now. What I propose is to make an appointment for an interview for you with the manager at Lilybank," and he picked up the telephone and spoke.

Then he wrote on the back of his card "To introduce Miss V A Drummond, 11 o'clock Tuesday, Lilybank."

I felt delighted and thanked him as I gazed at the framed pictures of ships that adorned the walls. The manager nodded at them.

"All built here," he said, then shook me warmly by the hand. "Good luck."

The whole visit had taken less than 15 minutes, yet it seemed an eternity.

On Tuesday morning in my best suit with the card in my hand and a line from Mr Malcolm in my pocket, I presented myself at Lilybank Foundry. I could hear the noise of the boiler shop as I walked up the street to the lodge. The manager was expecting me and I was shown up to a large room where I met Mr Thompson, the son of the head of the firm. He asked me to sit down and tell him about the work I had been doing. I showed him my line from Mr Malcolm and explained when my apprenticeship was completed I intended to go to sea as a marine engineer.

His father then came in and asked me some more questions about my work.

"We will give you a fortnight's trial," he said. "you will be in the pattern shop, and you can start on Monday."

I asked if I should be there at six in the morning.

He said, "No, at 9 o'clock your first day, and then we can see how the trains suit."

I was so thrilled and my parents were also pleased. Nana and Frances were delighted. Jean was still at her explosives factory, and John had joined the Grenadier Guards as a cadet at Bushey, so they had to be written letters.

The only sad part was saying goodbye to Mr Malcolm. He said he felt it was a step up the ladder and gave me a lot of advice. He also gave me a small round metal wire gauge.

"Often when I had a drink, and wanted another," he said laughing, "I thought this was a five bob piece in my pocket. When I put my hand in, I found it wasn't. If you don't like it, come back. You are welcome to come and see us any time, and some day when you have been over the Southern slope and return on leave in uniform and walk up the High Street with your badge on your cap and your Chief's braid up with all your medals, it will be a proud day for us all." But he was not there to see me.

Chapter Seven
Apprenticeship at Caledon - 1918-22

On Monday morning I put on a new dark blue bib and braces, rolled up my trousers, threw myself on my bike and flew down to the station. At Lilybank I was met by the manager who took me over to the pattern shop.

"You will soon get used to the noise of the works," he remarked.

The pattern shop was long and low, with windows and benches down the side and cross benches down the centre. As I entered, I was engulfed in the noisy drone of machinery, driving belts and the scratch of a circular saw. A warm cloud of floating white sawdust enveloped me and I remembered the old flour mill at Didlington.

My colleagues-to-be were all hard at work on their various benches and I was introduced to the foreman, Mr Begg, who showed me to my bench at the end of the shop.

"I'll lend her some tools," he said to the manager, "till all is settled. Then I can get the tools she requires. That's easily arranged."

"Well, I'll leave Miss Drummond in your hands," said Mr Thompson.

"And whose better?" was the reply. The foreman then put the tools he had picked out for me on the bench and told me to keep them clean and sharp till I got my own. He then put a blueprint in front of me: it was a pipe arrangement, with details and the number of the ship stamped on it. "The keel of that ship has been laid," he told me. "Here is a contraction rule. One side is for brass, one side for cast iron. Don't mix the scales. You can make this T-piece pattern. It's a split pattern as you can see. Allow for machining on the flange faces and ensure the case prints are the correct length."

He tapped the sheet with his rule. "The next one you will make is that small bend. Its brass. You will need to make a case box for it."

Mr Begg showed me round the machinery: hand saw, circular saw, lathe, planing and thicknessing machines, sand papering machine and surfacing machine.

"Don't put any pieces under 16 inches over that." he said. "The last apprentice that put a short piece of wood over lost all his fingers off one hand."

He then took me to the wood store and among the piles of planks pointed out the various kinds of wood. "Patterns by rights should only be made of yellow pine which is 15/6 a cubic foot now. With the war we have to use white spruce and red deal, although these woods twist too much for pattern making. Over there is lignum vitae. Use that for wooding the stern brushes. I will give you a piece of mahogany to make dowel pins for that split pattern you are going to make. When you have it ready for the lathe I will show you how to take the corner off on the circular saw. It's an awkward job."

My first day was spent calculating how much wood I required without waste and cutting it off the huge planks in the wood store, dragging it up to the shop, dressing it and cutting it to shape on the machines. True to his word, the foreman showed me the safest way to take the corners off on the circular saw before putting the job on the lathe. I centred and turned the body of the T-piece before knocking off, and next morning I turned the branch, cut out the six half flanges and screwed them in position.

My bench mate checked it over with his rule. "That's all right," he said. "Mind and make the dowel pins early so the top half of the box can be lifted without destroying the pattern. The next time the foreman passes tell him you have finished that job."

So I did, and he re-checked it and marked it to go down to the moulding shop and also marked it off on the sheet, entering it in his pocket notebook. He then pointed to the small brass bend on the blueprint.

"You can make a start on that," he said, and looking at his watch added, "in the morning."

I was glad to get back home to a cup of coffee by the nursery fire with Nana and Frances. Frances and I had both had Spanish Flu in September, and although only a mild dose, I still felt far from strong. Like death with an indiscriminate scythe, the Flu had sprung up suddenly, striking people down all over the country. Thousands died with it, so we considered ourselves lucky. Jean had caught it much more seriously at Gretna and was sent to the hospital there. John caught it at Bushey where he was training as a Guards cadet. He said he hoped to get well enough to leave hospital and go to France with his draft, which was due to leave in the second week of November. He informed us proudly that when he came out of hospital we would receive only field letters.

During my first two weeks of probation, my fellow workmates gradually got used to the idea of having a woman working with them and would talk in the few minutes before the whistle went.

One day the foreman called me over to his bench and remarked, "It can't be T-pieces all the time, it must sometimes be a piece for tea," and he handed me a delicious slice of cake made by his wife. After this he often brought me a slice of cake.

When I had completed my two weeks of probation the manager sent for me. It was arranged that I should stay on and go right through the shops. He told me that after the pattern shop I would go to the finishing shop and then possibly to the drawing office. He spoke so encouragingly to me that I felt thrilled with the programme that lay before me, and exclaimed, "I will do my very best, sir."

"The foreman tells me that you are not the kind that doesn't," he smiled. "I was under him when I was an apprentice."

The foreman was as good as his word and went down town to buy me my tools. He chose two chisels, three gauges with boxwood handles, one tenon saw, one rule, two compasses, a machinery gauge, a square, a hammer, a metal plane, a stone and two good slips and a spoke shave, a tool the foreman said should never have been invented as he preferred only the use of a chisel. The tools cost me just under £5. I was delighted with them and the foreman gave me time to make a box for them and yellow pine to make it with. I made two trays and various fittings for it, stained it yellow inside and mahogany outside and fixed a brass plate to the top with my name.

It was the second week in November 1918, the early fog had vanished as I set off for work, and when I arrived at my bench the sun was beginning to come out; a glorious autumn day with pale blue sky and brilliant sunshine. Suddenly a whisper swept through the shop, "The war is over."

Hardly had the foreman confirmed the rumour, when every ship on the river sounded its sirens and hooters, and the naval ships lying in the Tay let off rockets as every works whistle in Dundee blew, including ours. The whole foundry had emptied itself within minutes and we joined the great throng of cheering, shouting people, as they rushed down the street. All the jute mills came out, too, and the Lilybank Ragtime Band headed the procession. The crowds were terrific. I managed to catch the last tram going down town. All the trams were stopped before 12 o'clock as the crowds in the streets were so dense they could not pass through.

The Lord Provost announced from the steps of City Hall that an armistice had been signed and the war was over. By now the town was bright with hundreds of flags. Wearing a red, white and blue bow in my buttonhole I threw myself on to a local train for home. They were just finishing lunch as I rushed in.

"The war is over!" I shouted.

Our excitement was unbounded.

That afternoon we joined the crowds at Errol Station going to Dundee. It was a half holiday and as I bicycled to the station, I noticed a ladder and a half-filled basket full of red apples in the orchard. My mind flashed back to the abandoned hoe on the garden path that hot August day four years ago. Now only old men and young boys were celebrating the end of the war.

Dundee was in a whirl of excitement. The Band of the Highland Light Infantry marched through the streets playing rousing tunes. We walked over to the quay. It was thronged with sailors, mill girls, shipyard and foundry workers, people from the shops, fishermen and wounded soldiers all dancing reels. Even the fisher girls laid down their creels and danced.

"Come on, Captain," someone called to Papa, and we all joined in. I saw Papa dancing with a mill girl and we danced with sailors, fishermen and soldiers. When it was time to go home, we heard the crowds singing *It's a long way to Tipperary* as our train steamed out of the station.

Jean came back from Gretna to recuperate wearing a pneumonia jacket. She had missed all the fun of Armistice Day as she was in hospital. John came home also, having gone to London on Armistice Day. He said he would never forget the excited crowds and the cheering. A group of people shouted, "There's a Guards cadet," and carried him shoulder high.

But the next day was back to work for me in the pattern shop and everything went on much as before. Sometimes I would go to the moulding shop and see my patterns cast, or perhaps watch the blades for a propeller being swept up. In the months that followed I made many patterns for castings, bronzes, brass pipe rings, T-pieces, water gauge collars and bends. The foreman had wonderful eyesight and nothing escaped him. He could see the smallest detail on a blueprint. He could split the finest pencil line with a chisel and read the time on a clock face 2 miles away. He had been an apprentice when the old Tay Bridge was built and he had made the patterns for the columns. He was also very clever at cabinet making.

About this time I went to work with my bench mate on the cylinders for the next ship. It was interesting work and gave one a good idea of the casing of steam ports. My bench mate always told me to come down to the moulding shop whenever one was to be cast. It was a wonderful sight to see the furnace tapped amid a shower of red and gold sparks, the ladle skimmed and brought over on the runway and gradually tipped by the wheel till a molten stream of bright light poured into the mould.

Sometimes I got permission for my sister Frances or brother John to see a very big cast when the grimy depths of the moulding shop were lit to brilliance. Often in the dinner hour I would slip into the nearby boiler shop and crawl and climb through a finished boiler examining the various riveted joints. I also wriggled up the furnaces to look at the back ends and tube plates before the completed boilers were dragged through the trafficless streets at night to the yard and lifted into position on board the ship designate by means of a huge crane. Sometimes I would go to the brass or iron moulding shop where the mysteries of dry green sand and loam were unfolded to me as I watched the moulds being prepared for both brass and iron casts. I was told that the metal composition and quantities required for each cast were worked out in the drawing office.

A moulder had to serve an apprenticeship of seven years in those days, so intricate and experienced was the work.

The drawing office was a Mecca that few apprentices were able to enter for even a short period during their apprenticeship. Sometimes I wandered into the copper shop and saw the huge copper pipes being bent, filled with pitch or sand and shaped to a template, or to the plate shop where I watched the boiler plates being cut, bent and flanged.

One evening I arrived at Dundee West Station to catch the train to Errol. Papa and Mummy were also awaiting the train, having been to a meeting in Dundee. I suddenly saw Mr and Mrs Thompson and his father, the head of the firm, come on to the platform. When they saw my black face, they came up and talked to my parents and introduced their companion, Mr Wirtley, one of the directors of the Blue Funnel Line for whom they were building some ships.

He turned to me suddenly and said, "Let me know when you have finished your apprenticeship, and I promise you, I will give you a ship."

Delighted, I thanked him very much and assured him that I would let him know. The Thompsons were surprised and my parents very pleased. On the way home Papa said, "Well, your future is assured, Vicky."

The winter of 1918 was very cold and stormy. I left each morning in the dark and flew down to the station on my bike, passing the postie on her way up to Megginch. The half hour by train passed quickly as I always had a technical book with me. Some mornings I would get to the station only to hear that the train was at least an hour late due to a hospital train. Then I had to jump on my bicycle again and speed about a mile down to the main road where I would beg a lift from a Dundee-bound lorry, climbing in bicycle and all. Then what a dash to lift my check on time.

There were many wild nights; strong gales blew in from the sea, bearing the smell of salt in the damp wind. "A real Tay Bridge," was the remark as the force of the wind hollered round the foundry buildings accompanied by driving rain and sleet. I would struggle to the station with straw and paper blowing high in the air, the wind moaning and crying round the street corners where umbrellas turned inside out. The train seemed to rock on the metals, so strong was the force of the gusts. As I pushed my bicycle through the darkness I could hardly walk against it; the strength of the gale was incredibly fierce as it swept through the open fields and howled in the black branches of trees, crashing the tops together. Once I had to scramble over a fallen tree, dragging my bicycle after me. By the time I struggled through the door, there was hardly any evening left.

We were always given half an hour before the whistle blew on Saturdays to fill in our time sheets and clean and sharpen our tools. After lunch at home I would get through the list of jobs that had accumulated through the week, pans to solder, chairs to mend and locks to overhaul.

While I was in the pattern shop, two new ships were laid down and there were many patterns to make. At dinner time it was always a rush. I would throw a mac or light coat over my overalls and, wearing an apprentice cap and with moderately clean hands and face, drop in my check and rush out the gate. I would dash down the street to the tram stop and jump on a moving tram to the town centre. I had my lunch in the restaurant of D M Browns. The manageress was a friend and she always kept a place for me and a cup of coffee ready. I allowed 20 minutes for lunch, 15 minutes each way for the journey, and 10 minutes for any messages I had to do. If it was wet, I had a piece at the works washed down by a glass of water.

Whenever possible, I went to see things of interest in the works, perhaps a marine engine completed and ready to be dismantled for erection in the ship's engine room. On holidays when the shops were closed in town I had a delightful invitation to lunch through the unfailing kindness of Mr and Mrs Begg. Very often I was given a piece of cake in the afternoon, or a paper of sweeties was slipped in my tool box by a workmate. There was no doubt that I was being spoilt by everyone!

In summer when strawberries were ripe I would bring in a large wicker basket of fresh fruit, pricked that morning and covered in cool cabbage leaves. All my mates helped themselves, though the best berries were kept for Mr Begg, who tactfully went to the yard before the strawberries were passed round.

Peace was officially signed in June 1919 and my parents gave a celebration garden party. Although run on the traditional lines, this was a party grandiflora. All friends, neighbours and relations were invited along with many of my workmates and several disabled soldiers. Tea was served on long tables under the thousand year old yew trees in the flower garden. There was cheering music from a band, shaded by the lime tree and a piper played in the park amid sheets of golden buttercups where the children's games were in progress.

Both Papa and John were in uniform. After tea there were speeches and cheering. Papa said, "Now we have won peace, we must enjoy it and be worthy of it, never forgetting those who fought for us and are not with us today."

As the sun went down, the happy children went home, summer shadows lengthened and dancing started on the grass.

Supper was laid on white cloth-covered tables under the yew trees and as dusk fell pink Chinese lanterns illuminated the dancers. Finally, Papa, John and I let off a lovely display of rockets which rushed into the summer sky in showers of gold as the glorious day ended.

Mummy said, "It was a perfect day from beginning to end."

And as one walked about in the sunshine meeting so many people and friends one had not seen for years, it was like heaven.

Once Jean had convalesced from Spanish Flu, she went back to the explosives factory at Gretna to finish her time. After which she went to London to supervise the Queen Victoria Girls' Club in, Lambeth. She was one of the first to take on a paid job of this nature, to try and give girls in Lambeth new interests in life, to help replace all they had lost during the years of deprivation when relatives and loved ones were killed. With the appointment she had a flat at the top of a large house, 122 Kennington Road, with the club rooms and hall below. Here I spent several days of the Dundee Holidays before going down to see my grandmother at Foulden.

Jean took me with the club party to see the peace decorations. Even the lions in Trafalgar Square had green lights in their eyes. We all had tea afterwards in a restaurant.

After London I headed for Foulden. Norfolk was lovely. The distant echoing of guns was gone now. All the summer wild flowers were at their best, purple loosestrife and fennel, poppies and daisies. Auntie Maggie and Auntie Sib were there as well as Auntie Flo. Granny was well, and very interested to hear of my work. I told her in another two years I would finish my time. She showed me some of her beautiful ivory carving.

When I got back to the pattern shop I found a lot more blueprints had come from the drawing office for a set of cylinders for the main engines of a new ship, so my bench mate and I were very busy. One day a drawing came for a new desk for the pattern shop office, and to my surprise the foreman gave it to me to make.

"I think you can make a nice job of that," he said. "Make it of yellow pine."

I dovetailed the corners and carefully made the lid with mortice and tenon joints, getting hinges and a lock from the store. When completed, the foreman was very pleased and showed it to the manager.

Shortly afterwards he sent for me and said there was a vacancy in the finishing shop and that I was to start there on Monday.

The foreman said he was sorry I was going and so did my workmates. They took my tool box to the lodge for me and when I left the shop sang *Will ye no come back again?* I felt very sad.

The next Monday I made a start in the finishing shop. The manager took me over and introduced me to the foreman there who told me I was to be in the eccentric squad where I would work on the valve gear. I was next to the leading hand on the bench who gave me a hammer, scraper, chisels and a note from the foreman to the store for files that I would require.

The finishing shop was very large with drilling and screw cutting machines. I had interesting work on the radians blocks and on the links, finishing them by frosting with a scraper. I had to go to the smithy when the rods were bent and down to the yard when the pins were shrunk in the links. There were plenty other jobs as well, such as fitting oil boxes to the rods between time and working on copper pipes and hand rails.

The leading hand got the carpenter to make me a tool box and I arranged my tools in it. Sometimes Mr Begg would come to see how I was getting on, and one or other of my mates from the pattern shop used to look in. I often went to the fitting and erecting shop as well as the large turning shop. Once when I was doing a job in the yard I thought I would climb to the top of the huge crane at dinner time. I had climbed up a long way when, unfortunately, the head of the firm saw me from his home and phoned the yard instructing that I was to come down. Down I came, but most regretfully as I had not reached the top. The view was wonderful.

The leading hand often told me about the sea in the early days of steam and how his ship had once stopped a "blackbird" or slaver, and many other thrilling tales. Sometimes he would bring me a piece of cake for tea that his daughter had made.

In October 1919 my grandmother died suddenly. I was especially sad as I had been very close to her. Within a few weeks of her death, my eldest aunt, Auntie May, also died. That year we had another very cold winter and I shall never forget the Monday morning cold of starting work in the finishing shop. The chisels were like blocks of ice and seared my skin. The windows were covered in frost flowers, and as the snowflakes collected on the window ledge outside I felt I could never be warm again, even with a blue jersey under my cotton overalls. I shivered and everyone else shivered, too. The cold was intense, but soon the fast moving belts and throbbing machines warmed the air, though the frost flowers remained on the inside of the window till well on in the day.

One evening a fellow apprentice and I slipped to the yard after tea to examine and sketch a type of governor we had heard of but not seen before. We climbed on board the ship and made our way to the engine room where the governor was temporarily placed on the engine. Alas, as we eagerly examined it, it dropped apart and our combined efforts failed to get it together again. So we departed and hoped for the best.

"Do you think we broke it?" my companion queried.

"I don't think so," I said, "if we only had a drawing it would have been easy to fix up again."

I was able to go to the Technical College more frequently now and was still carrying on with the correspondence course under the wing of Mr Martin, Principal of the Marine School. I had only another two years at the foundry before I completed my time and emerged as a fully fledged journeyman engineer.

The last two years seemed to pass far more quickly than the others, and I found myself thinking and talking of the day my time would be out. We apprentices used to sit along the bench before the whistle went and talk of the things we were going to do when our apprenticeship was completed. Most, including me, were going to sea. One or two had already planned which company they would sail with.

There were many tricks and practical jokes in the foundry. One was tying up the sleeves of a jacket and filling them with old nuts and bolts and waste, so that when the unfortunate owner grabbed it at dinner time he had to get the knots undone and empty the sleeves before he could wear it. Of course on April Fool's Day people were sent everywhere, such as to the foreman of the erecting shop or the turning shop. Even I never dared to bring the drawing office into it as that was a thing apart. Once, having quite forgotten what the date was, I was sent there in fear and trembling by the works manager. I was only pulled back by a fellow apprentice at the last minute and saved from delivering a note, the contents of which were blank.

1920 was my last year. I had undertaken many skilled jobs and my notebook was full of sketches. "You had better have a look at this or that before it's boxed," was a phrase I often heard.

The year passed quickly, as the day my time would be out came nearer and nearer. One morning just before the great day, I found a 2 inch cube of steel and a new file on my bench. This was the works test and I had to file each face of the the cube to exactly 2 inches with the sides dead level. I might only use file, rule and square.

As can be imagined, I tried to make a perfect job and put my very best into the work. When complete both my bench mate and the forman looked at it, after which it was handed to the shop manager.

He sent for me the next morning and told me I had passed top. It was under two thousandth out with micrometer on all sides. I was delighted.

On completion of apprenticeship, every apprentice celebrates by the time-honoured custom of paying off when the journeyman engineer treats fellow workmates on receiving the first journeyman's pay.

The "pay off" must take the form of a party or sing song. My joy and pride was unbounded when I received my first journeyman's pay and I paid off the standing treat to my workmates with a night's entertainment at the King's Theatre Music Hall where I booked the first row of the grand circle. In the interval the manager of the theatre came before the curtain and said a few words about my paying off and we handed sweeties and cigarettes round. In a little speech Mr Begg said that I had faithfully discharged the necessary festive function incumbent on an apprentice who has entered upon their trade or profession.

We all had a very happy evening and everyone said they were sorry when it was over. There were about 70 of us altogether.

I worked as a journeyman until transferred to the drawing office when a vacancy occurred. The work there was very interesting and it seemed strange to be clean again after being black for so long! I put the date and my initials on each drawing and it was always exciting to see how the blueprint turned out.

Mr Begg came to see me sometimes, and often said, "It was a fine clear drawing you sent down."

Then there were the trial trips. I enjoyed them enormously. The coal had to be measured, the cards taken and worked out. The engine room was always very hot and she rolled about a lot, I enjoyed every minute with the fresh salt breeze blowing on my hot face. We got ravenously hungry. By about 3pm when the directors and representatives of the shipping firm for whom the ship had been built had finished their lunch we would be given ours which we fell on like wolves!

I loved to see the ships when they were finished. Sometimes we slept on board the night before the crew arrived, and as we lifted with the tide it really felt like being at sea. I would peep into the officers' rooms with the polished desk, wardrobe, chair and drawers under the high bunk with blue and white counterpane, perhaps a white anchor on it, green shaded bedside lamp, and square of new coconut matting on the deck. The Chief Engineer's room would have a bookcase with glass, a white bedspread, and a square of carpet. I longed to sail on them.

In 1922 there were less orders for the Caledon Works and along with many others, I was laid off.

Mr Thompson suggested I write to Mr Wirtley of the Blue Funnel Line and remind him of the promise he once made on the Dundee station platform. So I wote straight away.

One day...two days...three days...for four days I heard nothing, and then I had a letter on stiff white paper heavily embossed with the name Blue Funnel Line on it, requesting that I come to Liverpool for an interview. All the family were very excited and wished me good luck as I caught the night train for Liverpool.

Liverpool seemed so large, I had no idea where to find the office. I did not dare spend my small supply of money on a taxi. More by good luck than good management I found it and was taken up at the appointed hour to a huge, overpowering and austere room or so I thought it was! I was 2 minutes early as I stood waiting in my best blue suit.

Suddenly the door opened and the Engineer Superintendent came in accompanied by Mr Lawrence Holt, brother of the Head of the company. He explained that Mr Wirtley, the director I had met at Dundee, had died. My heart sank, but he told me he would substantiate his promise and they would like me to start in the engineering record office. The Engineer Superintendent asked me a lot of questions, which luckily I was able to answer. I was told that they would arrange lodgings for me through their office superintendent and I would start work next week.

The Thompsons at Lilybank were delighted for me, but many and sad were the farewells at the foundry. When I walked for the last time through the huge gates on 7th July 1922 I felt I was embarking on a new stage in life.

Chapter Eight
SS Anchises - 1922-23

My new life in Liverpool unfolded rapidly. The lodgings arranged by the company were in Canning Street in the same house as Miss Alexander, the superintendent. I had a comfortable bed-sitting room. The windows faced the quiet street and I paid 35/- per week for breakfast, something to eat at night and three meals on Saturday and Sunday if I wished. The company paid me £12 a month.

Being the newcomer, I was there first to take off the covers from the tables and ready them for the day's work. Everyone was friendly and I enjoyed my work, the large Liverpool shipping office was a community in itself, the focal point that controlled the fleet of passenger and cargo vessels, built on distinctive lines, each surmounted by a large blue funnel hence the name Blue Funnel Line. The main fleet numbered about 85 vessels at that time and individual gross tonnage varied from 4,000 to 14,000 tons. Each vessel bore a classical name and was maintained in immaculate order and run under the strictest discipline and far-sighted economy. The performances of the various vessels were scrutinised and any deficiency in speed or increase in consumption was instantly noted, analysed and corrected. Before the First World War, triple expansion engines using saturated steam were used, but now super-heated steam was being introduced. This was the idea of the Chief Engineering Superintendent, Mr Freeman, who took a keen interest in the training of young engineers.

I soon felt adjusted to my new life and my working day fitted into an orderly pattern. I had lunch in the office canteen, but sometimes went out to a tea shop or cafe with some of the girls, or walked over to the nearby quay where the ferries plied to and fro over the grey river and ocean going vessels made their way to the open sea.

Every time I saw one of the huge Cunarders alongside I strolled past and gazed at her through the gate admiring her brilliant red and black topped funnel, black hull and shining white paint. In the evenings I enjoyed joining the girls from the office and going for a swim while they talked of their holiday plans. On wet evenings I would stay in my room and work out various formulae that interested me using my slide rule. I was still working on my correspondence course with Mr Martin of Dundee Technical College.

During this time my work at the office had become increasingly interesting and absorbing, and I became oblivious to the various people who came into the office with items to discuss or messages from other departments. One afternoon one of these migrants spoke to me, and while he was engaged in entering something in his notebook, I asked the girl next to me who he was.

"Oh," she replied, "he is the man who measures the coal."

When he spoke to me a few minutes later, I replied quite unconsciously, thinking he was one of the company's employees and later forgot the incident.

But there was a sequel. To my great astonishment a piece about me appeared in the morning paper, to which I paid little attention. I didn't connect it with the man "who measured the coal". But during the morning, Mr Freeman sent for me and as I stood before him in his office, he told me I must never speak to a person I did not know without asking for his card.

I promised that I would not and the matter ended.

A few days later a man I did not know walked up to where I was working and spoke to me. Promptly I asked him for his card.

He said, "Is that necessary?"

"Yes," I replied, "very necessary."

There seemed to be an awful stillness in the office. One could hear the proverbial pin drop.

He handed me his card and at the same time invited me to tea next Sunday. Then he was gone. When I looked at the card I saw to my horror that it was Mr Richard Holt, the head of the company.

Next morning I was again sent for by Mr Freeman, and the magnitude of my crime was expounded to me.

"But," I protested, "you told me, sir, I was never to speak to anyone I did not know who came into the office and spoke to me without asking first for his card."

"Use your discretion," was the crushing reply.

However all ended happily as I spent a delightful Sunday afternoon, had a lovely tea, and Mr Holt said he quite understood.

So the summer went on. I had regular letters from home where John was busy with his rabbit breeding and Frances with the small fruit and the Perth Show, four firsts for rabbits. Jean, in Kennington Road, had got Princess Alice to present the prizes to the Queen Victoria Girls' Club, a great occasion.

On 25th August I was again sent for by Mr Freeman.

"What can I have done now?" I thought to myself.

"Good morning," he said smiling. "You are to join a ship that has discharged here and is going to Glasgow to load. You are to sail in her from Liverpool to Glasgow. You are to sign articles here as Assistant Engineer and sign off in Glasgow. Otherwise you will be a deserter," he smiled. "You may go home for the weekend from Glasgow, travel down Tuesday night and return to the office on Wednesday morning. You will of course take the stand-bys and will be on the Second's watch, 4 to 8 bells. Take a bathing suit with you," he added, laughing. Then he told me where and when to sign on, where the ship was lying and the time to go on board. As he shook hands with me he said, "Good luck."

I was sent to sign on at the shipping office, which seemed to me an enormously imposing building.

"Just wait a moment," one of the officials told me. "We have been expecting you. You are Miss Drummond, signing on as Assistant Engineer."

As I waited I watched a crew about to sign on a ship. Piles of thumbed discharge books were stacked behind the bars that divided the broad mahogany counter. Behind this stood the Master with the ship's articles before him; the large crowd of men started calling for the articles to be read. The hubbub was indescribable. I was so absorbed in this scene and the noise was so great that the official had to beckon me over and point to the line and small pencil x where I was to sign.

I don't think I shall ever forget the feeling of excited elation on signing my first articles, and while the official filled in the necessary information, he said, "Work hard, obey orders and you will have V G when you sign off in Glasgow."

The noise had died down by now and the captain of the other ship was addressing them. Suddenly the noise started all over again. The man beside me said, "When you are Second Engineer you will have to handle a crew like that."

It seemed unlikely.

The hours seemed to fly past and in no time I found myself mounting the gangway and stepping on my ship to be. In a whirl I was introduced to the Chief and Second Engineers and shown my room. I quickly changed into a boiler suit and reported to the Second, Mr Quayle.

Everyone was busy preparing for sailing. The surveyor arrived to float the safety valves of the central boiler and the Second told me to come up to the boiler tops and hold a light. It was very hot.

The surveyor asked me if I was getting too warm.

I said, "I am quite cool compared with the heat over those boiler tops."

Everything was hurry and rush, then stand-by and cast off and, with the aid of tugs, the ship moved out of the dock and into the river. I was told to stand by the desk between the engines and take down the engine movements.

When we got down the river and outside it was getting dark and a strong wind was blowing; I could see white crested waves through the gathering gloom. Being a light ship she was rolling about. When we finally got out to sea it was delicious to feel the cool breeze on my hot cheeks as I stood on the deck. The wind seemed to be increasing in strength and spray was splashing on the deck.

After I got some tea and something to eat, I was called to go down to the engine room again, as the bilges had got away and all were required to help. As the ship moved, the bits and pieces left from shore repairs washed about mixing with coal, ashes and grease, silting up the strum boxes in the bilge well and choking the pumps. After some hours of lying flat on the plates trying to keep the strums clear, or crawling under the plates cleaning the tank top, the bilges were under control just as the streaks of grey dawn showed in the sky.

I was soaked through and the Second told me to change. Lucky it was that I had brought two boiler suits. Hardly had I changed when I was called to go on watch at 4 am and then stand-by went. Again I took the movements until at last "finished with engines" was rung down and the Second told me to go up to the boiler tops and help shut down. It was hot and black and the various valves were pointed out to me. We had just finished shutting down when Mr Quayle sent for me and told me to get washed and changed, pack my gear, have breakfast and be ready to go up to the shipping office to sign off.

"I hope you will sign on again," he said.

How thrilling to be home again, everyone asking questions and so pleased and excited that I really had been sent as an engineer officer on a ship from Liverpool to Glasgow! The hours flew past and it seemed no time at all till I was sitting in the corner of a crowded carriage speeding towards Liverpool.

The next day Mr Freeman sent for me. "You have been appointed to a ship. You are to sail as Junior Engineer and you will rejoin the *Anchises*, when she has finished loading, and sail with her. You may go home when you have arranged about getting your uniform and gear here, and they will let you know from Glasgow the day and time you must sign on as Tenth Engineer at the Glasgow shipping office."

I was so terribly excited I was outside the door before I realised I had not asked where she was sailing to, so I rather timidly knocked on the door of the sanctum.

"Excuse me, sir, but I forgot to ask where she is going?"

"Australia!" was the reply.

In the office I was given a printed list of clothes I had to get: a uniform patrol suit, cap covers and cap, white shirts and collars, black tie, white handkerchiefs, white suits, shoes, boiler suits, engine room cap, and shoes and socks, a formidable list. I had never had so many clothes all at once in my life. Miss Alexander told me where to go to get my uniform made.

I wrote home and Papa said he could help with expenses while Mummy said she could get a few things in Dundee. I shall never forget the thrill of being measured for my first uniform and being shown the material from which it was to be made. Equally exciting was trying it on for the first time, with its gilt company buttons, the company badge on my cap, and on the cuff the purple and gold single band. With my uniform jacket and patrol jacket with its epaulettes, purple stripes and gold buttons packed into my new suitcase, I returned home for a few days.

There were more new clothes for me at home. Mummy had got me a dark blue serge coat and skirt, two felt hats, and a simple white evening dress. Also, to my surprise and delight, I was presented with a weekend leather suitcase with my initials on it, and a looking glass from friends and well-wishers. Mr and Mrs Thompson of the Lilybank foundry gave me a travelling clock in a green leather case, and Mr Martin a copy of his book on engineering. When I departed for Glasgow, I felt a new feeling. All these friends had confidence in me. I must never let them down.

"A good voyage, Vicky," Papa said. "Write home from every port, and go to church when you can. You have been brought up to know what is right, so do it."

Frances and John came to Glasgow with me, and saw me on board. As Tenth Engineer, I was paid £10 a month. After tea Mr Quayle, the Second, told me to sort out my gear, "As you won't have much time tomorrow."

So I unpacked my cases before going to sleep with all the sounds of the port and ship's life about me.

After breakfast on 2nd September I met a superintendent engineer who had come aboard to give me another book on engineering and to introduce me to some friends of his who were passengers.

"I wish you all the luck in the world," he said. I thought I might need it when I went below to go on stand-by. There was quite a send-off from passengers and friends as the ship moved out, but I did not see for myself as I was in the engine room writing down engine movements for the 3 $\frac{1}{2}$ hour stand-by down the Clyde, until "Full Away" was rung down and I entered "F A W" as the huge port and starboard engines gathered speed and momentum.

On my return, the Second told me to keep an eye on things in the stokehold for a couple of hours. There were three double ended boilers and 24 fires, twelve fires in the fore and twelve in the aft stokehold. The furnaces had common combustion chambers. As I pushed the heavy iron door open with its coal-dust grimed canvas curtain, a cloud of flying ashes met me. I heard the loud hiss of steam as buckets of cold sea water quenched the red hot ashes that were raked from the furnaces to the plates into black smoking heaps giving off thick sulphur smelling steam. Cleaning fires were in progress and the rattle of the fireman's shovel indicated opposite furnace doors must remain closed while the evening's operations were in progress. Then there was the noise of the trimmers' barrows as they rushed them through the narrow passage between the boilers from fore to aft stokehold, their white rimmed eyes shining in black faces as they dumped their load of shining coal on the plates, ready to feed the insatiable fiery mouth of the boiler. The orange glare of the fires reflected on the black-begrimed, sweat-bathed faces of the fireman as he opened his hand for the regulation boiler checks increasing or decreasing the supply of water to the boilers, his eye ever sweeping like a hawk the array of water and steam gauge glasses. His dungaree jacket and trousers were of the brightest blue through much washing and rinsing in brilliant Chinese blue powder. In time to come my dark blue boiler suits would also experience this transformation. A sweat rag was neatly tucked round the leading hand's neck.

I introduced myself and we shook hands.

"You will soon understand the difference in the water levels between the fore and aft stokehold," he said. "It's a bit different from a single end job. The trouble on this ship, one might say, is two Bs, excuse the expression, I mean bilges and back ends, but there is plenty of time to think of that as we won't be in Australia this side of 50 days."

Suddenly there was an awful roar and a deafening rush of steam. A gauge glass had burst. I dashed forward and shut off the gauge and the noise ceased. The leading hand appeared instantly from the after stokehold. "That's shore work," he said with contempt, and advised me to ask the Second for a new glass. But the Second was there in the stokehold as if by magic, a glass in his hand.

"I heard it go. Which one is it?" he inquired.

"Fore stokehold, port boiler, outboard glass," I replied.

Later, when I got into my room I found a surprise wire of good wishes signed "All at Home". I washed and changed into my patrol suit as we were not allowed to go into the messroom in a boiler suit and went down to the messroom for tea.

The evening light shining through the ports danced on the white painted deck head and I could hear the swish of water as it passed the ship's side. I saw Ailsa Craig and a big copper moon rising in black clouds which seemed to swing up and down with the movement of the ship. I read my wire from home again and turned in.

By 3.45 am, I was back down the engine room ladder in the pale light of dawn. I was initiated into the routine of watch-keeping. Round the main engines and auxiliaries I went, by the switchboard, down the tunnel into the stokehold, inspecting all bilges en route. Once each watch I went down the after well to examine stern gland and well. It was a long climb down an open ladder into the gloomy depths and as long, of course, back up to the bright blue sky.

"A good thing I can climb," I thought.

One of the tunnel bearings was heating up a bit so I had to inspect it every quarter of an hour. We had tea, coffee or cocoa brought to the engine room at 4.30 am, then at 6 am we had hot buttered toast and coffee or cocoa in thick white mugs with the company flag on them.

Mr Quayle instructed me very carefully in all my duties, and I felt a weight of responsibility descend on my shoulders as I listened to him. He told me that in addition to my watch-keeping duties, I would have the evaporators to scale on the morning watch and on the afternoon watch I would start overhauling certain auxiliary pumps. On the homeward passage after I came off watch and had finished breakfast I would assist in checking the stores and painting the engine room. He told me that all engineers must be on stand-by leaving and entering port or in an emergency. He also told me that I could talk to the passengers, go to dances and concerts in the evenings and also Sunday morning service, if I were not required for work. The service and the concerts were held in the saloon while the dances were on deck. I must always wear my uniform for these occasions and in warm weather a white uniform suit.

After breakfast I went on deck where I saw the Chief Engineer, Mr Waite. He looked at my uniform, and said, "Quite right. You must always wear your uniform when you come on deck, never a boiler suit except when you put steam on deck, or work on the winches, or some such job. This is a passenger ship and all engine room officers must look smart and tidy."

As we passed Land's End in the sunshine, two Australian passengers I had met gave me some chocolate and a *Windsor* magazine, and later the Master, Captain Inkster, came along and spoke to us. He said, "Next Sunday I shall expect to see you at church."

On the evening watch I had to go on top of the boilers and help the Second tighten a gland.

"This super-heated steam is very hot and invisible. You can't see it till you're burnt," he remarked.

After we passed Finisterre the sky and sea became a lovely deep blue. We were in half whites and I played deck tennis with my colleagues. The evenings were getting much warmer and the engine room very hot indeed.

In the evening a ship comes to life as she glides through the night with all her lights on, and the passengers in bright evening dress move about the prom deck talking and laughing, or dancing to the strains of a gramophone. And aft the firemen dance among themselves to a banjo or concertina, or some patter dance, or sing sea shanties, and all the time the ship cuts her way through the smooth dark waters scattering the million reflections from her lights, making them wobble and dance over the black water till the golden ripples are lost in the darkness.

"The day after tomorrow we're due at Las Palmas," Mr Wigmore remarked. I longed to go ashore there and see all the flowers and trees covered in fruit, although I had seen the Second's work list and I knew that the 6 hours we lay off the island would be filled with hard work. Some passengers had invited me to go ashore with them, but I knew I could not.

All day on 14th September we plunged past Gibraltar and Madeira. We saw the Royal Mail boat coming out of Gib bound for South America, but we saw no other boats and of course no land. On the morning watch at 5.30 am the Chief told the Second that I was to go through the bunkers with him and hold the tape while he measured the coal. This meant crawling through holes in hillsides of coal, climbing up mountains and sliding down precipices with all the big lumps of coal rolling and bounding after me, always on the alert to hold the tape taut for the Chief while he measured off the coal. He told me I could come with him each morning to measure the bunkers. I was black, so black that only the rims of my eyes were left white, and I was glad I had such a good supply of boiler suits with me.

The next morning we arrived at Las Palmas. When I went up with the Fifth to help open up steam on deck it was hot and rather misty and I could see the outline of the island.

By 8 am when I went off watch the anchors were down and we were in. I came on deck into dazzling white sunshine and a crowd of people selling green and yellow canaries, red and green parrots perched on their arms, all talking and shouting in Spanish. Monkeys, fruit and coloured postcards, white drawn thread work, all were mixed up together. The island looked bare and mountainous. The town with its white flat roofed houses was a bit away from the shore. I looked over the ship's side into the clear turquoise water shaded with emerald, the reflections of the bright boats all clustered round the ship bobbing up and down on the little waves, almost overflowing with fruit and merchandise. The firemen were pulling up baskets brimming with fruit by means of a line dropped over the side. The passengers were all climbing down the companion ladders, embarking in open shore boats.

On deck I found one of the greasers.

"We came along as we thought you might like to come aft with us and see the parrots and canaries, and maybe, homeward bound or next voyage, you might like to take home a parrot. A Spanish-speaking parrot would be best for you, as all his sailor talk would be Spanish, and we could teach him nice English for you."

So along I went to see all the fun of the fair. Rope mats and buckets made from old ropes and tins were descending, and parrots and canaries were ascending from the boats. The men bought some lovely canaries.

"We will get you one when we come back," they said, "and you will be able to get some nice ones in Australia."

On 16th September I was sent down the after well as usual by Mr Wigmore, the Fifth. I had been down the after well twice every day since leaving Glasgow. It was 50 feet straight down an iron ladder into darkness, a glimmering electric light at the bottom. I went down okay and looked round everything, but stupidly I forgot to wipe my feet on a sack before coming up, so my shoes were oily. When I got to the top I caught the edge of the door with my left hand and had my right on the hand rail when both my feet slipped off the top step. I still had one hand on the sill but I let go of the rail. I thought I was done but a greaser caught me by the shoulder and I got my grip as he hauled me up and I pulled myself onto the deck. Another greaser gave me a cup of water and I sat for a bit on the hatch. Then I completed my round and returned to the engine room.

It was the first day of "whites", and when I had changed after breakfast the Chief took me for a walk on the top deck, but he said nothing about my earlier incident and I didn't think anyone knew. In the afternoon watch, when it was time for me to go down the after well, I said to the Fifth, "Shall I go now?"

And he said, "You are never to go down the after well any more!" Then he told me that the greasers had reported me to the Chief.

When I went on the next watch the Second gave me a good talking to about the after well. From what he had heard it was a very near thing. He said, "The last man who fell down was finished," and he told me not to go down till we had crossed the Line, and never without a rope round me like going for gulls eggs. He said the greasers were trying to take care of me and look after me.

"I thought it was very plucky of him to get hold of me," I said, "I might have pulled him down, too!" I had the marks of the greaser's fingers bruised on my shoulders, he grabbed me so hard.

On Sunday I went to church in the saloon with the Third, the other engineers were not very keen. The Captain gave us a lovely service. It all felt very comforting.

After the service some of the passengers wanted me to stand in the sun and be photographed. Luckily the Chief was there and he got rid of them for me. "You never know what they might do with a photo," he said.

Some of the female passengers didn't like me, I think. They were always having little digs at me. One of them said, "You were not at the concert on Monday night. We supposed you were too seasick to come." Another one talking to me in the passage glanced at my hands, and said, "Oh dear, I must go and clean my nails before lunch!" Another one seeing me coming up from tea in my blue patrol suit, which I thought was rather smart, said, "You must find it hot working in that, but I suppose you wear white linen in the engine room!" It was really two different worlds.

But some of them were nice, and showed me the white embroidery and sweet canary wine they had bought and gave me chocolates.

As we sailed south the nights became hot and the sky dark and velvety sprinkled with a myriad of stars. We crossed the Line on 21st September, but there was no ceremony as Captain Inkster said he once had a rough house where someone broke their arm and he wasn't having that again. The passengers seemed rather disappointed and so was I, but the Captain said we had all qualified just the same. Little droves of silvery flying fish skimmed over the blue water in the brilliant sunlight and we played off our cricket match with the passengers.

So the days slipped by, cricket in the mornings on the white scrubbed deck with the short sun shadows, roasting watches and hot, still nights without a breath of air through the stokehold or engine room ventilators no matter how the firemen turned them. Every night I would climb the engine room ladder when the watch was up, cast aside my dripping engine room clothes, bath in hot sea water and scrub clean with sea water soap before scrambling into an immaculate white uniform to glide with officers and passengers over the smooth deck, under brilliant flags and soft lights with the clear moon shining on the sea.

The weather changed between Ascension and St Helena and became cool with a roll and grey skies, and everyone remarked, "We should be in Cape Town by Saturday."

The morning of Saturday 30th September was dark and misty when I went up from the engine room to open steam on deck. I saw a towering shape emerging in the half light, its top engulfed in white mist.

One of the sailors said, "The tablecloth is down on Table Mountain."

When I next came up it was brilliant morning, everything bathed in bright clear sunlight and Table Mountain towered in its grandeur with not a cloud in sight.

On deck I went to find the Second to see what I was to work at. I found him talking to the Chief who grinned and said, "The Second has reported to me that you have worked well, and I have also noted that myself. As this is Saturday, you may go ashore now and need not come aboard till 6 pm. Don't get into mischief and come back sober! If you are not on board by 6 pm we will tell the police to look for you. And don't paint the town red!" he called after me, as I walked down the gangway into paradise.

A short car run in blazing sunlight with the bluest of blue skies overhead and I was in Addley Street. There I was overwhelmed by the brilliance of the scene, the coloured river of flowers that flowed along the side of the pavement, displayed by numerous flower sellers. It was a riot of colours with violets, daffodils, anemones, narcissi, bundles of waxy arums, golden proteas, heavily scented lilies and feathery grasses tumbling over each other in a bewildering mass on this lovely spring morning. I had to tear myself away to do all the commissions I had been given, passing the stone Cathedral of St George's, where a lobster claw creeper spiralled its scarlet blossoms over the lower stone work. I gazed at the city hall and municipal buildings, and further away to the green trees surrounding Government House and the botanical gardens. After a snack lunch of fruit and sandwiches, I jumped on a tram. I was enthralled by the beauty of the scenery: the Lions Head and Devils Peak rising from green clad slopes, and the rugged range of the twelve Apostles, mysterious, wonderful, bathed in a kaleidoscope of ever changing lights and shades.

I jumped off at Camps Bay and rushed on to the fine sand, a ribbon of white surf bordering the brilliant blue sea. Here I found several passengers I knew and the Wireless Operator, and ran to join them paddling in the clear water. One moment it was shallow and controllable, the next a big wave splashed up to one's knees. The sun glistened on small sponges and shells, strewn over the dry sand.

The return run was even more beautiful, past white bungalows submerged in brilliant geraniums, waterfalls of magenta bougainvillea and a blue mist of plumbago. Huge butterflies skimmed over the flowers, replicas of the specimens I had gazed at as a child in the old sailor's collections. The tram went on round the mountain and a blaze of wild flowers spread below me, bushes of golden candle-flowered proteas, sheets of yellow marguerites, and under the trees of a small pine wood, waxy arum lilies shone dazzlingly white against the leaves. In the distance trees with shining silver leaves shimmered. As we neared Cape Town high orange trees covered with golden balls and scented wax blossom appeared along with feathery palms and glossy camellias, a mass of waxen pink flowers.

In Addely Street I walked straight into one of the ship's officers.

"You know the ship's on her way to Australia and the Chief's in a frenzy," he remarked.

I stood for a moment thunderstruck, and then I burst out, "Why aren't *you* on board?"

"Oh, I have deserted," he replied blandly, and then as he laughed, light came.

I collected my parcels, and armed with a bunch of flowers, went on board and reported to the Chief.

"Five minutes too early," Mr Waite remarked. "Tell the Second you are on board in case he wants a hand. He's been in the hot back ends all day."

Bunkering continued during the night with a terrific din. I was on watch at 4 am. However, when I came up for breakfast the Second told me we were not sailing till the afternoon, so I could slip ashore to church if I liked.

I was back on stand-by at 3.30 pm and we sailed at 4 pm.

When I took the movement book up to the Chief, Table Mountain was becoming distant and the scatter of white houses below melted into the mist. As I went below, the Fourth called me to look at a large school of porpoises quite close to the ship, plunging and leaping about like slippery black pigs.

When still in sight of the Cape of Good Hope I came off watch and there in the white moonlight I saw a beautiful sailing ship. She was making bad weather of it which was strange on such a lovely smooth night. The Second was on deck too and he also saw her.

"I wonder where she's going to," he remarked.

"She looks rather an old-fashioned rig," I said.

Next day I mentioned her to the mates, and as neither they nor the lookout had sighted her, they said, "She must have been the Flying Dutchman, we will have bad weather."

And so we did. Just as the first part of the voyage had been bright and hot with blue seas and skies, the second part was cold and grey with heavy seas and rain. Soon after leaving the Cape it turned much colder. We had a few more cricket matches before she started to roll. Then it turned very cold and the ship rolled too much for cricket. Nothing but grey skies and heavy seas, with dead lights up in the messroom and fiddles on the table.

At 4 am I stepped over the combing of the door to the deck on my way to the engine room, into a foot of icy cold sea water, bumping and sliding my way below where the greasers were quite unperturbed. When going round the engine I followed my usual promenade and one of the bottom ends caught my elbow as she rolled. I found that there had been a lot of trouble with the stokehold and engine room bilges. The Second told me to try and clear the stokehold strums while the others dealt with the engine room bilges. I dropped down under the stokehold plates and found that as she rolled to and fro the water and ashes rushed from side to side unable to escape through choked strum boxes. The firemen were very helpful, and as I filled a bucket with wet ashes scooped from the box they hauled it up with a rope which saved me scrambling up and down each time the bucket was full. Every now and then the cold black water washed over my head with a roar. The stokehold was pandemonium, coal, red ashes, and trimmers' barrows were sliding about as she rolled, and the water in the glasses was up to the top and down again.

From their vast experience the firemen kept steady steam and even found time to bring me a cup of hot cocoa during the morning. By this time the bilges were well under control in stokehold and engine room. Firemen and greasers only kept their own watch, but the engineers worked through successive watches till the emergency had passed, and a procession of drowned rats ascended the engine room ladder at noon. I peeped out on a wind swept sky and storm-lashed world. Occasionally a heavy sea thundered over the deck in cascades of white foam and dark water before rushing out the scuppers.

The dull light illuminated enormous seas like grey mountains with clouds of white spray blowing off the top. One minute the ship was dropping down 50 or 60 feet, the next she was climbing up and up. Huge albatrosses sailed against the wind with extended wings, their white feathers bright against the dark seas and gloomy sky, their curved yellow beaks and watchful eyes visible as they planed in the storm-laden sky, now high, now low, now far, now near, scanning the storm-tossed water.

I asked the Second Mate the names of the small black birds I had seen.

"Oh, those are Mother Carey's chickens, a sign of bad weather like your Flying Dutchman," he said. "Their real name is stormy petrels and they say it is derived from Saint Peter walking on the sea as they appear to walk up and down the waves."

I felt I had had enough fresh air so after a sea water bath and something hot to eat I turned in and slept till wakened to go on afternoon watch.

It was much colder and the temperature was being taken every 2 hours in case of ice. We were about 180 miles off St Paul's and not far from New Amsterdam. The Mate told me there was a hut and food on St. Paul's for the shipwrecked and each year a ship calls to see if there is anyone there. The passengers were very quiet and hardly any were in the saloon.

The Chief Steward remarked, "This is how the company saves money."

After two weeks she steadied up and the passengers held a dance. I danced all the dances till it was time to turn in before the next watch. The night sky was wonderful, studded with silver stars and lit with their brilliance. I saw the Southern Cross and all the stars of the southern hemisphere. It seemed ages since we left Cape Town.

On the morning of 19th October, the Chief came to the engine room as usual at 5.30 am. I stood, tape in hand, ready to measure the coal. He called to the Second as he came down the ladder, "Have sighted Australia!"

We had come over from Cape Town without a stop, 5,600 miles, and for a fortnight of this time we never stopped rolling, not for one minute. It was a long time to keep the engines going.

Arriving was very exciting. The pilot came aboard and we had an early lunch. Stand-by went at 1 pm and we anchored an hour later. We were then all sent up on watch at 4 pm. The lights on the distant shore were ever nearing, and there was a scent of land in the warm off-shore wind. We tied up alongside at Outer Harbour, near Adelaide, and were finished with engines by 9 pm, by which time it was too dark to go ashore and as I was on watch again from 4 am to 8 am, I turned in.

When I came up from the engine room for breakfast, the Second told me the Chief wanted to see me right away. I suppose I looked horror struck, for he added reassuringly, "Don't worry, it's something nice."

Miss Neil, one of the passengers, had asked if I could go to Adelaide with her, about 15 miles distant, and he had agreed provided I was back by 1 o'clock. I was thrilled. I don't think I ever washed and changed and snatched breakfast so quickly.

So it was that I first set foot on Australian soil. The country was dry and hot with a lot of scrub gum and wattle along the railway line. There were brilliant multi-coloured ice plants, portulaceas, and boronia, its four-petalled bell-shaped flowers chestnut brown and yellow, set off by grey-green leaves. The hot breeze was fragrant with their scent. Miss Neil pointed out scrub pepper trees, gums and aloes, and as we neared Adelaide the gardens were bright with flowers and white magnolias, fig trees and peaches.

The town of Adelaide was built on a plain with distant hills in the background. Miss Neil told me these were the Mount Lofty Range, she explained that the city was divided into two sections by the Torrens River. The south part was the commercial section while the north was residential. She showed me King William Street, very fine and broad.

We went into the art gallery not far from the station. It was very hot, lots of big fan palms in streets and gardens, and masses of fruit, pineapples and peaches were sold in the streets. We only had an hour in Adelaide before we had to dash for the train, but I bought some peaches, so juicy they were almost impossible to devour without being drenched in stickiness. By a great dash I was on board by 12 pm and on stand-by at 2.30 pm. We sailed an hour later.

After my watch, as I turned in, I dreamt of Adelaide, named after the Queen, the city she never saw.

On Sunday we could see the coast line of Australia, wild looking country, hills, yellow sand beaches and bush. The Melbourne passengers were very busy finishing their packing ready for their departure next day.

"Steward, please strap this, oh thank you so much.... Stewardess, this case is rather full...."

The packing motif continued all day.

The darkness was pierced by lights from shore, a wet breeze blew from the land and the ship rolled in the heaving water. Stand-by went at 3.30 am, a long stand-by up the Yarra. I came off at 10 am and we were alongside the Victoria Dock. Some of the passengers looked for me to say goodbye, but I was down below. I was sorry to miss them.

After lunch I went ashore to try and catch the mail with home letters, and explored this dignified city with its long wide streets and fine public buildings. In Flinders Street near the station I came face to face with one of the passengers who was going up country. He showed me the way to the Post Office and most kindly taught me the geography of Melbourne. It was delightful to wander along the broad, tree-lined street and see the various buildings of interest.

Later in my room I found an exciting pile of notes and invitations to dinner or lunch. My parents had both been busy writing letters on my behalf.

We were in Melbourne all that week, but every day I had to work from 7 am till 5 pm, so there was not much time to avail myself of the exciting invitations. I discovered however, that all the shop windows were brilliantly lit at night so I could stroll along and do my window shopping. One day I had coffee after dinner with a Miss Drummond, a relation of General Sir Jack Drummond, and on Wednesday I dined at the Alexandra Club with Lady Mitchell. I had put on my best white frock and at dinner I somehow tipped a glass of lemonade over it. It flowed straight across the polished table, where I heard it dripping to the floor on the other side. The Mitchells were charming about it; I loved them both and became firm friends with their daughters, Margaret and Lizzie. When I got to the Clock in Flinders Street, I found the Chief and the Second waiting to escort me back to the ship, as the docks were very dark, and several people had been sand-bagged. Even going in a party we had to walk in the middle of the road.

On Friday, the last day before we sailed, we had a half day, so I was able to accept an invitation to lunch at Government House from the Stradbrookes. Alas, I didn't realise there were two Government Houses in Melbourne and when I arrived after a great rush at the Federal Government House, it was the wrong one. I telephoned and said I was coming, but even so I was half an hour late.

We sailed at 8 am the next morning and came into Sydney Harbour on Monday 30th October. I was sent up to do a job on deck so I could have a look. There are two strips of headland which overlap each other and a passage between into the harbour.

Piles of letters and invitations were waiting for me here too. There were also lots of reporters and they came into my room, into the engine room and even into the stokehold to take pictures, but the firemen hid me as they knew the Chief would be annoyed.

We were in Sydney for nearly a week and as I had to work from 7 am till 5 pm again, most invitations had to be turned down. On Wednesday night I dined with Miss Beulah Bolton who had been introduced to me by Lady Novar. She was to become a lifelong friend and I came to regard her wisteria-covered house as my home in Sydney. On Thursday I dined with the Archbishop of Sydney and Mrs Davidson at Bishop's Court and after dinner we sat on the veranda which overlooked the harbour.

Again the Chief and Second both arrived to escort me safely back to the ship. They were more and more fussy about my safety, since the night before two of the crew had got badly done in, their money and presents taken off them, and one knocked out for 3 hours.

We left Sydney on Saturday 4th November and arrived in Brisbane the following Monday after a long, hot 45 mile stand-by up the Brisbane River; the temperature was 101°F. Black, boiling hot, and soaked through I emerged on deck for a breath of air before changing for breakfast. As I leant over the rail, looking at a jacaranda tree covered in dazzling amethyst blossoms and watching the river water slip and gurgle past the ship, a man from the port authority put a note into my hand from the Governor of Queensland, Sir Matthew Nathan, asking me to stay at Government House and spend my free time there. I rushed to the dock phone and rang the Private Secretary at Government House to explain about my work and duty hours, and we arranged that the ADC would pick me up for dinner at 6.30 pm the next evening, and that the following day I should go to lunch and the races to see the Queensland Cup.

Next morning at 7 am the Second gave me the job of putting new rings on a pump gauging the cylinders, renewing parts and joints and setting the valves. I had it ready for inspection about 4 pm when he commented, "A nice job."

This emboldened me to ask tentatively if I could have the following afternoon off in order to go to the races and dinner that night at Government House. He agreed but showed me a heavy programme of overhauling the bilge master valve in the tunnel for next morning.

That evening some of the firemen went ashore, and after drinking unwisely and far too well, chased the Second round the well deck on their return to the ship. I happened to be standing on the prom deck and witnessed the scene; it looked so funny I couldn't help laughing. However, the Chief was not amused and the men had to appear in court before we left Brisbane.

At Government House a large party assembled for the races the next day and I felt overcome as I was announced into the large drawing room. But His Excellency was so kind and reassuring as he took me into dinner and sat next to me, that I soon recovered. Afterwards we had coffee in the cool drawing room, the lights of Brisbane glittering below and a breeze scented with strange flowers whispering through the open windows.

Next morning I started work at 7 am and had my job well advanced by breakfast time. I got the valve filled up and ground in, and never stopped till I was finished at 11 am, when the Second came and passed the job and knocked me off. So at 12 pm I was ready in my pretty blue frock, white shoes and white felt hat when the ADC came to the door.

We had a delightful lunch and a very exciting afternoon. I was told that last year's winner of the Cup was Lawn Mower, whose sire was Flying Machine, quite a coincidence as this year a biplane had been flown from Charleville stopping overnight at Longreach and completing the flight to Cloncurry, a 577 mile trip, the next day. This had been achieved about a week before on 2nd November. The biplane flew at 60 miles an hour, as fast as an express train. Bullock wagons had taken over six months to make the same trip 50 years ago. Now there was going to be a flying service between the two towns, even though horse-drawn coaches were still running in some parts of Queensland. I longed to have a flight with the new Queensland and Northern Territories Aerial Service Ltd.

I picked a horse and gave the Private Secretary 5 bob to put on it for me, and it proved the winner.

Sir Matthew invited me to dinner and a dance that night, but I could not go as we had a "shut down job" and would not be finished till late. But they all wanted to come down to the ship. So the next day I gave the party from Government House a tour of the ship which they all enjoyed and we had tea in the messroom with plenty of cakes and biscuits. Sir Matthew sent a message to say he hoped to make the acquaintance of the Chief and Second at Government House on the next voyage.

The ship was to move up river early in the morning to load frozen meat and I was just wondering what time I would be able to get ashore when the Second came along and told me that he and the Chief were going to court the next morning in Brisbane. Then he added, "You are to come with us for laughing." I wished I hadn't, but it did look so funny. He said, "You can send a message to His Excellency that you can accept his invitation and will be outside the Court House when it opens tomorrow morning."

Next morning the Chief was very smart in a blue double-breasted serge suit, the Second equally smart. I was in a summer frock and wore my white hat and shoes.

"Never think we were off a ship," the Chief remarked with pride.

Off we went to Brisbane, walking to a local station, down the dusty road past white-painted frame houses raised off the road because of the ravages of white ants, wide verandas festooned with passion flowers, with ripe fruit. Each white-fenced garden was bright with flowers, blue plumbago hedges and brilliant zinnias and geraniums, the colour intensified by the contrast with the gum leaves.

Outside the Court House we met the ADC and my friend Grace Deshon. While the Chief and Second were in Court, we wandered down Queen Street and gazed in a jeweller's window at a collection of opals. Grace said, "Why not get one with the money you won? You'll never get one cheaper. I'll choose it for you!" And she did. Then we purchased a basket of fruit for the men and I treated her to a leisurely morning tea. Later the ADC joined us and we were whisked off to lunch at Government House.

Sir Matthew asked me a great deal about my apprenticeship and life and work on board ship. He promised that on my return to Brisbane he would give a dance for me.

Then the Secretary ran me back to the meat wharf, where the river water was thick and polluted with the discharge from the meat works and the smell and mosquitoes were equally bad. We sailed in the morning.

And so the marvellous pattern of kindness and hospitality continued as we retraced our steps to Sydney, to Melbourne, and to Adelaide. Australia had unfolded a brilliant panorama of brightness- flowers, fruits, beautiful birds, peeps of mountains and blue sea, framed by grey gum, cities that possessed a dignity all of their own, and the warmest and kindest of invitations in every port.

Of course all this brightness was superimposed on a background of hard and strenuous work from 7 am to 5 pm, and often on Saturday afternoons or all day Sunday.

There were more reporters on my return to Sydney, people coming and begging for a word with me, hundreds of letters to answer, and presents and baskets of flowers. The Australian Institute of Engineers presented me with a beautiful inscribed gold brooch in the shape of a rudder.

We left Sydney on 20th November but there was very little time off now as we had so many repairs to do for the long voyage home. In Adelaide I waded on the beach, but was not allowed to swim because of the sharks.

On the way home I acquired a white sulphur-crested cockatoo as well as a small possum and two white cockatoos, which I fed on boiled sweet corn. The firemen were particularly attached to the birds and often fed them for me if I were on watch. There was a dreadful storm as we came up through the Roaring Forties and I worked 25 hours out of 26. One minute I could see nothing but green water and foam through the ports, the next nothing but storm-tossed sea and dark stormy sky. This free seesaw went on and on. The piano in the music room got loose and smashed a bookcase, two or three chairs and two tables before turning over on its back. Then there was a leak in our messroom and so much water on deck we all had meals in the nursery.

However, the ship survived and we made Durban and later Cape Town, with Table Mountain rising straight in front. I could smell the land, a lovely scent of trees and soil, as I hung over the side watching the water lapping and the white gulls and cape pigeons dipping in and out. Green woods covered the lower slopes of Table Mountain while the rugged red-grey peak pierced the brilliant South African sky.

In Las Palmas there was plague, so we could not land, but the sea looked like watered silk, all shimmering lights and shades with now and then a drove of flying fish. As she glided along through the velvet blackness of a tropical night, I was awakened by stewards singing Christmas carols about 11.30 pm. If one imagined that there were 100 steam heaters on it felt quite like Christmas. The Chief, the Second and I went to church in the decorated saloon where we sang Christmas hymns. Later there was a Christmas dinner with wine, crackers and nuts. The Second and I were the only sober ones on board.

We arrived back in Birkenhead on 11th January to a raw bleak world, and I had three weeks leave before the *Anchises* left again on 2nd February for Australia. I had such a welcome at home, with Papa and Mummy wanting to hear every detail of my voyage, but some things I only retailed to my sisters, like my fall down the after well. Aunt Ayia came over and there was little Nana sitting in the nursery upstairs. The possum and the cockatoos were duly exclaimed over and my aunt took the birds to live in her aviary. There was so much to tell, so much to talk about that I never thought three weeks could pass so fast. I felt quite proud of myself, having made a voyage half round the world as Tenth Engineer. No one ever thought I would stick it out, but I did.

Chapter Nine
More Voyages on SS Anchises - 1923-24

In all I made four voyages on the Australian run in the *Anchises*. I became used to the routine, used to the different ports of call, and looked forward to meeting my many Australian friends. After my short break at home it seemed quite familiar coming back to my cabin in the *Anchises*. I was given one of the smaller passenger cabins, but had to change about as fresh bookings were received. Both Mr Waites, the rather austere Chief, and Mr Quayle, my friend the Second, were the same, but some of the other engineers changed. When we were not on duty I had taken to calling Mr Quayle Hedgehog because of his sometimes prickly manner towards me, and he usually called me Kate which he told me was because of my shrewish temper, although he also called me Dormouse because I sometimes found it so difficult to wake up for the 4 am to 8 am watch.

We left Glasgow at 12 noon on 2nd February 1923 and it was cold and rather wet going down the Clyde. After passing Ailsa Craig a strong wind sprang up which continued during the night. Sunday was a lovely day, bright sun, as we sailed past Land's End and crossed the Channel in the early afternoon. By Monday night we were in the Bay of Biscay when it became cold, rather wet and blowing. This continued until we were out of the Bay and past Finisterre. All day she rolled, and more at night. There was a high sea by the time we reached Gibraltar and so it continued until we reached Las Palmas.

Here the Second sent me up on deck to see where we were. The sun was rising, the sea all liquid gold, and the island veiled by a pale pink mist, all its rugged peaks a deep rose melting to gold. The crimson and gold edge of the sun as it rose was cut by a white-sailed fishing boat, floating out from this enchanted island. I was soon down to earth, or rather the boiler room, when the Second sent the Seventh and myself down to open the HP cylinder, which only a few minutes earlier had contained super-heated steam at 520°F.

Now we were into the Tropics again: the Southern Cross and a blaze of stars shone down as the ship glided over a silver sea with the deep velvet sky overhead, lit by the brilliant stars. There was a boxing match between the firemen on one of the hatches; one man got knocked out first round. Then there were the usual cricket matches between passengers and officers. They had a very good bowler, but I made a lot of runs and he didn't get me out. I was eventually bowled by a very elderly passenger, who bowled under-arm, and was delighted with himself. However, our side still won.

I had been making some copper bracelets for the ladies to wear for the fancy dress dance, for which I made about five and finished and polished them neatly.

"What are those for?" asked one of the new firemen.

"The Chief is going to make a present of one to each female passenger as a small mark of respect," said the Second. The fireman believed him.

The only thing which marred this was that one of the engine bearings went and I got a small splinter of brass in my eye. The Second was at hand to get it out at once, and then put olive oil on to soothe it. It was so sore I thought I would not be able to see again. But I did, and thanks to the Second's first aid, recovered quite quickly.

We arrived at Cape Town on 23rd February and I got ashore next day. As I came back round the corner of the docks my heart stopped as I watched a blue funnel slowly steaming out of harbour. I felt certain it was the *Anchises*, but then I saw her still at anchor: it had been a sister ship.

As we left port, the sea turned clear green with violet shadows and a big ground swell. We stood on deck and watched the coast as we rolled along, distant Cape Town, Devil's Peak, Lion's Head, the Twelve Apostles.

"If you don't want a job, get out of your boiler suit," came the voice of the Second. I went at once, but another engineer who didn't was sent on top of the boilers.

As we sailed down into the Southern Ocean the bilges gave trouble, as usual, but then she settled down. The Southern Ocean was nothing but silver grey sea and grey sky, quite smooth, with a slight wind. We were right in albatross country and I watched them gliding along silent and watchful with never a move of their great wings. Sometimes they dipped, curved and swooped through a wave, but their unmoving wings were always outstretched. When the birds rested on the water, they untucked their yellow, webbed feet from the white down. One day I saw one 16 feet across the wings. They were always silently searching the water with hawks' eyes.

On 4th March one of the greasers on afternoon watch told the Second a fog had descended, and sure enough a white blanket was all round us. Not what I call a really bad fog, having known London peasoupers as a child. One could still see along the deck. I had just gone down and reported to the Second when stand-by went and then the order from the bridge, "Shut watertight doors and sound the whistle every few minutes."

Which we did, but really there was noone to hear it but the albatrosses and the cold dark sea. We were about 600 miles from St Paul's and Notre Dame in the Roaring Forties. Now there is wireless to tell if any boats are about, but in 1923 they sounded the whistle every minute till 6 am the next morning. Every time they blew the whistle they wasted precious water, a fact the Chief didn't like. It was very cold indeed in Latitude 40° South, wrapped in our white blanket of fog.

On 5th March I was finishing the vaporiser, hardening up the nuts, when the Second said, "Don't mark the brass," and gave me a file. He started on some of the nuts near me, but slipped and caught his hand on the file and scraped it, just a scratch.

After breakfast he went to the Doctor to have a bad finger dressed, and the Doctor asked what was the scratch.

"Oh," replied the Second, "Miss Drummond hit me with a file on watch this morning."

So the Doctor went to the Chief and they all came out to where I was on deck.

The Chief asked, "Miss Drummond, can you tell me if this is the time the incident occurred?" and entered into his log, "Between Cape Town and Adelaide Miss Drummond attacked the Second Engineer and hit him in the engine room."

"It comes under the Merchant Seaman Act attacking Senior Officers," said the Chief. "You will be put in irons and tried in Australia. So surprising after such a good record."

And we all had a good laugh. But unfortunately the passengers heard and the story spread over the ship, so it had to be explained that it was a joke. However, it cheered things up, and the Second said, "They all knew you were a person of exemplary character."

As we neared Australia it became warmer, and I played football with the children and some of the engineers in the mornings. The children followed me about like dogs and I made paper boats for them and played Tom Tiddlers' ground and catch with a ball.

One could smell the land down the ventilators as we came in to Adelaide on 16th March. At 4 pm I slipped ashore to meet Tommy Barr-Smith and his mother, and we drove up to the hills, past olive groves and vineyards, orchards of fruit trees covered with peaches, oranges and lemons. I saw wild parrots flashing among the trees. The Barr-Smiths were staying at their house in the hills, so later they drove me down to Adelaide and gave me dinner at the South Australia Hotel.

Next day I was fishing over the side when two enormous sharks came up. One, about 12 feet long, smelt my line; it looked purple and shadowy as it glided along just below the surface of the clear water, showing its white underside and hoop-shaped, cruel mouth as it turned.

When I came on deck after putting my tackle away the youngest passenger, a little boy of two, had somehow climbed up on the rail and was standing poised above the shark cruising below. I went over quietly to take him down, and just as I got near, saw him slip. As he went over the edge of the rail I grabbed him by his woolly pants. Luckily the elastic held and I hauled him back, otherwise I imagine the shark I had seen underneath would have got him. I handed him to the stewardess who gave him to his mother. Perhaps it was as well she never knew how nearly she had lost him.

We arrived at Melbourne on Saturday 17th March and here I found a charming letter from Lady Mitchell inviting me to spend the weekend at their country house near Macedon. I caught the express. It took nearly 2 hours to go about 50 miles up country; there had been no rain for a year. The stock were very thin and all along the line the gum scrub and prickly pears were limp with the heat and drought.

There was a trap to meet me for the 4 mile drive up the steep, wooded hills. I looked back along the dusty road with the old gum trees shedding their pale bark, leaving silvery patches on huge stems, their leaves hanging over the road where their shadows lengthened against a milky pink sunset sky. I really felt I was on the other side of the world as I breathed in the clear air laden with the scent of eucalyptus.

Sunday proved a hot autumn day. I lay on a deck chair in the garden among Michaelmas daisies and the turning leaves of scarlet oaks and Virginia creeper in brightest red.

In the afternoon I walked with Margaret and Lizzie through the gum woods up 700 feet to the top of a hill called the Camel's Hump, 3,700 feet above sea level. There was a lovely view, miles and miles away to the north over the burnt up plain. The woods were lovely, though very dry: wattle, blue and red gum, peppermint gum, and lots of bracken. All the leaves in Australia seem to be starched.

Our return walk was through Ferny Creek, a deep glen with a burn of ice cold water running among a forest of tree ferns. Some 20 feet high, and with stems 3 yards in circumference, as I measured to my cost, stretching my arms round a mossy damp stem in my clean cotton dress.

We arrived back at Sydney on Friday 23rd March and on Palm Sunday I was invited for tea by the Archbishop, after which I went to church at 7.30 pm.

On Monday I worked in the boilers all day, putting on zinc plates, carrying them up a few at a time from the engine room slung round my neck on a rope. I cleaned up the studs nice and bright before hardening up. There was a lot of creeping and crawling over the furnaces, I was absolutely black. Afterwards I dined at Green Club with Miss Henderson, Private Secretary at Government House where we walked among the shadowy palms and cape jasmine. Later the Second took me back to the ship.

There was a great scramble in the boiler and an awful noise on Tuesday as they were scaling it as well. Someone had cracked the isolating steam valve from the live boiler by mistake, and the boiler became very hot indeed. Instantly a big Australian scaler picked me up and pushed me out of the manhole door. I had to get into uniform afterwards and go to a dinner they were giving in the messroom for the Doctor who was getting married that weekend.

On the 28th I went with Lord and Lady Fosters, the Governor-General and Miss Henderson to the Royal Agricultural Show where 1,000 children formed the map of New South Wales, and spelt out the words *SUGAR AND WOOL*. It was so pretty on the bright green grass under the floodlighting.

On Thursday after work I went with the rest of the crew to a football match, a long way by tram, and came back afterwards on my own having done some shopping. I decided not to return to the ship on my own again, as I was followed closely by some very alarming looking types; I made it to the gangway just in time.

We sailed at 9 am on Easter Sunday for Brisbane. I heard the Easter bells ringing over the water as we slipped out to sea. I had forgotten it was also 1st April.

"Quick!" shouted one of the greasers. "The Second wants to see you at once."

So I rushed off.

"First of April!" he called after me.

I had had a letter from Sir Matthew Nathan in Sydney telling me to be sure and telephone the moment I landed at Brisbane, which we did on 3rd April, so at lunch time I managed to slip ashore to phone. Colonel Parsons said His Excellency had invited the Second and myself to a dance.

"Oh," I said, "but I have only a very simple white evening frock."

"Don't bother about that, my wife can fix you up. And His Excellency said tell the Second to come in uniform."

Our arrival at Government House was like a dream. I was taken to a room where there were about a dozen of Mrs Parsons' beautiful frocks laid out for me to choose.

"Put on any one you like," she said, the nicest thing that had ever happened to me. So I chose a white lace embroidered muslin gown with elbow sleeves and went downstairs with another girl who was staying. I sat next to His Excellency in the cool dining room, the lights of Brisbane twinkling through the open windows and later I danced my shoes out gliding over the slippery floor, and went into supper on Sir Matthew's arm. Feeling like Cinderella, I danced until 3 am, the thought of starting work at 7 am the next morning quite out of my mind.

On Friday we sailed to Tasmania, my first visit there, arriving at Hobart at 10 am on Sunday morning. We docked at the foot of Mount Wellington on the River Derwent, about 12 miles up from the mouth, in a deep sheltered harbour. After lunch I went ashore to a lovely beach where I paddled and collected shells. I tried to walk to where the fern trees grew, but some people I met told me it was not safe to go alone into the bush. So I had tea in the town instead and went to evening service at St David's Cathedral. Here too I had invitations and the MacAuleys took me to a lecture in the University and a reception. We were due to sail on Tuesday at 12 pm, so I had only time to go ashore and buy a crate of New Yorker apples and be back on board by 11.30 pm. However we didn't sail till 4 pm, so I fished off the deck and caught a small shark.

We docked at Melbourne on 19th April, but having been on stand-by at 3 am and working continually since, I was too tired when I finally knocked off at 5 pm to do anything but tumble into bed, ignoring my three invitations for dinner.

Next evening, although working all day, I felt strong enough to go ashore and dine with Miss Ivory, who had a large girls' school, full of lovely old furniture, which her family had brought out with them. The Second met me afterwards to escort me back to the ship, and on the way we went into a restaurant for a cup of coffee.

Suddenly a man jumped up and started shooting.

"Under the table!" said the Second, and under the table I went. It got pretty bad. The manager locked the front entrance and called for the police. The Second spied a door near us a chink open, so we crawled over to it. Luckily it led into a side street, and we ran. People were lying on the floor of the cafe bespattered with blood, and the shooting had started again. I was jolly glad to be running down the street.

"In a fight like that," the Second said, "the only thing is to get out. We don't know what it was about and would just have got killed."

My last day in Melbourne I went ashore and bought a pair of lorikeets. They are quite small, about the size of a cockateel. They live wild all over Victoria, in marvellous colours of yellow, red, blue green, white and black. They whistle tunes, though mine didn't, but the sailors said they would eventually.

I made boxes for the birds in my spare time on deck, covering them with felt and canvas, and two sand trays, so they were all comfortably housed. The firemen loved looking after them. One day when I was coming down from the poop, I got caught in a heavy sea and rolled over and over. The firemen picked me out of the scuppers where I was washed, and I had to dry my uniform in the engine room.

We were in albatross seas, the wild expanse of sky and water at the end of the world, when an albatross was killed. I am perfectly certain that was the cause of all the bad luck which afterwards pursued us. I was below at the time so I missed all the excitement, but the albatross hit the wireless and came down on the deck. The sailors couldn't get it to fly and it couldn't rise from the deck, so some bright spark painlessly put an end to it. The Doctor was photographed with it, but I refused to be.

And bad luck did come. Doctor Lawrie left the ship on his return home after one of the crew had severe appendicitis, and we had to put into Lisbon to get him into hospital. The Captain said the Doctor should have operated, but he would not try an operation without the proper equipment. Everyone was very sorry he left.

But by 13th June we had docked at Liverpool, and I was away home for three precious weeks before the *Anchises* sailed again to Australia on 30th June.

Mummy, Frances and Nana came to Glasgow to see me off. It had been lovely seeing them all, and on my way back I bought a second white jersey for the cold voyage across the Southern Ocean. That night Mr Richard Holt came on board, and my friend from the office, Miss Jean Alexander, took me over the new boat which was sailing for China and on which the Holt family were travelling.

We arrived at Las Palmas on 7th July at 5.30 am and stayed all day coaling, taking 1,200 tons, the longest I had yet been there. As I was coming out of the engine room one of the coal shore gang, a rough looking Spaniard, caught me with a shovel on the head as I walked past. There was a huge bump on the back of my head and Martin, the leading hand, made me sit down and gave me a cup of water. He wanted to tackle the man but I dissuaded him as I thought a melee would result and they might be fighting firemen and greasers.

We arrived at Cape Town on 21st July, but there was a lot of work to do for the long run over to Australia.

After the Roaring Forties it got very cold indeed and we took the temperature on deck every 2 hours for ice. We passed a two-masted schooner making very heavy weather in a part of the ocean where one never sees anything. They were having a pretty wet time and although we passed within 200 yards of her, one could hardly see the hull at all. She was bound for Australia too and I watched her till she was lost to sight in the mountainous seas. The new Doctor cut his leg very badly after getting knocked over by a heavy sea, but fortunately one of the passengers was also a doctor and stitched it up for him. The Chief got his finger caught in one of the laundry machines, but that too was mended. Writing wasn't easy, mainly because of the cold. I had five blankets on my bed and was glad of my thick new jersey under my patrol coat.

The 10,000 ton liner drove her way along laden with cargo for Australian ports, her powerful twin screws thrashed through the great seas. She was a steady boat, a good sea boat, but these were the Roaring Forties. A green indigo sea slashed with white, a sea with waves mountains high and many valleys filled with foam. A sky of flying clouds and gleams of sun, with a long roll now to port, now to starboard. Just listen to the wind howl, how it howls and sobs, then sighs and lulls and rises again in a long weary wail that reaches a hoarse scream, then dies and moans again, and the great Southern Ocean seems to answer with a mighty roar, that deadens the throb-throb of the engines. Swish, a sea dashes against the cabin ports and for a second the white foam is lit up by the electric light within. Hark, a crash like thunder, another has landed on deck. One can hear the amazing lash and hiss of water as it dashes to and fro seeking an exit through the scuppers.

Sounds of hurrying feet, the water has found entrance through the heavy teak door at the after end of the alleyway, and is flooding the rooms. The stewards are rushing with mops. That was a big roll. Is she coming back again? Yes. Sounds of objects falling, the coal in the bunkers shifting, cracking, breaking, excited passengers ringing bells, everything swaying, slipping, sliding. The whole boat is creaking and straining. There she goes again, she has taken another sea.

I turned in and slept sound until I heard a knock above the noise of the storm wind. "The Second says to come to the engine room at once. Trouble with the boilers."

And I was there in a split second, 2 am on the engine room clock.

We had two leaks in the back ends. One started in a low fire on the starboard boiler, and although they drew the fire, the metal was still white hot. The Second put on two boiler suits and went in to stem the leak and when he came out his boots were burning. I had a bucket of water to put his feet in before he went back and finished. As he came out the planks were burning and the tools were so hot I had to throw them in water before I could hold them.

At last on 10th August we sighted land, and lay outside the breakwater at Adelaide waiting for daylight.

We sailed for Melbourne the next day and then on to Sydney where we arrived on Monday 20th August.

On our last evening in Sydney I met and dined with Beulah Bolton and Miss Macarthur Onslow at the Queen's Club. Later we went to the Science Congress at Government House where lots of people wanted to be introduced to me, including Sir Gerald Leonard Conynghame, the head of the Congress. His daughter said, "Are you really who you say you are, or are they pulling my leg? Are you really an engineer?"

If she had seen me coming out of the back ends that day she would have had no doubts. Miss Macarthur Onslow took me back to the ship in her car; there were two men having a fight on board with men from another ship, I hoped she wouldn't notice.

As we were on stand-by for sailing, the Chief called me up on deck. So I ran up, and saw what seemed like thousands of bright blue jelly fish all around the ship, with long feelers spread swimming as only jelly fish can, a very wobbly stroke.

We arrived at Parmont, near Sydney, on 3rd September. One of our men was stabbed that night, Parmont being a particularly dangerous place and I was not now allowed over the Parmont Bridge alone.

Just before sailing on Sunday I got a piece of brass in my eye. The Second couldn't get it out with his handkerchief and the Doctor said it was too risky to touch. So I had it in until Wednesday morning, when I went to a hospital in Melbourne. I was sent to the surgery section, a perfectly horrible scramble, where a very small and cross lady in a yellow jumper was hauling things out of people's eyes with a pair of pincers. Some of the eye whites were bleeding and they looked awful. Someone shoved some colour in my eye, but it was too much for me and I asked for my note back. They wouldn't give it to me, nor would they let me out. I saw the note on the table, however, so I took it and ran. I went to the secretary and asked for the name and address of the best eye specialist in Melbourne. When I had got it, I walked out.

I went to his home address and his housekeeper, a Scot, opened the door. It might have been very difficult to get an appointment, but thanks to the housekeeper I saw him first. I told him I had run away from the eye hospital and was off a ship. He gave me another two lots of cortisone and tried first to take the brass out with a pincer, but it was too firmly embedded. He then used a knife and the piece came free. There was instant relief. My eye swelled up for a day or two but was soon all right.

We sailed for Adelaide on 15th September, and after lunch two days later, the Second and I went up to Adelaide and met Ursula Barr-Smith at the South Australia. She drove us to a lovely place, all gum woods and wild parrots and big bushes of wattle full out, the ground covered with brown and yellow cypripedium orchids. Here we met Molly Barr-Smith and her friend who had come in another car, and then we went to Long Galley, where there was a burn, and arum lilies stretching along the bank under weeping willows. We looked at orange orchards and lemon orchards and had tea on the veranda, the garden filled with the scent of orange blossom, huge violets and freesias. Later we had dinner at the South Australia and Mrs Barr-Smith sent me back well supplied with two big cakes, two boxes of chocolates and a huge bunch of flowers.

After we left Adelaide we had bad weather which delayed us about three days. We had to slow down for the gale, with everything slipping, sliding and bumping in the mess room, tea and food all over the table, rollers floating in water on deck and everything wet with spray. But it passed and the sun came out, and the firemen and sailors played cards and cricket and danced to the strains of the mandolin, while all the tropical birds were brought out on the hatch to sun themselves. There were rose-breasted cockatoos, cockateels and gallinules.

However, the long way back was nearly disastrous. The Second became seriously ill with pneumonia and nearly died. And I was also very ill with what I thought was gastric flu, but the shore Doctor told me it had been typhoid. With my friend and protector Mr Quayle laid low, I found myself persecuted by Mr Howard, the extra Second. None of the other officers were able to help me, and I did not feel I could bring it to the notice of Mr Waite, who although gruff, was always kind and fair. So I gritted my teeth and stuck it out, and we arrived home in November.

Even in a chilly November in Scotland, it was nice to be home and petted by Mummy and Frances and John. Papa, who was nearly blind, always sat downstairs in the little sitting room by the front door, with a bright fire. Another cosy room was the old nursery upstairs where Nana Watt held court. I had decided that if Mr Quayle were not well enough to sail again, I could not risk the persecution without his support. The ship was due to sail from Glasgow again on 8th December, and great was my relief when I had a letter from Mrs Quayle to say that her husband, although still very poorly, was feeling much better after the quiet time at home and had every intention of sailing again on the *Anchises*.

So off I set again on my fourth voyage to Australia. Mummy, who came to see me off in Glasgow, said, "My only recipe for Mr Howard is to use the magic spell of the Litany: say to yourself, 'That it may please Thee to forgive our enemies, persecutors and slanderers and to turn their hearts, we beseech Thee to hear us, good Lord.' This will ward off the evil thoughts and unkind actions from you, my beloved child, so brave and good."

I felt very shaky as we left Glasgow that morning. The cold was intense and the hills were all brown heather and snow. I wondered whether I had made the right decision to sail again, or whether I should have stayed and helped John and Frances with the series of amateur theatricals they were putting on. We sailed past Ailsa Craig as it was getting dark and then had a long stand-by coming up the river to Liverpool. We got into a landing stage for passengers by the afternoon. We heard there was a gale in the Channel and plague in Las Palmas, but we were putting in there for water, so perhaps it was better.

After the Channel Islands the weather improved, and off the coast of France it was really warm and sunny and the sea became bluer and bluer until we got to Las Palmas. The island looked just as sun-baked and rocky as ever. Little white-sailed boats and many rowing boats clustered thickly round the ship selling their wares, though not so many were allowed on board because of plague.

Hotter and hotter it got as we went south, the pitch on deck was soft and bubbling. We glided along under a blazing tropical sky. When I tried to print some photos the glass in both frames cracked across with the heat. We crossed the Line on Thursday after Las Palmas, my seventh time.

On Christmas Eve we had a Fancy Dress dance on the prom deck, all hung and bedecked with flags. I went in whites and enjoyed myself tremendously. Later the stewards sang carols and as many had good Welsh voices, it sounded quite Christmassy. All the men wished me Merry Christmas when I went on watch and when I came off there was a large box of chocolates on my table. On Christmas Day we went to church in the saloon and in the evening I came up from watch to a nice Christmas dinner in the messroom, with balloons and crackers, Pouding de Nöel and Pâté de Mince!

On 28th December we arrived at Cape Town at about 6 pm. I found a letter from Mummy telling me that Auntie Maggie had died on 19th December of pleurisy and a bad heart. Jean had been to see her the day before and she had been her old cheerful self. "Whatever happens you must have a merry Christmas," she said to Jean, and added, "there comes a time when one's number goes up, and I think my number is up now." I felt very close to her in the Southern Ocean.

I loved gazing at the southern stars and watching the sky at sunset, iridescent with pale flickering greens and yellows, stretching as far as one could see, or the fully risen moon making a silver path over the restless waters of this lonely sea. Heaven and earth didn't seem so far apart after all, and I thought of the cloud of witnesses.

We arrived at Adelaide on 17th January and in Melbourne on Monday 21st January. The next day, Lord and Lady Forster invited the Second and me to dine at Federal Government House, and on Wednesday I dined with the Barr-Smiths. They came all the way down to the ship to invite both the Second and myself. I was very black in a boiler suit, having just been working on the back ends. Mr Quayle was also in a boiler suit. I did wish I hadn't been quite so dirty! We were a little late arriving as Mr Johnson, the new Ninth who was on his first voyage after working in the drawing office, fainted in the engine room from the intense heat and it took us half an hour to get him round.

Next morning we left for Sydney. The day after arriving I caught the 9.45 am train to Omanangle, where Denzil Onslow met me. He took me to the creamery and dairy, where I saw butter being made, and the export packed in square wooden boxes. I saw milk being strained and screened and had a lovely cool glass of milk to drink. After my childhood work in the dairy, I felt I knew all about milk and butter making! It was wonderful to see the quantity of milk and cream and golden butter. The fat content must have been very high.

Then Denzil drove me to Camden Park, a charming old house with an English atmosphere, blue and white china bowls of roses, old furniture and pictures. The house had been built and was still owned by the family who introduced merino sheep to Australia, a gift from the King of Spain. I saw descendants of the original sheep.

After a delicious lunch, I saw the wonderful collection of orchids, the kitchen garden, beds of water melons, melons in nets, vines covered with grapes and peach trees. Denzil told me they were troubled by parrots eating them. Then we drove to the 200 acre peach orchard and the farm and saw pigs fed on skimmed milk from the dairy.

It was really a day to remember, pastures with scattered gum woods and the Blue Mountains far in the distance.

We sailed for Brisbane on Saturday, where it was very hot, 105°F, just like being on a hot stove. The mosquitoes were very bad on the river, as bad as wasp stings.

From here we went to Hobart in Tasmania for apples. The change in climate was amazing after Brisbane, where I had spent a hot week in whites and sleeping under one sheet. Now I had the doors and ports shut, and piled blankets, a coat, rug and uniform on my bed, but even with a hot water bottle I was still cold.

There was a bit of a roll on our voyage back to Melbourne, where I found Mr and Mrs Neary, immigrants from Glencarse, waiting on the quay to see me.

I had been invited with the Second to dine at Government House the next night by Lady Forster, so after work I changed into my French grey evening frock with the frilled muslin and lace collar and cuffs. After dinner we played card games until it was time to go. We walked back to the ship along St Kilda's Road. In spite of my dinner, I was still hungry, so the Second took me to a cafe for fish and chips.

On our way home we put into Albany in Western Australia, where I spent a lovely day with Mrs Haslet, a friend of Lady Forster.

Then back we sailed, across the Southern Ocean, Durban, Cape Town, Las Palmas and Liverpool. Next voyage, they said, we were going to China, and perhaps Japan, which would be interesting and take three and a half months, much shorter than Australia round the Cape.

I lost no time in catching a train from Liverpool to Perth where John met me in his car. It was an icy April, with gusting snow showers and I had to wear two pairs of combinations and all my winter woollies. However, my new parrots were quite warm with their friends in the big conservatory in the front garden, where the mimosa tree was already in flower. There was a gum tree too, and the warm scents of gum and wattle must have made them feel at home. Jean was home on leave and so we were all together. How lovely it was all to be together again, everyone wanting to hear every detail of my Australian voyages.

I had barely a month at home before we left Liverpool again. It was still cold when we slipped away down the Mersey, quite a sea high road with its ever moving stream of outward and homeward bound boats, ocean liners for the most part. Bustling foggy Liverpool soon dropped away behind us and in a short time we were lifting to the Irish Sea. As I stood taking the stand-bys in the hot, heavy, oily atmosphere of the engine room with the steady beat of the engines and the electric lights reflecting on shining steel, brass and copper, I felt we were really outward bound. I was going to China at last. We dropped the pilot off at Holyhead about midnight and when I went on watch at 4 am we were well down the Channel. By afternoon we were off Ushant and the clear blue twilight of Northern France. There was fog in the Bay of Biscay, watertight doors shut and the whistle blowing but by night it had lifted and we were through it in about 30 hours, and so down the coast of Portugal and past Cape St Vincent.

When I came up for dinner on Wednesday night there was the coast of Morocco on one side and Spain on the other. We were in the Straits of Gibraltar. It felt quite strange turning up to Gibraltar instead of heading right down to Las Palmas. There was talk of putting into Gib as one of the trimmers was thought to have appendicitis, but he recovered. However, the Second let me slip on deck as we passed, and I saw the Rock splendidly. It looked lovely by moonlight. It was a regular southern evening with clear eau de nil sky and oyster sea, the Rock looking very big and dark against the sky with a little cluster of lights at the foot, a few scattered lights on the mainland, lighthouses blinking and silvery stars overhead. The whole place looked very familiar to me, as if I had been there before, and just like the picture I had drawn in my drawing book from imagination.

From looking at my school atlas I had thought the Mediterranean quite small, but I revised my opinion once we were sailing through it. I was surprised at the number of small migratory birds, swallows, martins and yellow wagtails which came on board to rest. The Second had a busy time saving them all from the ship's cats, who thought them a particular present. But the little birds were so tame and friendly, and came on board almost as though they were seeking protection for themselves. On 19th May we passed Crete and then about tea time Alexandria. All one could see was a sandy coastline and a lighthouse. We were on stand-by at 8 pm and an hour later arrived in Port Said. I had been on watch since 4 pm in the afternoon and we worked straight through till 1.30 am in the morning. One of my jobs was to help the Second pack the telemotor on the bridge, so I had an excellent view of Port Said. In the Red Sea the temperature under the ventilator in the engine room with the wind blowing down on the thermometer was 106°F. On the middle platform it was 118°F and in the stores and round by the vaps anything you like! At night one could see people walking about with a pillow trying to find a cool spot, nearly everyone slept out, passengers as well. The deck was littered with them. I only fainted three times from the heat, and only once in the engine room was it a really bad faint. The Second got me round and gave me a hand to my room where he rubbed my hands and face with Florida water. He then fetched Miss Moodie, the stewardess, and left me with her. She helped me out of my boiler suit and gave me sal volatile and I was soon all right again. But the Second made me stay in my bunk. All the same I did not miss my watch. My skin peeled with the heat, and I lost quite a bit of weight.

The hottest part was the Strait of Bab-el-Mandeb. I saw Port Sudan on the starboard side almost opposite Mecca, and looked at the hills thinking of the stories Papa had told me of the Suakin Campaign when he had been fighting there. When we got to the Gulf of Aden we had a monsoon warning by wireless and all the canvas awnings were taken down, but the rain never materialised. Later we came to Sumatra, a nice looking island with high hills, and into the Straits of Malacca where it was boiling hot and very damp and steamy after heavy tropical rain. We passed a small rock island covered with palm trees which smelt so fresh after the rain.

When we arrived at Singapore on 7th June, I received a telegram that Papa had died on 29th May. It was a dreadful shock to me and somehow I could not take it in. All this time as I voyaged through the great heat, he had died and been buried at Megginch. It had been most sudden and unexpected. He had been going on his annual holiday to Oban and my mother had been at Perth Station to see him off on the train. He was nearly totally blind, although he would not admit it, and while Mummy was at the bookstall for a moment, he had suddenly taken a step forward and fallen off the platform. He had been rushed to Perth Infirmary where they found he had broken his leg. This was on 16th May and to all appearances he seemed to be recovering. However, on the 24th his condition deteriorated and pneumonia set in. He often spoke of me, they said, and was talking about my coming exam the day before he died. Mummy, Jean, Frances and John were all with him when he died. "It was a beautiful May morning, with all the birds singing," Frances wrote. She could write no more.

They all wrote; they told me of the funeral, of the coffin covered with the Drummond tartan plaid, the Drummond holly wreaths, and all the friends who came to pay their last respects, while the Atholl Highland pipers played a lament under the Megginch holly trees. "Your mother was so brave.... John arranged it all so beautifully.... It was just as your father would have wished.... He was so proud of you...." I could see it all, and yet here I was on the other side of the world in China, and no longer part of it.

The Second was very kind to me, so were they all. I cannot remember anything much of that time as I was so sad inside while on the outside I went on with my work, doing everything with a kind of mechanical precision and feeling nothing. I still could not believe that Papa would not be sitting in the Front Hall just as usual when I got home. When I saw a camphor wood chest I thought, "Oh, that's the very thing for Papa." But there was no Papa to buy camphor wood chests for. Then I saw the Chinese market returns in the paper. "I must send this paper home," I thought. "It would be nice for Mummy to read to Papa."

It had been boiling hot after we left Singapore and it stayed hot as we went past the Gulf of Siam, Cochin China, French China and the South China Sea. We reached Hong Kong on 12th June. John's old school friend, Jock Jardine, had written to his relatives that I was coming and they sent down a car to the boat. We drove into the country through coconut and rubber plantations, and little native villages. It was so lovely, birds' nest ferns on the trees and orchids and greenhouse ferns on the banks, and all the air smelt like a greenhouse. It helped a little to put things into perspective for me, but then I came back to the ship and thought about home so far away. They were all kind to me, but I still felt numb inside.

From Hong Kong we sailed to Shanghai, where the Second took me for a walk in the country through paddy fields and through the native villages. There were no roads in China, only mud tracks between paddy fields. The rice looked like young corn, grown in water. All the fields were irrigated and water lay between the drills. It was very flat and every scrap was cultivated with rice, corn, or strange kinds of vegetables. Strewed about the fields were the coffins of dead Chinese, lying in the fields open to the air and not buried. The villages were very dirty, full of mangy dogs and poorly clothed inhabitants who looked at us with hostility, curiosity and terror. The houses were made of bamboo and matting. Seeing all these strange new places and being in the country with the Second somehow made me forget for a time to be sad.

From Shanghai we sailed right up north to Taku-Bar, near Peking, and although I went on with my work I was so sad I could feel very little. Taku-Bar was not much of a place. We anchored 9 miles from shore, as it was too shallow to go in, so we had to discharge the cargo at sea. The sea looked quite yellow, which would explain its name, and I saw lots of junks sailing about. The crew discharging were all Chinese and ate with chopsticks.

On 27th June we left Taku-Bar at 7 am in the morning and sailed to Ching-Wang-Tu which is really in the Gulf of Pe Chili, practically in Chinese Mongolia. We lay out that evening, a warm still night with a shot yellow and green sky. On the shore the lights of Chin-Wang-Tu twinkled against the rugged hills, very mysterious looking. Somewhere in these hills was the Great Wall of China, which they said was only 5 or 6 miles from the town.

From here we sailed to Dalney. Before the Russo-Japanese War the area was Russian, then the Japanese took it, and the population became very mixed, Russian, Mongolian, Chinese and Japanese. The town was laid out on the lines of a European city with wide boulevards planted either side with fruit and acacia trees, massive stone buildings and heavy war memorials. The formal gardens in the plazas were also laid out in European style, but planted with Japanese trees and Japanese plants.

"It is very strange to walk in a European town inhabited by oriental people," the Second said. He was unaccustomed to people from different races. We bought some canaries, and a Mongolian we met in the street brought them on board for me.

From Dalney we sailed south to Tsingtao which was a regular German town, having been their one possession in the East when war broke out. They had spent millions on it, built red roofed model houses, paved the streets and made German cafes, docks and a fort, and had put up many notices both in Chinese and English stating the things one might not do. I was not allowed on shore on my own, but in the evening the Second took me and we went in rickshaws which was great fun.

And so we came down to Shanghai and the Yangtse, thick like muddy yellow soup, with paddy fields and junks. We lay off shore, which was perhaps as well as there was a lot of cholera in Shanghai and black smallpox. Both the Second and I were ill, overwork and the heat, I think, and I was sick at heart.

At the beginning of the voyage I had written to Mr Freeman, the Engineer Superintendent in Holt's office to ask for a reference as I planned to take my Second's ticket when I came home. But I did not want to stop sailing with the *Anchises*. I did not want to go on sailing without my dear Second constantly to supervise, advise and protect me. Although we came from different backgrounds, our minds were perfectly attuned: we loved birds, the sea, engines and the British Empire. We shared the same wry sense of humour, the same love of travel. If there had been no Mrs Quayle, no Malcolm, no Helen, it is possible our relationship would have ripened into romance. But my dear Hedgehog was too honourable a man to abandon his commitments. He coached me constantly for my coming exam, he escorted me ashore, he took me round and guarded me in the foreign dockyards of the world, but he would never allow our friendship to become more than just that.

We were both very tired on the China voyage of the *Anchises*, neither of us had recovered from our illnesses on the previous voyage, I was totally overcome by the death of my father, and the heat was ever present, ever debilitating. At Port Said on the return voyage I received a letter from Mr Freeman saying that this must be my last voyage on the *Anchises*. I at once wrote back suggesting that Mr Quayle should be made a Chief (as he had a Chief's ticket) and that after I had sat my Second's exam I should go with him as Chief's Assistant. It would have made such a good and grand finish to my career; I could have gone ashore, not tied by watches, I could have painted and written in my spare time. It was a splendid plan, it seemed to me. After two years in the engine room, the work was getting me down. "You are knocking up," said the Second, "and I am too."

So I wrote all my splendid plan to Mr Freeman. It was only years later that I could see what a mistake this had been; it immediately convinced him that the relationship between the Second and me was closer and quite other than it really was. "If only" and "perhaps", what sad words they are. It had been a sad voyage.

But when dear Jean and little Nana came to meet me when the *Anchises* docked at London, I did not know it was my last voyage on her.

Chapter Ten
TSS Mulbera - 1924-27

When I came back from my last voyage on the *Anchises* everything was different at Megginch. I had never thought I should miss Papa standing in the middle of the house shouting for people to come, miss the enforced turns sitting with him and reading the daily papers and the letters. Mummy was still there, busy with her garden and flowers, making potpourri and painting. Nana still held court in the nursery with the cats curled by the fire. Frances was still there, working late at night over the fruit, doing the hens and very often the cooking. But without Papa, it was not the same.

Financially we had always been in low water. When Papa died a whole room was discovered full of bills, where he had thrown them unable any more to cope. Mummy worked out with the lawyers that by using every scrap of rent from the tenants for the next few years, living off her own small income and what we could grow in the garden, by scrimping and saving, and buying nothing new, we could manage to pay off the Death Duties and some of the bills. But it would be an uphill struggle.

Jean now lived at Queen Victoria's Girls' Club in 122 Kennington Road, Lambeth, where she had a flat and a small salary. The Reverend F O T Hawke was Vicar of St Philip's and Jean often lunched with him as he helped her with the Club. It was a slow and long-standing romance and we always hoped it might blossom into matrimony, but it never did.

John went south with a friend to seek his fortune in London. At first he stayed with Jean, but later found digs of his own. His first venture was a restaurant where all meals cost one shilling. It might have been a good idea, but of course all John's friends had free meals and eventually the whole enterprise collapsed.

When I got back from the *Anchises* I was determined to sit my exam at once and go with her on the next voyage, but it didn't happen like that. I became ill and it was over six months before I was well enough to take the exam. Sometimes I went to London and stayed with Jean in her flat and studied there, sometimes I studied at home. Mr Martin from Dundee sent me constant help and advice, and so of course did my dear Second, who corresponded regularly and sometimes came to Megginch when the ship docked at Glasgow.

During the next two years I took my Second's exam three times and the third time I passed it. During this time John had become engaged to Gladys Pullar, a very nice local girl, and then unengaged. He had then become engaged to Rosamond Cholmeley, and again unengaged. None of us seemed fated to marry. At home everything was very quiet. Although Mummy, Frances and Nana worked very hard, the financial situation seemed worse than ever.

After I passed my exam I wrote at once to the Blue Funnel Line to take me back. It was a great shock to me that they would not have me. I suppose they feared a scandal. I could have told them it was not like that, but they wouldn't listen.

In a frenzy I wrote, and got Mummy to write, too, to everyone we could think of. Suddenly I heard that the British India Line would possibly take me. I rang them and Mr Lesley, who answered, said, "This is just to tell you, Miss Drummond, that Lord Inchcape is agreeable to your sailing with the company and therefore I think I shall put you on the *TSS Mulbera*, 9,100 tons, turbine driven, oil fuel burning, running out to East Africa. She goes to just below Mombasa. The Chief and the Second are both very nice. The best plan will be for you to come to London about 19th March when the *Mulbera* comes in. I will take you down myself, and you can talk the Chief and Second round." I was so excited I could hardly speak.

On 11th April I went down to the office and saw Mr Wilson. "Your powers of persuasion have prevailed," he said, and I replied, "It is now up to me to do my best." I thought this a suitable remark.

He then sent me to a superintendent who gave me a book of rules and a slip stating that my pay was to be £11 10/- per month. There were nine engineers and I was sailing Fifth. After this Mr Wilson took me to the Royal Albert Docks to meet the Captain, who was tall with a dark thin face. We then went to the shipping office where I was introduced to two more supers and given a dock pass. I was also introduced to the Chief Engineer, who was very Scottish

On board the *Mulbera* I was taken to see my room, a nice cabin with two ports opening out on to the top deck, but there was too much to see and take in at once. I was introduced to all the other engineers; first to the Second, Mr Lamb, who seemed a nice young man, and the others who were all boys without tickets except for the Third and Fourth. There was quite another feeling about the company. They all seemed quite superior sort of people.

On Tuesday I went down again and took my suitcase to the engineers' quarters. I was sent along to sign on and when I came back Mr Lamb sent me ashore for the night, telling me to catch the early train in the morning. Luckily I did, for whom should I find getting off at the dock station but Mr Lamb. After lunch he took me to the engine room and the Third Engineer showed me round.

The passengers did not come on board till the afternoon, and we did not sail till the evening, so I had time to get my room straight. It was a much more comfortable room than the one on the *Anchises*, with a bunk, wash hand basin, wardrobe, chest of drawers, opening desk and a settee. The woodwork was light oak and the carpet red bristles. The curtains were grey, the cover on top of the desk blue, and all the walls white. The only trouble was that there was not much privacy as both ports opened on to the deck and any passer-by could look in. In addition, I had to share a bathroom. Still, one cannot have everything in this life. I had an Indian steward to whom I could only speak Hindustani, so I started working at my Hindustani books.

I was on the 4-8 am watch and while I was on watch the Second rang for me to come up and say goodbye to the Dock Company's super.

At 8.30 pm I went on stand-by and on to the port engine to answer the telegraph and work the go ahead and go astern valves. I had never worked a turbine engine before and going out of port there is always a lot of manoeuvring to be done. However, I thought nothing ventured nothing gained and I managed okay. I was let off at 9.15 pm and turned in for my early start at 4 am.

My steward called me at 3.30 am and I was down in the engine room by 4 am. When we dropped the pilot at about 6 am, Mr Lamb let me go up on deck to have a look at the white cliffs of Dover through the store port. After breakfast I went on deck where it was very cold and grey, almost as grey, cold and foggy as leaving London. By noon we were off Weymouth and I saw the Isle of Wight, and by tea time off the Scillies.

Mr Lamb was 34 and as tall and thin as the Chief was short and fat, with straight, fair hair. Both he and the Chief seemed very respectable, as did the Third, Mr Gladstone. The Fourth was Scottish and came from Dumbarton and the other three Mr Miller, Mr Chater and Mr Wilkes were all boys of 22 or younger and very much the schoolboy type.

I didn't think the ship was as steady as the good old *Anchises*. Of course the engine room was very clean and everything shining. The oil fuel made a big difference, but this was balanced by the noise of the turbo generators, which was so strong I could not hear myself shout in the engine room. At first it made my head ache a great deal, but I soon got used to it.

The wind continued strong as we rounded Cape St Vincent and passed Gibraltar. The Mediterranean was rolling with white horses .

The food on board was very good, there was chicken and ice cream, salad, lots of vegetables and pickles. The messroom was large and airy and my room was also very comfortable, though it still took me some time to get used to walking to the bathroom preceded by my Indian steward carrying my soap and bath towels. One of my troubles was the washing. On the *Anchises* my dear Second had found a stewardess to do it. Here Mr Lamb said, "Just give it to a steward. He will do it for you." He did not understand, and I could not explain, that there were certain personal, feminine things which I could not possibly give to a steward. Nothing in those days was disposable. It made life very difficult for me.

By the time we had passed Majorca, hazy and blue in the distance, I had finished the ballast pump and overhauled a valve. Luckily I enjoyed climbing and thought nothing of going 40 feet hand over hand, up and down straight ladders.

Our first port of call was Marseilles which we reached on 21st April. I was allowed off at 4 pm, but Mr Lamb said I must be back by 8 pm because it was not safe on the French docks after dark. It was just as hot as June and all the home summer flowers were out.

By next Sunday, 24th April, we passed Stromboli. "Don't you want to see Stromboli?" Mr Lamb called through my open port, so I dressed quickly and went on deck, and there was the volcano rising straight from the sea, the lower slopes terraced for vineyards and white villages with flat-roofed houses along the shore. After breakfast and inspection I went to church, as the Captain asked me specially. I sat up on the left with the other officers, just opposite the table covered with the Union Jack, and felt every eye was on me. The Bishop, Chaplain-General Taylor-Smith, preached for 40 minutes. The Captain tried to stop him as we were going through the Straits of Messina, but he would have his full 40 minutes.

Eventually we got out to see the Straits which were quite narrow, less than the width of the Tay at Dundee. There was snow on the hills and snow on Etna with orange trees and vines on the terraces. The town of Messina was all white houses with green shutters.

At 4 pm I was back on watch again and Mr Lamb said, "You see, you are in sole charge when I am out of the engine room and you will also be when I go up to dinner, as I don't want to have to send a relief."

So when he went up to dinner, I was in sole charge, as one might say, of the ship! In full charge of engine room and stokehold. It took some doing keeping the steam, regulating the oil fuel pressure and temperature, feeling round every hour and taking the counter, taking the temperatures, seeing to the oil lubrication pumps and keeping the bilges free of oil, seeing to the boiler gauge glass and starting up hot salt water on deck.

As we sailed down the Mediterranean it became warmer all the time; a yellow wiggie-woggie came on board (as I always used to call wagtails) and a gramophone played on deck. All the officers put on clean collars for breakfast, a really smart ship.

We reached Port Said on 27th April, but as I was on watch when we got in I was too sleepy when I came off to do more than look at the lights and turn in. We went into the canal about 11 pm and when I went on watch at 4 am it was still too dark to see more than the outlines of the desert stretching out on either side. By now the sea temperature was 83°F and it was 109°F in the coldest part of the engine room.

We were about 30 miles through the canal and had passed Ismailia when Mr Lamb sent me up to see why we had stopped. Out of the store port I saw the sun rising over the desert. It was a wonderful sight, all grey and gold shadows, just like one reads about in books.

When we got into Port Sudan Mr Lamb let me off the evening watch. There seemed so much less to do than on the *Anchises* and the engineers spent a lot of time wearing white suits in port all day. The city was built on coral and the glare from the white sand was intense. After lunch Mr Lamb said, "Don't change, just go ashore as you are." So I went in my white uniform and put on a double felt hat, and Mr Lamb lent me some green glasses, as it was quite impossible to see with the glare.

When I came back, I found the others were going for a swim, so I slipped on my bathing dress with my whites on top and we went over in a boat to the other side. Some of the passengers were bathing, too. The water was warm and clear in a big sea pool with white coral sand and rocks all round, yellow seaweed growing on the bottom. It was so lovely rowing over, the sun setting behind the palms, the desert stretching out to the hills, the sky every shade of orange and yellow from the palest primrose to the deepest apricot.

We sailed on Monday about 7 am and the coolest part of the engine room was 115°F. On the 12 pm-4 pm watch it went up to 120°F. We passed Cameroon, then Perim in the Gulf of Aden and we passed through the straits of Bab-el-Mandeb to arrive in Aden at 1 pm. They may well speak of the "Barren Rocks". I have never seen anything so dry and bare before, high walls of sheer rock rising straight out of the sea with not a blade of grass or anything green growing on them. Along the bottom of these cliffs there ran a rocky road where one could see camels harnessed to carts, shimmering in the white heat. I walked round the deck and looked at the shore boats and watched people diving for coins, they would only dive for silver. I bought some limes and squeezed them in iced water with sugar; they were delicious.

After leaving Aden it got even hotter and the engine room temperature rose to 118°F. Early on Friday morning we passed Cape Guardaput where there is a false cape or second headland which ships often mistake for Daput. All day we passed along the coast of Italian Somali land, wild bare rocky cliffs plunging sheer down into the sea with here and there a little bay of sand. I saw a good many gulls flying about and a dear little rising dove, a dark green stone colour, came and rested on the deck.

We were to cross the Line on Monday 9th May and I was asked if I would take the part of Lady Neptune in the ceremony for crossing the Line. They had to ask me four times, but in the end I agreed to do it. My costume consisted of a sacking slip with a hemp fringe round the waist and neck, and on my head a cream coloured wig of jute and a high paper crown.

As we crossed on Monday, Neptune should have come aboard Sunday night, but the Bishop would not have this. So it had to be fixed up for Saturday night. It was a pouring wet night and the tropical rain was dashing down in white sheets by the deck house and bridge, a real cinema sea-storm effect. The ship was rolling and the white tops of the waves were lit up by flashes of blue electric fire that shivered across the sky in one of those electrical storms that only comes in the tropics. I dressed in my kit and went aft to the fo'castle head where the rest were crouching behind the windlass. When the right moment came, Neptune, who was Chippie the carpenter, hailed the ship as green and red flares were let off from the fo'castle head.

"I see a black light. What craft are you?"

The answer came back from the bridge: "The good ship *Mulbera* of London."

"Where are you bound?"

"Mombasa in East Africa."

"Have you any greenhorns on board?"

"Yes."

Then Neptune climbed over the windlass and we all climbed down from the fo'castle head and proceeded across the well deck and round all the decks. They howled all the time and beat on tins till we arrived on the prom deck where all the passengers were gathered. The Captain presided over a table with glasses containing tots of "good rum". He shook hands with Neptune and with me since we headed the procession. The Clerk (who was the Second Mate) read out the charges, which of course were all quite ridiculous, and after the charges were read we shook hands again with the Captain and proceeded back to the fo'castle and crouched behind the windlass until the red flares had gone out.

On Monday afternoon Mr Lamb let me off watch for a bit so I could take part in the crossing of the Line. I put my costume on over my bathing suit and once again we all marched along the deck to a table where Neptune and I sat surrounded by the mock Court: the Clerk, the Doctor and his Mate, the Bishop, and on a platform by the deep canvas bath the Barber and the Barber's Mate. All the passengers and officers who were not in the ceremony watched from the foredeck.

The first girl came dressed in a cream silk frock, expensive shoes and stockings, and freshly shampooed hair. I felt sure she did not know what she was in for. The charge was read and she was taken to the Doctor who gave her two large round pills, about the size of a small egg, made up of carbolic soap, pepper, mustard and vinegar. She tried to avoid them, but they forced the pills in and held her mouth shut and then poured the tonic down. This was made of vinegar, quinine, salt, sugar and pepper, and I believe was too nasty for words. She was then dragged up the wooden ladder to the Barber where she was lathered with a mixture of whiting, glue and syrup all over her hair and face while the Mate shaved her with a big wooden razor. Then the Barber threw her into the bath (which was quite a drop) where the Bears, people detailed to duck the victims and give them a rough time, finished off the poor girl.

All the passengers who had not crossed before were done. Some of the men tried to get away, but they were dragged down by four policemen, taking a hand and a foot each. The ones who knew put on bathing suits and several went and changed when they saw what their fate was to be!

One man pleaded he was seasick but they gave him three pills all the same. They hunted the whole ship for one cadet till long after it was over. They got into a great fuss as they thought he might have gone overboard; the Mates even came down to search the engine room. In the end they found him in the store.

Finally the passengers raided the Court. They turned the hose on us (and there is some strong pressure in a ship's hose) and then they threw Neptune in the bath, the Doctor and the Bishop went, too. They got hold of me and pushed me up the ladder, so head first I went into the bath. I quite enjoyed being Queen of the Sea, especially as so many of the passengers told me how pretty I looked!

On 13th May we arrived at Mombasa but anchored 2 miles out at Kilindini where we were unloading cement. I had to work all day but went for a refreshing swim in the evening. On Saturday I got ashore after 2 hours work and Mr Lamb took me to see the *Modassa*, a sister ship berthed next to us, but not as nice as the *Mulbera*. In the afternoon I took a taxi and went exploring on my own. The town, if it can be called that, was quite small. There was an old fort built by Vasco da Gama, for at one time it was a Portuguese settlement. I walked right round by the cliffs to the lighthouse, following a rocky path. The soil was deep red and all the rocks and cliffs were of dazzling white coral, discoloured in parts to a deep cream. Every kind of greenhouse plant tumbled over each other wherever they could get a footing, bougainvillea, plumbago, bright yellow trumpet flowers and frangipani.

The town streets were bordered with flamboyant trees, ferny leaves like acacias and bright red flowers decorated the boughs.

We sailed on 15th for Tanga, a coral island, black with palm trees and then to Zanzibar. After I came off watch I took a walk under the bridge and the Captain came down and asked me to have a look at the chart which was most interesting. He took her in himself without a pilot. It was very pretty sailing from Tanga to Zanzibar, the misty palms of the island faded into the hazy heat of the mainland, and wide streaks of turquoise patterned the deep blue of the sea. These were the coral reefs through which we had to pass, and although mostly sunken, they were as sharp as knives with long spines running right out under the sea.

We sailed that night for Dar-es-Salaam, formerly capital of German East Africa. The entrance to the harbour was between white coral reefs and with the low spring tide I could see the coral as we passed between it. We lay right out in the harbour. The town was built round the landlocked harbour and there were coconut palms and plantations right down to the shore. It was a long way to get over from the ship to the stage. However, I got a boat, and with three Africans rowing and me steering, I got ashore. Boats did come alongside to take passengers, but sometimes it was rather difficult to get one.

We sailed the next day and arrived at Beira on the 22nd where we lay at the mouth of the river a long way from shore. The mosquitoes were very bad and the water thick and muddy.

The Second put me on night work from 6 pm to 6 am. We did not need to stay down all the time and I just went down every half hour to look after the freezer, the boiler and various auxiliary engines. Twelve hours was a long time on my own and how I missed my old Second, my dear

Hedgehog. If I had been getting down on a job or getting done up on watch, the old Second would say, "Slip up and have a blow," or "slip up the tunnel and have a sit down." Some mornings he wouldn't have me called till 6 am. But on the *Mulbera* I had never been offered a "blow" and at sea I was up every morning at 3.30 am, so I missed the Second a lot.

The Portuguese Governor-General arrived at Beira on Thursday, so the ships in the river were decorated in his honour. The ship's officers were invited to a dance in town given by the Club for Empire Day, but I felt too ill to go. Mr Carlin, editor of the *Beira News*, came on board the next day and put a piece about me in his paper and invited me to the Governor-General's state ball, but I still felt too ill. However, I did spend the afternoon with his wife who fetched me in a trolley car, a small tram for two people which was pushed by two boys. The trolley rails were laid in streets of soft sand between houses of wood and corrugated iron. There were palms, red-flowered shrubs, violet-coloured jacarandas, red and white hibiscus and trees bearing clusters of bright yellow fruit. The Portuguese had done little to improve the town and it was dusty, hot and below sea level with a large wall built to keep out the sea. They did not seem to like the British much and all the Europeans seemed a washed-out lot, drinking too much.

In Beira we loaded oranges and chrome ore from Rhodesia and then sailed back to Dar-es-Salaam where we loaded ivory. I watched them stack the tusks into a big net and take it aboard like that; we also loaded tortoiseshell. It was so hot and bright that I could hardly look at the shore. But despite its scenic beauty, Dar-es-Salaam was not a healthy city because the Germans had run all the sewage drains into the harbour.

We sailed that day for Zanzibar where the channel ran quite near the coast and I could see the ruined palaces of former Sultans standing amongst coconut trees and overlooking the sea. Each new Sultan had to have a new palace built for him as he could not live in the palace of the former Sultan! The water was a clear blue shaded with lilac, and emerald green islands dotted the surface of the sea. Zanzibar was built on a low promontory and came down to the water's edge.

The Chief said I could go ashore but must be back by dark at 6 pm. I went in the agent's launch and the agent, who was called Nichols, said his mother had been a Drummond-Hay, and invited me to dinner.

We landed on the white coral beach and I jumped over the side into the warm, shallow waves and set foot on Sinbad the Sailor's Isle of Cloves where the air was perfumed with the spicy scent. Mr Nichols and I walked up the beach and got into his 6-cylinder shooting brake. He ran me through the narrow, twisted streets crowded with every nationality Arabs, Swahilis, Africans from the Congo, Syrians, Jews, Chinese, Turks, Indians, Abyssinians, inky black Nubians and Hindus all populated the Eastern streets of Zanzibar!

Date palms and trees with sweet, starry flowers like cape jasmine grew outside his house which was large, white and cool with a broad veranda and polished floors covered in Persian rugs. Mrs Nichols and Captain Forbes were just finishing tea so I had some chocolate biscuits. Later they fitted me out with a bathing suit and we set off in the car for a Sultan's ruined palace where we swam in warm water on a white coral beach. When evening fell we returned to the palace and sat on the veranda, talking to the Adamsons who lived there. I don't think I've ever been in such a creepy place, oil lamps cast a flickering light as we sat or lounged in long wicker chairs on the veranda and the only sounds were the wash of the sea and a faint, sighing breeze. Now and then a bat flapped past or a lizard ran across the wall. The palace was decorated in Arab plaster work and the floors had been whitewashed since the marble squares had gradually been stolen till little remained. The doors were of mosaic native wood embellished with pointed brass studs to fortify the entrances against elephant charges when the place was attacked about 100 years ago.

We got back in the car and shot along narrow, tree-lined roads; Mr Nichols never drove less than 55 miles an hour, which seemed terribly fast for these narrow paths. This house was large and white, and we found the owners sitting at the front door drinking sundowners and listening to a gramophone. I watched the lizards running about on the wall snapping at moths and the bright fireflies flitting in and out of the hibiscus. When Mr Nichols told his friends I was an engineer, they could not believe it.

After dinner we went on a 17-mile drive to see some clove trees. I saw the grove beautifully spotlighted in the car headlights and picked some leaves. They are a bushy kind of tree, like a rhododendron, and if you look at the seeds of a rhododendron you will see they are shaped rather like cloves. The Nichols told me how some Americans had come to make a film of Zanzibar and took about 60 feet of a giant mango tree thinking it was a clove tree.

Finally Captain Forbes took me back to the *Mulbera* loaded with cloves and Zanzibar oranges which are really sweet limes.

We left Zanzibar at 4 am for Mombasa, where we stayed for about four days. I learnt a great deal about the history of Mombasa and how the Portuguese had built a fort which was always being attacked by the Arabs. In 1696, the fort was besieged for eighteen months before the Portuguese could get reinforcements, and when they did the Arabs redoubled their siege for another fifteen months until at last, overcome by sickness and starvation, the garrison surrendered and all were killed. Two days later the relieving fleet despatched from India arrived off the coast and hearing there were no survivors set sail again. I saw the old Portuguese guns and lookouts built of coral rock in the fort and thought how they must have gazed from the loopholes over the dazzling waters of the Indian Ocean for the relief that never came.

All this part of Africa was Ethiopia and it was from here that the Egyptians drew their slaves, gold and ivory. Right down as far as Rhodesia there are surface gold workings known as the "Queen of Sheba's workings"!

It was so pretty sailing up the Gulf of Suez, the jagged purple hills tinted with orange and when the sun set the whole sky turned clear duck egg green. We entered the canal about 4 pm and were not out till 2 am the next morning. As I was not on watch till 8 am, I saw the canal very well. There is something very mysterious about the desert. Now and then as we passed along I would see a drove of camels feeding, and towards evening I saw three Arabs mounted on camels, one of which was white. They sat like statues watching the boat pass, then turned away to the desert. I watched the sun set over the desert and all the sand seemed to turn pink in the afterglow, till it was dark and I could see nothing but stars and sand.

We were in Port Said in the evening, and as I came on deck to read my home letters, I saw it all beautifully, the houses with green shutters, scarlet flame-of-the-forest trees and the statue of Ferdinand Lesseps who built the canal.

On the way back we called at Malta. I was able to get ashore there and one of the passengers, Mr Henderson of Lawton, a neighbour from home, kindly drove me up to the town.

We saw the Governor's Palace, Parliament House with its wonderful old tapestries, and then the Church of St John where the Knights of Malta are buried.

It was nice to get away from the boat and from Mr Lamb whom I now realised was a wolf in sheep's clothing. He told me on the first day that he didn't want me there and since then had been alternately kind or nasty, often saying things against my work to the others. Once or twice he swore at me and he was always shouting at me, which wore down my nerves.

One day he was so bad I went to the Chief and told him in confidence about my trouble. The Chief was very understanding and I felt better now that he knew my position.

After Malta we went to Marseilles and from there through the Straits of Gibraltar, past Cape St Vincent and Lisbon, all gold in the setting sun, and finally reached Plymouth on 6th July. It was then that I began to realise the difficulties of sailing with the *Mulbera*, for unlike the *Anchises*, when I had done a long voyage there was time to go home and relax before the next one. With the *Mulbera*, we moved round London, Middlesborough and Antwerp with no real time to spare before embarking on the next voyage. If it were not for this shortage of leave and the unpleasantness of the Second, the *Mulbera* would have been a very good ship as she had a kind crew. But I was so afraid of Mr Lamb getting me into trouble in some way or giving me a bad report that my peace was shattered.

When we got into the Royal Albert Docks I was able to slip over to Kennington Road and see Jean. I also saw John, who had now moved on from his restaurants to taking a troupe of dancing girls round the provincial theatres. They were called The Sporty Girls and although John had always loved the theatre and was enjoying it, I found him tired and overworked.

I managed to persuade the company to allow Frances to come over to Antwerp when we were there. I was on night duty, but after a short sleep in the morning, we were able to slip ashore together and tour the city. Frances had never been abroad before and was entranced by the cobbled streets, the long straight lines of poplars down the roads and the canals with their barges. We found a park with a lily pond in it, Frances' especial favourite, had tea at marble-topped tables in tea shops and explored the art galleries. We went to Bruges and fed the swans and Frances was enthralled with the flat open country, the windmills against the panoramas of clouds, bright balloons being sold in the streets, continental coffee and hot croissants. She stayed in one of the passenger cabins and was soon a firm favourite with the dear Chief and the rest of the engine room staff. Even the Tiger showed her a smiling face. The Captain's wife, who was paying a visit, came to tell me how much they had enjoyed having Frances on board and the Chief and the Doctor were quite heart-broken when she left.

In Middlesborough I did have a few days off and went home, but much of my time was spent visiting the dentist and getting ready for our voyage to India. Once again Mummy arranged to write to people in Madras and

Calcutta who might entertain me and look after me ashore. In Colombo there was my Cousin Harry Drummond-Hay whom I had seen on the platform at Euston Station returning from the Boer War so long ago. We had heard rather disquieting reports of him from various people and though all the Drummond-Hay cousins and Mummy wrote, I was nervous of meeting him.

We sailed at 11.30 am on 13th August 1927 and were soon dropping away down the Channel, shrouded in cold, grey mist, rolling on the chalky sea.

We dropped the pilot off Dover at 9 pm and by next morning were off the Channel Islands. We got through the Bay of Biscay in about 28 hours and passed Oporto near enough to see the white walls and yellow and red roofs of the houses. We passed Lisbon in the night and Cape St Vincent about lunch time on Wednesday. There was a lighthouse and a convent on the Cape.

"The lighthouse keeper must have a fine time with all those nuns," said the Chief.

All afternoon we sailed along the coast, where bare red hills and sandy bays were all that was visible, with here and there little groups of houses. We passed Gibraltar at about 4.30 am in the morning, faintly lit by an orange dawn.

On 18th August we passed Algiers and I was working at maths in my room when the Chief came round and asked me to come and have a look. There were white houses with red roofs, all much larger than I had expected. All day we went along the coast of Algeria.

Since leaving London I had not done a stroke of work as I had hurt my hand in Middlesborough and it was still very sore. The new Doctor was in a great fuss over it and said that it might never get right unless I kept it up. He clapped my hand in wooden splints and went straight to the Chief and asked how I had ever been allowed to work with such an injury! The wood splint went right up my arm and I had to sleep with it, which was not at all comfortable. I offered to work with one arm, but the Second was furious that I couldn't work, although I could not help feeling that it was his fault. If he had sent me home when the accident happened at Middlesborough, I might have been perfectly all right now. I hoped the Tiger Cat got a ginger-up.

When I next went to get it bandaged, I asked the Doctor if I could work, and he said quite firmly, "If you take your hand out of that sling you do it without my consent and at your own risk. I am not at all sure that you may not have a thumb with a good deal of stiffness all your life."

So I could do nothing but rest and work at my maths, and although the Second was longing to make work he was too scared of the Doctor. There was a new Third on board, Mr Martin, to replace Mr Walsh who had scalded his foot and he would have noticed if I were bullied.

We reached Port Said on 23rd August and it was dark by the time we got to the oil berth. The new junior, Dixon, was in a great state of excitement to see everything he could.

As we went through the canal, I thought how the character of the East had not changed much since Biblical times. Towards sunset I saw a shepherd standing on rising ground, counting his flock of sheep and goats as they filed between two sand hills. He was dressed in a black robe with a white turban on his head, sandals on his feet and a staff in his hand. The flock snatched at the scrubby bushes as they went along and all around the desert sand glowed pink. He might have been Moses or David or Jacob—the Good Shepherd. Further along was a house built almost entirely of empty kerosene tins, perhaps this was where the shepherd lived.

On Sunday in the Red Sea I went to church, taken by the Skipper. There was a parson on board, but he wouldnt preach, which was perhaps as well since the Skipper kept the service nice and short.

After church one of the passengers, a rather grand and tiresome lady, spoke to me. She asked me if I knew anyone in Auchterarder where she lived. I couldn't think for the moment and said something about the boot factory, which was quite the wrong thing, so I fled.

On deck I met the Purser and the Chief Officer, Mr Cleves, who said, "I saw Miss Nichol go for you. She is an awful bore and we are all fed up with her. Do you know the other day she said to me, 'I am sorry for Miss Drummond, having to work with so many of her social inferiors!'"

We all had a good laugh.

Another doctor, who was a passenger, also looked at my thumb and said he had no doubt it was broken. He said he could feel the broken bone close to the joint, but that if I were careful I should be able to use it some time. He said it was using it and rubbing the broken bones together which had caused all the inflammation and soreness.

We did not put into Port Sudan this time. A passenger on one of the ships had died of heat there, so the company made a rule that no ship was to take more cargo for Port Sudan than they could unload in a day. However, another ship had been short of cargo for Calcutta and so loaded cargo for Port Sudan. It took four days to unload, and two more people died of the heat. A great row ensued and now we do not go there at all.

In the news from home, John was seeing a lot of his childhood sweet-heart, Violet Buchanan-Jardine. Since they first met at Castle Milk in 1915, she had been married and divorced and was now living in London with Hugo, her little boy, aged seven. When I heard that the Sporty Girls had been dispersed and that John now ran a cinema in Leighton Buzzard, I felt that perhaps Violet's influence was making itself felt.

Aden was hot, but not as hot as Port Sudan. When it became cooler we had a concert. The Skipper was really a very good conjuror and even took a dove out of a box. Later there was a fancy dress dance and one of the female passengers came dressed up as Lux in white with a gauze ruff that looked like soap suds. After we got out a bit from Aden we got into the end of the monsoon. On 1st September we passed Socotra where the in-habitants are said to be cannibals. It looked a most desolate place, dry rugged hills and a rocky coastline.

A few days later the Doctor took my hand out of the splint and discov-ered that my thumb had mended all bent over. Although it did not hurt, it was a bit stiff, but I thought with gentle massage and exercise it might eventually come right. I was so pleased to have the splint off at last, but when I went to see the Doctor next day he took hold of it and forced it straight. This nearly finished me and I felt like nothing on earth. The Doc-tor called Mr Chayter who was standing near the door and got him to hold my thumb tight while he lashed it to a splint. On deck Mr Chayter helped me along and we got as far as the first deck when I suddenly felt very sick. One of the passengers got hold of me and held me up till Mr Chayter got a deck chair and a glass of water.

By 6th September we arrived at Colombo. At first I could see nothing but a faint shadow and then the white line of the beach with a dark blue line above it. As we came nearer, the lines sharpened into distant hills and feathery forests of coconut palms while a thin ribbon of pale sand bor-dered the dazzlingly white surf. Here and there were fishing boats with brown-red sails. Soon I could see the town of Colombo, the breakwater, the War Memorial, the Galle Face Hotel and Government House. In the harbour tall-masted native dhows sailed amongst the steamers.

In Colombo the Second said I could do night work, which was quite difficult with one arm in a sling. However, I managed and came off watch at 6 am. After 3 hours sleep, I got up and had my thumb dressed by the Doctor. Then, wearing my double felt hat and white spongebag dress, with one arm in a sling the other carrying a camera, I sallied forth and took a shore boat.

We rowed past native dhows which had come from India and were unloading rice. On shore I hired a car from Cooks with a good native driver, as I felt safer than a local taxi, and we drove through narrow streets teeming with people sitting in shop doors or carrying water pitchers, bunches of bananas, or baskets of fruit on their heads. There were people and bullock carts everywhere and it was quite difficult to drive past. Along the way there were shops with bright coloured wares for sale, earthenware bowls and jugs, silks of every colour, brass vessels of every shape, beads and shells and carved wood.

Eventually we got out of town and drove on through some small villages. The driver pointed out a bread fruit tree and I got out to have a look at it. It was about as big as the walnut trees at home and bore bright green fruit about 10 inches long and 5 inches wide. In the village we saw women making lace. They had paper patterns marked with pin holes mounted on pillows and all the different threads on bobbins; whenever they get a few stitches down, they put a pin in the hole on the paper pattern.

On the beach the blue green breakers of the Indian Ocean were dashing themselves in white foam. A fisherman from a boat which had just come in showed me some of his catch, a bright red fish, perhaps mullet, and one like a shark. We visited a coconut plantation where a little boy climbed a tree, just like Jocko our monkey, and dropped a big green coconut down. Another boy picked it up and split off the outer skin, exposing the light brown nut all covered with silky white fibrous threads. He then neatly cracked the top round with a stone and, in a final blow, knocked it clean off. I drank the delicious clear milk and nibbled the cream white flesh of the nut.

On the drive back to port, I saw the *Mulbera* framed in a sunset, like a living well of fire.

We arrived at Madras on the morning of Saturday 10th September. It was very hot indeed. I was hanging over the rail watching the bright Eastern scene when one of the deck stewards came up to say there was someone to see me. Following close behind him came a smart woman in apricot georgette, with a shady hat and parasol, pearl necklace and smiling face.

"Miss Drummond, isn't it? I am Mrs Middleton. His Ex asked me to come and look you up as they are up country. Can you get leave now? I hope you can come and stay with us. I have the car here."

This was just what suited me, a proper car and invitation, so asked the Second if I could go ashore, and to my surprise he said yes, if I was back by 6 pm for night work.

I changed into my cream silk and muslin with the flame tie and the smart little handkerchief and my white silk stockings which had washed cream, so they matched. Off I went with Mrs Middleton and set foot for the first time on Indian soil.

Mrs Middleton's husband was a major in the R A M C and they lived at Fort St George where he was head medical officer. They were both so welcoming and made such a fuss of me that I felt gloriously spoilt. Mrs Middleton took me to their club that morning and told me a little of the history of Madras. The Portuguese had once sailed from a place near here to rescue the people at the Fort of Jesus in Mombasa, but, discovering they were too late, they returned to Madras. In the late 15th century they settled at Mylapore, the 2,000 year old Peacock City of the ancient Hindu world. The settlers found remains of Christian churches and local tradition claims that St Thomas made his way east and settled in a cave on a small hill called the Little Mount. Here a spring of drinking water sprang up and he was fed by birds. So many converts came to him that the Hindu priests attacked him, but he got away to another hill called St Thomas's Mount, where he was eventually killed; he was buried at Mylapore. When the Portuguese came they built a church on the ruins of the ancient church which enclosed his tomb and this was succeeded by the Portuguese cathedral.

There was much cholera in Madras and cholera tents had been pointed out to me in case a camp was necessary. I heard there were 80 deaths a day and I was glad to be lunching with the Middletons where everything was properly boiled and sterilised.

Major Middleton showed me round St Mary's Church, the first Protestant church in India, built within the walls of Fort St George in 1680. Inside the church the air was sweet with the scent of frangipani. I looked at the white marble tablets of all the people who had died. They were all 22 or 23 years old. One tablet had the names of eight officers who had all died within three years. The Major said they were victims of fever, drink and dysentery that is, the ones that didn't die of sun stroke. "Of course they never wore topees or white suits. They just went about with their military caps and their scarlet uniforms buttoned tight up to their necks. They had no fans, and no ice, bad sanitation, and how they didn't all die was a marvel."

After our tour of St Marys, the clergyman asked me to sign the church book which had very few names in it, only those of great note. My hand was hot and quavering and the pen sputtered, but I signed my full name *VICTORIA ALEXANDRINA DRUMMOND*.

We arrived at Calcutta on Thursday 15th September. The Hooghly is a bad river of shifting quicksand and we had to take two pilots. Sometimes the sands shift as much as half a mile a day. The James and Mary Quicksands where the barque the *James and Mary* was sucked down with all hands is the worst, but there is another bad point where one can see a steamer's funnel and masts sticking out where she sank. We anchored out in the stream where the current was very swift, like a mill race at times.

Finally on Thursday 19th we came alongside the jetty and I was sent ashore to see Doctor Bradley, the medical adviser, about my hand. He told me he would come to the ship that evening and take me off to have it X-rayed. So I was taken off night work and he arrived at 7 pm and drove me through the hot, lighted streets. The hospital was large and cool and smelt of anaesthetic. After they had X-rayed my hand in three different positions, Doctor Bradley said to me, "No wonder it was sore. The bone is damaged and smashed at the joint, and has become inflamed, so you must go on using a sling and not take the splint off." He said the ship's doctor had made it worse by re-breaking it and always trying to bend it.

In Calcutta I discovered that the Army and Navy shop was the same as the one at home, so I put several things down to my mother's account, photos for developing, new stockings, a white dress and a new evening dress which was very pretty, magnolia coloured with lace and cost £2, but I couldn't get anything for less.

During our second week we had to shift down river to Garden Reach where we were to load for home. The Chief took me to dinner with Mr and Mrs Campbell, the Head Engineering Super and his wife. I nearly did not go as the Tiger discovered the invitation and made such a row about it, saying I was always going ashore, so I said, "Very well. I shall tell the Chief I can't go."

Of course the Chief fixed the Tiger Cat good and proper.

I also went to lunch with Mrs Bremner, who had been Miss Lornie from Errol. After lunch she took me back to the boat via the Black Hole, now marked by a black marble square hardly the length of an average sized car. A tablet on the wall says that on the night of 23rd June, the hottest time of the year, 1856, 146 British civilians were imprisoned in this prison of the old fort called the Black Hole, and that next day only 23 persons were taken out alive. There is another tablet on the street wall saying "This is the site of the door where the 123 bodies were dragged out from the Black Hole," and there is a white marble memorial with the names of the persons who perished. The horror of it struck me very much as I actually saw the size of the place and understood about the temperature.

That evening Cousin Algy came down to the boat and I put on a white suit in his honour. I showed him my room and the engine room and introduced him to all the others. The Chief invited him to his room for a drink; the whole visit was a great success. "Any time you can come ashore," Algy said, "Ring up and let me know and I will come for you."

Our last day in Calcutta, 3rd October, was a poisonous day. The heat was intense and the dust from the iron ore, castor seed and jute was choking. The stinging green mosquitoes were eating me up and the noise of the winches continued unceasingly. To add to the enjoyment, the bodies of three dead natives were floating about in the water, one of them jammed between two barges and one stuck between the *Mulbera* and the wharf. There was also a dead cow. The smell was awful. Even the bargemen had something around their mouths. I felt nearly sick with it even though my constitution can stick most things. The heat in my room was like an oven, and in the end I could bear it no longer and rang up Algy. He said he would be down the next day to take me ashore. It was the last day in port so I had an evening free.

Unfortunately they altered the hour of the medical inspection to 4 pm, after which no one was allowed ashore. However, I put my frock on underneath my uniform and I watched my chance and slipped past the two policemen who were guarding the gangway. I dodged through the sheds, hopped into Algys car and we drove through the gates to safety. He was rather surprised when I said, "Let's be quick, I am dodging the police."

We drove in his open-topped car to the Golf Club where we had coffee and chocolate cake outside in easy chairs. As it got dark, fireflies began floating amongst the mango trees. Such a hot still night.

Later we drove to his house where we sat in the cool drawing room and talked and talked. He and his brother had been children of a younger son and were first cousins Cousin Henry Effingham who had come to Megginch with his grand cars when I was a child. But Cousin Henry was not, it seemed, as splendid as we had supposed. Cousin Algy fought in the South African War and the last war, had been wounded and won the Military Cross, and all his life he had struggled to support himself while his rich cousin had been living like a fighting cock. Now Cousin Henry was dead, but he had left his enormous inheritance the house, the family pictures and treasures, the money to his friends and nothing at all to Algy's brother, the new Earl, or poor Algy. One of the friends had even cut off the weekly supplies of vegetables and butter to their old Aunt May.

We talked of his happy visit to Megginch and how Mummy had made him dig the flower garden. After dinner I drew him sketches of the *Mulbera's* oil fuel system and the boilers. As he ran me back to the ship he said, "I am quite old enough without being called Cousin, perhaps you might just call me Algy." I got on board safely, dodging the police, and my lovely evening had quite taken away the horridness of the day.

By 8.30 am the next morning we were down the Hooghly and away from the floating corpses and dead cows. Between the last two tides the sands had shifted $3\frac{1}{2}$ feet. The river banks were emerald green with paddy fields, jute, groves of fan coconut and toddy palms. Here and there were small villages with thatched-roofed houses while further along were the great jute mills, Riven, Chivette and Budge-Budge. We passed a whole flock of vultures eating something washed up on the bank. Better not to inquire what, I thought.

We arrived at Madras on 8th October and Major Middleton was there to collect me. Off we set to the club where I had an orange cobbler, which is mandarin orange cut up into little bits and put in a glass with chopped ice, sugar and several straws. In Madras everyone sits all morning sucking orange cobblers or cocktails and gossiping. Later they have a light lunch and sleep till about 4 pm when they go out for tea or a drive in the car. Dinner is usually about 9 pm and afterwards they play bridge.

The next day Major Middleton took me to have my hand X-rayed. The doctor said the break had healed up and the inflammation was down, so I was fit for proper work again and I could go back on watch.

We arrived at Colombo on 13th October, and sailed again the next day, my birthday. I wondered if I would see Cousin Harry Drummond-Hay this time, but although he sent me two large baskets of fruit, a huge bunch of bananas and twelve boxes of sweets, he wrote that he was unable to come down himself as he had fever.

As I was sailing back to the ship in the dusk, with still a long way to row, the oarsmen stopped and said they wanted more money. I didn't like it one bit, alone in a boat with a most villainous looking set of natives, but I gave them a good dressing down and this appeared to do the trick. They continued rowing and got me back to the ship. The same thing had once happened to me in China, going back to the *Anchises*, and the same treatment had worked. But for anyone who was not an old sea-dog like me, it might have been more difficult.

We had the most perfect weather after leaving Colombo, warm spicy breezes off Ceylon, and then wonderful nights with a blue-black tropical sky spangled with stars. As the ship slipped along, the water was bright with dancing green and blue flashes of phosphorus. The sunsets were spectacular, particularly when we passed the Maldive Islands. The Skipper took me up on the bridge and showed me the chart as we passed Small-pox Island where there was a leper settlement. I had heard that many of the natives got leprosy from living on so much fish.

That night the sunset was magnificent, sky and sea were like the inside of an oyster shell, all pinks and greens and pale blues and creams and yellows, and as smooth as glass. As the dark came down, the water by the ship turned into long ripples with green phosphorus flakes dancing into foam as we sailed onwards into the darkness.

We were a night at Aden taking cargo and it was very hot, 116°F to 120°F in the engine room. We got a wireless from the *Dardistan* about 200 miles off saying they wanted a doctor and we both steamed towards each other. On board the *Dardistan* was a six month old baby ill from heat, but it died before the doctor got there. They flew their flag at half mast and so did we.

We called at Malta and Marseilles on the way back. I did not get ashore, but bought fresh lemons and a sponge from the shore boats. We had a proper dust going through the Bay, 50 hours, and the weather in the Channel was so bad we were slowed down to 5 knots. However, we docked at Plymouth, and then reached London on 11th November. I had two days off to see Jean before we were away up to Hull. Luckily I went to the shipping office while I was in London, so although the Doctor had put in a very bad report about me from Calcutta, saying I was not strong enough for the work, the Chief stoutly said that I had worked all the way home and there was no need of a report from him because he was entirely satisfied with my work.

There was another row with the Tiger when we got to Antwerp, for in London the shore staff had left a bit of jointing under the shaft of the LP turbine which they couldn't remove, so they forced in the casing and screwed it up. Naturally I thought the Chief knew about this, as it was such a big thing, and when we were talking one day in Antwerp, he said, "It was such a rush getting away from London."

"Oh, because of the jointing?"

And it turned out that he did not know. The Second had not told him. Of course the Chief went at the Second, who went round asking everyone who had told the Chief. When he got to me he was about at white heat.

I said, "Yes, I mentioned it to the Chief in the course of conversation since I thought he knew. I was not aware there was any secret about it."

The Chief said I was right to tell him as there could have been serious consequences. He wanted to know exactly what the jointing was like, so I showed him the piece.

On leaving the Scheldt at 2 am on 28th November, I was standing with the Chief on deck in the cold, dark fog.

"It's very narrow here," he said, "if they aren't careful we will be on the bank."

About 2 minutes later she gave a sudden lurch Full Astern, Full Astern went in the engine room and we were aground. It was pitch dark and through the thick fog the shore lights looked blurred and far away. The ships screws churned the inky water to white foam which lashed round the stern and the fog bell clanged in the darkness. We were right up on the bank, but after a bit she slid off and then swung round and came back on again, bows first. There we were stuck.

"This is a pretty kettle of fish," said the Mate.

And the Chief said, "Yes, we are aground sure enough, you may turn in." At 3 am on an icy November morning I needed no second telling. She was aground for over an hour and then came off with such a bump that I thought she was going to swing round again and go on the other side.

After our grounding we were in dry dock for ten days before we eventually sailed for Middlesborough and I was able to dash home for a few days.

All was excitement at home as John had at last got engaged to Violet Peel, and this time they thought they would really get married.

Chapter Eleven
More Voyages on TSS Mulbera - 1927-28

My last three voyages on the *Mulbera* were all to India. On the first we sailed from the Royal Albert Docks on 17th December 1927. It was icy cold and when we got round Ushant into the Bay, we didn't half get it. My room was upside down and down side up, all the drawers were out and everything was on the deck. So it continued all night, but it did not bother me much, though I could hardly stand when I got into the engine room and the Tiger gave me the job of putting brass strips on the turbine casing which the shore staff had not had time to do in London. So I got all the benefits of the roll as well as the full vibration of the turbines and the steaming heat. On top of this I had a rotten cough and heavy cold. However I wasn't seasick.

Everyone else was seasick, including the Tiger, who looked sea green and didn't come to lunch. All the passengers were laid low except for four. On the morning of the 18th a huge sea came on deck and smashed in the heavy teak door of Chippie's room and everything inside was smashed like matchwood.

The Chief said, "As you have not been seasick in the Bay this time, I do not think you ever will be."

However, the weather improved going past Cape St Vincent, and by the time we were going along the coast of Algiers it was warm enough to have a fancy dress dance. I met two of the passengers who had been at the Caledon Works. One said, "You see, Miss Drummond, there are Caledon people all over the world."

Then it was Christmas and I had a cable from home to hang up in my room. The passengers were well away; on Christmas Eve they began by singing carols and by 2 am were singing just about anything. In the messroom Mr Miller stood drinks all round. I saw a lovely star in the East even though I was only drinking lemonade.

"A merry Chrissy-muss," said my boy as he woke me, and we had mince pies for breakfast. I went to church and sat between the Mate and the Second Mate, and we had an excellent lunch with crackers and champagne from the Chief. When I was on watch that evening one of the Quartermasters came down wearing a yellow paper hat and said he was going to take over the watch. Luckily he relented. I was very relieved.

We reached Malta on Boxing Day but were only there for 6 $^1/_2$ hours so there was no chance of going ashore. One of the shore boats brought me some lemons still with their leaves, smelling of lemon blossom and verbena.

The new wireless man on this voyage had been on the Blue Star boat that picked up the SOS from a passenger boat which recently sank off the coast of South Africa. There were 1,200 passengers and over 500 of them drowned. The starboard shaft had dropped out in a calm sea, but they could do nothing as the watertight doors were not working. When the water got to the dynamos all the lights in the ship went out and everything was in darkness. When other ships came to help they could not get near because of all the people in the water. Four hours after she went down there was nothing but a long line of wreckage and sharks showing over the surface. The story haunted me.

When we got to the Gulf of Suez it was still cold and I had to sleep with two thick ship's blankets, a rug and a hot water bottle, and I still was not warm. New Year's Eve was a wonderful clear night with bright stars and a sandy sunset. An old coal-burning tramp with battered iron decks heading for Bombay signalled "A Happy New Year" as she passed us.

At midnight they sounded umpteen blasts on the whistle as the Quartermaster rang the ship's bell forward while Mr Miller struck sixteen bells in the engine room. The passengers all sang *Auld Lang Syne* and *God Save the King*. I went to the Chief's room which was filled with Scottish people and an old Glasgow lady sang some old Scottish songs which even I did not know.

We finally reached Colombo on 12th January. I had a charming letter from Cousin Harry with two baskets of fruit, bananas, chocolates and biscuits, although he was unable to come down to see me. I went ashore several times to try and ring up Sir Matthew Nathan at the Galle Face Hotel, but he was always out. However, by 7 pm I found him in and he said, "Come round right away." What a rush it was, but by giving the man on the launch backsheesh not to pick up people off other ships I got ashore, jumped into a taxi, and sped to the hotel. It seemed very large and grand and I was glad when Sir Matthew came and met me. There were several import people in his party and a few were looking me over like something the cat had brought in, surprised, I think, that a female engineer could turn out looking so presentable. The Chief was in the lounge with some of the Scottish passengers so I introduced him to Sir Matthew. Three ladies in particular were very superior and kept looking me over but none of them suggested that I might like to come to their room and tidy up, which as I had had to change in my cabin, climb a gangway and come over a mile in an open boat and 2 miles by car, I would very much have liked to do.

Sir Matthew asked me to lunch the next day, so I set off for shore in my lavender voile dress and white felt hat. The boat going ashore nearly capsized and I think it was only my weight which saved it. This time I took the precaution of going to wash at the place at the docks before going to the hotel. This time also I was able to identify Mr Kindersley, Government Agent of Central Ceylon, and Mr Drummond Shields, Labour Member for East Edinburgh, who said, "Oh are you the lady Engineer I've heard so much about? I admire your pluck." Before he left he came round and made quite a little speech to me. I could see the three ladies of the party looking crosser than ever.

After lunch Sir Matthew said to Lady Donoughmore, "I believe Miss Drummond is free until this evening, perhaps you might invite her to your dinner party."

"Oh no," said Lady Donoughmore, "she would be much too shy. And this afternoon after I have had a sleep, I am going to play tennis, so I can do nothing more for her."

As all this was said loudly in front of me, I was so cross that I said, "I would like to have a sleep, too, if I wouldn't be in the way."

She said most grudgingly, "Well, I suppose you can sleep in the sitting room." Upstairs in her suite she had a huge sitting room as big as the library at home with fans, open windows and sofas, an equally large bedroom, and a beautiful bathroom, all paid for by the government. I stretched out on one of the sofas and had one of the best sleeps I had had for weeks. When I woke Lady Donoughmore was just going off to play tennis with her friends, so I spent the afternoon and evening wandering round the town and beach on my own.

We sailed next morning and arrived at Madras on 16th January, where the Tiger at once put me on to night work. About midnight that night I was sent for to repair a passenger's fan and light. When I was in the middle of doing this the passenger, an old very irate Indian Colonel, came in and demanded, "What are you?"

I replied, "An Engineer Officer of this ship."

He said, "But can you do it? Can you mend it?"

I said, "That is what I am here for."

He then became very polite and explained that he had been chasing mosquitoes with his bath towel. When I had mended the fan and the light, he bowed and thanked me profusely.

After leaving Madras we sailed up through the Bay of Bengal and took on the Sandheads pilot at 2.30 am in the morning. We were at Sangor Roads by 7 am and reached Calcutta at 2 pm. All the way up the Hooghly the country on either side looked burnt and dry, rice had been cut in the paddy fields and the jute had been harvested. We eventually discharged the passengers at Garden Reach and went on up the river to anchor at the buoys. I had been looking forward to having a weekend off and being put on day work so I could have the evenings off in Calcutta. But this was not to be, the Tiger put me on night work which meant an 84 hour week for me with about fifteen days of night work. It was impossible to sleep during the day as they were chipping paint, caulking the decks and discharging cargo, besides everyone talking and shouting outside my room.

On arrival I got a note from Algy and a formal invitation from the Governor of Bengal and Lady Jackson to have lunch on Monday. I did not leave the ship on Sunday as the river was so dangerous here, but on Monday the Chief sent me ashore with a Hooghly pilot. The smell of the river was enough to make me sick.

The pilot walked with me as far as the Post Office and I then took a taxi to Government House, a huge place which used to be the Viceroy's when Calcutta was the capital of India. Arriving was quite alarming with armies of red-robed, gold-trimmed natives taking me though paved marble halls and passages hung with crystal chandeliers to the drawing room. It was all amazingly formal and we waited a long time for His Excellency and Lady Jackson. They told me they had heard of me from my cousin Kitty Atholl.

For lunch there was a placement list with our names put up outside; the table was long, polished and decorated with red roses.

Afterwards we went into the Throne Room. Lady Jackson asked if there was anything she could do for me. I said, "I wouldn't mind coming up for a sleep, as I am on night work," and I explained about being unable to sleep with all the noise on deck. So she suggested I come up on Wednesday at 11 am.

I enjoyed my sleep on Wednesday enormously. I was met by the ADC who took me up to a huge suite prepared for me, a sitting room, bathroom and bedroom, all with beautiful flowers, clean sheets and soap. I slept until 4.30 pm when they woke me for tea and, as the Jacksons weren't back, they sent up a lovely tea of ham and eggs to my room.

On 1st February we moved to Kidderpore, which was even worse than Calcutta. Some of the deformities and horrors I saw in the streets were terrible. I saw a man with three legs and a boy covered with smallpox. I think their families just threw them out of the house to wander about the streets.

One day while we were there I lunched with the Browns and one evening the Chief took me to a dance at the Engineering Club. He also took me to dinner with Mr Campbell, the Head Super.

But after this the Second put me back on night work again. He managed to get Mr Walsh and Mr Dixon, the two nicest Engineers, transferred to a coast job, and retained Mr Chaytor, who was always horrid to me, sneaking behind my back.

While I was in Calcutta this time I tried to find out about my ancestor, John Drummond, the Admiral's uncle, who had gone out to Calcutta. I found a record of his burial in St John's Churchyard on 5th October 1765. He was just twenty nine.

We sailed on 7th February and when I was between Calcutta and Madras, John and Violet were eventually married. John had stayed with Jean and Frances the night before and they had helped dress him for the wedding in his morning coat, pale grey waistcoat and a gardenia in his buttonhole, which Jean had procured with the greatest difficulty as the only one in London. He had a bath first in the tin bath, which was all the flat at 122 Kennington Road ran to, and then set off by taxi to the Chapel Royal of the Savoy while Jean and Frances followed. Mummy and Nana had stayed at Megginch to deal with the amazing crowd of joiners, builders, carpenters, painters and slaters who had descended to rebuild the old house, but they hoisted the flag and invited a large party for cake and wine and to drink the health of the young couple.

Violet's mother, Lady Buchanan-Jardine, was too ill to come to the wedding, so all had been arranged by her Aunt Eva, Mrs Bell-Irving. The whole church was filled with white lilac and lilies. Afterwards everyone went to Mrs Bell-Irving's house at 7 Grosvenor Crescent. Jock Jardine, who gave Violet away, and his wife Jean filled the newlyweds' suitcases with rice before they drove off to Cornwall in Violet's Rolls. Jean, Frances and Mummy all wrote me endless accounts of the wedding; I was so excited to hear about it and wished I could have been there.

It was a very cold run on the way back, though sunny in Port Said. The hills of Crete were streaked with snow and the temperature had fallen 28° to 46°F. We went to Marseilles on the way back, and then London, Dundee and Antwerp. We were held up in the Forth by a 78 mph gale on our way to Dundee. However, everyone came on board the ship and I had one glorious day at home before we set sail again for Antwerp.

I managed to persuade Frances to come over to Antwerp again, which made it much better. The weather improved and we had a marvellous time together, drinking French coffee and eating omelettes at little cafes. We went to Brussels for the day by car, driving past dogs in carts, magpies' nests in trees and cowslips in the fields. Another day we went down the Scheldt, exploring picturesque villages, where people working in the fields wore blue blouses and sabots. We saw windmills and three huge black and white storks. On Palm Sunday we went to church in the Cathedral in Antwerp carrying pieces of box wood, and on Monday we had a glorious excursion into Holland. It was a perfect day with blue sky and white fluffy clouds, long cobbled roads with poplars each side, plum orchards in blossom, canals with barges and brown-sailed boats, villages like toys, and houses with trim little gardens.

I signed off at Middlesborough on 11th April and signed on again for my next voyage on 12th April. We were to have less than a week in London before we sailed again on 21st April 1928. By 28th April we were in Malta, and after I had come off watch at 12 pm, knowing I was free till 8 pm, I asked the Second if I could go ashore.

He said grumpily, "Ask the Chief," thinking of course that the Chief wouldn't let me go. But the Chief only said to be back by 5 pm. On shore I found a telephone book to try and ring the Baroness Inguanez, an old friend of Mummy's, but someone told me she was not on the telephone and lived about 7 miles from Valletta. They got me a car to go there and back for 10/-, saying, "The driver, he will go very fast." He did!

Baroness Inguanez had an old house with a palm court entered through big gates. The long rooms were crammed with furniture. I was shown up and introduced myself. The Baroness Inguanez and her husband Colonel McKeen were very kind and gave me an excellent tea with lots of Maltese cakes.

When we arrived at Port Sudan the Second put me on day work cleaning the oil filters, and it was 4.20 pm before I had finished and could go ashore. I changed into my pale pink dress and white hat and set off.

I was on day work again when we reached Aden on 11th May, and I had just gone down to start work in the engine room when the Chief handed me a bundle of letters. I ran to my cabin to open them since whenever I saw "Air Mail" I knew it was something bad. There was no letter from the Second among the bunch as usual. Then I saw the black edge, and the cross, and I knew.

My dear Hedgehog had died on 13th April aboard the *Anchises* on the way to Cape Town, where he was buried. It was a knock out blow to me. I felt quite frozen and unable to do anything.

I went down to the engine room and Mr Lamb gave me a job at the back of the boilers, but I didn't feel hot even though I was soaked through. I cut the lockjaw bit of my thumb right through, but I didn't feel it though it bled all over the place. The Tiger saw it from a distance and rushed to the Doctor. He couldn't stitch it because he was afraid of stitching in the dirt, so he just bound it up. I didn't feel any pain and worked all day, but by the evening when I was beginning to thaw, it began to feel sore.

I did not know how the Hedgehog had died. I knew nothing. I could not believe I would never see him again. I wished I had gone to Glasgow to see him last leave when he was back. When he was in Glasgow and I was in London, I could have caught the train and gone up. If only I could have seen him I would have known how tired he was. We had just said "July" on the phone when both our ships were to be in London at the same time. There were so many people in the world who could have died except him. It just knocked the bottom out of things for me and my whole career felt like a collapsing pack of cards. Everything in the engines reminded me of him, every tool, every job, it was almost more than I could stick. How I wished this was my last voyage, but my time would not be in till 8th October and the *Mulbera* sailed again on 7th September. I simply had to do one more voyage on her; I could not let Mr Wilson down and I knew the Second would have wanted me to get my ticket.

But at that moment in Aden I was at the end of all things. I had no one to talk to, no one to tell anything to. I only knew the fact that the Second was dead, no details, nothing. When Papa died and I was on the *Anchises*, I had the Second. Here there was nobody.

I kept on waking up in the night and wondering if it could be true and if I just wouldn't get a letter from him as usual at Colombo. Then it all came back to me. I would now never be able to show him the *Mulbera*, my room, my uniform and the engine room. I wrote to the *Anchises'* Doctor and to Martin, the greaser, and also to Miss Alexander of the Shipping Office to try and gather any details I could.

He had not been happy, I knew. He had said in one letter, "It is no better than a gaol here. I should either like to be Chief or get out."

He always wrote to me and I just didn't know how I would get on without his kind helpful letters. I was quite lost without him. I told the Chief, the Mate and the Wireless, as they were the only nice people on the ship. But I told no one else.

A long time ago the Hedgehog had told me, "You are never down until you say it yourself." Those words were very valuable now.

But I was so unhappy. It was such a miserable world. If only I had asked for leave last time we were home. I only had one day at Dundee and one day in London. But the horrid Tiger was spreading such nasty stories about me that I thought it best not to stir anyone up so that I could just get my last two voyages in.

I dreamt about the Second all this long, hot time and one night I saw him in the engine room. When I looked again he was gone.

We arrived at Colombo on the evening of 18th May. In the darkness, the lights of the city looked beautiful, but I no longer had the heart to enjoy anything. I got a cable from my mother telling me he had died of pneumonia. I had been wondering and wondering what had happened, whether it had been a back end that went on him or something else. He had nearly died of pneumonia four and a half years ago when he had a temperature of 104°F for two weeks, but he put up such a fight. I was so terribly, terribly unhappy, and I wished and wished I had gone to see him in Glasgow that last time. I knew he had wanted to have a long talk with me. He kept saying so in his letters and now he never would. The last time we spoke on the phone he said, "God bless you, Kate. God bless you and keep you always." I had thought it was not like him to say that.

We worked all morning on arrival in Colombo and in the afternoon I went ashore and had my hair done by a native hairdresser. While I was waiting he told my fortune: "You have two sisters and one brother. He has married and is a great help because of his marriage. There will be a very special child soon. You have mother, but you are no help to her as you are very extravagant and spend all you get, though you work hard. Your father had nothing, always nothing, and he is not here now. Just now you are in great trouble. You will see gentleman in India but will have nothing to do with him. I see many countries, much work. Then it is finish. No more."

These people were funny about what they saw and how they saw it. Jean would have got more from him, she was very good on fortunes and very particular. I just wrote it down as he said it.

I walked on the beach in Colombo and looked for shells and then went back to the ship. The flame-of-the-forest trees were all out and a big acacia was covered in yellow flowers, but I could enjoy nothing. Nothing at all.

We were late leaving Colombo as one of the passengers died. She was 23, travelling alone to the Andaman Islands. There was a great stir up, police and shore doctors and they took the body ashore. It was the heat, they said. I was soaked through working in the engine room and, as I lay down in my cabin, I thought she was lucky.

A lovely basket of fruit had been sent aboard at Colombo by Cousin Harry. He said he hoped perhaps we might meet next time. He had heard all about the visit of the *Mulbera* to Dundee and John's marriage, so was well in touch.

Every day I thought, "I must remember to put that in my letter to the Second," or "That will just do to tell the Second." I had written to him every week. And he to me. In his last letter he wrote, "Take care of yourself. I am always thinking of you." It was only posted three weeks before he died.

We had such a perfect understanding, and I used to talk to him about everything. He had such a nice way of looking at things. After he was so very ill before, he said he had been on the Border Land and if he had gone over he would have waited for me on the other side. I said that I didn't think there would be anything wrong in that because there was no such thing as marriage in Heaven. Now I felt as if he were trying to get me over. Of course I was just sticking it out, but it wasn't as if it were a matter of a little time. I knew the blank would be there as long as I lived. Of course everything must be for some wise purpose, but I could not see why the dear Second had to go. I just could not see.

I went to church the Sunday after I heard and they had the hymn *Forever with the Lord*. I think the Captain chose it specially for me because he knew a great friend of mine had died.

The Goschens and the Middletons were both away when we got to Madras, but there was a kind message from the Goschens to go and sit in the garden at Government House whenever I liked. The heat was intense, but we were not there for long and were soon going up the hot Hooghly towards Calcutta.

The horrible Tiger put me on night work, of course, largely because I was the only person who knew anyone ashore or was likely to get asked out. And it was impossible to sleep in the day. My cabin was like a furnace or the hottest water lily house at Kew. Besides, the noise was terrific as the iron sheets and bars were unloaded, bang, bang, bang, crash, crash, crash! Then everyone was talking in the messroom, dishes were being handed round, the sun blazed into the side of my cabin and the side of the ship was so hot I got burnt if I accidentally touched it. The smell of the sacred river Hooghly was beyond description or imagination.

On the jetty there was nothing but piles of iron rails, and when the sun shone on them the glare was so intense I could not bear to look at them; it was enough to burn one's feet to walk on them. Past these piles of rusting cargo and long, boiling dark sheds, just beyond the dock gates ran the Strand Road. There the ground was thick with heavy dust while all the pavement and road were splashed with bright red stains where people had chewed betel nut and spat it out again. The betel nut sellers squatted along the pavement and rolled up the white paste in green leaves which they kept fresh and cool by washing in the gutter, again indescribable. The road was scavenged by pariah dogs all covered with sores and huge water buffalo dragged awful loads, their mouths streaming with froth.

So this was India, or rather the India I came in contact with.

There was a note from Algy, so I rang him and he took me to tea at the Tollygunge. It was very restful there under the mango trees. Afterwards he took me back to the boat, and I began for the first time to feel human again. I must stick it, I told myself, I must stick it.

To my surprise that night the Tiger said he would arrange for me to have a passenger cabin with two fans to sleep in as it was so hot and noisy. I suspected they had been going at him for treating me unfairly.

On Wednesday I was able to get away in the evening, which was a great relief. Algy came down and collected me in his car and we had a delicious lunch with orange pudding. Afterwards I went up to his spare room to sleep. There were green shutters up, gauze curtains and two fans. A room in an Indian bungalow was quite different to a room at home. In the first place they were very high, large and bare with a great many windows. The doors were double folding and went nearly up to the ceiling, and they were always wide open with a curtain across them. The bed, festooned with mosquito netting, was always in the middle of the floor because of beasts and insects crawling up the wall. Oh it was so lovely to get on to a cool bed; I slept from 2.30 pm till 6 pm.

Later we drove round the Midan where all the flowering trees were so beautiful, scarlet flamboyants, golden michelia, purple jacaranda, golden Indian laburnum and bright pink queen of the flowers. As it got dark all the lights twinkled out one by one.

Friday was so terribly hot. I had a faint turn going up the gangway, which was almost perpendicular as the ship was empty and the tide was high, and I had to go up hand over hand. Because of the noise, sleep was impossible on the boat so I rang Algy and asked if I could come up and sleep. I found my own way there and slept soundly till Algy woke me and insisted we should have iced coffee before he drove me back to the ship.

I spent a long weekend with the Browns and was allowed to go to their house as he was Chief Agent for the Company. I would much rather have gone to stay with Algy, however, since although very kind, the Browns were very social and gossipy and I felt more at home with Algy.

On the last day there was trouble with the Doctor's Inspection, but I did my dodging act with the police as before and was just getting away with it when a European policeman pounced on me.

"I am just going to the post," I said, smiling sweetly and showing him a bunch of grand letters which the Chief had advised me to take. By a fluke he let me go and I ran to the gate terrified Algy would not have waited. But he had and we had a delicious dinner and a long talk to make a lovely evening. If it had not been for Algy's kindness, I think my bleached bones would have been left in Calcutta.

The skipper on a Dutch boat near us died of heat and one of our stewardesses got sunstroke. She complained of a headache and her temperature rose to 109.8°F. She was packed in ice for an hour and it dropped to 101°F, but she lost consciousness and never came round; she died in Calcutta Hospital on 12th June. I lost $2^1/_2$ stone in the three weeks we were there and I thought I was lucky that was all.

We left Calcutta on Sunday 10th June and arrived in Madras early on the 14th. I was on anchor watch from 8-12, then the Fourth left me to finish running the freezer so I didn't get up till almost 2 pm by which time I felt about finished. None of the others went ashore and when I asked the Tiger if I could go ashore for an hour, he was very rude to me, but he finally said, "Go."

We had hit the mooring chain of a buoy going into Madras, and we had also hit the bank going down the Hooghly. The mooring chain damaged the propeller so our speed was very slow.

The heat of the voyage was upsetting everyone. One of the quartermasters broke his leg and we thought another one was going mad because when he was told to hoist the Blue Peter he said he couldn't find it. When he was then asked what it looked like, he replied, "Oh a white flag with Peter in blue written across it!" In addition to this, one of the passengers got sleeping sickness and it seemed as if everything was going wrong.

I got a lovely basket of fruit as usual from Cousin Harry. This time he wrote he had fever and couldn't come down. The only thing which cheered up the homeward voyage was that Frances came down by train to Marseilles and travelled back to London with me on the *Mulbera*. She enjoyed it enormously. All the talk was of the garden party which John and Violet were going to have at Megginch to celebrate their wedding. Frances and I were busy drawing up lists of people we wanted to invite, and yes, the fortune teller in Colombo had been right, there was to be a baby in December.

After Frances had gone back to help with the great garden party, I treated myself to a ride in an aeroplane when we docked in Hamburg. I had never been flying and was very excited. My first impression of the aeroplane was that it didn't look very big. However, they filled the radiator with water, put a ladder against the side and after we climbed up they shut the door. I found myself in a little box with two windows on each side and one in front, four seats covered in red car leather, red carpet on the floor and a board to fix our feet against in case of nose diving. The pilot's cap and scarf and the mail bag completed the equipment of the aerial cabin. The pilot took his seat while the ladder was removed and the ropes eased away.

The engine went with a roar and we tore bumping over a huge grass field, faster and faster, leaving behind the rope men and officials all waving enthusiastically. We went so fast that we got off the ground and took to the air. We went on rising and tilted first to one side and then on the other; the pilot beckoned to us to shut the window in case we fell out.

We went up over 1,000 feet till the canals looked like silver thread and the long lines of poplar trees like rows of very young corn. Over Malines we flew and then started coming down for Brussels, rather like coming down in a lift. My fellow passenger got very excited and felt rather seasick, so I had to keep her calm. Then we touched the ground, bump, bump, bump, and came to a standstill.

My fellow passenger nearly embraced me and was hurried off to her waiting car. I was taken to the Hamburg-Amsterdam Mail. This plane took eight or ten passengers and there were four or five places each side covered in brown velvet. The windows had sliding glass panels. We were just three passengers, the rest being occupied by luggage and mail. The crew stuffed their ears with cotton wool, shut all the windows tight and settled to it.

We tore humming along the ground and took to the air. As we rose higher and higher, we saw the Cathedral at Malines a mere dot. Then Antwerp. There was the *Mulbera* in the harbour, just a speck. When we got to the water before Dortzatt, we hit thick fog and banks of cloud that dashed past the windows. We had to come right down and just skimmed over the tops of the poplar trees. I could see the purple heath and wildflowers, the spotty cows and windmills, the villages and people who came running out to look at us. We came near Rotterdam and slowed to 130 miles per hour, but even at this speed I would have had my finger taken off if I had put it out the window. I did not think I would advise anyone to go by air, since although I was used to bad weather and noise, I had never experienced anything like that day.

We came down with an awful bump, tore along and stopped. Everyone looked so pleased to see us. I had my camera in my hand and a man seized it and took a photo of me.

My letters from home were getting shorter and shorter, and everyone was in a tremendous state of excitement about all the alterations at Megginch. Violet was very much in love with John and had agreed to pay for everything. John was very much in love with Violet and wanted to turn the house into an enchanted castle for her. Reports came in to me and I could hardly wait to get home and see for myself. The old pillared front door which the Admiral had built was taken away and the pillars made into a folly in the garden. The front hall and little sitting room on the right where Papa always used to sit were merged into one big billiard room and there were now three windows in the front instead of one. A new front door and long entrance passage had been built on the side of the house, with iron gates and battlements indistinguishable from the original stone.

Everything was moved and changed round. John and Violet were to move into Mummy's old bedroom and Ayia's room was divided up into a bathroom, dressing room and passage. New windows were knocked out everywhere. We were to have a little flat upstairs in the old part of the house and a new bathroom was put in for us.

New papers, paint and carpets were everywhere; there was an orange velvet pile up the stairs and a new purple Turkey carpet for the dining room. A butterfly house was built in the kitchen garden, the Rose Garden was laid out in brick paths and there was a new herb garden made. Over 68 builders worked day and night in shifts, often by flare which lit up the house and could be seen as far away as Errol. All had to be finished for John and Violet's grand arrival on 15th August.

They arrived in Violet's Rolls driven by Reid in a smart grey uniform and chauffeur's hat. A horde of dogs poured in; people came to stay. All was bustle and activity. Violet was a wonderful organiser and had written out 150 invitations for the party and invited all the workmen. It was planned for 1st September so that both Jean and I could get leave for it

Tents were laid on and there was to be tea and games plus races for the children and endless prizes. I thought back to the many garden parties there had been at Megginch, each one had been splendid, but there had never been a party like this one. A thousand people came to it, including many of my old friends from the Caledon Works, friends from Errol, cousins and relations and neighbours.

There was so much to see and do on this leave. John had got a motor boat and we all went out in the Tay, picnicked on the sandbanks and fished. How the Second would have enjoyed the motor boat, I thought, but then I always thought of him whatever I was doing, wherever I was.

Hugo was a dear little boy. He followed me everywhere calling me Aunt Victoria. It was funny to be an aunt. We went to see a witch at the Dundee Flower Show and when Mummy asked about the new baby, she said, "The baby will be a girl, and a very clever girl, but SHE will have sons. And one day there will be very great rejoicing at Megginch."

So of course although we thought a boy would be nice, none of us minded, any baby would be lovely. Jean started to make a satin cot cover embroidered with the Drummond arms and holly leaves, and Mummy started on a Christening robe.

All too soon my leave was over and I returned to London to rejoin the *Mulbera*.

There were three new juniors in the engine room, one a boy from Stornoway who told me almost with tears in his eyes, "I think the coast of Africa is a little like Mull, only Mull is more beautiful because there are yellow gleams of sunlight through the mist on the hills." Quite *Lochaber No More*, I thought, and started teaching him maths in my spare time.

I heard from one of the passengers that Broughty Ferry was in a great state over the Megginch party and no one could talk of anything else.

This trip we had four race horses on board and a white and brindled bull dog.

When we got to Gozo the two new boys said the heat was terrible.

"Wait till next Wednesday when you are in the Red Sea," said the Fourth, "and you will wish that you weren't alive, let alone at sea."

We arrived at Malta about midday the next day. There was a nice note from the Baroness Inguanez saying they would unfortunately be in France, but that she hoped I would go up to Casa Inguanez where the housekeeper would have lunch and tea ready for me. I asked the Tiger if I could go ashore when I came off watch and he was, as usual, very rude. But the Chief let me off and told me to come to him if the Second was rude because when I asked a civil question I was entitled to a civil answer.

As we had predicted it was burning hot in the Canal. We got through in 14 hours 47 minutes, the quickest I have ever done it, because we were carrying mail and flying the Royal Mail P O flag. With the *Anchises* we took 22 hours outward and 19 homeward bound.

When I woke next morning we were well away down the Gulf of Suez. It was one "burning fiery furnace" below and old Nebuchadnezzar's wasn't a patch on the engine room of the *Mulbera*, I am sure. Every night before going on watch I swam in the moonlight. The water was phosphorescent and the temperature of a hot bath.

We reached Aden on 25th September and despite the heat, I deciced to go ashore since I had never been. It was the hottest, driest place I have ever been, there wasn't a scrap of grass anywhere, nothing but rock and dust, and camels through the main pass. From Aden I took a taxi up to the water tanks which were said to have been made by the Romans or Cleopatra. There wasn't a drop of water in them now, but when they are full the water is sold by auction. No one knows how the water gets there.

The temperature dropped after we passed Socotra as we sailed into the cold current that runs up from the Antarctic; the sea temperature went down from 90°F to 75°F in just 4 hours. After this it got hot again though and one of the tail-wallahs on my watch had a fit one night caused by the heat. He looked terrible. The Fourth carried him under the ventilator in the stokehold and I went for the Doctor.

We passed Minicoa and sailed through nights of moonlight and silver seas into Colombo on 4th October. This time I wired Cousin Harry before we arrived, but he wired back saying he hadn't realised we were in so soon and that now it was too late to do anything. So instead I went ashore and had my hair washed by the fortune teller. This time he said, "You have come from England and are going to Calcutta where you will have a letter from a gentleman, an European one, me think English. In three months you will see him again in London. You have good friend in him, but better friend died. Your father dead. You are having heavy work now. Take off your shoe," so I did, and he said, "you have a very lucky toe." These Orientals were strange.

As I did not have to be on board till late, I went to dine with Captain and Mrs Trefusis. Captain Trefusis asked if I had seen my Cousin Harry.

I said, "No, but he will probably come next time."

He laughed and said, "Oh he is the funny old man who keeps snakes."

They had lots of muskrats and lizards running about the bungalow as well as five cats. It was a hot still night, scented with sweet smells and spicy scents only found in the tropics.

The run up the Hooghly was green and pretty after the rains and we arrived at Calcutta on 12th October. We discharged the passengers and horses at Outrun Gatt, which took us about 32 hours, and then we went out and "dropped the pick" about 70 yards from shore.

Algy was still in Simla or Darjeeling or somewhere, which was a great loss to me as I was depending so much on getting into his cool room for a proper sleep. Mrs Brown was away, too, in Japan, so it looked like a grim three weeks.

It was too. There was a plague of green flies. One couldn't see the lights for them. I went up to get supper about midnight and I had to give it up, it was impossible to eat or drink as I had about half an inch of them on top of my glass. I could hardly see the end of the messroom for them, and they bit, too. Next morning the deck was covered in a thick, green carpet of dead flies.

As soon as we moved in they started chipping paint just outside my room and it was quite impossible to sleep at all. The noise was terrific. Without the sleep at Algy's I was about all in and just hanging on by my eyelashes, which seemed to have grown very long. I thought I could perhaps hold out to the end, but at times I longed for a whole week in bed.

The smell of the sacred river was appalling, made worse, no doubt, by the dead bodies. One day I saw a dead body floating down the river with a vulture sitting on top, it was tearing one of the arms to bits.

I had my fortune told again by a Calcutta fortune teller. He said one day the whole world would admire me and I would astonish my friends. I rather liked that one, but I didn't have enough money to hear any more. Tiredness continued to dog me and several strange things happened when I was on watch. One night I had to change the settling tank over as there was not enough fuel oil to last the night in the other tank. I remembered at the beginning of the night, but after that I was so tired I forgot all about it. I was sitting on top about 2 am when suddenly I heard a voice behind me say, "I say, Kate old thing, slip down and sound the settling tank." I looked round and there was nothing, but the old Hedgehog might have been at my elbow. I nipped down to the engine room and found the settling tank stood at 1 ton, the least amount that could be allowed before changing over. If I had not changed over then all the fires in the boiler would have gone out! Another time I was taking a blow on top and I felt someone close behind me, and then the Hedgehog's voice said, "Kate, a freezer engine connecting rod bearing is hot." I ran down and it was!

We had a good run to Madras where we arrived on 30th October. On arrival I found a note from Government House inviting me to spend all the time I could there. "Come up to lunch," the note ran. "Keep the car and come right away, or send it away if you are working and order it when you want it. There is just me and another girl for lunch," and it was signed W. Goschen. It caused quite a stir on the old ship with the driver in red and gold and the huge Government House car waiting for me.

When I arrived I found the note was from the Goschens' nephew, Captain Goschen, who was on his own at Government House. The Goschens were away, but he pressed me to stay, so I said if he asked for me to get off I would, but I couldn't ask myself. He said, "After tea I will come down to the boat with you."

So after lunch we set off back to the boat and I showed him the whole of the engine room. This took some time as he wanted to see everything. Unfortunately the Chief was ashore so I felt my chances of getting off were slight. However, Captain Goschen got it fixed up with the Tiger and after we had exhausted the engine room, as he still showed no signs of wishing to go, I took him to see Mr Ash, the wireless operator with whom we talked for ages till it was almost dark. Then I showed him my cabin, threw some things together and he took me back to Government House.

He had to go out to dinner, so I had a huge and solitary dinner on the white marble veranda where the reflections of shaded lights highlighted the silver moon rising behind the mango trees. I was very tired when I turned in. My room was the Court Room on the ground floor and outside I could hear the splash of the fountains, the night cries of the lizards and the pad pad of the sentry outside my room and I slid into the first deep dreamless sleep since I had been at home.

I spent the next morning reading under a mango tree until Captain Goschen fetched me for lunch. Besides their Excellencies, there was another ADC, a Private Secretary and two otherguests. After lunch I rested in the garden and later had a swim in the pool, so cool and delicious. They sent me out a big bath towel, bathing suit and cap.

As we were supposed to be sailing at 5 pm, Captain Goschen came for me at 4 pm, and insisted on running me down to the boat himself. When we arrived I asked him on board to have tea with me and I got the mess boy to bring lime juice and cake. On board we heard that the *Mulbera* was not now sailing till midnight and Captain Goschen seemed to be enjoying his tea and showed no signs of leaving. So after tea I went out sailing with him in his yacht. While he was bringing her round to the jetty I changed into a clean white skirt and felt I looked very smart. It was simply marvellous, gliding along into the sunset through the iridescent water.

When it got dark we went to the Yacht Club and sat on the terrace. The lights of the harbour were all reflected in the water. At the end of the evening, I didn't let him come back to the ship, but made him drop me half way, as I felt everything had been so perfect I didn't want the Tiger to come and spoil it.

I had a wire from Cousin Harry saying he couldn't come when I was in Colombo, but he kindly sent me lots of fruit all the same. This was my tenth and last visit there, so I had long given up expecting him to come.

I had determined to leave the *Mulbera* when she docked in London and not trail on with her to Hamburg if this could be managed. Hamburg in December sounded cold and depressing and I wanted to stay with Jean and Frances in Kennington Road and enjoy the splendid new London house in Eaton Place which John and Violet had bought.

We were due in on 3rd December and I was relieved from duty that Monday night. After five long voyages I was sad to leave the *Mulbera* and if it had not been for the terrible Tiger and the lack of leave when we came home, perhaps I would have stayed on her longer. Afterwards I often thought this. But at the time I knew I could not have stuck it. Mr Stuart, the splendid Chief, gave me a first class reference: "attentive to her duties, civil, willing and obliging and I hope to hear of her future success. She is of exemplary character." How Jean and Frances laughed when they read that, or had it repeated to them by me, as they often did.

Chapter Twelve
The Thirties

When I came home from my last voyage on the *Mulbera* I moved in with Frances in John and Violet's new house in Eaton Place. Violet had gone to Princes Gate to stay with her mother for the birth of the baby, and John alternated between the two houses. It was marvellous not to have to get up at 3.30 am for the morning watch or to be on night work. I loved looking at the bright London shops and having the company of the family. Mummy and Nana were holding the fort at Megginch and we promised we would all be up for Christmas.

Jean Cherry arrived at 6.30 pm on the evening of 17th December, a blue-eyed, fair-haired girl weighing $7^1/_2$ lbs. As soon as we had all seen the first of a new generation of Drummonds we sped away north to tell Mummy of her new grand-daughter. Christmas in Scotland was only saddened by the death of Cousin Jim Drummond-Hay, who had tripped over the door-step when running out to chase holly thieves. But for us at Megginch there was much to rejoice over. Afterwards I arranged with Mr Martin to attend classes at the Marine Engineering College in Dundee to work for my Chief's Certificate. Now however, there was no bicycling down the cold snowy drive to catch a train to Dundee as Violet had bought me a blue and silver Baby Austin as a Christmas present.

We came down for the christening at All Saints, Ennismore Gardens, on 21st January 1929. It was a splendid affair; Jean's friend, F O T Hawke, now Bishop of Kingston, performed the ceremony. We all had a grand lunch and Lady Jardine's chef made a magnificent christening cake.

Afterwards I returned home to my studying and Lady Jardine swept Frances off to South Africa for a cruise on the *Walmer Castle*. It was the chance of a lifetime for her and we were all busy trying to supplement her rather meagre wardrobe, so she should do us credit with the other first class passengers. I knew too well what passengers could be like.

John, Violet and Jean Cherry came up to Megginch in early February to the new nurseries. How excited and happy Nana had been about the new baby. All the old toys and dresses had been got out and washed and ironed. Sadly a few days before the arrival she fell ill, becoming very weak. Evenso she was determined to see the baby. It was heart-rending for us seeing her fading so fast.

Violet brought the baby up to see her and she put out her frail hand, so kind and loving, and touched the tiny young one with her fingers. Her ivory prayer book was on her bed as usual and she pointed to it. She had her finger on a verse of the Psalms:

"My flesh and my heart faileth, but God is the strength of my heart, and my portion for ever."

So many prayer books and Bibles had she and Mummy given out to the children of the Sunday School, each lovingly marked with a text. I held the prayer book up to the baby and Nana smiled. It was her last gift. We buried her by the chapel at Megginch, and felt that her loving spirit was still near us.

Somehow without her, home felt quite different. Not the amazing re-building, the armies of servants, the change over of our rooms to the flat at the top of the house, none of these things had made such a difference to me as the loss of Nana Watt. As I drove home at night from Dundee, I felt a deep sadness that she would no longer be there waiting to greet me and discuss all the events of my day.

John had made a splendid new workshop at Megginch in the old sta-bles and Lady Jardine had paid for an electric light engine. I would be able to make and turn so many things when I came home.

After much discussion we decided to get a bolt-hole of our own in Lon-don and took up the lease of 143 Kennington Road, almost opposite Jean's club. Mr Garnish, Jean's friend from the club, started putting in a bath-room, renovating the staircase and making a breakfast room behind.

So many friends of Violet's and John's were being invited to stay at Megginch that summer, that we felt there might not be room for us all, so we planned a holiday of our own on the Island of Texel in Holland. We all four sailed on 31st July on the *RMS Vienna* and stayed in the Hotel Lindeboom, in Den Burg, with 23 pieces of luggage. It was an enchanted August: white sand beaches, marvellous birds and the sea warm enough to bathe in. Frances and Mummy spent their days sketching Dutch churches, fields of wild flowers, markets and fairs While we were there we met Alfred de Booy, an officer in the Dutch Navy, who took us over his ship and later introduced us to his parents with whom we were to become lifelong friends.

By October I had determined to try the Board of Trade exam.

I took it three times in the next two months. Each time I failed. Mr Martin wrote from Dundee that he thought my work was going back, which was a pity as I had worked so hard, and that I really needed private tuition. On 19th December we all came north to Megginch for Christmas, exam failures and past irritations forgotten. We filled the house with holly, the Christmas tree stood in the drawing room and on Christmas Day Hugo rushed in with Jean Cherry shouting, "Look at the walking baby!" as she toddled unsteadily round the dining room table.

By January 1930 the family party had broken up. Jean and Frances returned to London to work, as Frances was getting quite a few commissions for her paintings, designing shop displays, chocolate boxes and wallpapers. In fact she intended to call the new house The Studio. Mummy went to Nice to visit her old friend Edward Woodall at La Selva, acting as hostess to his tea parties. Many of the guests were rather elderly and she was thrilled to have made friends with the girl in the villa next door, Olga Seydoux, a bright, pretty girl about the same age as John whom she took to calling "my fourth daughter". John and Violet went off to Jamaica and Lady Jardine swept up Hugo and Cherry to her house Earlywood near Ascot. So I was once more alone in the castle, working at my studies.

It was cold but rather nice to have the house to myself, and I entertained Mr Page, the Engineering Super who had been so kind to me during my last time in Calcutta, to a dainty afternoon tea, presiding over the silver teapot.

Jean and Frances were regular correspondents from London, telling me all the family news there. Mummy returned full of energy from the South of France to organise a concert for the Girls' Club which was, as usual, woefully short of funds. Cousin Kitty Atholl was persuaded to play the piano and other friends joined in.

Mr Stuart, the Chief of the *Mulbera*, had retired soon after I left and set up house in Chingford, Essex. When I visited him there in the autumn I found him ill and depressed. He said the one thing he wanted was a dog, one like my black cocker spaniel, Sox. So with great difficulty I found him a little black replica which he called John. He was devoted to him and his sister told me after he died that the little dog was the only thing which made his last months happy. He would sit in his chair in the dark, with the photo of me pulled close to his side, and listen for the scrape of little dog's feet on the floor. After he died there was the problem of what to do with John. Dogs were not allowed at 122 Kennington Road and we were not yet moved into our own house. Frances managed to get him moved comfortably into a kennel and re-christened him Glen.

By summer 1930, Glen was back at Megginch with Sox and the pack of Megginch dogs. Mr Tim, the giant tabby cat, had deserted Nana's quarters and taken up residence in the kitchen where he held sway over the vast pack of dogs, but only just. Besides the dogs, there were the horses which Violet had put in to Oldwood, looked after by the groom who had taught her to ride.

We picnicked at Lunan Bay, sliding down sand dunes, and at Earlsferry in Fife. By now Cherry was old enough to come and dig in the sand, while John and I wrestled with the engine of the motor boat. F O T Hawke even paid a brief visit when Jean was up and everyone held their breath, but nothing happened. We enjoyed every minute of that enchanted summer.

By September Mummy, my sisters and I were off to Texel again to stay in Hotel Lindeboom, where things were more peaceful and there was time for sketch books to come out again. One morning as Frances and I sat outside the hotel, we suddenly saw Mr de Booy. He had retired from the Navy some years ago and was now Secretary of the Dutch Lifeboat Society. He invited us to accompany him on a tour of life saving equipment on Texel.

We jumped up at once, leaving our things behind on the table, where they remained until we returned. We stopped in the market on our way to buy bread, cheese and fruit for our lunch and a square of bright checked cotton in which we tied it. Up and down the dunes we climbed, slipping on the fine white sand, which was sprinkled with wild flowers and topped with sharp sea grass. When we rested for lunch the scent of wild flowers and honey was strong. The sound of the sea was ever with one on the island, only broken by the shrill cry of gulls and sea birds wheeling overhead.

After Mr de Booy had inspected the lifeboat station and tried out the telephone, he let off a rocket. He told his men in Dutch that we were shipwrecked English sailors. They did not believe it, so he asked us to speak in English and they thought it a fine joke.

Another day I went to Den Helder and Alfred de Booy gave me a boiler suit and let me inspect the engines of his ship with the Chief Engineer, a most interesting experience.

The days of our holiday sped past, swimming in clear blue sea, sketching, studying wild flowers and picnicking on the sand dunes.

But even with all these holidays and jaunts, I had been working all the time for my Chief's exam. This time even Mr Martin was hopeful that I would pass. I failed.

By the end of 1930 we had moved into the Studio at 143 Kennington Road, and besides Frances' artistic work started a small business importing and selling goldfish. We were registered as the Golden Fisheries and kept the tropical fish in tanks and the others in the pool we had made in the garden.

Summer was reserved for holidays at Megginch, which were action-packed with children and dogs. John had started a recording studio and made gramophone records called Great Scot Records, as well as his films. There were always amusing and interesting people being recorded, bands and singers, and the dairy had been converted into a record factory. It was difficult to work for my exams at Megginch, but I was determined to pass and went up for it every time there was an opportunity. If only I could do a perfect paper, then they would not be able to fail me.

Violet was expecting another baby in the autumn of 1931 and again we all hoped for a boy. There was no Dundee witch at the flower show, and if there had been it would have made no difference, for the baby, born on 9th November, was a girl. She was called Heather Mary.

And so the years slipped by, with never much money, though Frances was always earning a little with her painting, and I tried to mend cars, do odd engineering jobs and sell my photographs. When I was working on some electrical repairs in March 1932, I slipped and broke my wrist and strained a ligament in my arm. All that year I was poorly with it and it remained strapped up all summer. It curtailed my plans for getting to sea again. I continued working for my exam and I continued failing it. After some years even Mr Martin had become convinced that it was because I was a woman they would not pass me. Of course I was not deterred. It even became quite a joke between us.

"What did they fail you for this time?" Mr Martin would ask.

Sox died and was buried at Megginch. I was happy to have Glen, another little black velvet shadow, who was there to take his place.

In August 1933 Olga Seydoux and the de Booys came to Megginch and we took them on a tour of Scotland as far north as Caithness where we visited my friends from Calcutta, Captain and Mrs Dewhurst. Later in the summer Frances and I took Hugo camping in Sutherland to pan for gold. I found a clump of white heather which was especially lucky. Perhaps now at last I would be able to get back to sea again. However, I continued to fail my exams with the utmost regularity.

In early 1934 Frances received a commission to paint spring flowers in Switzerland. I was suddenly fed up with endlessly sitting an exam, which it seemed I could never pass, and of having my hand and arm permanently stiff. We planned to do a grand tour, take in the flowers, and come back together, perhaps via Germany. There were so many places in Europe I had not been to and the itch to travel was strong. "Perhaps I could take photographs of flowers and sell them," I thought.

On 26th May we went by boat train from Harwich to Antwerp. Then we proceeded by train via Brussels, Cologne and Basle to Interlaken, where we arrived on the 28th May. We spent two nights walking in the mountains, where every meadow pasture was a carpet of multi-coloured flowers. In the high Alps the crocuses were bursting into flower as the snows receded and lemon thyme smelt sweet beneath our feet. The marvellous deep blues of the gentians, deeper than the skies behind the mountains, were her especial favourite and she painted a picture of a bowl full of them.

We left Interlaken on the 30th to go by train to Venice. All was new and exciting to us and we gasped with surprise as the train galloped into the black depths of the Simplon Tunnel and then rushed out into green chestnut forests which gave way to vineyards and peasants leading white oxen in carts. The setting sun caught old villages in a rosy light, and when the still waves of Lake Garda appeared under a rising moon we understood why so many Victorian artists substituted glass for canvas in their pictures of the Italian lakes. We arrived at Venice in the evening to the excitement of having our cases put into a gondola and being rowed through the streets to our hotel.

Next morning all was blue and green and gold, sunlight reflecting on aquamarine waters. As we strolled along the hot paving of Saint Mark's Square, we watched a man trickling grain from an open sack in the form of a large *S*. As he did so, from everywhere, pigeons arrived in a cloud of silver, blue and beige. In an instant we were engulfed in pigeons; they perched on our arms and heads, But then as the clock of St Mark's sounded, the pigeons, having finished the grain like lightning, disappeared as quickly as they had come. As we walked around we marvelled in the dim, jewel lit beauty of St Mark's, the gold of the High Altar sparkling from afar.

After St Mark's, we went to look at the Doge's Palace. "It may be too expensive to go in," I told Frances, "but we can at least look."

A marvellous stroke of luck then happened. A guide approached us, hat in hand, and asked if we would come as guests of an American lady he was escorting who did not on principle want to go round alone with a male guide, so we saw it all: the Tintorettos, the Bridge of Sighs and the magnificence of the Doges.

Before we left we passed through the flower market at the Rialto to see all the bundles of waxen madonna lilies, their combined scent almost overpowering, displayed for Lily Week.

It was Lily Week in Florence too, where we spent a night in a small hotel. The market was piled with wicker baskets of lemons with leaves and blossoms still clinging to the stalks of the fruit, amongst them bunches and bunches of madonna lilies scenting the air.

We left for Rome at lunch time the next day and on arrival were over-whelmed by the maelstrom of speeding traffic, motor horns blaring, brakes screaming, and cars skidding. This hideous cacophony continued una-bated throughout the night. Everywhere we went, Rome was full of places we had seen in picture books: St Peters, the Coliseum, where a large tabby cat was sunning itself in the ruins, the Arch of Constantine, the Forum, the galleries and the fountains all delighted us. That evening we received a message to go to the Scotch College to be prepared for an audience with the Pope next day. We were impressed by the immensity of the Vatican, the brilliant colours of the uniforms of the Swiss Guard and the crowds of people. We went up a crowded staircase, spying a scarlet Cardinal's hat bobbing ahead of us. At the top we were beckoned over by one of the papal servants who took us to the Pope's Secretary, who was writing at a table in a large, dim library. He rose and we made low curtseys.

We were then taken to a small room with windows open to the summer day where white muslin curtains hung motionless. A few chairs were ar-ranged round the room, their backs to the wall, on which people were seated. Presently we were all told to kneel and soon after a breath of air stirred the curtains as the Pope entered dressed in white. He raised his hand and gave a blessing in Latin as he entered, and then he passed round giving an individual blessing and extending his hand for each person to kiss. After he left we all remained kneeling and then were shown the way out. As we passed through crowds and crowds of other pilgrims, we felt the blessing we had received would remain with us through life. And I think it did. We were both in some very tight corners in times to come and I feel that the Pope's blessing gave us strength and courage to come through safely.

Later in the day we went to tea with the Giustiniani-Bandinis, whom we had known in Perthshire before the war. The old servants remembered us and had even made cucumber sandwiches in remembrance of long-ago Scottish teas. Their son had been killed in the war and so the servants all wore black arm bands.

On 6th June we left Rome for Genoa, glimpsing the sea and Elba from the train. Passing through Leghorn, Frances even spotted some white leghorn hens scratching in a farmyard. We passed Pisa and glimpsed the cathedral and the Leaning Tower from the window, and Carrara, famous for its marble quarries. We stayed in Genoa in an hotel that had been an old palace. Our room was enormous with a painted ceiling. We did not dare unpack in case we would never find anything again in the shadowy depths. We explored the narrow streets and carved stone doorways of old Genoa, and after an early lunch made our way to Nice.

Here we found Mummy on the platform waiting to meet us. Edward Woodall had left La Selva, where she was staying, and she and Miss Laking, the housekeeper, were engaged in packing up for the summer. The silver had been stored in the bank, pictures and china put away, so we were camping in a house covered with brown holland covers. It was lovely to see at last the yellow Italianate villa with its terraced gardens on the side of a hill where Mummy spent so many of her winters. The valley at the bottom was filled with huge eucalyptus trees and carpeted with clumps of flowers. There was a pergola and hanging garden of wisteria, enormous palm trees and hundreds of plants. The views through the town and over the villa of the Russian Prince towards the sea were spectacular. It was far more beautiful than Mummy had ever been able to describe. Sadly, her neighbours the Seydoux were away. One day we went to Monte Carlo to the famous casino and then back to Interlaken via Milan and the Italian lakes. Mummy and Frances stayed glued to their sketching pads among the flower-spangled meadows, while I went off for more adventurous walks.

While we were away that June, we heard that Aunt Ayia, who had been increasingly frail and forgetful, had died in Perth and been buried at Megginch. We had not even been able to get to her funeral, although of course Jean had been there, and John and Violet, but we felt very sad.

The winter of 1934 was a worrying one for us, as Mummy was ill with her old arthritic trouble, so we all spent Christmas together in our snug nest in Kennington Road. Afterwards she went to Lytchett to stay with Auntie Allie and then up to Megginch. My hand was still very stiff and sore and I was getting out-patient treatment at St Thomas's Hospital, where the doctor said I was fit only for light work. This clearly did not mean going to sea.

In February 1935 Frances and I collected together various commissions, enough to justify the expense, and set off armed with a special card to the Trade Fair at Leipzig; this meant that the rail fares were reduced by as much as 33 percent in Britain and 60 percent from the German border. And there were other privileges, too.

It was bitterly cold in Leipzig; there were icicles over 3 feet long hanging from the roofs. There was a mechanical polar bear handing out leaflets for the Trade Fair in the street. We stayed in a small hotel with huge feather beds and there was a high white stove in our bedroom which the landlady stoked during the night while we were in bed. Even so there were frost flowers on the double windows by the morning.

1935 was the year of King George V's and Queen Mary's Silver Jubilee, and we had a party to watch the procession go down Kennington Road on 18th May, having decorated both the Club and our own house opposite for the occasion. As they drove past, I thought of the time I was presented to them so long ago, it seemed, and how the King had smiled at me.

Later that year I picked up a small repair job in Hamburg which would pay the fares out, so Frances and I set off via Groningen and Bremen. The trees and gardens were just touched with the first colours of autumn, we noticed from the train.

We had intended to return by one of Ericsson's sailing ships which was bringing grain from Australia to the Aaland Islands, and while we waited for her to come in we went round the old town of Luneberg, with ancient gabled houses.

Early next morning we inquired when the ship would be in and were told she had been delayed and as far as they knew she would not be coming in to Hamburg at all. By this time our finances were running low and with some nervousness we made our way to the Hamburg Amerika Line. The *Albert Berlin* was sailing next day, but she was apparently full up. Suddenly a thought struck us. We knew she had a fish room and carried tropical fish to America. By a curious stroke of luck we had the name of a firm in Berlin from whom we imported fancy goldfish. We also had a Golden Fisheries card.

It was miraculous! They said they were short handed in the fish room, and if we could help out they would find us two berths at a considerably reduced rate. The fish room was lined with glass storage tanks full of magnificent fish in perfect condition, fresh weeds for the voyage and all systematically arranged. In no time we were back at Southampton.

That year we did not spend Christmas at Megginch. In fact when we had left in the summer, Jean and Frances and I felt as if we had shaken the dust off our feet. It was not that we weren't welcomed, we were. Violet always pressed us to stay and I think she really liked us. But we didn't like the friends she and John had; they all seemed to drink and smoke so much. Some of them used language which would have gone down well in the stokehold. Of course the children were sweet; we loved them, but we couldn't spend all our time in the nursery or camping out in the hills with

Hugo. And there was so much noise and hurly-burly, and people always wanted to know where we were going and who we were going to have tea with. I suppose we had become rather secretive in the last days with Papa, as he made it so difficult to do anything if he knew. So we had made certain that he didn't. It became quite a game with me and I would always tell them something different to keep them guessing.

There was the question of money, too. Violet paid Mummy an allowance to compensate for the farm rents, and she let us have the rent from the Mains. When she first came she had paid all our old debts, and when we had slipped in a few extra things, she had of course paid those, too. She had said we were all to buy new outfits at Draffens, and so we had, but we didn't realise this was only once and not every year. The bills kept coming in to Mummy, who naturally left them as long as possible before paying them and it finally resulted in her account being closed. I wrote to them at once and told them what I thought of them, but it did not help matters.

So we spent Christmas in Lambeth and a whole chapter of our lives seemed to have closed. There was no open fight or row, just simply a moving away down separate paths.

Hugo spent a night with us in January 1936 on his way back to school. He had left the Grange, Crowborough, and was now at Stowe. We took him to the pantomime at Drury Lane, though it was hardly a festive period as the whole nation was aware of the grave illness of the King. As we drove along the lighted streets the hurrying throngs seemed bathed in sadness and gloom, and the brilliance of the performance did not dispel this from the audience. When the curtain rang down, the manager stepped in front of it, and said simply, "The King's life is drawing to a close."

The National Anthem was played pianissimo and the whole audience filed silently out from the theatre, and we found ourselves walking in silent pilgrimage up the Mall to join the thousands quietly standing outside the gates of Buckingham Palace. The only sound that broke the stillness was the sound of thousands of approaching feet, and still more in the distance, tramping through the night.

The same announcement was read out by one of the crowd from a small sheet of paper posted on the railings of the Palace. The words were whispered back to the waiting throng who stood bareheaded on that bleak January night remembering all the times they had stood to cheer.

"The King's life is drawing to a close."

Later, on our return home the Archbishop of Canterbury announced that the King was dead. The queues for the lying in state stretched over

Westminster Bridge to Vauxhall and back over Lambeth Bridge, a sad-faced crowd of people shuffling slowly to file through Westminster Hall.

In February 1936 Frances and I went to the Trade Fair in Leipzig again. This year the de Booys came to us, and we arranged a tour for them and Olga Seydoux through Yorkshire and on to Caithness and the far north. We lunched at Megginch, but did not stay, as we said there were too many of us. I think they were quite relieved, as they already had eleven staying in the house besides the family. Our tour of Scotland proved the brightest spot in a year which began with the death of the King and ended with the Abdication, an event which left us all bewildered and sad.

In October we went to Paris with Mummy and stayed at the Hotel d'Albion, just behind the Madelaine. I was still trying to take my Chief's ticket, although Mr Martin had earlier that year finally tackled Mr Pemberton, one of the examiners, who admitted that it was a question of sex. They would not pass me because I was a woman. The examiners would not admit this but had told Mr Martin privately. If it had not been for this we would have been very happy in our nest in Kennington Road.

For the Coronation in May 1937 we had our house crammed. "The army of occupation," as Mr de Booy called it, for of course, the de Booys came over, and there was Gloria Rossi, an Italian friend of mine, Olga Seydoux and Mr and Mrs Wilson. The house was decorated with flags and we joined in the street parties, contributing sweets and cakes for the children's teas. Long tables spread with white cloths were laid out in the middle of the street. Everyone was given a Coronation mug. On the actual day we all had seats along the procession route. What fun it was! Afterwards we surged to Buckingham Palace to see the royal family appear on the balcony. There were peers in their robes jammed in the traffic as the crowd swept past. Some people climbed on to the roofs of taxis for a better view.

"I shall never forget the kind and good mannered people and their strong attachment to the Crown," wrote Mr de Booy. "I hope that Britain will remain a leading power in the world, and I trust it will not give the lead to madmen like Mussolini."

In June we took Glen and went over to visit Cherry and Heather who were staying at Seaview on the Isle of Wight for a seaside holiday. They had Miss Bon-Bon, their nursery governess, with them. We hired a car and drove to Carisbrooke Castle and over to the coloured sands of Alum Bay where Glen became covered with coloured sand, a most unusual looking spaniel.

Later that month we all went to Rouen and up the Seine to Paris on the *St Brieuc*, past misty lines of poplar trees reflecting on the water. Mummy and Frances sketched while I took photographs. Jean did not come with us, but she came on our trip north to Scotland in August when we drove. Now we had started seeing my cousin Hamish Murray again. He had a house at Cuil-an-Duin, near Ballinluig, which he seemed loath to let us see. However, in 1937 we managed to get in for tea.

With the Coronation and parties and small jaunts abroad, it had seemed a very safe world. I did not like the unease behind Mr de Booy's words in his thank you letter. But February 1938 was anything but uneasy as Frances and I sat in the breakfast room in Kennington Road with its red, Dutch enamel pots and pans and its bright checked table cloth, spreading my latest batch of marmalade on to hot buttered toast opening our post. We had accumulated lots of commissions for the trade fairs in Leipzig, Prague and Vienna. There were to be commissions on the things we bought, enough to pay for the trip and perhaps a bit over. Our eyes sparkled as we mulled over time tables. We made lists, arranged currency, and in no time at all had disembarked from the Hook boat and were boarding an express for Dresden.

Staying at Hotel Union in Dresden entailed travelling to Leipzig daily on our fair tickets. The white polar bear still stood in the street and it was just as cold as it had been before. We had a lot of work to put in at the fair, but by slogging at it we had a free day in Dresden at the end.

In the Gemalde Galerie we gazed on Raphael's *Sistine Madonna* and Rembrandt's *Portrait of an Old Man*. We had time too to visit the Museum Johanneum with the marvellous collection of china and porcelain from China and Japan, very large vases of deepest blue.

There was a terrific crowd at Dresden Station and in the confusion Frances and I were swept apart. She got on the Prague express while I found myself on the Berlin express. The officials refused to let me leave the train which was on the point of departure, and while we argued fiercely, the whistle blew and the express was off. I could see Frances waving to me from the other train, still unmoving. In a panic I slipped down to the end of a corridor and on to a balcony at the end of the coach, which to my joy was unlocked. By a great stroke of luck, the train was brought to a halt by signals in a wilderness of rails and points.

Like a flash I was out of the door, down the steps and on to the track. I glanced quickly to left and right, nothing coming, no electric rails, and darted across two lines to the very end of the platform.

By this time officials were screaming at me from the train, but I was away for all I was worth, and putting my good hand on top of the wall vaulted on to the platform. By a miracle another train interposed itself between me and the screaming officials. I sprinted down the platform to where Frances was holding the door open for me against great opposition. In I bounded, a whistle went and we were off to Prague.

Such an enjoyable journey through forests of pine, even a glimpse of snowflakes glowing in silver patches amongst the fallen leaves of winter as we rushed on. Larger and deeper patches of snow appeared, and when we arrived in Prague on 8th March snow was falling. After dumping our things in the hotel we went out into the town of Good King Wenceslas under a sky of stars. We dined in a small restaurant where each table had a wooden bowl of red pepper and one of salt. We had thick potato soup with dumplings, Bohemian cakes covered with poppy seeds and hot black coffee from a long handled pot.

"This really does taste of coffee," Frances said, "the stuff we had in Leipzig tasted of ground dry leaves." Men in fur caps came in and hung their fur-lined overcoats on pegs as they entered. The women wore wool shawls or coloured handkerchiefs over their heads and short brightly patterned padded skirts with high boots. The melting snow from the overcoats ran in rivulets along the wooden floor and there were snowflakes in the bitter wind as we returned to the hotel.

Next day we reserved for our business with the fair. There were over 3,000 exhibits. I was busy in the machine tools section while Frances had commissions to buy textiles. Afterwards we moved towards the porcelain and glass and my special favourites the Christmas tree decorations. We couldn't resist buying golden boots, spotted red toadstools and golden nutmegs for our Christmas tree at home.

That evening all the buyers were given tickets for the opera, which was sung in Czech in the opera house. We had marvellous seats quite near the President.

On 11th March after a final look at the fair we boarded the afternoon train for Vienna. We were told that all trains would be late because of the examination of papers at the German frontier and the movement of troops.

"Why?" we asked.

"We have little news," was all they would say.

"I have always wanted to see Vienna, city of my dreams," Frances remarked, as the train rushed past forests of fir trees, dark boughs laden with cones sprinkled with glistening snow. Piles of cut logs stood neatly stacked. Czech soldiers were on the frontier and after we crossed the bridges, both lines and stations were guarded by German troops, which we thought odd.

The train windows became veiled with ice crystals and snow flowers. By now it had become quite dark and when we drew in to the station at Vienna and glided to a standstill in a cloud of steam, the ice-covered windows sparkled with light.

On mingling with the crowd we at once became aware of an indescribably tense feeling and the grave anxious faces that surrounded us. However, we jumped into a taxi and sped through bright streets, made noisy by crowds and the marching feet of youth processions promenading the city, bare-headed with Nazi armlets. They were all shouting "Sieg Heil!" as they marched.

As we passed the propaganda office our taxi was held up by the crowd, which pressed against the windows demanding that we should make the Hitler salute. We refused and the taxi went on.

"How ridiculous they are," I remarked.

"They seem very worked up," said Frances.

On arrival at the Hotel Munchnerhof we registered and showed our passports. "We must have them," said the porter.

"Why?" Frances asked.

"To send to the police," was the disquieting answer.

"If the police wish to see our passports, they can come to the hotel," I said.

While we waited for the police to arrive, we asked the dazed-looking clerk at the desk to book us good seats for the opera next night.

He stared at us, and replied in amazement, "Not the Opera?"

"Yes," we retorted, "the opera," and glancing at the entertainment guide we added, "for *Tristan and Isolde* tomorrow night, please."

By now the police had arrived and checked our papers. Even they seemed very rattled, but were most polite. The eerie feeling seemed to increase. We were escorted to our rooms on the first floor facing the main street.

"A good thing we had dinner on the train. They all seem to be too moonstruck to get us anything," I remarked.

"Not even a sandwich or a cup of coffee," Frances replied rather regretfully, "a cup of hot coffee would have been nice."

The night was disturbed by ominous distant shots, shouts, cries and screams, marching feet sharp orders and rattling rifles.

The morning of Saturday 12th March was very cold. No morning coffee was brought and we were not called. On opening our door to descend for breakfast we found the banister rails hung with heavy German military overcoats, bespattered with mud, as were the army boots outside each door.

"It looks as if the hotel has been occupied during the night," I remarked.

"And by German troops," Frances added.

Chaos reigned in the dining room. The waiters wearing red armlets marched round the tables. At last a waiter marched up to us with cups of cold coffee.

Service was practically nil, except for the ashen-faced head waiter who tried frantically to rally his staff with poor success. Finally he served the guests himself. The red armlets had proved too much for the staff and they could only march. Everyone spoke in whispers and there was a strong feeling of tension, heightened by a blaring announcement on the radio that Dr Goebbels would speak.

As we were making the best of our cold coffee, a man from the British Consulate arrived and asked if he might sit at our table.

"We are here for the fair," we explained.

"I know," he said, and gave us a quick resumé of the position. "All frontiers are closed. Hitler's advance troops have arrived in Vienna. Have you got train reservations?"

"Oh yes," we said, "for Monday 14th March on the Hook Express."

"You might look round during the day and see us at the Consulate," he said. "The German troops and Austrian police will probably be skirmishing. Keep out of crowds."

"We won't make the Hitler salute," we said firmly.

"Then put your arms in slings," he advised, "and make two Union Jacks out of white card and pin them to your coats."

After he had gone we sat in the deserted dining room making cardboard Union Jacks. As we were doing this the wireless blared again. This time it was Dr Goebbels himself, speaking from Berlin. "Since morning the troops of the German forces are marching over the German-Austrian frontier," he said. "Their infantry divisions are marching with also detachments of SS units, accompanied with tanks. The German Air Force is in the blue sky above. All are summoned by the new National Socialist Government in Vienna unanimously, to decide their future by real plebiscite."

We had scribbled the speech down as it had been given. "Could he really have said blue sky?" I asked.

"Yes he did," said Frances, "such a strange mixture."

We walked along the Karntner Ring and straight into a clash between

German soldiers and Austrian police. As the Germans tried to take over command, the Austrians resisted. Remembering the warning to avoid crowds, we quickly looked round for a side street or somewhere to shelter. We found we were outside a large hotel, and the manager who was standing at the door beckoned us to enter.

As we were about to go through the swing door, one of the German soldiers stepped forward and stamped deliberately with his enormous boot on my foot. Like a flash, I turned and hit him squarely with my strong left hand, as hard as I could.

To my great surprise and relief, he stood to attention, saluted, and then held open the inner door for Frances and me to pass through.

"Why?" Frances asked when we could get our breath. "I thought he was going to run you through with his bayonet."

"Unpredictable," I replied, and the manager took us out by a back door and directed us to St Stephans. "British!" he said smiling and patting us on the back.

We walked through side streets to St Stephans Cathedral and enjoyed its austere beauty. After we had been round we found a restaurant that was open, and even at this early hour almost full, but were shown to a table set for three.

Hardly had we sat down than the double doors swung back and an SS officer entered and seated himself at a nearby table where a man was lunching. He glanced at this Jewish gentleman and then jumped up like a cat off hot bricks and seated himself at our table.

We called the head waiter and said carefully in our best German, "Please give this officer another seat. We have not asked him to sit with us."

The restaurant was now full and there was no other vacant place except at the table where the company was not acceptable. He therefore took his coat off a peg and went out. Both the Jew and the manager gave us a sidelong smile.

As we made our way to the British Consulate many planes flew low in the sky and over the roof tops scattering leaflets. The din created by the aircraft was terrific and nerve-racking. We picked up one or two leaflets as they fluttered down in the cold wind. The noise from the sky seemed to increase till we could hardly hear ourselves speak and everyone looked bewildered and dazed under this tension of sound.

We managed to reach the Consulate, avoiding crowds and marching troops, and a long queue stretched into the street. We showed our passports on arrival and were ushered in. After our passports and reservations for Monday night had been checked, we sat a few minutes and talked.

"I'm afraid the fair will be a flop when it opens tomorrow," Frances said.

"Could we not leave now by one of the other frontiers if the German one remains closed, perhaps returning via Hungary or Yugoslavia and pick up the Orient Express to Belgrade or Paris?" I asked hopefully, as the prospect of a delightful trip flashed through our minds.

"I am afraid your trip is out," the official said, "all frontiers are closed."

On returning to our hotel, we changed into frocks for the opera and managed to find a taxi that got us through the crowded streets to the magnificent opera house. We were dazzled by glittering crystal chandeliers, thick soft carpets, the fine staircase ascending from the entrance hall, the statuary, the velvet covered gilt furniture. The richness and grandeur of this huge opera house seating over 2,000 people was breathtaking.

Our seats were excellent; we were told we had been given the best seats as the house was not so full.

The orchestra took their places, white shirts gleaming, and we heard the soft sound of instruments being tuned. The conductor bowed to the audience and the thrilling overture swelled through the house; we were lost in the charm of the production, oblivious to all the trouble outside.

In the interval we had a delicious series of dishes from the cold buffet, crystal chandeliers glittering above. We felt in a wonderful dream of music and beauty as the last curtain fell and we passed out on to the grand staircase, only to a terrible awakening.

Leaking hoses were trickling water over the rich carpeting, down the grand staircase to the vestibule where camp kitchens had been set up. Greasy smoke billowed from them and the smell of cooking was heavy in the air. German soldiers were everywhere in mud-stained uniforms, trampling mud into the carpet. We stood at the top of the grand staircase gazing down at it, unable to comprehend what had happened. Then we were swept down in the pressing crowd.

The crush in the vestibule was indescribable, people struggling to get out, more crowds in the street and German soldiers pushing their way in with more and more equipment. We somehow forced our way to where we had left our coats. Tears ran down the elderly attendant's cheeks as she handed them to us. We stood, with our Union Jacks pinned on our coats, looking round helplessly.

Suddenly the manager, immaculate in tails, came up to us and led us back into the now empty opera house. He pointed to where a few members of the orchestra were still putting instruments into cases. "They will get you out," he said, and making a low bow added, "till happier times."

We went out the stage door with about a dozen musicians, scarves and overcoats over their evening clothes, instruments clutched in their arms. We all went to a cafe, where we sat drinking hot coffee.

"There will be no performance tomorrow night," they said. Some of them were in tears. They told us that Hitler had arrived in Linz, and that Himmler, head of the Police, and all the police forces of the Reich were now in Vienna.

The cellist added, "They say we will be given our freedom, but how can you give freedom to people who are already free? If he is at Linz, he will be here soon." No one dared mention Hitler by name.

Next day, the fair was, as we had expected, a complete flop. Buyers and sellers alike spoke in undertones. It was bitterly cold and depression hung over it like a pall. Frances went round the stalls with her Austrian schillings, determined to buy all she could before they stopped the currency and made people use marks. One of the buyers told us that Hitler would arrive tomorrow and perhaps after that the frontiers might be opened.

We left the fair and drove to the Vienna woods, where blue hepaticas were peeping out from leaves under the still bare trees. We had an early tea in a cafe, gazing out across the blue distance to Vienna below, while the planes still flew overhead. The people in the cafe were always talking in whispers and looked jumpy.

"He comes tomorrow," whispered the waiter as we paid our bill. "What will become of us? British always good."

We went back to the city and wandered round the streets trying to avoid Nazi troops who were patrolling everywhere. The city of dreams was fast becoming the city of nightmares. We didn't sleep well; people were still shooting, shouting, marching about, and we were becoming more worried as to whether we would be able to get out that day. Breakfast in the dining room was more of a turmoil than ever, but we insisted crossly that we be given coffee and rolls, for we felt that with Hitler's arrival everything would come to a standstill.

There was a guard at the door who refused to let us out. "You must be in the hotel not later than noon," the officer told me. "This is the procession route."

"But this is a holiday," I said, having just heard this announcement on the radio. "Can we not all do as we like?"

"No," he snapped, and then added, "but there will be singing and dancing for the liberated people afterwards."

We went for a stroll in the park purely to prove that we were free and British. Lorries were already taking factory workers to their viewing points and the pavements were packed. We were back in the hotel on the stroke of noon. The officer saluted us and detached a guard to take us to our room and lock us in, posting a sentry in the passage.

However, they couldn't stop us looking out of the window.

"I don't think the pavement could hold another person," said Frances. "It's absolutely packed." A line of soldiers was holding them in position. Hitler was not supposed to pass until 3 pm.

Presently a lorry came along, very slowly, laden with small bundles of swastika flags on sticks. At meticulously regular intervals, a bundle was thrown out on each side of the street. A soldier picked it up, cut the string and distributed it to his section of the crowd. An officer instructed the people how to wave them when Hitler passed. Then a camera mounted on a car came by and the officer told them to wave the flags, which they did. What a picture, I thought, of waving flags and gloomy faces.

We were getting hungrier and hungrier by the time that Hitler himself drove past. He was standing erect making the well-known salute. I had seen it so often in news reels that in real life it seemed a boring repetition. A man sat beside him and he was guarded by crouching soldiers with machine guns, which we felt sure would make mincemeat of the crowds should anything unforeseen occur. The crowds cheered and waved as he passed, but not enthusiastically, perhaps they had done it too often. I leant as far out as I dared to take photographs, with Frances holding my legs.

After he had passed we watched the handle of our door for release. The sentry was so moved that he said to us, "Was he not wonderful?"

I said coldly, "There were so many people, we did not know which one he was."

We had coffee and ham in the dining room and then went to our travel agency to ensure that our tickets were in order. We heard Hitler's address to the people of Vienna from the balcony on the Imperial Palace. Enormous crowds stood listening to his words, which were relayed by so many loudspeakers that they seemed to bounce back from the buildings.

We went back early to our hotel, as the travel agency had impressed upon us that although the train was not until 11.30 pm we must be there well in advance. We got a taxi to the station where we were stopped by police. However, our British passports and fair vouchers worked wonders and we were able to struggle through the crowds to the barrier, where the same performance was repeated. Even in this short time the crowds had increased enormously outside the barriers and people were shouting and crying to be let through. The express drew up alongside and the attendant showed us our two adjoining sleepers.

He asked us in a low undertone if we would mind sharing one sleeper; he had already arranged an extra bed in one. "The train is so very crowded," he said apologetically.

Then he asked us for our passports so that we should not be disturbed at the frontier.

We explained firmly that we always kept our passports with us.

He dropped his voice very low, and whispered, "But this is a matter of life and death."

We handed them to him.

"You will have them in the morning," he said and shut the door.

As the time of departure approached we heard shouts and screams and cries from outside the barriers a long distance down the platform. Then suddenly we were moving and gathering speed with every second in clouds of steam, and the lights and horrors of Vienna became a thing of the past as we rushed through the dark.

Much later we were awakened by a long stop and a conversation in German outside our door.

"The frontier," I whispered.

"Two English ladies occupy these sleepers," we heard the guard say, "these are their passports and Trade Fair vouchers. They handed them to me as they did not wish to be disturbed."

There was some rustling of papers, and then another voice said, "Ah, English! And the vouchers all in order."

The conversation ended and they moved down the train.

It was daylight when we awoke and the sun was coming through the edges of the blinds when the attendant brought us our passports with hot coffee and rolls.

"They thank you," he said as he handed us the steaming cups of coffee, "British always good."

Later, before we dropped off to sleep in our berths on the Hook boat, Frances said, "But *who* were they that thanked us?"

"That we shall never know," I told her.

The rest of 1938 followed a more usual pattern. We went up to Caithness with our round of visits on the way, though this year I had an accident when I collided with another car and broke my collarbone. The other driver tried to sue for damages, but luckily the Procurator Fiscal refused to press charges. Unfortunately a small paragraph about it appeared in the Scottish papers and I had to take a lot of teasing from John and Hamish..

Later that year we went to Holland to stay with the de Booys for Queen Wilhelmina's Jubilee. Every room I looked into was lit up, the shutters were wide open, and everyone wore orange bows and drank the Queen's health.

Afterwards we proceeded to Antwerp where I met Frances at the station carrying two rucksacks ready for our planned walking tour. She had left the suitcases at the office of the Harwich boat until our return. We started early for Dinant, a lovely sunlit morning, wild flowers covered in dewdrops, pale blue sky breaking through earlier mists as the sun came out. We followed small footpaths along the Meuse, planning to reach Dinant before dark. Soon we saw some chairs and tables outside a general shop, where we breakfasted on coffee, brown bread, cheese, butter and sweet red apples. The lovely border of wild flowers continued all along the river path. Here and there we passed a house and garden bright with flowers and butterflies, or a small fruit orchard with laden branches. At midday we picnicked on the grass by the banks of the Meuse and then pushed on till the high Basard Rock at Dinant appeared. We crossed the bridge at dusk and came to the small hotel for a comfortable night.

Buying our picnic lunch next day in the baker's shop, we noticed a new tense atmosphere of excitement. Conversation was in progress and we managed to pick out a little here and there through the torrent of excited words. "Army papers...recruits called...bridges mined...and this one mined, too!" a boy cried in great excitement, pointing to the bridge we had strolled across the night before.

We walked through wooded paths and meadows lilac with autumn crocus and only saw one man driving sheep. Towards dusk we entered a thick forest. Presently we met a French couple and asked them the way to the hotel but they were strangers. As we stood rather uncertainly a woodman appeared from the shadows with a gleaming axe on his shoulder and offered to show us the path. The couple looked very dubiously at our guide with the axe as we followed him into the gloom. The light had nearly gone by then and all we could see as we climbed the slippery path through the ravine was the shining steel of the axe head resting on our guide's shoulder. We seemed to be going deeper and deeper into the forest. Suddenly we reached the top and saw the lights of the hotel.

Our sinister guide raised his hat, smiled and said, "British good," and disappeared into the forest. Next morning the French couple turned up to find out if we had arrived safely: they had feared the worst and were delighted to see us still alive.

Next day we walked through pleasant villages along tree-lined roads till we came to a ferry with high rocks on each side. A very old woman sat in a boat at the water's edge and took us over.

"They have all gone," she said. "All our men have gone. My grandson has gone. There is no one left for the ferry. I am the only one here. It is 1914 again," and tears rolled down her cheeks.

We stayed several days in Han and explored the subterranean caves and grottoes near by.

On our last day the proprietor very kindly took us to the station in her car and off we set for Luxembourg. Everyone spoke either French or German and was friendly and helpful, although they all had a worried look.

"I would like to stay here." Frances said, but I said, "No, we must go on, the people here look as if they had seen ghosts," so we walked on through woods and forests to Diekirch, a bright market town with a square. At the hotel there was a student from Oxford, who had trouble with his car. I soon fixed it for him, and he offered us a lift to the coast.

"Not yet," we said, "we haven't finished our walking tour."

"You'd better," he said, "I've just come from Germany and they're almost off."

"Oh, we don't think it will be quite yet," we said airily.

We walked in the late September sunshine along the Sure valley until we came to Vianden, its ruined castle high on its ramparts above the river. This was the castle from which the House of Orange descended, and from whom we, too, were proud to claim ancestry, so it was with special feelings of history that we climbed round the castle.

The River Sure was the Luxembourg frontier with Germany and terrific activities were in progress on the German side. Rocks were being blown up and picks and shovels were in action all along the rocky bank. The people of Vianden told us this was the Siegfried Line under construction and that the work continued at night with floodlights.

We then headed south along the river to Echternach. It was a lovely walk through autumn flowers, only spoilt by the activities on the opposite bank. We noticed a lorry full of youngish German boys who looked tired, and when it pulled up they ran to the river to wash in the clear water, but were at once driven back to start work by an armed guard. We saw the German town of Bollendorf on the opposite bank, but did not cross the bridge to it. In Echternach we discussed our future plans for the walking holiday with the manager of the hotel, who was very worried.

"The situation is very tense," he said, "and we are very close. If troops were moved for any reason, travel would be impossible."

However, he told us that he had a member of the French government staying, and that the moment he made a move, it would be time for us to go, too. We had one day exploring the romantic walls of the medieval city.

Suddenly the manager appeared and said, "Will you please give me your reservation numbers for the Harwich boat, and I will change them immediately by phone when it is necessary."

By midnight we were woken by the manager, who said in a sinister voice, "He has gone. You must leave at 6 am tomorrow morning by car for Luxembourg."

So next morning we sped off to Luxembourg, to Brussels, Antwerp, Harwich and London. It was our last visit to Europe before the war.

On 3rd April 1939 John and Violet had a third daughter, who was christened Margaret April Irene, but was always called April. By now Cherry had started at boarding school and Hugo had left Stowe and was due to start Cambridge in the autumn.

In June Frances and I turned our backs on the old world and sailed across the Atlantic in the *Queen Mary* to New York. It was a brief but thrilling visit. We went to the Exhibition and visited the wonders of New York, ascending the Empire State Building in lifts that did not seem to move but just the same deposited us at the top, where we gazed down from 1,250 feet at the tapestry of New York City spread far below. This great building was only eighteen years old. We window shopped, strolled into the stores and had tea with Gladys Stewart-Richardson at the Barbizon. The days flashed past and in no time we were in the train, dashing through the country heading for Philadelphia, not in the morning, as the song says, but in the afternoon.

Our first impression of the City of Brotherly Love was of straight, tree-lined shaded streets with rows of red brick houses. Transport was easy by the fast street cars and we crossed the two-mile long bridge over the Delaware and went to Wanamakers, where the windows were all arranged for the King and Queen's visit.

"The King's visit made me wish we were still a colony," someone said to me.

There were many memories of a bygone age. In parts of the town there were still wooden houses with porches and rocking chairs, and old fashioned gardens with peonies and roses, where on hot summer evenings people sat out on their porches.

Back to the train and south for Charleston on 12th June. It was a very hot morning when we woke and looked out as the train rushed past cypress swamps, then woods and thickets of trailing creepers, then cotton fields, tomatoes, corn and magnolia trees covered in huge white flowers, the scent drifting into the train windows. Black-eyed Susans grew thick along the railway tracks, tumbles of magenta bougainvillea filled the gardens.

CHARLESTON WELCOMES YOU read a sign in huge letters and we were there. As we drove to our hotel, we passed Georgian houses with fanlights and brass knockers. They might have appeared from an English village. The church bells of St Michael's were pealing out. "The spire is like St Martin's in the Fields," Frances exclaimed, and later we were told it was a 1761 copy.

On arrival at our hotel we found the blinds in our room drawn, and a dish of cold oranges, squeezer and glasses were brought to us.

We wandered out into blazing sunshine, keeping to the shady side of the street. The service was over in St Michael's Church, so we went into the churchyard where the old stones revealed many inscriptions of the long ago past. Some had apparently died of strangers' fever and we wondered what it was.

In fact we wondered so much that we went into a store and each bought a large straw hat. A lady accosted us in the streets, and said, "You cannot wear those, they are plantation hats!"

However we thought of strangers' fever and kept them on.

Later we visited some of the beaches round Charleston, where coloured shells were collected to make ornaments. The elusive scent of magnolias pervaded the hot air. Eighteenth century wrought iron work appeared on grills and gateways and cast attractive scimitar shadows. At our evening meal we were introduced to Southern cooking with sweet potatoes and pumpkin pie.

From Charleston we went to Spartenburg, which we thought was the nearest station to Biltmore, where we were going to stay with our cousin Jackie Cecil, who had married Cornelia Vanderbilt. It turned out that we had misread the map and the nearest station was Asheville. Poor Jackie had had to drive 100 miles to get to us. Yet there he was waiting on the platform to greet us with no word of reproach for our mistake. We were very apologetic.

Biltmore was amazing, a vast house built like a French chateau, and filled with period furniture, with acres of marvellous gardens. It felt rather like going back to Didlington where everything had seemed so superlative, and I thought of the dinner tables for the royal visitors. It was all marvellous, and all too much. But Jackie was just the same and we so enjoyed seeing him.

When we left he took us to Asheville for the train trip down to New Orleans. Wrought iron work and magnolias, oleanders and beautiful houses, New Orleans was all we had dreamt. We explored the French Quarter, the Garden District with beautiful houses, but even in June it was too hot.

Back to the train again and over the Mississippi, a sweep of yellow water.

About 100 miles from New Orleans the everglades country continued, then we were into sugar plantations, peanuts, rice and corn. Here people worked in the fields protected by large hats, though sometimes we saw tractors.

Texas was even hotter. All day we travelled through Texas, a state nearly as big as Europe, full of cattle ranches and wild rugged country. "Look! Cowboys, real cowboys!" exclaimed Frances, peering from the window. And oil wells, too, pumping up and down.

We crossed the Mexican frontier at Del Rio and sped on to Los Angeles where we found great contrast between the public buildings and the poor, squalid houses.

But San Francisco was the golden city of the golden state, built over the hills where the trams rushed up and down, to the circular bay and the Golden Gates. Here was the Pacific with great rollers and rocks where sea lions caught the slightest breeze. When the mist suddenly came in from the sea, the air turned cold and damp and dewdrops hung from the trees. It was the end of the Lincoln trail where everyone came to make a fortune. Beyond were the redwoods with their soft bark and dark green leaves. At night we looked down at the glittering mass of lights, stretching over the Golden Gate like a string of topazes. We too had crossed America.

The way back was more streamlined, 2,000 miles in 39 hours to Chicago, past fruit orchards, vineyards and into mountainous forests. The sky became deep blue after sunset, and darkness fell quickly. We travelled through the desert of Nevada and past the mysterious Salt Lake where stretches of salt water were bordered by white sand as the distant snow-capped mountains loomed above all.

Then into the prairie, miles and miles of sagebrush, hundreds of white-faced Hereford cattle, thousands of sheep and prairie dogs sitting on their lodges.

We flew home to a house we had taken at Stratford-upon-Avon for the summer. The garden was filled with bright flowers stretching down to the Avon, where our canoe and punt were moored and where the grey willow branches swept to the water. Here we were joined by Mummy, Jean, Olga Seydoux and Mary Mitchell, my Australian friend, now a celebrated authoress. We used the punt to go to Stratford for our household shopping and the canoe for pleasure trips up the river. Occasionally we went to the theatre in the evenings.

Mummy and Frances painted, Jean read and I embroidered, and we all lazed in deck chairs, Glen stretched at our feet. The sounds of nightingales, bees and the river floated on the faint breeze, while the scents of rose, lavender and mignonette lay heavy on the hot still air.

We explored the Cotswolds, Glen hunted for water rats in the willow roots and occasionally a blue dragonfly or brilliant kingfisher flashed into sight.

As August advanced the news became more and more disquieting. On the 23rd Olga left as she felt war was imminent and she might not be able to get home across France. Later that day Mary left to join her sister at Manchester University. On 24th August Jean went back to London to report to the ARP as an Air Raid Warden. Frances and I took Mummy and Glen to a friend in Hampshire before driving back to London where Frances too enlisted as an Air Raid Warden. Everywhere people prepared for war.

Chapter Thirteen
Bombs at Sea - 1939-40

The Saturday before war was declared was a lovely hot day. Everyone in London was digging trenches and filling sandbags because we had no doubt that war would strike at the heart of our city. Hospitals were being moved and schools evacuated to the country. Everyone was being fitted for gas masks, for we knew it would be a chemical war, a war of hideous new weapons. Frances and Jean were run off their feet as Air Raid Wardens. So many people came to the club or to our studio house across the street asking for advice, that my sisters had a leaflet typed.

Mummy was safe at Crookham and at Megginch they had come to see if the house was suitable for a hospital, but as in 1914 it was turned down because of the uncertainty of the private water supply. "An awful mossy taste," Chrissie Cowie, the old housemaid, used to complain, and it usually was, though on that occasion we found it was dead rats in the water tank. Although over age, John joined the Black Watch and was sent to guard a canal at Grangemouth. Violet and the children had their own flood of evacuees from Glasgow, but none of them stayed. They all found the country too quiet.

Now at last, Chief's certificate or not, I felt it was time for me to get back on a ship. I was desperate. I wrote sending my certificates of competence, my list of voyages on the *Anchises* and the *Mulbera*, recommendations from the captains and chiefs I had served under, to anyone I could think of: the Board of Trade; the Ministry of Defence; the various merchant shipping companies. No one would have me. They might be short staffed, but that was no reason to employ a woman engineer. And certainly not in war time.

But I could not just do nothing, so, on 26th August 1939, like Jean and Frances, I enrolled with the Lambeth Town Clerk as an ARP Warden. Jean still ran the Queen Victoria Girls' Club and was busier than ever. Frances was co-opted into the Admiralty Draughtsman's department and was drawing secret weapons and parts of ships.

When I was not on duty in the Air Raid Post I went down to the Royal Albert Docks. Surely someone would want to employ a first class ship's engineer. One day as I walked into a cafe, I was hailed by a cheery voice, my old donkeyman from the *Mulbera* whom I had last seen in 1928.

"Hullo, Fifth! Come and have a cup of tea on us and we'll give you the news."

On sitting down I was introduced all round.

"We're all right," he said. "Just signed on and have our gear with us going aboard at noon. How are you faring?"

I told him I was trying to get back.

"Have you heard of a berth yet?" he asked.

"No, not yet."

"Take our tip," said my friend, "I tell you what I would do: sail under a foreign flag. If the Red Duster won't have you, go foreign."

"We could get you a job right away," said his mate. "There's a man here who owns a number of small international tramps running down the Med. We have to meet this chap this afternoon and tell him we can't join one of his ships after all, as we have got fixed up and signed on this morning."

"Come on," said the donkeyman, "we said we'd meet him by the Underground. You got us out of a spot in Hamburg with your German. One good turn deserves another."

They then shouldered their sea bags and I followed them out. A tall, elderly man was waiting. The donkeyman went up to him, touching his cap. "We've come to tell you, sir, we can't come as we're all fixed up British, signed on and all. But we've brought Miss Drummond who is a qualified engineer and we've sailed with her. Cheerio and good luck," they called to me, and then off they went.

The stranger looked rather alarmed when he saw me, but took me to a cafe and ordered black coffee and asked to see my papers. When he had read them through, he looked a lot more reassured.

"Yes...I see you have plenty of experience: four voyages to Australia, one to China, one to East Africa and four to India. And you have been in two of the best companies, too: Blue Funnel and British India. Our ships, of course, are rather smaller, some two or three hundred tons while the biggest is 2,500. She carries a Chief Engineer, Second, Third and a donkeyman. We're looking for a new Second. Give me your address and I will write when you are to join her."

He scribbled something on the back of his card, handed it to me, paid the bill, picked up his briefcase and was gone. Written on the back was: "To introduce Miss Drummond engaged as Second Engineer". Once more I felt the old sea dog was about to take to the sea.

On 19th March 1940 Frances and I set off down to the docks and I joined the *SS Har Zion*. Frances and Jean wrote to the Lambeth Town Clerk and reported that I was no longer able to be an ARP Warden and he thanked me for my services. It was nice to be appreciated even when I was only marking time for something else. I had to send back my tin hat and warden's kit, but they promised I could have it all back the moment I was able to rejoin.

Frances came on board to see my cabin which had two ports, a wash basin and pegs to hang my clothes. I slung my sea bags onto the berth and said goodbye to Frances, watching her bravely making her way across the docks in the blackout, back to her warden's job.

After she left I went down to the engine room and had a look round. The Chief, Mr Miller, introduced me to the international crew. The Third and Fourth were Spanish and the donkeyman was a Gypsy. The three greasers were Hungarian, Egyptian and Russian; the firemen were equally assorted, Czech, German and Arabian.

One of the nice things on the ship was the beautiful ginger dog from Poland called Ginia which howled, "Wo wo wo!" She had been on the ship for four years and slept in the Bosun's cabin. On cold mornings she refused to get out of bed. They warned me she was rather cross, but so far she had been all right with me.

The Russian was very slow and peasant-like. One day I asked him for a piece of rope in a hurry, and he came slowly ambling out of the store with it, saying, "This rope it is from the oxen that came to the ship in Constantia. It's a good rope. The oxen were good, so the rope is good."

We went down river that night and anchored with the northern convoy, my first experience of being in a convoy. The food was good and I liked the ship very much. That evening I had to move to a cabin on the other side, and although I lost the basin with running water (which was not much of an asset since I think it ran straight into the lavatory drain and smelt very strong), I gained a proper desk with drawers underneath for stowing my things. Mr Miller was a great sport and I found all the others nice to work with. In fact I liked it more than the British India. We had no gun and I suspect that only two of the lifeboats were actually seaworthy. Never mind, that did not worry me.

Wednesday morning, 21st March, we sailed and lay off Gravesend for one day. It was lucky we did not sail any earlier because the ship that took our original course went down, struck amidships by a mine. We lay with a big convoy and I could see three sunken ships with their funnels and masts sticking out, and while we were there a Dutch boat came limping in badly hit. If I had been nervous it would have made me worse, but I was not.

On Friday morning, 23rd March, we were given a different course. I was on stand-by all the time we went through the minefields and when the Lookout saw a mine he shouted, "Mine to port!" or "Mine to starboard!" and the Captain took avoiding action. The mines floated about with horns on them and could be seen quite clearly as we passed very close to them. In the middle of the minefield, we had a joint blow out on the oil pump, so we had to stop to fix it. A torpedo missed us by only 15 feet while we were stationary. Then when the joint was mended we set off again, slowly, with the Lookout shouting his warnings. We left England at 11.10 am and did not arrive in Antwerp till 5.10 am the following morning.

After breakfast I told the men to wipe down the engines, which they did not want to do and they started to fight. That put me on my mettle. There would be no fighting on my ship and no knives either. Quite quietly, with my voice becoming softer as it became more determined, I told them they must do as I said. They did, which was a relief, though I never doubted that I had control over them. At 12 pm I knocked them off and the Chief let me have a sleep. In the evening I worked at the store list.

In the drama of crossing the Channel, I had somehow lost count of time and season and forgot that today was Easter Sunday. However, ships don't celebrate Easter and we moved into dry dock. It wasn't so easy to get her started as there was a steam leak on deck, but we eventually got into dry dock. Then the Chief told me to blow down the boilers, and after that I did the stores and fixed up a light from shore. Not much of an Easter Sunday. However, I got the afternoon off and went up town to the Queen's Hotel, where I had a bath, not before time!

The men were off for four days that week, but I had to knock in the boiler doors, a big job as all the top nuts were rusted, finish the stores list and get everything ready for inspection. It was snowing and freezing cold and a parcel of knitted things arrived for the men which they fell upon with joy. By 10 am they were all wearing woolly socks, gloves and scarves. The engine room filled with snow while we were working on the skylights.

There was a great deal of work to do as everything had to be opened up by the shore staff who were inspecting for the Lloyd's Certificate. The boilers were leaking badly, as were the oil fuel tanks, and there were huge cracks in the boiler furnaces to weld. However, she was a jolly ship, with rather the touch of a pirate about her, and I was enjoying myself.

By the next Saturday I had got the work in hand and was able to walk up to town, an hour of brisk walking. No taxis were to be had with the war and lack of petrol. Antwerp was just the same and there were beautiful Easter cards in the windows. Most things were expensive except for food, so I went to my old cafe and had coffee and cakes. On the walk back I got a lift from one of the dry dock lorries. "No good walking in docks," they warned me.

All this time I was working very hard on the ship to get the engines ready to pass the survey. The Chief left the boilers entirely to me and really I was the only one who could get into them as there was only about 12 inches between the tubes.

There was no water in the ship which made washing difficult. One morning there was not even enough water to make coffee. I had complained for some time that the water smelt and tasted funny. I finally discovered we were drinking water out of the dock.

By 14th April all the repairs had been done and the *Har Zion* moved out of dry dock ready to sail for the Mediterranean. Wild rumours had been flying round about the escalating war. The dock workers, who were avidly pro-British, brought me old valves and any old bits of metal "to kill the Germans".

I was quite glad to go. We lay in the mouth of the river till the 16th, then joined a convoy leaving at 6.15 am and sailed back across the minefields in the Channel to Gravesend. I was excited to see three mines blow up as we passed, the sudden whoosh of water shooting into the air and the noise of the explosion. German planes flew overhead as we lay at anchor in Gravesend, but we were not allowed to move. It was a beastly place. The first night we had an air raid and the next morning German planes flew over as mines exploded in the harbour quite near us. The noise was terrific. I was shutting the water-tight doors in the engine room when one went off and water shot into the air about 50 or 60 feet. It was much more alarming to see them go off so near us.

Later we had the Navy inspection. When they saw the Second Engineer they looked amazed and disgusted. I could almost hear them thinking, "Fancy having a woman Second, you can see it's a foreign ship!" I was rather amused.

The next day was awful, there was gunfire and mines exploded all night, shaking the ports. The ship was a complete blackout, all the dead lights were off, and every now and then there would be a fantastic bang which shook the whole ship. I kept thinking, "The next one will be us."

We carried our money and papers on us and the Chief told me to carry my certificate, too. The Spaniards called me San Pedro because I always carried the keys of the store. "When we go up you can go straight to heaven and open the doors for us," they said. This was a great joke, but at night in the total blackness with the fantastic explosions from some dread leviathan of the deep, it was not so funny.

On Saturday morning 20th April I was just coming on deck when there was a terrific bang. A ship moving anchorage had struck a mine forward and, as I watched, her foremast crumpled and she sank in 2 minutes. Two minutes! It was an awful sight, one minute there, the next minute gone.

By chance just after she sank there came over the wireless the prayer for those at sea and a blessing. "Well," I said, quite overcome. However, I pulled myself together and went down to the engine room and we sailed to join the other little sheep in our convoy, which was so secret that a naval boat, when she gave us our orders, only called out "P m".

The Mate said he had never seen such a convoy. We were all straggled across the bay, smoking hard, and we did look an awful collection! We had tough weather and it was a difficult job keeping the revs they set. So much for the engine to turn, then changing it every few minutes, and no smoke in case the enemy spotted it over the horizon. We anchored outside Lisbon as it was getting dark and moved in the morning. I was on at 4 am and as we came into harbour the fan engine broke down. Also the cargo light wasn't working, so I didn't finish till 10 pm, quite a day.

In Antwerp we got a new Third, a Greek, who was a real pig. It was his day aboard, but he said he had a date that night that he had made yesterday.

"All right," I said, so as not to make trouble, "I'll come back at 7 pm."

Just as I was going off he came to me and said he was going off at 5 pm. "Very well," I said, as the Chief was ashore.

But of course it curtailed my time ashore. In the afternoon I went up to the town where I discovered aloe plants, Moorish tiles and fountains upon which bright sunlight played leaving deep purple shadows. What a lovely place, I thought, and planned to come back after the war with Frances. In the dusky light the harbour was coloured like the inside of a shell, and the Portuguese boats were painted bright colours with men in striped trousers climbing over the huge barrels of wine they were loading, just like a picture. I thought the *Har Zion* looked a real pirate ship when I saw her tied up from the shore.

I had to buy a pair of shoes as my engine room ones had shrunk so much with the wet. I also had my hair done, mostly in sign language as the Portuguese spoke no English and little French. The shore police were teaching me Portuguese at night, or trying to. They were very pro-British and asked me to go to a bull fight, but I refused.

When we left Lisbon one of the greasers was one over the eight, so I had to see things were all right till the next greaser came on at midnight. The Third was due to go on watch at 12 am, but he came on board quite tight at 2 am and I had to report him to the Chief for his conduct. The Third vowed to get me for reporting him, but luckily the Spaniard overheard him saying this and warned me when I came on watch at 4 am.

When we got to Gibraltar the Spaniards left and I was sorry, as they had been friendly and kind. Now there would be a lot more work with just me, the Third and the Donkeyman. That morning when I went into the engine room the Third went for me and I had to call the Chief. Mr Miller fixed him, I was glad to say, and changed my watch to the 8-12 with only a greaser to help me.

We reached Beirut on 11th May where the news from Europe was becoming more and more alarming. Beirut was such a lovely place, but the greasers said not to drink the water, and I felt if they said it, there must be reason.

On Whitsunday I went ashore and took a tram into the country. I walked towards the mountains, through orange and lemon groves past pink houses with blue shutters and gardens on the roofs. There were trees with dark, glossy, leaves and scarlet waxy flowers, stone pines on the mountains and strawberries and tomatoes grew round the villages. I saw flocks of lop-eared sheep and their shepherds. The men wore fezzes and the women had skirts and trousers.

From Beirut we sailed to Haifa and on the way I broke one of my fingers, the first one of my right hand. It had happened some time before but I didn't like to say. When the Doctor came on board at Haifa, I showed it to him, and he said, "The bone is broken between the first and second joint and there is a piece loose so I must put it in splints." However I managed to keep on duty with it.

One of the dock pilots here was a Dundee boy who had lived near Mr Begg, so I showed him round the engines and he brought me a bag of enormous oranges, very ripe and juicy.

The sad thing that happened in Haifa was that the Captain had the yellow dog put to sleep. He said she was an old dog and had been on the ship since a puppy, and he didn't want her on board in war time. I was very sad and the whole crew were seething against the Captain.

From Haifa we went to Port Said, then to Alexandria and up to Marseilles. When we arrived we found one of the bombed boats still burning. There were air raid warnings every day, but luckily nothing much happened. Our cargo from Marseilles was very different to our usual one, it was human. We took the Consul, all his staff and the remains of the British expeditionary force and landed them at Gibraltar, where we loaded up with more refugees whom we took across to Casablanca in North Africa. Here we loaded rice for London. On the way home our convoy was attacked, but again we escaped injury and sailed proudly up the Thames on 20th July.

On 25th July, the Mayor of Lambeth, Mr Lockyer, invited me to give an address to the Council in Lambeth Town Hall. It was a great honour, but really there was so much censorship and secrecy about that there was very little I could talk about except the mines and the cargo of rice.

In London I left the *Har Zion*, although I had enjoyed being on her despite the dangers and hard work. The Chief Engineer, Mr Miller, had been very kind and I was sorry to leave him, but the Third and I had a mutual antipathy and I felt it was only a matter of time before he fulfilled his vow to "get me". Also I had never felt the same about the Captain since poor Ginia had died.

I had three weeks at home and then on 6th August joined the 7,000 ton *SS Bonita* as Second Engineer. I was paid £46 10/- a month, £5 more than I had been earning on the *Har Zion*.

I joined the ship at Southampton and had not been on her long before we were bombed at Portland. I was on the engines at the time. My watch was smashed and I hit the side of my head on an oil box from the vibrations of the bombs. They missed us by 10 feet and we were only 20 feet away from having one down the engine room skylight. It was once more a very frightening experience.

From Portland we sailed on to Fowey in Cornwall, a harbour that winds several miles into the country from its narrow mouth which is barely a ships breadth in places. On the west side the town stood on the steep hillside with the houses clustering down to the water's edge, overhanging the water in places. Old stairs led down to landing stages. In places the high rocks hung with wild flowers, in others green meadows sloped down to the shore. About a mile beyond the town were the jetties and elevators where the steamers came to load china clay, the principal trade of the port. It was at the farthest of these wharves that my ship loaded her cargo. The trees here almost overhung the ship as she lay close under a high cliff at the foot of which was the elevator that took the clay from the trucks and poured it down chutes into the ship's holds.

The powdery china clay was put to such varied uses as making fine china ware, a base for most tooth powder and paste, many cosmetics and face creams, and for polishing gold and silver ware. When loading, especially on windy days, the clay dust was everywhere, always 3 or 4 inches deep on the deck and in drifts of several feet near the hatches. The whole air was full of it, cabins and cupboards were penetrated and it thickly powdered my clothes. On wet days the dust became slippery mud and it was almost impossible to keep one's feet.

The streets of Fowey were narrow, hilly and winding, breaking at unexpected points from the hillside to the water's edge. Neat, well-stocked shops lined the main street and from my favourite dairy I could send Cornish cream to London, delivered next morning. France had recently collapsed and there had been an inrush of strange craft with their pathetic burdens of refugees. I heard Dutch, French and Flemish tongues mixed with the west country accent. The townspeople welcomed them all, as they did us.

On my days ashore my first objective was the hotel. Here the manager always had a bath ready for me and an excellent supper afterwards, with a seat overlooking the whole sweep of the harbour, north and south. Later in the gathering dusk, I would walk along the path back to the *Bonita*, the dim mass of the ship lighted only by the glow from the china clay. And so to sleep till awakened by the arrival of the wagons and the rattle of the elevator as another day's work began. How quickly and pleasantly those summer evenings passed.

On our last Sunday in England, I went ashore early, crossed the harbour and climbed the steep road, little more than a lane beaten deep into the soil from centuries of traffic and the feet of generations of Cornishmen. Turning into a meadow near the crest of the hill I found a shady bank and settled down for a completely lazy and happy afternoon. The whole air was heavy with scent of wild flowers and new mown hay. Beneath me the inlet stretched dark between green meadows and yellow cornfields, and the harbour mouth shimmered in the bright light. Beyond, a white fringe of breakers marked the Channel, deep blue and stretching into limitless haze.

Here in that place of peace, on that perfect day, the War became remote and unthinkable. Yet beyond the haze-dimmed horizon, the forces were already in motion for a grim struggle on which the fate of my country would depend, the Battle of the Atlantic.

On 23rd August I telephoned Mummy and Frances and told them we were off. Crossing the Atlantic in a convoy seemed somehow more of an adventure than threading one's way across the Channel in a minefield, or cruising up the Med with the BEF. It was going into Tom Tiddler's ground with a vengeance, submarines and planes would both be on the lookout for us.

After I got back to the *Bonita* I was busy getting everything ready for sailing, running the fridge for the sea storage and so on. As dusk settled over the town and harbour, tugs forward and aft manoeuvred the deeply-loaded *Bonita* round the bends in the canal and we headed seawards on the first stage of our journey. Hundreds of people turned out and waved to us. It was a long and laborious business in the engine room and entailed innumerable movements of engines "Full Ahead" to "Full Astern" alternatively for several hours. I envied the officers on the bridge or on deck who could see and exchange greetings and farewells with their friends on the jetties as we drifted slowly past the town. It was dark when we cleared the entrance and the pilot left taking our last letters for home. The telegraph rang "Full Ahead", then "Full Away" and the ship swung slowly to her course, lifting gently like some great animal waking from sleep as she felt the deep ground swell of the Atlantic. The night was dark and the land soon faded into the blackness as we steered well south to avoid the danger of mines in the shallower waters. Shortly before midnight flares were dropped, presumably from enemy planes, but well astern of us and we did not come within their fatal radius. Through the night we drove the engines at their maximum, working full speed in the hope of clearing the danger area during the hours of darkness.

We were a Panamanian ship with a Hungarian Captain, in effect an enemy alien, so we were not thought to need the protection of a convoy.

Next day we saw a dozen St Malo fishing boats with sails strung out in a long line. I thought they looked so pretty, but the Mate, Mr Warner, muttered darkly that they came from St Malo which was in enemy hands. All was smooth and calm and I thought nothing more of it. We had taken up sea watches and I was on the normal Second's watch of 4-8.

On the morning of Sunday 25th August I came up on deck after my watch and was talking to Mr Warner when we saw more of the St Malo fishing boats. The Second Mate was also with us.

"I don't like those fishing boats we passed this morning," the Mate said, "and last night, too. They are spying on us. What are they doing fishing here? The water is too deep and we are 300 miles out from the nearest land." He had hardly said this when there was a burst of firing from a plane that had just appeared overhead. It was 8.55 am.

Within 2 minutes I was in the engine room standing by the main engines. I gave her all the speed I could, for I knew that our only hope of survival was to dodge the bombs. Herbert the fireman was in the stokehold where he stood no chance at all if the ship were hit, and indeed there was little chance of survival even in the engine room. I called Herbert up and then Tommy, the greaser, to stand on the main platform by me. Hardly had I done this than vibrations began shaking the ship. Never had I known anything like it. The bombing at Portland had been bad, but this was ten thousand times worse. We got it, all right, and I thought we must be hit as the vibration was so terrific. I counted eight separate bursts of firing from the guns and bombs. All the lagging came off the pipes and fell like snow. The feeling was as if the ship were lifted up and dropped each time. With the bombs, the machine gun fire and the engines of the plane, the noise was terrific and magnified even more in the enclosed space of the engine room. In fact, with all the noise going on, the engines seemed almost silent.

Flying debris hit the main water service pipe to the main engine and scalding water began to gush out; the end of the speaking tube to the Bridge broke off, too. I had my ears stuffed with cotton waste to deaden the noise but pulled it out to hear the Captain's orders. None came through. We were on our own. I got the engineers to open out the fuel injectors and the main steam throttle, and then I pointed to the door.

"Get out," I shouted. By this time some oil from somewhere was running down my face and I could only see out of one eye. The engine was a hissing, bubbling inferno and everything that could shake or bang rattled like marbles in a drum. The ship must be doomed, I knew that now. My duty was to keep the engines going as long as they would turn. For the rest of the crew their chance of safety lay in being outside and getting to the boats. Tommy hesitated, then he too went and I was alone.

Was this the end, I wondered, banged and buffeted in this inferno of noise and steam? It didn't seem a good way to go.

How many times had the plane bombed the ship? Was it three, was it four? Each time she came and we were miraculously unharmed. I began, against all reason, to hope.

Suddenly the noise of the bombs and firing stopped. I heard a slight noise behind me and saw that Tommy and Herbert were back. I scrawled a chit to tell the Chief the engine room water service pipe and the end of the voice tube to the bridge were damaged and I wished to repair them. It was 9.25 am and it was all over.

The plane had exhausted her bombs, finished her bullets and gone. Not a single bomb had hit us. It was a miracle and one due in part to the brilliant seamanship of Captain Herz, who had held the ship steady on course and then, as the bombers were ready to unload, had jinked the bow away in time to avoid the bombs, putting her hard to port or hard to starboard so that they were always just behind. I thought perhaps it was also due to the fact that the engines were kept going so he could avoid the bombs.

When it was all over the Chief came down and took charge of the engine room. The donkeyman came down with a bullet in his hand which he had picked up off the deck. After I had examined the boiler and engine room for damage and seen to the pipe and tube, I went up on deck and we all looked for bullets and bits of bomb. The plane had been a large four-engine bomber, they thought a converted air liner, so she could not turn easily and had to go about 5 miles, take a huge circle, and come back. Even though she came over four times, flying just over the mast, not one of the 25 bombs she dropped hit us, though they fell within 10 or 15 feet of the ship. The water was all black like ink where some had fallen. These were thought to have been mustard gas. The explosive bombs were different from the ones we had in Portland as they detonated at a much greater depth, getting under the hull to blow the ship sky high! It was a marvellous escape.

I went round with the Captain and Mr Warner to see the damage. One bullet had gone right through the deck sheet of the poop and hit the deck in the crew's quarters. Another had gone through the deck above our bathroom and made a long dent. Another had gone through the deck above the Second Mate's room, through the ceiling of his cabin, through his bunk, through his chest of drawers and made holes in lots of his clothes. We found the bullet in the bottom drawer, resting among his silk pyjamas. There were two kinds of bullets: one large and copper covered, one small and steel.

The port lifeboat was holed and the bullets cut grooves in the iron decks and through the hatch covers. If we had had a gun, I think we could have knocked spots off her. The Mate said, "If we had taken to the boats we would have had 300 miles to go, which at a rate of about 4 miles an hour, would have taken 77 hours." We had lovely new ships' biscuits in the boats, and I tried a bit of one, but thought little of it. Sparks sent three radios: *BEING ATTACKED, BEING BOMBED AND MACHINE-GUNNED, SEND FIGHTERS QUICK!* But they never came.

After it was all over, the ship's cat and kitten came out and sat on the hatch, not minding a bit; the cat cleaned her whiskers and the kitten played with little bits of string. We all felt a bit like the cat and the kitten, I think, with the relief of it.

The Mate wrote quite an account of it all in his diary, which was later published in the newspapers:

...Our Second Engineer, Miss Drummond, is quite a famous person: the only British sea-going woman engineer. She was sent here by the Ministry, who couldn't get another engineer to take on the job.... She is about the most courageous woman I ever saw. She seems to be without fear or nerves, is very good at her job and has an uncanny power over the engines, for which I once thanked God. She gets from $^1/_2$ to $^3/_4$ knots more out of the ship on the same fuel in her watch than any of the others. I once asked her how she did it, and she said, "Oh, I just talk nicely to them. You can coax or lead engines to do what you want, but you must never drive them," which, of course, is as clear as mud.

...We had a hell of an attack on the second day out. More than 400 miles from land, a big four-engined brute went for us for 35 minutes till all his bombs and ammunition were exhausted....

...All were most damnably close and the noise was hellish as the guns (he had two in three turrets ahead and astern) kept going till near the end, when apparently they were out of ammunition or seized up with heat.

...Besides almighty God, we have to thank the coolness and skill of the Captain, who had to judge every order in terms of seconds (and never once made a mistake); but perhaps even more, that very noble lady the Second Engineer. She took charge of the engine room and in 10 minutes had "talked" to those engines to such good purpose that our miserable top speed of 9 knots had risen to 12 $^1/_2$ and was still going up when she eased down at the "All Clear". That speed had never before been recorded in all the ship's eighteen years.

It is only in the last few days that I have heard what happened down below in that ghastly half hour. She was talking to the Chief Engineer and me on deck in her Sunday best uniform after breakfast when the alarm gongs went. She went at once and took charge down below. After the first salvo, which flung her against the levers and nearly stunned her, she realised that there was little hope. She told the engineers to open up the fuel injectors and began opening the main steam valve bit by bit. Then, calling the engine room and stokehold staff, she gave them the last order, pointing with her long arm to the ladder: "Get out".

She gave them a chance for their lives and stayed alone where she knew she had none. Two cast iron pipes were fractured, electric wires parted, tubes broke and joints started, but her iron body and mighty heart stood it. The main injection pipe just above her head started a joint and scalding steam whizzed past her. With anyone less skilled down there, that pipe would have burst under the extra pressure, but she nursed it through the explosion of each salvo, easing down when she judged from the nearness of the plane's engines that the bombs were about to fall, holding on for all she was worth to a stanchion as they burst, and then opening up the steam again. If the pipe had gone we would have stopped and it would have been all up. By getting the speed, it gave the helm a chance to move the clumsy hulk, and literally every second mattered in the swing.

I saw her once during the action when I had to dodge along to the W T room and looked down through the skylight, hoping to shout a few words of cheer to her. She was standing on the control platform, one long arm stretched straight above her head and her hand holding down the spoke of the throttle as if trying by her touch to urge another pound of steam through the straining pipes. Her face, as expressionless as the bulkhead behind her and as ghastly white in colour, was turned up towards the sunlight, but she didn't see me. From the top of her fore-head down her face, completely closing one eye, trickled a wide black streak of fuel oil from a strained joint. That alone must have been agony. She had jammed her ears with oily waste to deaden the concussion and then in a panic tore it out again for fear she would not hear some vital order from the bridge, not knowing that all connection with the bridge was out.

She was about all in at the end, but within an hour was full of beans and larking about picking up spent bullets and splinters. All round her, by the way, the platform was littered with bullets that came down from the skylight. They still sweep some up every day.

A few days later I was on watch at 5.30 am when the fireman came to me and said, "British convoy." He had been up top for our jug of hot coffee when a big, homeward bound British convoy had been spotted. We did not slow down though I stood by and managed to peep out of the engine room port to see the convoy. It looked lovely in the lemon sunrise, the great grey dragons like sheep dogs protecting the mixed collection of ships. We were so close that the Commander was shouting through his mega-phone. I could see him from my port.

"ARE YOU ALL RIGHT?"

"YES!" Captain Herz shouted back.

"YOU'RE VERY TOUGH!" shouted the Commander of the destroyer. They had heard all about us being attacked. The Captain shouted to them to watch out for the fishing boats, for we were all sure that they had be-trayed us to the enemy.

As we sailed into the Gulf Stream, lumps of yellow sargasso weed floated across the sea. It reminded me of the book *The White Squall of the Sargasso Sea* which I had bought in Macdonalds in Oban when a child for 1/8, and felt it was wicked to have spent so much on a book.

Then we saw a full rigged Swedish sailing ship, a wonderful sight, skimming across the ocean. We also saw a real water spout with water rising straight from the sea like a tree. I could smell the coast, so I knew we must be getting near to land. The sea temperature rose to 84°F.

After our assault by fire, I found I thought less of the Chief Engineer. There was something creepy about him and he had a bad temper. Also he was in an absolute jelly over the bombs and no good at all. I had to do everything.

We got into Norfolk, Virginia, on September 8th and there was such a fuss about landing. The immigration people came aboard and even took our fingerprints. They also asked me for the name of a relation in the States, so I gave Jackie Cecil, as I was so afraid they wouldn't let me ashore if I didn't.

We were 7 miles from the town on a wharf, and they started unloading the china clay. There was mess everywhere. I managed to get hold of a newspaper which was full of bad reports of the bombing of London. This made me very worried about Frances and Jean. I heard we were due back some time in mid-October and I determined to ask for leave right away so I could still catch the Michaelmas daisies and dahlias, late roses and autumn trees.

By 12th September, the story of our bombing raid had come out and we were a three days wonder in Norfolk. Captain Herz and I were featured as the hero and heroine of the piece. Everyone was complimenting everyone else.

"Miss Drummond is one of the most competent engineers ever employed on this vessel," said Captain Herz.

"We owe our safety to the excellent seamanship of Captain Herz," I told reporters. "He handled the ship in such a masterful manner that the bombs exploded too far away from us to do any great damage."

We were headline news in the *Norfolk News Index*, the *Norfolk Ledger Dispatch* and the *Norfolk Virginian Pilot*. I was photographed in the Captain's quarters with Captain Herz and the Mate, in the engine room with the Third and the Fourth, and on my own wearing whites. The reporters even penetrated my cabin and reported that I had a soft blue woollen blanket on my berth and a pastel blue plaid blanket at the end of my bunk.

Once the blaze of publicity had reached the press other people came to see me and none was to prove more dear to me than Mrs Julia Johnson Davies. She invited me ashore to speak to many of the organisations with which she was concerned. So many of these were striving to send bundles to Britain, or to provide home comforts and food for those who most needed it. Of course there were a lot of repairs to do to the engines and I could not get ashore often, but when I did I went with Julia Davies and addressed the Red Cross Production Headquarters and the Norfolk branch of the Bundles for Britain as well as many more.

While I was in Norfolk, a telegram came that our little house at 143 had been hit by a bomb, all the windows had gone and half the side had been blown down. Frances and Jean had been on duty as Wardens and when they came back could only stare in horror at the desolation. Frances went straight into the garden and to her joy found that the goldfish in the pond were all right. Thinking of all this happening at home while I was the other side of the Atlantic made me feel very homesick.

Before we left, the kind ladies of Norfolk loaded me with warm garments for the people of Lambeth and tins of fruit, tea and milk for the Queen Victoria Girls' Club. We had now loaded up with scrap metal for Britain, but instead of sailing straight home we went north to Halifax. On 13th October the Mate and I had a day off and went to look at the maple woods, turning scarlet and gold. I filled myself with the beauty, for I could see there was still the long crossing of the Atlantic ahead of us.

We came back in convoy, a rough winter voyage with huge seas and many of the merchant ships with us were blown up by submarines.

Our first difficulty was with smoke. "She is making a very black smoke that can be seen for miles," the Mate wrote to me, "will you do something about it if possible?"

"I am sorry, but I have had to slow down the fan owing to a hot rod, but will be OK now I hope, " I wrote back.

Later we began to lag behind in the convoy. "Please give her all you can with safety and try to avoid smoke," wrote the Mate. "Please increase to maximum speed," he added later.

Dark was coming down over the Atlantic and the convoy was slipping further from sight. Night was the best time for submarines. "Could you give her a spurt for just a little while to get her in place before dark and then we can let her ease down. They let her get a long way behind last watch," the Mate wrote.

Things did not become better. "Miss D., smoke was very bad but is becoming a little better. We have seen four 'suspicious vessels' and there are more in the vicinity. Will want all the speed possible by daylight. Please give her full ordinary speed without smoking, if possible."

This was my moment to talk to the engines clearly, and I did—response from the Mate on the bridge was most satisfactory: "Please let me know what you are revving now as it is just what the doctor ordered."

The next message was even more encouraging: "Convoy is in sight. If you give her the works we might get in station this watch."

Well, we managed to close that watch, but the trouble was that the other watches always let her slip back out of convoy. And once the convoy was out of sight, that was the moment for the submarine wolf pack, which was following us so closely, to close in. Without the convoy we were virtually doomed.

Even the nearest ships in the convoy were difficult to see in the rough weather. "Miss Drummond, convoy has practically dispersed," wrote Mr Warner. "I am trying to maintain touch with our 'next of kin' on the right which shows sometimes through the squall. Will you please now increase carefully one revolution only. If she takes too much water we will have to reduce speed again."

Next morning the weather was better, but the convoy had again slipped out of sight. "Miss Drummond will you please give her all you can till I let you know to ease down. Convoy was nearly out of sight when I came up. Second and Third officers say they have been waiting for more speed all night but could not get it."

I could have told them that was because I was not in the engine room. The next message after I had got to work was more cheerful: "Good business, D. We are closing with the rear lines of the convoy now. Inside the next half hour should be in station. I will ring two longs when right station. Please then reduce two revs and reply with two long whistles and we can adjust the revs as required later."

Next time I came on watch the same thing had happened, we had slipped back out of convoy. "Come on, D, do your stuff," the Mate wrote desperately. "You are only playing with it now. Shake her up. Tear the tripe out of her. Sea is down now and there is a chance to catch up. It is going to blow again from the southward soon."

Luckily after this the speed of the convoy was reduced a bit and we were better able to keep up. However, by now we had trouble with the bilges and we had to slow right down to clean them out.

"Have just sounded No.1 starboard," Mr Warner wrote desperately, "and there are now 13 inches. Are you quite sure it was pumped out? If so she must be making water fast."

Things did not improve. "Actual speed now through the water is $5\frac{1}{2}$ knots!!" wrote the Mate. "At this speed we have no chance at all of either intercepting the convoy at another rendezvous or of meeting the destroyer escort. Please, what revs are we doing? There must be something wrong. What is the steam pressure? Sorry to trouble you but these are the facts."

After this things improved tremendously. "I know it is very wrong, D, by the Gospel according to Judas, but will you please send me a note of the different alterations of speed since 4 am and what are revs now? We are in good station. Weather is getting bad."

However, fine weather was forecast and later the note said, "Wind and sea are moderating rapidly. You can proceed at the best speed compatible with the safety of your heap of scrap metal."

And at last, at long last, land was in sight. "Please give her all you can, D. I want to see Donaghadee before I turn in. A little smoke won't matter now." On 3rd November while I was on duty in the engine room, I was suddenly telegraphed to "Stop Engines" to avoid collision. I managed to stop them, but was thrown with such force against the engine room bulkhead that my jaw became dislocated and remained out of its socket for over 24 hours. I was in agony, but nothing could be done, as there was no medical assistance available and I was on duty the whole time, carrying out my watches. After 24 hours, to my unbelievable relief, it somehow snapped back into place and I felt human again.

The next day, 5th November, we at last made it into dock at Port Talbot, South Wales, where I was able to get ashore and see a doctor. Of 39 merchant ships in the convoy, only four limped home. We were lucky.

I was tired and worn out and longed to leave. As soon as I arrived I telephoned Jean and Frances. They had moved in to stay with the Sisters of Consolation. Our cousin, Maurice Drummond, Head of Scotland Yard, had taken the goldfish to his house in Hampshire. Most of them survived. Mummy was now living at Green Shallows near Fleet with a Miss Stanley, and as soon as I could leave the *Bonita* I planned to join her.

"The bad raids started on 7th September," Jean told me. "All the girls were having tea in the club when the alert sounded. They helped to carry the tea perfectly calmly across Kennington Road to the shelter in Walcot Square, where we continued our tea. I got them to sing *There'll always be an England*. Overhead we could hear the German planes droning and trying to shoot down the barrage balloons. We could hear machine gunning from the dog fights and heavy fire from the batteries in action. Since then we've had to plan our club round shelter life."

In Scotland John demobilised himself out of the Black Watch and came back to Megginch to farm, starting up the Megginch branch of the LDV with himself in command as Sergeant-Major. Hugo had left Cambridge and joined the Welsh Guards and Violet and the girls had potatoes growing in the flower beds, chickens in coops and cows on the lawn. The house was so full of people from the Victoria League that although I was invited up on leave, I feared I might have to sleep on a sofa. Lady Jardine had turned her house at Binfield Park into a convalescent hospital, with herself as Commandant, staffed only by the prettiest VADs. "So nice for the soldiers to look at," she said.

There had been much talk of disaffection because the *Bonita* was sailing under the Panamanian flag and the Captain and many of the officers were Hungarians. When Hungary entered the War with the Axis, it was thought safer to change the crew for British and when we reached Newport, this was done. It happened after I left the ship on 8th November, which was perhaps as well. Shouldering my kitbag and with all my tins of milk and fruit, and the boxes of woollens for Lambeth, I made my way by train to London, where I found Jean at 122 Kennington Road, although she and Frances were still living with the nuns. We had so much to say, so much to talk about. We had both been in battle: I in the Battle of the Atlantic, they in the Battle of Britain.

Later I went to stay with Mummy at Green Shallows, too late for the dahlias, but there were still some Michaelmas daisies and late roses. The Mate came to stay, and Jean and Frances when they could. It was golden and quiet. Mummy read Kipling aloud in the evenings and I gave her the scarlet maple leaves I had brought from the other side of the Atlantic. She pressed them and put them into her Bible, as she read in her soothing voice:

"They that go down to the sea in ships and occupy their business in great waters: these men see the works of the Lord and His wonders in the deep."

Chapter Fourteen
The War at Sea - 1940-45

With the peace and rest at Fleet, the injuries to my head soon recovered and I felt more myself. I was able to go to London and join Jean for her Christmas party at the Girls' Club with many of the things which had been sent over by the ladies of Virginia. Jean used some of the ingredients to make her delicious cakes. While we were getting the tea ready, three huge bombs fell without warning on St George's Road near the Elephant and Castle, rocking the club.

"Perhaps you should go to the shelter," Jean suggested to the girls.

"Oh no," they said, "they've dropped their stick now."

I also had to see the Mayor of Lambeth and distribute the other things which had been given to me in Virginia, mainly wool to knit forces comforts while in the shelters, but also magazines, packs of cards and warm garments to put into packages for sailors. The Mayor was very pleased, particularly as there was the exciting prospect of more things being sent over from Virginia.

We had a happy Christmas all together at Fleet. Jean and Frances were preparing to move to a flat of their own at 2 Restormel House, Chesterway, still near the Kennington Road. Mummy was talking of getting a house of her own. We had found a flat above Milward's, the shoemaker's in the High Street, which had three nice sized rooms upstairs, a tiny bathroom and two small bedrooms, and downstairs a small cupboard-sized kitchenette and a dining room. It was also very sunny and had a garden with an apple tree and a large shed, which could be filled meantime with furniture.

In January 1941 I had heard to my great sadness that the *Har Zion* had gone down with all hands except one. I could not help feeling that if the yellow dog had still been with them, perhaps they would have been all right. Sailors are very superstitious people.

By 3rd February Mr Warner had signed on as Captain and I as Second Engineer on the *SS Czikos* as part of a skeleton crew. There were two other ship's officers and four quartermasters. We were to travel to Liverpool by train and there join the *SS Avoceta* as passengers for Lisbon where we were to pick up the *Czikos*. She was meantime sailing under a Panamanian flag with an American crew and a cargo of iron and steel scrap.

I was relieved to be sailing with Mr Warner again. The *Czikos* belonged to Messrs Craggs and Co, Winterbourne, Devon, and had originally been an Ellerman Hall cargo ship, flush-decked and built in North-East England about 1913.

Before we left I wrote to Mr Isaac of the Ministry of Shipping to see whether I could take a Chief's Certificate with only a verbal exam, as many people were allowed to in wartime if they had sufficient practical experience. Although I had by now gained a Panamanian Chief's certificate, I still did not hold a British one and I felt if I had to go down, I would rather go down as a British Chief.

I told Mr Isaac that I had already completed the Chief's exam 31 times and that I felt my whole career and work might be taken into consideration if I could just take orals. "I want to be all the help I can during the war period," I wrote, "or as much of it as I am spared to serve through. I would rather go down with a Chief's certificate than with a Second's."

Mr Isaac replied that there was no way such an unprecedented step as counting the number of times I had applied and my practical experience could be considered. He said there was no shortage of Chief Engineers, only of Seconds, for which I was adequately qualified.

He ended by saying, "Writing as I do after many years of experience as a marine engineer and knowing so well the present dangers and difficulties pertaining to that calling, permit me to say that I think it very courageous of you to take a watch on the starting platform in the prevailing conditions. I venture to suggest, however, that your talents would be equally well employed, for example, in the training of women as assistant engineers ashore or other similar duties where your experience could be of value."

"You cannot teach an old sea dog new tricks," I thought, and wrote back firmly, and more fully than I had done before:

"I know you will understand and I feel I may explain the matter fully, dropping all formality with a marine engineer of your vast experience.

"I explained I would rather go down with a First Class than a Second Class certificate, but I did not like to explain my true reason for fear of being misunderstood. Please do not think I am telling tales if I say that my last Chief always became totally incapacitated, apparently through nerves, under enemy action. The foreign engineers were absolutely unreliable in action, although good engineers at other times. I therefore had to assume full responsibility and take over in the engine room on all occasions, and be ready to take a sudden Stop or Finished with Engines. This must all be done with decision, judgement and rapidity as you know.

"I am now going to serve under a Hungarian Chief, and have a foreign third and donkeyman, but as I know you will appreciate I would be in a much better position to carry out these duties as Second holding a Chief's certificate.

"As to the training of women, it was suggested to me that I should take a shore job but I felt that this work could be carried on by a very elderly man unsuited for a sea-going life, or a man who was unfit for sea through bad health or war service."

It was no good though. I had all the answers. I was a better and more experienced engineer than many then serving under Chief's tickets. But I was a woman and they would not let me pass the exam.

So, with all my sea gear once again securely packed into little bags, Captain Warner, the crew and I set out on the train from London to Liverpool. On arrival in Liverpool things began to deteriorate when we saw the disgusting state of the hotel where we were supposed to stay overnight. It was really a doss house at the back of Lime Street Station, and the Mate, as I still called Captain Warner, said it wasn't fit to go into; it was so dirty the smell nearly made me sick.

So off we went to the Exchange Hotel, where I was afraid we would have to pay the difference. Then we had to go down in the pitch dark to the sailors' home to see about the men. It was bitterly cold and they had not been ordered food. However, we got it fixed and there were more forms and papers to get them to fill in.

Our night at the Exchange Hotel was very comfortable, but the next morning we had to go down again to the sailors' home, which was freezing. I went to the Mersey Mission, the Flying Angel, where they were so nice, and the Mate and I paid the sailors' tea and pies.

When we got to the ship it was very cold and I was glad of the new blankets Mummy had given me. I was lucky enough to have a cabin of my own with three berths. Besides our skeleton crew, the *Avoceta* carried her own crew and a torpedo crew, a tough lot, using every spare scrap of accommodation. The torpedo crew were from St Vincent, all intensely British.

We had some very rough weather going down towards Portugal. One huge sea came on deck and when I looked out of my port all I could see was swirling grey water. Three of the ship's crew were hurt, one with a broken arm, and one with a broken hip. Although I was lucky to escape injury, I contracted a bad cold, which was largely due to the bad food and the constant wetness and chill in my cabin. Dr Jackson gave me a splendid bottle of stuff to stave off my flu.

We had mouldy rice and sago puddings for sixteen days and no fruit since leaving port, living primarily on salt meat out of a barrel. The coffee was undrinkable. The only thing which made life bearable were the cosy evenings in the Chief's room with cake and tea. Sometimes the Captain came and joined us. Except for the Mate, I was the eldest there. Afterwards, I would slip down the galley and fill my hot water bottle with boiling water.

On the whole I was enjoying myself and soon we got into warmer weather. On 8th March we reached Lisbon where it was already spring and flowers were coming out. We were two weeks in Lisbon and had to recruit the remaining members of the crew at the dock gates, with no help from the British Consul because the ship was registered under the Panamanian flag. Many of the crew came from Eastern Europe, Romanians and Yugoslavians, fleeing from the Nazis. We left on 22nd March for Gibraltar, passing close to a warship at sea that same evening, *HMS Sheffield*. She made us heave to and Commander Burry and a Captain of Marines came aboard, but it was too rough for us to coal from them. The weather was very bad; we were rolling a great deal and kept on stand-by duty all day. We saw several submarines, but managed to keep enough steam going to escape. "There is a sub on port beam and a big ship following. Keep a good head of steam" the Mate scribbled down to me. It was not a thing he needed to tell me twice.

We loaded with more steel at Gibraltar and then set off north again. After we left port we sprung a leak in the fore peak. We all helped to shift the cargo in No 1 hold and Captain Warner shored up the bulkhead, which was a job as she was rolling a lot. We all pumped with a hand pump to keep the water down, but there was a split 2 feet long.

Then the Chief Engineer told the donkeyman to cut a hole through the bulkhead and let the water into No 1 hold. He wanted to do this because the bilge pipe was broken in No 2 hold and the bilges from No 1 were running back through the broken pipe to No 2, which I was unable to pump out. Luckily Captain Warner stopped him. If he had done this, we would have gone down easily.

At Gibraltar we joined a convoy sailing for the Clyde, which meant sailing southwest from Gibraltar, halfway across the Atlantic, then north and finally southeast to the Clyde. It was rolling something dreadful in the Atlantic. However, we got the water under control with the pump and were just getting on nicely when we were attacked by a large plane about 300 miles northwest of Ireland. She was a Focke-Wulf Condor, a long-range four-engined bomber which I thought had probably come from

Merignac near Bordeaux. The weather was fine and cloudy and the plane suddenly swooped on us out of the clouds. The bombs didn't hit us, though each time they fell the ship rocked in the water; the first attack put the engine room telegraph out of action. I was off watch at the time they attacked and dashed down below where I found the engine room full of steam and ashes. I thought a boiler had gone, but it hadn't. The watch had all done a bunk and gone on top.

The officer on watch sent down to tell us to give him maximum speed, so I chased the men down again, and the men off duty too. She was an old triple expansion job and there was a valve which could be opened in an emergency to admit steam at full boiler pressure to the low pressure cylinder, but of course this could not be sustained for a long time.

In order to terrorise the crew, the plane came in again with a machine gun attack. James Clegg, one of the quatermasters, had taken over the wheel and was machine-gunned and died in the arms of a young Romanian boy. The Third Mate was wounded and so were two of my engineers; we had no protection at all. By now the ship was leaking badly and there was water under the cargo. Captain Warner, as cool as ice, went down and plugged the leaks even though she was rolling heavily.

The Third Mate was transferred to a naval escort vessel, but died aboard her and so was buried at sea. By the next day we had limped into Moville, Donegal, on Lough Long. The two wounded men were got off to hospital, but the ship was a total shambles. Skylight glasses, the mirror on the wheelhouse, the bridge clock and telescope, were all smashed. Ladders were pulled off from the iron funnel, jolly boat planking was in splinters, hatches and tarpaulins were damaged, the engine room was a fearful mess, and most of the crockery, oil lamps, saucepans and electric bulbs had gone. In my own room the wash basin was smashed, as were the water bottle, oil lamp and globe. The bridge of the ship was open to the four winds, with only a canvas wind-dodger in front of the wheel since all the wheel-house had been shot away. We were very shattered by it all. Even worse, most of the engine room crew who had tried to sink the ship had to be arrested. An armed guard came aboard as soon as we landed, but of course could do nothing because Ireland was neutral.

We were in Londonderry for about a week and Captain Warner and I managed to get ashore and have a slap up meal in the local restaurant, real farm eggs, thick Irish bacon and fat sausages.

That night Hitler decided to give himself a pre-birthday raid on London. It was one of the fiercest and most dreadful yet. The Lambeth ARP Post where Jean and Frances were was struck by a bomb and they were among nineteen others buried in the wreckage. Air Raid Wardens from all the surrounding districts rushed in to help, a mechanical digger was got in, and Jean and Frances and three others were dug out alive. Everyone else was dead. They were moved to a hospital at Fleet, near Mummy, and it was from here that I received the telegram. Knowing they were all right was a great blessing, but I do not think I should have survived if it had not been for the kindness of Captain Warner.

We were ten days at Moville before we sailed across to Ardrossan where we arrived on 29th April. Upon arrival the Chief Engineer, one greaser, one fireman and two trimmers were removed under guard for London. The next day Mr Duncan came aboard as Chief Engineer along with other replacements and we immediately started on the huge list of repairs which needed doing, starting by removing the ashes from the deck and blowing down the port boiler. I was desperate to get down to Fleet and see for myself how Jean and Frances were. As soon as the cargo had been unloaded and the new engine crew settled in and started on the repairs, I wrote to Messrs Craggs and Co at Budleigh Salterton to be relieved on 16th May.

"I spared no effort to bring your ship in safely and remained with her till the cargo was discharged," I wrote.

I then set off south. Mummy was still at Little Anstice, Crookham, but the move to 202 Fleet Road was all in hand and Glen of course was overjoyed to see me. Jean and Frances had left the hospital and were their own plucky cheerful selves. All those terrible 15 hours they had repeated hymns and Bible texts to each other which enabled them to carry on. They had been sitting in water, with little air, and their legs were never the same afterwards.

"But God delivered us out of the depths of the earth," said Jean, "we put our trust in Him and were saved."

In the midst of all this I was particularly delighted to hear that Julia Davis had gathered together a committee of ladies and between them they had raised £400 towards an ambulance to be named the "Victoria A. Drummond Ambulance" for the people of Lambeth. What the people of Lambeth needed far more, however, was a canteen which would serve hot food to those whose houses had been bombed. So instead the "Victoria A. Drummond Canteen" was set up near Lambeth North Underground serving hot meals for a cost of 6d a head. It was amazing how much money had been raised. Julia told me how she and Mrs Leitch had got Robert Frost, the poet, to give a reading of his works, and many people all over

Virginia had contributed. I eventually made my way to London to see the canteen for myself. Painted bright green and yellow, the "Victoria A. Drummond" was proving an immense morale booster to the bombed out people of Lambeth. I felt very proud.

By July 1941 I was trying to return to sea. I applied initially to Townsend of Leadenhall Street and they agreed I could go to San Francisco to bring over a tug, sailing as Chief. I stood by, waiting every day to be called, and when Messrs Jacobs, Barringer and Garrett of Fenchurch Street offered me a job as Second on a 12,000 ton ship, I was unable to accept since I was already standing by for Messrs Townsend.

On 8th July I had a very exciting letter from the Admiralty informing me that on the recommendation of the First Sea Lord, the Prime Minister had obtained the King's approval for my appointment as a Member of the Order of the British Empire for my services on *SS Bonita*.

On 29th July I took Frances as my guest and, wearing my Merchant Navy uniform, set off to Buckingham Palace to receive my MBE from the King. I was rather nervous, but when the time came the King had quite a chat with me. He asked me about the bombing of the *Bonita* and I told him, but of course not at great length.

"You were very brave," he said.

"I had to do my duty and save the ship," I replied. He caught my eye and smiled, and I thought, "Well, we both have something in common then."

After this I went back to my endless trailing round shipping offices. I continued to call at Townsend, but nothing came of it. I tried the Counties Ship Management Company and was told they only had a foreign crew, the ship was 35 years old and it was not very likely she would get over in bad weather.

I tried the King Line to bring the *King Gruffydd* from Durban. I was told the pools had already promised them a man before I called.

The Crest Line had no vacancy and were not changing their Second Engineer after all.

I tried the American Commercial Attache, the American Chamber of Commerce, the USA Maritime Commission, the Operating Manager of United States Lines and the Marine Operating Company in New York. They all said they would take my name and particulars and would let me know.

And so it went on. Nobody seemed to want me I thought. But Lloyds Of London did. On 30th September they sent me the Lloyd's War Medal for Bravery at Sea, awarded to me by the Committee of Lloyds as an acknowledgement of "your bravery when your ship was attacked by enemy aircraft in August 1940." I was immensely proud of both my medals. They reassured me that at least someone believed my work was worthwhile.

For a long time I hoped to get on another ship with my friend, the Mate, Captain Warner. I knew he was sailing as Captain of the *Fort George* which was due to be in Montreal in April or May, and so I determined to find a ship going there, so we could meet and discuss our tactics of finding a ship together. By luck the Manchester Liners said they had a job for me on the *Manchester Port* sailing in April.

CAN YOU REPORT MANCHESTER LINERS 8 DOCK SALFORD FRIDAY MORNING AT 10 SIGN AS FIFTH-NAUTICUS read the telegram. I travelled up overnight and next morning signed on. There was a great deal of work to do as the ship was very dirty and ill kept and one day I had to go after one of the firemen, Pollard, who just walked ashore with his suitcase.

"I'm not sailing on that filthy ship," he said.

I explained to him carefully and in words of one syllable that the alternative to sailing was gaol. After some argument he returned to the ship. But I did see his point. Everything on the ship was dirty, even the stores had been neglected.

On 20th April we went to Eastham, a pretty village with hedges bursting into spring leaf. I climbed the ladder over the ship's side and ran to the village where by some amazing luck I was able to buy sweets, a rarity during the war.

The next day we moved down the Mersey and formed up in convoy with 53 ships in all, under Commander McKay. We were made the Commodore ship. It was cold as we steamed out into the Atlantic and very hard work for the engineers. The firemen made complaint about the dirty cook and his assistant and also complained about the way the food was dumped on their plates like a dog's dinner. They were quite justified. I went into the galley and it was filthy. It was a wonder we did not all have food poisoning. In the morning I reported the state of the galley to the Captain who paid little attention and did nothing. He seemed to be drunk.

On Sunday 26th April we picked up another convoy of twelve ships from Ireland. I think a submarine must have been following them because the American destroyer in our convoy sunk one in the afternoon. They said she was French. There were no survivors.

The weather eventually cleared, although it was still extremely cold, and by 28th April we had one of those silvery days when the sea and sky were all pearl grey. Standing on deck well wrapped up, I thought the convoy looked rather fine steaming away across the Atlantic in formation. During the next few days we heard several depth charges and on 1st May a wolf pack of four submarines was reported to be after us. The weather deteriorated again to hail storms and several ships dropped out of the convoy, unable to keep to the revs set. The next day we heard the that *British Workman* was torpedoed. She had fallen behind with boiler trouble and was told to join the slow convoy which was coming up behind. Instead, she tried to catch up with our convoy and, on her own, the submarines got her. That morning the convoy split up and we were now only fourteen ships. We were within sight of Newfoundland, however, and patches of snow and amethyst hills rose in the distance.

When I woke on 6th May there was bright sunshine and out of my port I saw Quebec above the blue green waters of the St Lawrence. The town was bathed in sunlight and I thought of General Wolfe climbing up from the Plains of Abraham in 1759, of Uncle Adam and my great-great-grandfather coming here ten years later, of Sir Gordon playing here as a boy and later coming back as a general. Above the high, wooded cliffs there were green lands sloping away to foothills clear blue in the distance and the rainwashed May sky was as blue as a hedge sparrow's egg. The scent of pine trees came down the engine room ventilators and sunlight flickered on the bulkhead. We were the first ship up the St Lawrence since last autumn, we were told.

In the afternoon the Fourth and I sat on deck. I loved the contrast of the powdered green of the maples with the dark of the spruces, and a different green again of the meadows where cows browsed. The French Canadian houses were white or buff with brightly coloured roofs and shutters and each village was dominated by a slender church spire. We arrived in Montreal on a clear spring evening with everyone walking home from work.

We were there until 14th May, and although I worked a great deal, I was able to get ashore a bit. As in Virginia, I was overwhelmed with kindness and hospitality. Commander and Mrs Stewart took me under their wing and they, along with the Sharpleys, invited me to their house, to lunch at Eatons or to have tea in the Merchant Navy Club. Sometimes I lunched on my own in a little French restaurant. And although it was May, I bought decoration chains for our Christmas tree, a message of hope for the future.

In fact I would have been very happy if only the Mate had been there. As soon as we docked I went ashore to look for him, but he was not there. He had written to me on the way over, "I expect we will make a US port and proceed by rail to Montreal." But by 6th May the *Fort George* was not there and there was no word in the pools of Captain Warner. He had ended his letter, "You will probably have torn this letter into small pieces, jumped on it, and then thrown it in the fire long before you have got this length...." But I hadn't. Instead I had brought it all the way across the Atlantic with me, hoping to join my old shipmate.

On 17th May after loading dynamite at Three Rivers, we sailed into the Gulf of St Lawrence in a convoy of seven ships, and as we swung into the open sea the wind freshened and became colder once more. We reached Halifax on 20th May. I felt the time had come for someone to say something about the Captain and, as I had already given in my notice, it had better be me. So I went ashore and reported to the agents that the Captain had been drunk since leaving the Mersey. The next day Captain Davis was taken ashore by naval escort at 11.30 am and at 12.45 pm a new captain, Captain Middleton, arrived on board. I went ashore to look at the boats, but there was no *Fort George*.

It was snowing heavily when we left Halifax and there were many depth charges, and so it continued all across the Atlantic. On 6th June when I was on watch there were 36 depth charges dropped by a single corvette, but I could smell land through the engine room ventilator and knew we were near home. The next day we were in Ellesmere Port and then going up the Ship Canal. As the dangerous cargo was unloaded I was able to leave the *Manchester Port* and head south by train for Lambeth. Frances had had a letter from the Mate from the Pacific, dated 25th April, in which he said, "I waited in Montreal for three weeks and several other drafts came out without her, and then I had to go on to Vancouver." He said he was coming home in June in a new ship with very nice accommodation. If I would come on it, he would stay with it, although he did not think I would like the Chief Engineer. Otherwise he would change and we could try to get a ship together.

"I miss Victoria very much," he ended. I missed him too. We seemed fated never to meet.

The worst ship I ever sailed on was the *Danae II*. I was appointed to her as Second Engineer on Monday 31st August in London and I joined her at Boston Links that same evening. She was owned by the Ministry of War so I thought she would be a good ship to serve in. How wrong I was. She was managed by Messrs Ambrose, Davies, Matthews of Whitting Avenue, London. They were very averse to my appointment, as they had another engineer in view, but I had precedence over him and my appointment was carried through against considerable opposition.

The *Danae II* was built as a French coaster and should have been a nice little job, with good accommodation and a well laid out engine room. However, when I arrived I found the condition of the ship was filthy and verminous. The men slept without bedding for two nights and I had no bedding either. We fumigated the ship at Boston to get rid of the bugs, but it didn't work. I had been told on joining the ship that the back ends, smoke boxes, tank top and bilges were clean, but I found that this was not the case. As she had to sail, however, I decided to carry out the work in North Shields. The real reason I was so keen to sail on the *Danae II* was that the Mate was going to be on her as First Officer. At last we would be back on a ship together. But it wasn't at all as I had hoped. That first evening in Boston Links the Mate went off with Captain Cheek and the other officers, who were no better than criminals, and I was left on that revolting boat.

In North Shields we discovered that the repairs required on the boilers meant that we had to first blow down the starboard boiler and then do the same with the port boiler. When I went up to inspect the starboard back ends, I found them full up with ashes approximately one foot over the furnaces. The next day we could do nothing as the ship was fumigated with cyanide, and certainly after this it was possible to sleep without being bitten to bits. We eventually dug the back ends out, but of course they were still very hot because of all the ash, the smoke boxes were cleaned, and steam was raised on the starboard boiler as the port boiler was blown down. When I went to inspect the port back ends, I found them just as bad as the starboard side, so they all had to be dug out and the smoke boxes cleaned. It took the men two days to get the ashes on deck in order to facilitate inspecting the stokehold bilges. By Friday morning we were at last able to get at the stokehold plates, and the Chief Engineer inspected the bilges and tank tops and told me to have them cleaned. There was so much work for the engine room staff that some of the sailors on deck also helped us and finally we were ready to sail for Methil on Sunday 13th September.

In Methil the Captain tried to give me notice and get me off the ship. He used the pretext that my burnt hand was too bad to allow me to sail, but a shore doctor soon disabused him of this. The Third and Fourth engineers were both uncertified, one a promoted fireman, and nearly always drunk; the greaser told me that they had not bothered to turn up for their watch. I reported this to the Chief Engineer, who also drank, as did the Captain, who was always shouting at me and abusing me along with everyone else on the ship. The general turmoil on the ship, largely created by the Captain, was beyond belief. The Second officer, a friend of the Captain's, had been sacked from his last boat for being drunk on watch.

In Aultbea there were more repairs on the engine room, which I had to do while keeping steam up for constant moves. On the afternoon of Tuesday 22nd September I was sent for by Captain Cheek and told, without being given any reason, to leave the ship next morning at 8 am This was without giving me 24 hours notice and I had, I understood, signed articles for two years. The firemen, greasers, donkeyman all told me they also wished to be paid off as they would not sail without me. The sailors said they also wished to be paid off. The whole ship was in a turmoil and the entire crew left. The Mate, who had been very much "in" with the dreadful Captain, refused to join me and stayed on the ship.

I immediately went ashore and telephoned the Minister of War Transport in London and, believing the telephone line to be a private one, I explained the entire situation. When I left, I went straight to London. I naturally had to explain in detail what had happened both to the Ministry of War Transport and to Messrs Ambrose Davies and Matthews Ltd.

On 23rd October I received a solicitors' letter which read: "it would appear that you have made defamatory statements of and concerning our client to Messrs Ambrose Davies and Matthews Ltd and to Representatives of the Ministry of War Transport. These statements were to the effect that our client was under the influence of drink when in command of the *SS Danae II* and that he was not competent. We are instructed to say that unless you withdraw your allegations and apologise to our client in writing our client will at once commence proceedings claiming damages."

I think I had the last word. I wrote back: "There are certain statements in your letter which might be open to dispute on my part, but if any slanderous statements were made by me regarding the sobriety of Captain Cheek while I was with him on the *Danae II* these are unreservedly withdrawn."

They could take it either way, and I hoped they would see what I meant. Certainly I never heard from them again.

I did hear from Captain Warner, however, whose apparent desertion had upset me dreadfully. He explained to me that only by keeping in with the dreadful Captain and his vile crew was he in some way able to mitigate their behaviour towards me.

"They were a dreadful crowd," he wrote to me later. "You were perfectly right. I never knew a worse crowd. Absolutely awful. Regular criminals. I do not regret at all that you did not sail on the ship. It nearly killed me. The voyage was pure Hell from start to finish, and I can only thank God you weren't there.... Do you know if anything is going to be done about that man Cheek? The amount of trouble and expense that he causes apart from his habits should be inquired into."

It was five months before I got this letter from him, during which time I had written him a great many cross ones first. I had told him he could jump on them, and I expect he did. I was glad that he had really shared my opinion of that dreadful ship.

On 31st October 1942 we all went to Hugo's wedding in the Guards Chapel. He was married to Leila Cookson, one of Lady Jardine's prettiest VADs. Cherry and Heather, now thirteen and ten, were bridesmaids. We hadn't seen them for four years and they had grown a lot. In fact it was a great family reunion and everyone had stretched their coupons to produce wedding finery—the two bridesmaids were in ivory taffeta and the little bride, who was scarcely the same height as Cherry, looked enchanting in white lace. Hugo wore his uniform, and so of course did I.

A week later I was staying in the Central Hotel, Glasgow, going round all the Glasgow ship owners trying to find a berth. I also wrote to the Manchester Liners and to my old friend Mr Freeman at the Blue Funnel Line. If only I could get to Canada, I was assured of a place back on one of the new boats. Several people wrote and suggested I should try going out as a stewardess.

By luck Mr Freeman managed to get me a job as fridge engineer on the 10,000 ton *TSS Perseus*, which was going to Australia and then back round the Cape. I travelled up to Liverpool overnight and signed-on on 29th January 1943. By 1st February we were off, sailing down the Mersey with a cargo of high explosives forward, general armoury stores aft and five planes on deck—two bombers, two fighters and a sea plane. There were also 24 passengers, all men and mostly naval, going over to pick up ships. It was dark and blowing with snow showers and heavy seas as we set out in a convoy of 41 ships to sail "over the Western".

My room was comfortable and the food was excellent. There was usually meat served twice a day, good hot soup both for lunch and dinner and substantial steam puddings or jam rolls, just the thing for warming up after working on the freezing bilges. Because of course there was bilge trouble almost at once.

We sailed close up the Scottish and Irish coast, picking up more ships as we went due north. It got colder all the time and the Chief had to give me a pair of socks to prevent my feet dropping off. The new moon seemed to make it colder than anything, if that had been possible, but the displays of Northern Lights were magnificent.

I think 15th February was the coldest day I have ever experienced. I thought of the icy conditions in the garage in Perth and in the Caledon Works in Dundee, of bicycling up the drive in an arctic wind, of the cold of the southern ocean, and I still came to the conclusion that this was worse. The snow came down like Jack Frost crystals and the polar wind whipped round the deck and froze all the winches. I helped to make torches of old condenser tubes or anything I could find and we used these as well as waste cotton lit on shovels to thaw out the winches on deck.

On 22nd February we entered the Chesapeake Bay and arrived at Newport News. We were alongside by 11.45 am, where we disembarked the 24 passengers and tied up at a coal wharf. I worked all day on repair work, but at 7 pm I was able to dash ashore and telephone Julia Davis. How wonderful the warmth of the south felt, the lights, the scent of flowers, and above all the ground under my feet after 22 days at sea. I felt inclined to run and run and run. Dark coloured faces smiled at me from all sides and the stores were heaped with oranges, apples and red peppers.

I had to work solidly from 7 am to 7 pm all three days we were in port, but on Tuesday the ship's chandler ran us down to the ferry for Norfolk. Julia was waiting for me at the Navy Quay and her house was full of friends, her mother and sister Josephine, Mr and Mrs Osborn, Mr and Mrs Hughes and Mrs Whitehead, and smelt deliciously of the bowl of white apricot blossom on a table. Julia promised to do all my shopping for me and said she had collected more parcels for Lambeth.

Afterwards, carefully carrying a red camellia given me by Caroline Hughes, Julia drove me back to the ferry, and so back via another ferry and a taxi to the ship, which had meantime loaded 3,500 tons of coal. Everything was black and covered in coal dust. Our crew had diminished at Newport News, for three men had been landed sick and five had jumped ship. We moved to anchorage in Chesapeake Bay that night, and the next day, when we thought we were again moving anchorage, sailed to New York.

We had a marvellous view of New York sailing in on 26th February despite the intermittent snow storms. We anchored out and took on another 24 passengers, mostly soldiers and naval personnel. We were to have gone out with a convoy, but had to stay behind as the men had sent in a petition to have their accommodation improved, so we moved into the wharf to have it done up.

It was bitterly cold and even the stars looked icy. However, to my joy I was able to get ashore one afternoon to Broadway, where I was overwhelmed with the glorious lights. I had hot chocolate in the drug stores and peered at shining new books. I had tea with my friend Mrs Marjoribanks and did a great deal of shopping to take home, as well as an eiderdown and, of course, chocolate. But it was ever so cold; the water was all frozen solid on the ship and there were long icicles everywhere.

On 9th March when we thought we were moving anchorage again, we suddenly found we were putting to sea, and at 4.30 pm on that icy cold evening had joined a convoy for the south. In two days it was bright sunshine and boiling hot. We sighted Cuba on 14th March and next day were expecting an attack. I was woken by an explosion and Chips sounded all the tanks at 3 am in the morning, but we were undamaged and anchored the next morning in Guantanamo Bay.

All the time through the Caribbean I was working very hard and now found difficulties with the Second Engineer, who always gave me extra work, kept me on ship when in port, and was consistently rude to me. The Chief told me to pay no attention.

By 21st March we had arrived at Panama and the next day we started through the Canal, it was terribly hot. There was an armed American guard on board and another one in the engine room, and every move on the telemotor they checked by phone to the bridge. They told me they were there to prevent sabotage, to stop a ship being sunk to block the Canal. They had had trouble with two ships already, they said.

The lock was a magnificent structure of concrete and stone with great gates. At 9.30 am we anchored in Lake Gatun and I lay under a life boat in the shade. The shores and islands were covered with thick tropical growth, with here and there high palms standing out. The flowering trees in the forest made it look studded with jewels. The sky was grey with rain-wet clouds, and the thick air full of butterflies. Huge black butterflies with crimson wings, white ones, orange and yellow ones, and iridescent blue ones flew over the ship. By 11.45 am we were on our way through the lake again and came to a part where dead trees stuck out of the water, as if part of the forest had been flooded to form the lake.

By 2.30 pm I was back on stand-by in the engine room, but I managed to slip on deck when we came out of Lake Gatun into the narrow canal where we passed between high cliffs of orange-red stone covered with burnt grass and scrub. The water here was intensely green, almost jade.

We came through the second lock where there were several houses on the bank with flower-filled gardens; I saw two little black monkeys tied to a stick, dancing about with bananas in their hands.

By 5.30 pm we were through the third lock and out of the Canal into Balboa Bay. We unloaded the armed guards who came to say goodbye and wish me luck and then we were off again, lifting to the Pacific swell. Away to port were the brilliant lights of Panama Town, and as we passed the Perlas Islands green shapes loomed black against the tropical night sky. The halo of the moon illuminated the clouds which drifted over the water. I sat eating my supper of coffee and biscuits on the hatch, watching the lights of Panama sparkling like a string of golden necklaces.

We sailed down the coast of Columbia, out of sight of land, and crossed the Line at Ecuador at 2.30 pm on 25th March. It was very hot and I was tired; the Second was very rude to me and told me to work faster. My feet burned from the deck and my hands with touching the tools that had been on the deck. Round white clouds floating on the horizon cast purple shadows and it was difficult to tell which was sea and which was cloud. Little droves of flying fish planed across the calm water and dipped into tiny waves, sun shining on their steel blue bodies and wings. In the evening the passengers held a sing song on the deck to a violin and we sang *There'll always be an England* and *White Cliffs of Dover*. And as the night deepened there were stars in the sky and stars in the sea as bright phosphorus "witches' fires' drifted beneath the surface of the black water.

I developed a cold and heat cough from working in the burning sun, and on 3rd April I scalded my foot badly while scaling the evaporators. By tea time it was so bad that the Chief said I must show it to the Doctor. He cut the blister, bound it up and gave me cough mixture for my cold.

By 4th April it had begun to get cooler and we were into blues. I was still working, although my foot was so sore I could not get a shoe on properly. Next day my foot looked so much better that I didn't have it re-bandaged and sat on deck learning splicing and fancy knotting from the Bosun. But next night my foot suddenly swelled up and became unbearably sore. In the engine room I looked for leaks on the fridge and cut a joint for the brine pump, but all the time my foot was feeling worse and worse. By lunch time I could hardly bear it, so I showed it to the Doctor, who sent me straight to bed. It was blood poisoning and pink spots came out all over my leg and I felt sick, sleepy and alternately burning and cold. The pain was unbearable. Four days I was in bed with it and four days I had to sit with it up, but we lost 15th April altogether when we crossed the date line, so I suppose that would have made it nine days in all.

Fourteen

By 21st April I was able to start work again, although the Doctor was still dressing my foot. That day we sighted a small cargo vessel, the first we had seen, though in the night we were nearly run down by a huge tanker. The following day we sighted land, the blue hilly coast of Australia, all in a gold and pink sunset.

On Good Friday we tied up at Miller's Wharf where the Air Force came to take the planes off. I went to sleep with the ship at rest and the lights of Sydney reflecting through my port.

Next day I was ashore by 10.15 am excited to be on Australian soil after nineteen years. The people at the dock gate remembered me and I rang up the Boltons at Hunter's Quay, who said to come at once. It was lovely to be welcomed so warmly. The day was hot and sunny and I sauntered up Windmill Steps under the sombre Morton Bay figs and through Argyle Cut to Circular Quay. Armed with papers, bananas and chocolate, I boarded a speedy little ferry boat for Valencia Pier.

The Harbour looked bluer than ever and the bridge more splendid. We passed numerous cargo ships with extensive torpedo damage one had a great hole completely through the stern. I thought how extremely lucky we had been to cross the two great oceans without being sunk.

I took a bus to Hunter's Quay where Beulah and her sister met me with the warmest of welcomes. At their rambling stone house, I sat on the veranda in the sun, watching the sparkling waters of the Hudson through half closed eyes. They picked oranges and lemons for me and gave me a huge branch of scented wisteria blossom.

On Easter Sunday the Chief said I could go to early church and have the whole day off. I woke soon after 6 am. The whole day was mine! In George Street, I picked up a tram for St Andrew's Church, decorated for Easter with lemon chrysanthemums and pale gold tritoemas. After the service I had a milkshake then bought a ticket to Katoomba in the Blue Mountains.

The countryside was burnt yellow, with here and there a small holding with cattle huddling under the shade of a few gum trees. There had been a drought here for seven years.

Presently the country became more wooded and we climbed among hills densely covered with bush, gum and scrub in all shades of blue. At 3,336 feet stood Katoomba, a cheerful town which in some ways reminded me of Ryde in the Isle of Wight. I took a bus to the Three Sisters where there was a magnificent view looking 700 feet into the valley below, over miles of blue green forest and hills with clouds like shadows on an enormous lake. No wonder they were called the Blue Mountains.

After lunch in Katoomba I wandered among the fern trees, some up to 25 feet high, and heard now and then the laugh of a laughing jackass. Long strips of bark peeled from the gum trees leaving silver patches on their trunks and the path was strewn with crimson sickle leaves. It was quite cold.

Later I caught the 4 pm train back to Sydney, which was packed, but I sat on the platform behind the coal truck and ate my hamburger and fruit as the Blue Mountains faded into blue dusk.

We were in Sydney for another fortnight and I was busy the whole time working on fan engines, bilge valves, steam valves and watertight doors. But I managed to get ashore most evenings, although the Second tried to prevent me when he could. They were busy unloading the explosives most of the time we were there.

On 26th April a cargo worker fell in the dock and was drowned, and on May Day the cargo workers were all on strike and the military had to unload the cargo. This meant that when I went ashore the customs officials usually sent a man with me in case there was trouble with the strikers. One night I came back from dinner at the Boltons carrying a huge bouquet of red zinnias, roses and dahlias, and the strikers kept calling out, "Cheerio, sister! Give me one for May Day!" I think they must have thought I was a most militant Communist.

After they had unloaded the explosives they started on the bags of soda ash, which blew all over the place. I heard on 3rd May that seven ships had been torpedoed and sunk off the east coast of Australia that week. These things should not have made me nervous because when one's number is up, that is it. But they did.

Our bathroom on the ship was unusable for a time and none of the hotels on shore would let me have a bath.

"Is it an unusual request?" I asked.

"Most unusual," they told me.

One night about 10 pm I was all washed and clean and ready for bed when the Bosun came and said a pin had come out of the valve gear on one of the forward winches. The soldier who was working on the winch said, "I am a trained mechanic."

What luck, I thought, and replied, "Well, this job is nothing to you, you slip in the pin," and so I got the job done without getting dirty.

The next day we sailed to Newcastle, which took about 5 hours. It was a lovely day with bright sun and powder blue sky. We were keeping a careful lookout for submarines, but all we saw were jolly porpoises, their round backs bouncing through the waves

We were berthed in Newcastle by 6.45 pm, but by the time I had washed and had dinner, there was just enough evening left to take a walk along the quay. The next day I was working on deck all day and we were coaling hard all that time, so that there was a thick black fog round us, but I could still see that Newcastle was an attractive place with wooden houses and forests surrounding the harbour.

We saw more porpoises on the 12th when we returned to Sydney, and the men were very cheerful, saying, "Our nose is pointed the right way now, for home!" When we arrived I had the same old trouble with the Second, who simply would not let me go ashore, and kept me hanging about till half-past seven. However, the moment I could I dashed ashore and caught the ferry to the Boltons where I spent the evening relaxing by the fire.

The next day it rained and was cold and dark when I went on stand-by at 6.30. When I came out of the engine room at tea time we were clear of Sydney Heads in a small convoy of fourteen ships accompanied by a destroyer. We headed into stormy weather and of course the bilges gave trouble, so I was soaking wet and chilled after a 6 hour stint and delighted with the hot roast chicken they had kept for me from supper. We had been rolling and plunging through huge seas with scudding icy rain and kept on losing sight of the convoy in the mist and waves. After two days there was no convoy in sight but we could see land.

When I came up at 9 am there was a ship alongside us and we were found.

Sunday was a beautiful day and after breakfast I asked the Chief if I could go ashore. "Yes," he told me, "but you'd better mention it to the Second."

When I did, however, he shouted at me worse than ever, "Get out and bloody well stay out!"

Such rudeness seemed to me uncalled for, so I told the Chief.

"Think no more of it," he said. "Run away ashore."

And so I did. I caught the bus to Perth over the Swan River and along King's Gardens. In Perth I caught another bus up to the hills, past the orange orchards and vines and into wattle and big gum trees. At Waterman's Bay, a lovely bay of white sand with little rocky coves, sponges, red seaweed and shells, I talked to a fisherman who told me to go to the caves where I would find good shells. The tops of the low cliffs were covered with pink-flowered pelargoniums and silver leafed plants of cotton lavender. I went to Evensong at St George's Cathedral and the bishop preached about travellers and wanderers, which I thought very suitable.

On 7th June we sailed on our own for Durban, nearly a three week voyage. The seas were cold and the ship was rolling, though there were flashes of sunshine and on occasion beautiful sunsets and sunrises. We saw a lot of albatrosses, some of the crew had never seen one before, and once we saw whales spouting in the distance. We had twelve Australian passengers on board and a sweet little spaniel with a blue nose, who reminded me of Glen. I made a press for my flowers and saw nothing but sea, sea and sea. We seemed safe enough sailing without a convoy.

On 26th June the water became green and milky and I could smell land. After anchoring in the bay we came and tied up alongside at Bluff, Durban, where we finished with engines at 3.42 pm. I was quietly washing my hair when the pump for the starboard auxiliary condenser stuck and I had to dash down to mend it.

However, the next day I was due to go ashore and visit some of my relations who lived near Durban. Charles Smythe, son of my grandmother's sister Emily, had emigrated to South Africa in the last century and had fourteen children, and now there were at least 34 grandchildren who were all my Second cousins. I rang up the family home, Strathearn, and spoke to Effie Smythe. She said she would spread the word of my arrival round. Another cousin, Adrienne, said she would meet me in Drummond, so I got a train and was met by Cousin Elaine who took me to her bungalow surrounded by scarlet poinsettias.

Adrienne arrived after tea and we set off through the Valley of the Thousand Hills, where everlasting flowers and oranges grew wild by the road, so of course we stopped and picked some. After winding through crumpled green velvet hills we came to Pietermaritzburg and their comfortable house where we had dinner and sat by the fire, telling fortunes and eating sweets.

On 4th July Adrienne drove me up to Strathearn, climbing all the way. The country was all shades of brown with yellow patches here and there. There were cattle, white ibis, wattle and gum woods, which had formerly been used for pit props in the mines. A large hawk skimmed over and we saw a vulture in a tree and a 360 feet high waterfall. Strathearn was a red brick, red roofed bungalow, with verandas round and large trees. There was a very warm welcome from all the assembled cousins. There seemed to be hundreds of them, but we only sat down twelve for lunch, which for them, I suppose, must have seemed very few. The drawing room had muslin curtains and rather collapsed sofas from Methven, and a lot of Perthshire prints hung in the passage. The best room of the house was the store room, full of hanging hams and shelves of jam and bottled fruits, and parcels of salted bacon. Afterwards Adrienne drove me back to her home for tea after which I returned to the ship by bus.

After coaling we left Durban on 9th July as commodore ship in a convoy. All day we hugged the coast, blues and greens and stretches of white beach, and I worked at intervals on the tunnel watertight door plate, the super heat drain valves and the broken ashpit door. There were eleven ships in the convoy and we picked up another ship at Port Elizabeth and got to the Cape of Good Hope without incident.

On 16th July I was working till 12 pm and after my lunch, I still did not know whether I should be able to knock off or not, so I appeared in my boiler suit at 12.50 pm, when at last the Second said I could knock off. Little did he realise that I was changed into my shore clothes underneath. I dashed ashore and did my shopping, still buying things like jellies, tea and stockings, and then took a taxi to where the Hedgehog was buried. It was a peaceful spot, very well kept, with flowers and cool trees. There was a plain granite coping round it engraved with the words:

MALCOLM CHARLES QUAYLE, DIED 13 APRIL 1928, ANCHISES, LIVERPOOL.

I stood for a long time in that quiet garden, thinking of other voyages and other days. Then I got back to Cape Town and took a bus to Camps Bay where I walked on the white sand, watching the rollers, thinking of the wide oceans of the world. I thought of the great company of the dead, who lived on some other shore, and yet in my mind they lived as clearly as when I had last seen them. It seemed inconceivable that I should go back to Cape Town and find the *Perseus* and not the *Anchises* with the bright face of the dear Hedgehog waiting to greet me. I knew it was not so, but just for a moment I could not believe it.

Then I went into a Chinese restaurant, the Purple Cherry, and what should I see but my photo cut from the papers and pinned to the wall. They asked me to do them the honour of staying to supper with them and the owner told my fortune with tea leaves and insisted on loading me with oranges and shells. Seeing me arrive with all my parcels, the police at the gate gave me a lift back to the ship. Only when I got back on deck did I really believe that it was the *Perseus* and not the *Anchises*.

On Saturday 17th July we sailed, and four of the crew were very nearly left behind and had to do a pierhead jump just as we were casting off. I thought we would just be moving out to the bay to wait for a convoy, but instead we were full away by 12 noon with Table Mountain, Devil's Peak and the Lion's Head melting away blue into the distance and the white waves curling back on the sides of the ship as she clove through the water.

Now there were no more albatrosses, only molly hawks. The work continued heavier than ever, though Chips and some of the sailors helped me. I had a poisoned finger and sometimes I did not break for lunch as I was too hot and black, and just drank coffee. When I had time off I sat on the hatch feeling browned off and cross, determined to leave the ship when she got back to Liverpool and not do another voyage on her. It was perhaps as well for me that I did, for she was torpedoed and sunk by a submarine in the Indian Ocean on 16th January 1944. The fortune teller in Cape Town had told me she saw a ship lying helpless, but a new appointment was coming for me. Perhaps I had known in my bones, but I certainly knew that the voyage had gone sour on me.

We crossed the Line and I lay on deck and began to feel better. On 1st August when I came out from breakfast there was a big armed merchant cruiser. I thought privately she might be a raider and I think the rest of the crew did, too. However we ran up a signal and she answered it by flash. So that was all right. Later, about 11 am, a camouflaged plane flew over and circled us once or twice, but then she flew away, too.

On 3rd August it was pouring heavily with tropical rain and I was in the store room when Stores came in. "The Old Man is looking through glasses at two objects on the horizon," he said. "He thought they were subs."

So I came out on deck and looked. Chips and the Bosun and the Captain's Steward were all looking. It turned out to be one of ours and the other object was a carpet!

At 4 pm, Stores came bursting in again, "Land ahead!" So again we rushed on deck and there were the lights of Freetown. It was very hot indeed and I lay on deck on a deck chair under the stars, thinking, "Well, that's another lap of the voyage got through safely."

It was very hot at Freetown and there was quite a lot of work, as usual. The bum boats were round the ship most days and I got some lines for fishing from them and arranged for someone to bring me a lizard skin. We took about 400 tons of coal altogether, which didn't seem enough to me.

The river where we were lying was about as wide as the Thames at Gravesend. The town side was all hills and the other side swamp with blue grey palms. The river was salty, a strong greenish colour and very warm. One day I saw the men all swimming round the ship joking and laughing and holding on to an old lifeboat. "We are survivors!" they called out.

There were marvellous sunsets, but very often it poured with rain, tropical deluges. But that didn't stop the bum boats, which came round crowded with people who rowed with long swings, umbrellas up, chanting as they rowed. Some of the boats had brightly coloured handkerchiefs on sticks as flags. I bargained with soap for baskets and a small bunch of bananas which I hoped to take home.

We left on 14th August in pouring rain and when I came up after a long hard stand-by we were right out in convoy and the west coast of Africa was a mountainous green blue, fast being lost in steamy clouds.

We passed Cape Verde and Dakar on 17th August and it was very hard work and boiling hot. I ended up in a proper sweat and the man working with me was quite done in. One night I sat on deck after dinner listening to the gramophone until the Mate stopped it. "The submarines might hear it," he said. A naval commander who was a passenger said, "I never heard such nonsense! Submarines haven't got bat's ears!"

Another day I had trouble with the Store Keeper. As I was working on the leaking deck exhaust pipe, the Store Keeper walked past with about ten men to put down the watertight doors.

"Come on," I said, struggling with the pipe, "give us a lift."

Two of them pushed forward to help, but as they did so, the Store Keeper shouted from the main deck, "Come on! None of that. I won't allow that."

"Awful cheek," I said to them. "You'd better go on," as I didn't want to make trouble.

On 25th August the deck started on gun watches and we changed course and headed westward. I thought we were still off the African coast, somewhere near Casablanca. I saw a bird which looked like a hoopoe flying over the ship and next day the ships of the Gibraltar convoy joined us in the morning, so I saw my guess had been right. At 10 am, a destroyer came alongside and asked if we wanted to go in to Gib for coal. We had very little coal indeed, so at 3 pm on 27th August we left the convoy and with two destroyers proceeded to Gibraltar.

It was a great disappointment to us all, as we felt we were so nearly home. Still, I thought, one must never be too disappointed about anything and just take things in one's stride. It was a funny sight to see the great convoy of 60 ships sailing off in the other direction for home while we were outward bound again. It was perfectly still and as the light faded, the destroyers gleamed out pale and grey in the descending darkness until finally, with the Great Bear overhead for company, we steamed on alone.

The passengers were cross and depressed, as they had all thought they would be getting home. I tried to buck them up and cut my coconut on deck into a tortoise shape. We would have gone into Lisbon, but that would have meant dismantling the guns. On 29th August we saw an outward bound convoy of fourteen ships taking up position; many of them troop ships.

On 30th August there was a call for stand-by at 5.45 am and when I came on deck it was quite dark and the light of Cape Trafalgar shone out brightly. When I came up again at 8 am, we were in Gibraltar Bay, and there was the dear old Rock. There were quite a lot of ships about, the blue lines of Africa on one hand, and the dried brown hills of Spain on the other. That night was quite lively, with depth charges going off all round us, searchlights crossing the sky and flares illuminating the bay.

On 31st August we saw one boat shooting at a swimmer. They came out from Spain to fix small torpedoes on the keels and blow up the ships or damage them severely. A diver went down to see if there was one on ours in the middle of the night and again at breakfast time. He found a split in the first after keel plate. We went in alongside that day and all the passengers went ashore. I felt fed up at not getting ashore, since we had been cooped up on board for over six weeks.

There were nothing but depth charges all night that night, too. Some of them seemed right under the ship and shook me to bits. I said goodbye to Commander Jackson who was trying to get a lift home in an aeroplane and gave him messages to take home for me. All day I was working at stores and sorting tools, even when we moved in alongside, and although all the passengers went ashore there was no shore leave for the crew.

On Friday they dragged under the ship with a diver as they thought there might be a torpedo attached to the keel. There were a lot of splits on the ship's bottom, but no torpedo. They were holding special prayers for the fourth anniversary of the start of the war and I wished we could have gone ashore for that. I thought back to those halcyon days at Avonmead and the hurried rush back to join the ARP, of Mummy and dear Glen being driven to safety. It all seemed so long ago.

Next afternoon I heard on the wireless that we had invaded Italy. As I sat on deck, listening to gramophone records and trying to sketch Gibraltar, it was a real picnic with heavy gunfire, more depth charges, planes flying over and searchlights from the Rock.

We did not get ashore on Saturday as we were sailing, though the foreman of the coal workers brought me some fruit. The bananas I got in Freetown had not lasted and I had to throw some of them away. The coal worker brought the fruit from Spain wrapped in a checked handkerchief. After a long stand-by we were into convoy by 7.30 and when I came up there were the lights of Cintra and the Straits of Gibraltar with a rose pink blush across the sky.

It was cold and rolling in the bay and as we went ever northwards it became cooler and cooler. On 12th September the danger flag was up on the Commodore Ship and there were depth charges, so it must have been a submarine.

And so after eight months of going round the world we sailed back safely into Liverpool where I had the herculean task of getting all my parcels, food, boxes and luggage back to London. Even getting through the Customs with so much stuff was a considerable job, but luckily Jean had got the Lambeth WVS to write and explain about the food for the Queen Victoria's Girls Club. Transporting everything to London was not easy either. When I got to Restormel House where Jean and Frances had their flat, I found that half of this had been bombed away, although their flat itself was all right. It shook something dreadful when there were bombs though.

We had so much to talk about, so much to plan, practically a whole year had passed since we had all been together. Mummy had recovered from her illness and all was well at Megginch. Hugo and Leila had a little daughter, Sarah. We also had to plan our special Lambeth children's party on 31st October with all the goodies from our kind friends in Virginia who had plied me with largesse. The food was a huge success–fruit, tea, cocoa, marmalade and candy, all the children ate sweets which for some of them had only been a dream. Afterwards we had a conjuror and the children presented me with a writing case and gave three cheers for the ladies of Virginia.

And there were the presents I had somehow carried home right round the world: warm overcoats for Jean and Frances from New York, frocks, watches, scent, jumpers, stockings, books, face creams and powder, presents from Virginia, Australia and Durban. There was melon and ginger jam, lemon marmalade, pineapple jam, honey, biscuits, flour, dried fruit, sugar, jellies and chocolates. My seaman's cases and bags were like magic cornucopias.

The Mate was now Captain of a ship, the *Flowerdale*, based in Hull. I went to see him several times that autumn, but he did not have a vacancy for a Second Engineer on his ship and after my very long voyage, I was not really ready to sail again. Besides, I had never felt the same towards him after the dreadful voyage on the *Danae II*.

By January 1944 however, I was back on the familiar old trail of hawking my credentials round the shipping companies, trying to get a job. The bombing continued, but it was different. Now there were doodle-bugs, those horrible mechanical flying bombs, and V2s, the giant rockets. For the first three months of 1944 I was travelling up and down to the docks, to Liverpool, to any company who would see me or give me an interview. No one would have me.

Then in April I got a job as Assistant Engineer on the *MV Karabagh*. I first met Captain Charlton at the gate of the Board of Trade at Tilbury on 10th April 1944, where we signed on to the *Karabagh* together and then went to a cafe at Tilbury Station and became friends at once.

We first sailed to Onega in the White Sea, a mission so secret that we were not even told where we were going and so had no really thick clothes. I was only saved by my fur lined, zip boots, which I had the forethought to pack with me. Even though it was light until quite late, the weather was bitterly cold. When I went ashore quite a crowd collected. I think they were surprised to see a British woman on a ship. What intrigued them most were my zip boots, they kept pulling up and down the zips. One little Russian girl came back the next day with a silver kitten with silver eyes which she wished me to take. Of course it led to all sorts of problems, a very expensive six month quarantine among others, but I found Silver too attractive to resist and eventually he settled with us in London.

I signed off on my return at Portsmouth on 22nd May and the same day signed on again as Fourth Engineer. We were now getting ready for the invasion of Europe, but our work was so secret that I was not even allowed to write news or give an address to my sisters. However, I was able to see Mummy at Fleet and Auntie Allie Rockley, who lived quite near Bournemouth. Sometimes Jean or Frances would meet me at Fleet, bringing essential things like strong patches for boiler suits, henna shampoo (my hair was beginning to lose its original colour, but I was determined to keep it as it had always been), plimsolls, strong cotton, writing paper and envelopes.

From Portsmouth we moved to the Isle of Wight and anchored off Cowes. I would sometimes go ashore with Captain Charlton and explore the twisty streets and red roofed houses, the air smelling of flowers and seaweed, and everywhere the calling of gulls. It seemed amazingly peaceful in the midst of wartime. Captain Charlton lent me books which I read in the intervals of doing my embroidery.

While we were waiting in harbour for the invasion to begin I started to do an embroidery map of the world with the British Empire marked in red. Later we had it framed and hung in our flat, but it always reminded me of those days of intense strain when we were waiting for the invasion to begin.

From D Day on 6th June when the beachhead was established we were on "Special Ops", which meant ferrying stuff back and forwards to Europe. We called ourselves the "Smugglers", for we sailed at night to avoid enemy attention, slipping past the coast line lit by moonlight. It was a difficult and dangerous time as there were enemy planes everywhere, although the submarine menace had been gradually contained by the British. There were still mines. Captain Charlton was a very nice man to sail under and I was gaining valuable experience with a motor vessel.

On 9th September we moved off "Special Ops" and I was back on my rounds looking for a job again. Mr Freeman, my old friend at the Blue Funnel Line, had now retired but still looked in at the office occasionally and I hoped to get a job through him.

To my great joy, through the kind offices of Mr and Mrs Horton, director of Trewent and Proctor, I was able to get back on the *Karabagh* under Captain Charlton on 16th April 1945 as Third Engineer. It had been a very sad winter for us all, for Hugo had been killed in his tank in Holland on 17th February 1945. Curiously, I had dreamt about him so vividly that night; he had been waving to me from the turret of his tank, "Don't worry, I'm all right, Aunt Victoria!" he shouted. It was so clear I remembered it when I woke up. But he wasn't all right.

The *Karabagh* was moving round the south coast, and finally settled at Newport, Monmouth, where I was working under a new Chief. There was a great deal of work and I often did not finish till 2 am in the morning. We thought we were getting ready to go to Europe, but we did not know.

Occasionally at Newport I was able to take days ashore with Captain Charlton. One day we drove to Tintern Abbey through the Wye Valley. The wet primroses, violets and wild cherry blossom dripped in the April downpour, serving to bring out more strongly the scents of spring. That was the day he asked me to marry him. I did not know the answer—neither then nor years later. I had wondered often about the Mate; if he had not been married to Mrs Warner, would I have married him? I did not think so, since our friendship, though close, was more that of two shipmates sharing dangers. His Northern Irish temper flared as quickly as my Scottish one. No, I do not think I would have married him. If it had been my dear Hedgehog and there had been no Mrs Quayle, there would have been no doubt in my mind. Earlier still, if my cousin Hamish Murray had asked me at the ball in Edinburgh I should have said yes. But he was not the marrying kind. And after all these years at sea, I did not think I was either.

And yet...and yet...I was so fond of Captain Charlton. He had a kind of calm seriousness which the Romans called gravitas; we shared so many things in common, our minds were so in tune. So I said, "Not no, but maybe." And we talked of other things. He did not ask me again.

In the end we did sail for Europe and were lying off Antwerp when victory was declared. We were loaded with 10,000 tons of high aviation spirit, so when the other ships let off rockets and tracer bullets to celebrate we had to signal to them to stop because of our cargo.

"You would make a fine bonfire!" they signalled back with joie de vivre.

But I didn't think so, as I thought we would just have gone up and forgotten to come down.

Because of our cargo we couldn't celebrate much, but we threw boxes overboard and shot at them with service rifles for a bottle of rum. I came in second.

"Well done, Miss Drummond," said Captain Charlton, and I felt quite pleased at that, and quite pleased, too, that I had survived the war.

I thought of Hugo and of my friends on the *Har Zion* and on the *Perseus*, and all our many friends lost in the Lambeth raids, and of other cousins and other wars. But I was alive, Jean and Frances had survived and we had won the war.

Everybody was drinking everybody else's health and the hooters and sirens were going on all the ships. The war was over!

Chapter Fifteen
Sailing in a World of Change - 1945-51

After we left Antwerp we sailed to Kiel. We were the first ship into Kiel after the war and Captain Charlton had orders to shoot the German pilot who was taking us through the canal if there was any funny business. Luckily there wasn't. We had mine sweepers searching for mines ahead of us as we went up the North Sea, which made us feel quite important.

It was dreadful in Kiel. It was flattened, bombed to bits, and there were ten million marks to the pound. There was also a lot of typhoid about and we were told not to go ashore, but of course I did. I walked over to the Baltic one evening to see if I could find amber on the beach. It was beginning to get dark as I came back through a wood and suddenly I heard a sharp whistling sound as something just cleared my head. It was a bullet from a sniper which missed me by a hair's breadth. I returned very quickly to the *Karabagh*. After that I didn't go ashore again.

We were to escort the German prize ships over to the Forth. They had German crews and Royal Naval ratings and we were the Commodore ship in the convoy. It was rough on the way over and when I was drilling a piece of brass, I slipped and it got in my hand. As soon as we arrived at Grangemouth, I had to go to Falkirk Infirmary to have it taken out. They gave me local anaesthetic, but it took 6 hours to cut it out.

I signed off and on again at Grangemouth on 18th June, and from there we sailed straight over to Houston, Texas, where we arrived in July. I had all sorts of plans for repeating my shopping successes in the *Perseus*, but here things were rather more difficult as you had to have points in order to buy canned fruit or sugar, and there were no radios to be had for love nor money. However, I was able to get a navy suit for Jean, and some light woollen things for Frances and Mummy, which I knew would prove popular.

I loved the Southern states which were hot and Spanish, and I was able to get ashore on the beautiful Gulf beaches and walk in the unspoilt country full of wild flowers, such a contrast from the terrible devastation I had seen at Kiel. On these outings it was hard to believe we were only 300 miles from the test site of the atomic bomb.

When we left Texas we sailed straight back to the Mersey, which is where we were for V J Day, but could not celebrate properly as we were on sea

224

watches, preparing to sail again for the Persian Gulf. I signed off here on 22nd August and after some leave rejoined the ship at Birkenhead on 18th September.

Our first destination was the Bouches du Rhone, where we were due to discharge our cargo of benzene and petrol from Texas. There was always trouble with the engines of the *Karabagh* and we had a breakdown at sea before arriving at the Bouches du Rhone on 27th November. We went into the Port de Boux for repairs.

One Sunday I decided to go ashore, so I left the ship and walked along the Rhone from Port de Boux to Martiques. On my way back it began to get dark and I got lost. Suddenly, to my horror, I found that I was lost in a minefield. All round me were notices saying "Danger!" and "Defendu!". The only way out seemed to be to go on, so on I went, over high heather and scrub rosemary, all through the minefield. At the other end was a 16 feet fence which dropped into an oil refinery. Of course if it hadn't been so pitch dark I might have found my way quite easily. I found a chemist on duty in the refinery who gave me directions back to the high road.

"Where have you come from?" he asked me, and when I explained and pointed out the way I had come through the minefield, he exclaimed, "Oh no, that is impossible! You cannot have come through the minefield!"

"But I have," I told him.

He still would not believe me.

However, despite the chemist's kind directions, my adventures were not yet finished, for I still had to walk a mile along a pipeline, through a bog at the other end where there were 10 feet deep bomb holes full of water, and over a double barbed wire fence. And so eventually, still clutching the little fig book for Mummy in my hand, I arrived safely back at the *Karabagh*.

The Superintendent had to fly out and inspect the damage to the *Karabagh*, and only after it was mended were we were able to set off across the Mediterranean to Haifa and then to Port Said.

When we were in Port Said I slipped on a patch of grease in the engine room and broke a couple of ribs; one was broken in three places. Of course I did not know that at the time, nor how much damage had been done, only that it was extremely sore. Captain Charlton was sent for at once and he was marvellous as he placed them perfectly in position and strapped them up. When we got through the canal to Abadan where we were to load petrol, I was sent up to the hospital for X-rays. Afterwards the Matron invited me to her house for tea and it was most interesting hearing about Iran.

We celebrated Christmas and New Year on board, while at home Jean and Frances were busy moving into another house in the Kennington Road, as Restormel House had finally been demolished. The new house was called Tresco, just a bit further up the road from the Girls' Club at 160.

It was a Regency house with a pillared porch, three storeys and a basement, standing back from the road with a small garden on either side of the path facing the street. It also had a larger area of garden at the back with a huge lime tree and some old figs, although the rest of it mostly seemed to consist of piles of old tins and bottles and a bomb crater. They managed to take the same telephone number with them which we had had ever since we rented the studio.

From Abadan we sailed back to Liverpool where we arrived on 12th February 1946. So much damage had been done to the *Karabagh* that she had to be laid up for extensive repairs. Captain Charlton had already gone on leave, and it was while he was away that the First Officer, who had been biding his time for just such an opportunity, laid me off. It was bitterly cold, the end of February and I had to leave the ship in a snowstorm. If only, I thought, Captain Charlton had still been there it would never have happened. I got soaked through and remained wet in the train all the way to London; when I arrived at Tresco I had a fearful cold and chill. Even worse was that it went to the spot on my lung which had developed after I broke my ribs and I became really ill.

Frances and Jean put me to bed in Tresco, a cosy room upstairs with a gas fire which they kept burning, and ran up and downstairs with trays of hot soup and coffee. Somehow I felt I should never be warm or well again. For two months I shivered and felt low like a poor, cold monkey and then gradually I began to recover. I must not be got down, I told myself. Now was a splendid opportunity to take my Second's Motor Examination; I had been so long on the *Karabagh* that I knew almost as much about motor vessels as I did about steam and this was surely another step towards being made a Chief.

So I settled down in my cosy room at Tresco and worked. Frances, Jean and I each had a bedroom on the top floor. Frances had painted hers green, her favourite colour, and Jean's was blue. There was also a bathroom. On the first floor there were two more bedrooms and a very large drawing-room which Frances planned to decorate in blue and cream. There was also the sitting room with a gas fire round which we sat in the evenings. The cosiest room of the house was the bright yellow kitchen. When one switched on the light it seemed like walking into a blazing summer's day. All the furniture was yellow, so were the plates, and there was a bowl of fruit and vegetables so artistically arranged that it always seemed a pity to touch them. Here, too, lived the resident household gods Coal, Sugar and Silver, which I had brought back from Onega. Coal was a black fluffy cat with golden eyes, inclined to bite, and Sugar was a huge white cat with deep yellow eyes and an affectionate nature. She allowed herself to be cuddled like a dog.

My room upstairs was always flooded with evening sunshine and outside I could see the lime tree in the garden bursting into yellow-green leaf.

The garden was full of daffodils planted by Frances to brighten my home-coming. They had paved over the old tins and begun to make a pond in part of the bomb crater. Some of the golden privet from the studio had been brought for a hedge in the front garden.

I took the exam in May and passed on my Second attempt, but it was too late to sail on the *Karabagh* which left on the 23rd. I could have kicked myself. There I was with my new Second's Motor Examination and no ship to sail on. My only hope was to wait until she came back from that voyage and try to join her again. So I went to see Mr Coward, the owner of the *Karabagh*, after I passed my exam. I told him I would take a temporary job and wait to rejoin the *Karabagh* when she came back from her voyage.

I marched with the Merchant Navy in the Victory Parade on 8th June, which was a great honour, and had lunch with them afterwards, meeting many old friends. Frances and our friends the Wilsons had special seats in the stand and Miranda Wilson, their grand-daughter, said she recognised Aunt Victoria from the picture in the programme.

Money was once again running very short, so I had to find a job of some kind. I was offered a job sailing as Second on two ships, but I turned them down as I feared it would mean that I would not be in Britain when the *Karabagh* returned. For the same reason I turned down two offers to go to the States and ferry vessels back. Curious, I thought, the thing I had once wanted to do more than anything and now, for different reasons, I felt unable to accept.

Once more my old friends from the Blue Funnel Line came to my rescue. They had two 10,000 ton vessels under construction at the Caledon Yard in Dundee and wanted me to come and supervise. It was a marvellous opportunity and I could stay once more at Megginch, where I had not been for eleven years.

It was funny coming back to this place I loved so much, especially as I had been away a long time. The house seemed curiously shabby when I returned—the garden overgrown and out of hand, and Violet and John had changed and grown older. Violet's hair was quite grey and John was very fat.

Another rather awkward thing was my lack of money. I only had 12/- on me and a season bus ticket for a month to Dundee cost £1 10/-. Until I was paid by the Blue Funnel I was going to be rather stuck. Fortunately James Gardiner, the butler, was back from the war so I was able to borrow money from him without losing face.

It was cold and wet to begin with, but I had a nice office in Dundee to work in, though most of my time was spent in the yards looking at the ships. Gradually I became more solvent again. The weather also improved and the country began to smell of new mown hay, bean fields and wildflowers. There was marvellous honeysuckle on the Kingdom hedge, yellow and sweet scented, and every hedgerow was alive with wild roses. The talk at Megginch was all of farming and the prospects of harvest. Violet was busy with the soft fruit and I helped her sometimes in the late summer evenings. Time seemed to telescope so that, sitting among the scented leaves in the walled kitchen garden, I could not quite believe that I should not find Mummy and Nana Watt distilling rose water when I came into the house and Papa shouting from the front hall.

I went to see the old Drummond-Hay cousins at St Kessoggs and visited many old friends and acquaintances. I spent a lovely day with Hamish Murray, who took me round Blair and showed me the family pictures and told me all the stories. Afterwards we had dinner at Easter Moncreiffe, where he was living, and walked in the garden and looked at the wet roses. Hamish played me old Scottish songs on the gramophone and they were beautiful, but made me feel sad. I loved my day with him, every single second of it, and when I got home I walked through the dusk to Lady Charlotte's garden in the shrubbery by the Beech Walk and smelt her rose, glimmering whitely in the summer night, and thought of many things.

When my job in Dundee finished at the end of July I was quite sorry to leave Megginch. Cherry and Heather had returned from school and the place livened up. I had even got used to the packs of dachshunds and cats which seemed to roam everywhere, and I had come to enjoy my evenings with Violet picking black currants and my talks with John about his new schemes. He was now renting an island on the west coast to grow seed potatoes free from disease.

I was back in London when the *Karabagh* came in and I met Captain Charlton. He told me that there was no chance of my being taken on for the next voyage as the engineering crew were remaining the same. It did not deter me. I decided to go on taking temporary jobs and try to get on the *Karabagh* when she came back for her next voyage.

In September I was relieving for Cunard on the *SS St Margaret*. She was bright and modern, and Mr Richards, the relieving Chief, was very kind. Although the appointment had come through the pools, I suspected the moving force behind it had been Lord Howard de Walden, a distant cousin who from time to time had helped me on in my career.

I spent much of my time on these short relieving jobs until the following spring when I managed to get a job as Second Engineer on the *MV Hickory Mount*. A 4,500 ton vessel, she sailed on 25th May 1947 from Fowey to Philadelphia with a cargo of china clay. The accommodation was marvellous, my room was 12 feet square with a full sized bed and hot and cold water. But the ship was an awful sea boat, as both the engines and accommodation were aft, and she rolled terribly in bad weather. I had never been in a ship that rolled so badly; I felt when she rolled everything would come back.

We arrived in Philadelphia in June but did not know the duration of our stay, nor the mode of our return. In fact we were more or less stuck in the mud, or at any rate at Pier 34 South. I was receiving £10 a week, but would not get paid until we got home. The Captain would not advance me any dollars out of my pay and only gave out the meanest of subs. This meant I was hardly able to do any of the shopping I had planned to replenish our depleted wardrobes. However, I slipped ashore and telephoned our cousin Jackie Cecil, who kindly sent me some dollars, which I repaid with English currency in his London bank account. Although I still walked everywhere and picked up things as cheaply as I could, his loan made a lot of difference.

In July, Frances took Cherry to Amsterdam to stay with the de Booys. It was her first trip abroad and she loved the trip over to the Hook of Holland. I was very envious as all July I was stuck in the mud at a pier in Philadelphia. There was a lot of work to do overhauling the engines and it was terribly hot and muggy.

By 8th August we were still stuck in Philadelphia. I had not been able to go down and stay with Jackie for a weekend, as the fare seemed too expensive, but I had once been down to Norfolk to see Julia and Josephine and up to New York to see Betty Richardson. We toured Radio City, visited the beautiful gardens and looked in all the shops. I bought some strawberry patterned material to make curtains and bedcovers for one of the rooms at Tresco and some strawberry patterned china.

Rumours of what was to happen to us went backwards and forwards, but in the meantime we worked on the engines. With the terrific heat we had some terrible thunderstorms, white sheet lightning and almost tropical rain. Finally by 6th September it was decided that the *Hickory Mount* would be sold and remain in Philadelphia. The Captain and Second Mate, the Chief and Third Engineer would stay on while the Mate and I took back all the Indian crew. We had to take them back by train from Philadelphia to Halifax, which took two nights and one day, and then we were to come home on the *Aquitania*. By this time I had spent all my money and had bags, suitcases and crates. Besides the clothes, there was Campbells' chicken soup, chicken and plum puddings in tins, jellies and fudge tartlets and chocolate fudge mix. I was determined to have a proper Christmas when we got to London. I had not realised, however, that we would not be fed on the 36 hour train journey to Halifax.

We were given absolutely nothing to eat and I had not a cent left with which to buy anything. Of course it did not worry the crew, who sat on the floor of the railway carriage making up fires and cooking curry and rice and chapatties. They were all going back to India when they got back to Britain, and for them this had been the job of a lifetime, so they missed no opportunity to take souvenirs. Every fitting that could be patiently and carefully unscrewed from the train was removed. Every time the Mate and I managed to extract the handle, or mirror, or whatever it was, and screw it back into place, someone behind us had unscrewed something else. There were 57 of them and it was like holding back the tide. Besides, except for water, there was nothing for us to eat. I have never known a longer journey and it was 46 hours before we arrived at Halifax and boarded the *Aquitania*, where we were at last able to get a square meal.

When I arrived home, I spent a lot of time painting and getting the house into order. After my experience in 1946 I had no intention of taking a job which started on Christmas Day. We all enjoyed our Christmas house, the children's party with the things sent over from Virginia, the decorated trees and the delicious meals. Jean always had bowls of hyacinths out for Christmas and the smell was of spring in our sitting room.

By 3rd January 1948 I had joined the *MV Bancinu* at Falmouth as Second Engineer. She was due to sail to Paris, but we were not able to sail until the weather calmed down and it was very rough. However, the ship was warm and comfortable, and although she had been a good deal knocked about, everything was made of solid mahogany. She was a tiny little boat, smaller than a tug, but somehow did not seem so when one was on board. The Chief was Dutch and curiously enough I had met him during the war when I went from Amsterdam to Antwerp in a train.

Soon after we arrived, the Superintendent came down and looked her over. There was a great deal of work to be done to make her seaworthy, but it was blowing so hard that it did not look possible for us to start out. In fact, a dozen Spanish fishing boats came in to Falmouth for shelter from the gale with other boats. The weather continued bad and there were so many repairs that a week later we were still in port. I wrote to ask Jean and Frances to send me on all my forgets—two balls of coloured string and a leaflet on knotting belts so I could make some in my spare time, some quinine and mouth wash tablets and, most important of all, two tins of henna. These all arrived safely three days later and for the first time in ten days I was able to get ashore.

It was warm and mild, sea birds drifted in the wind and Spanish and Greek sailors from the weather bound boats walked about the town. One tried to go out that morning, but was driven back by the heavy seas. The trouble with going ashore was that the last boat back to the ship was at 4.30 pm. Also I had to stay on board as the Chief Engineer's girlfriend had arrived and he was based on shore.

We tried twice to get out, but were twice driven back by the bad weather. The third time we tried unsuccessfully was also unlucky for me because I broke my wrist and was not able to sail with her when she eventually set off.

I left the ship on 2nd February and was quite glad because I would not have liked to have crossed the Bay of Biscay in her. But on the other hand I was sorry because I was being paid £50 a month, and although £12 18/- was clawed back in income tax, it was still some money towards the up-keep of Tresco and Mummy's house in Fleet. I had broken so many things in my life that I knew the only thing to do was rest and lie up until the bone had mended, so this I did.

By 25th April I was Chief Engineer on the *Eastern Med*, which was to sail from Plymouth to the Mediterranean. She was a rotten old tub, built in 1909, and although I was now Chief I had to work really hard from 7 am till 5 pm every day. There was great difficulty getting hot water on the ship, so when we reached Gray's Wharf in London in early May, I made a special effort to run up to Mr Chapman to get my hair properly treated before the voyage.

The crew were Arabs which meant that one had to be very careful when Jews were around. We sailed from London to Famagusta in Cyprus which was gloriously hot and full of orange trees.

Cyprus reminded me of Gibraltar in 1944, there was heavy gunfire and it was not safe to go ashore. I left the ship on 2nd June in Famagusta and returned via the south of France. From here I travelled home by bus by way of Grenoble and Paris so as to be back at Tresco to see Julia Davis and Josephine Johnson who were visiting from Virginia.

When they arrived we hired a car and travelled up with Jean to Megginch, seeing friends and cousins on the way. We spent a week at Megginch and visited Edinburgh, St Andrews and all the beautiful sites of Perthshire and central Scotland. Jean had to travel south on the 17th, as her holidays were over, but Cherry took her place and we went northwards to Inverness, where Cherry picked up a Mr and Mrs Nairn who took us monster-hunting in their yacht up and down Loch Ness and round Castle Urquhart. Hamish Murray turned up trumps and took us all over Blair. He was enchanted with Cherry, whom he thought just like our ancestress Jean Drummond.

Julia and Josephine were enthusiastic about everything, the beauty of the Highlands, lochs and waterfalls, the sheep and cattle, the little stone cottages and dry stone dykes. Nothing tired them, nothing made them cross. After a really long and flagging day when Cherry and I were exhausted and only just able to get down to breakfast the next morning, we found Julia and Josephine bright-eyed and cheerful, already wearing their hats, having "done Warwick" before breakfast. They loved Tresco as well, saying it was like a London daughter of Megginch with all the charm of the old castle at home. I was glad that we had been able to repay some of their amazing kindness and generosity to me, and to the people of Lambeth, during the War.

On 22nd September 1948 I flew out to Malta to tidy up the *Alberto Gianpaolo*, which belonged to Lambert Brothers, once more as Chief Engineer. At first we were put up in the Hotel Regina, as the boat was not fit to stay on. The *Alberto Gianpaolo* had been lying neglected in dock for six months, before which she had come from Italy, where she had been on the bottom after being sunk in the war. It was lovely staying in the hotel since I was able to get ashore to have a bath and dinner after working on the boat all day.

However, when the ship was fit for a crew they all came on board and so did I. I was working very hard all the time, so there was little time to go ashore and shop or sightsee, although the shops were full of every sort of thing. Unfortunately, as always, money was very short and I had to buy lemonade as the water was so brackish. However, I bought lots of Malta weave table cloths and napkins for the Tresco kitchen, and a pottery tea set with a design of green leaves for £3. There was so much work to do on getting the ship ready to sail home that I was not able to do any of the delightful excursions I had planned. We sailed after about three weeks and went to Sfax in North Afric from where we sailed to Gibraltar and then home on 8th December for a nice long Christmas.

On 20th February 1949 I was on the go again, this time as Second Engineer on the *MV Lenamill*, which I joined in London. We sailed down the Mediterranean in the now familiar way, but had to put into Trieste for lengthy repairs. I disliked being Second again, having served as Chief, and did not like the Chief Engineer, who came from Donachadee in Northern Ireland. I found the work on the boat far too hard and did not want to go to Australia with her.

"You are here for two years," they told me, but I argued that I had only signed on for two or three months. I was to be paid £44 a month and wanted to get home for the summer so as to visit Olga Seydoux with Frances.

We arrived at Trieste on 10th March and there was a great deal of work to do on the ship, besides painting out the engine room. However, when I was able to get ashore it was bright and sunny, and I found the shops full of Easter eggs and artificial flowers. I had the usual difficulty of getting money, Frances and Jean kept sending me £1 notes in letters so that I was able to buy things. I sat in cafes drinking coffee and went once to Monfalcone, a village in the hills full of pink and green houses and a tiny church with a fresco of golden saints. In the square, chestnut buds were bursting and stone tables clustered outside the little inn. I could see anemone pulsatilla growing in the fields.

But, and of course there was an enormous but, I did not know where we were going, nor when. The Chief was almost impossible to get on with and a greaser told me that the last Second was so annoyed with him that he attacked him. He was constantly rude and swore at me. I finally said, "Stop it! I have had about enough!"

He said, "I hate having you here and I would not have done if the owner had not insisted. So I will take it out of you all I can."

"All right," I retorted, "get another Second."

I knew he was inexperienced, young and a poor officer, not knowing what to do next, so I imagined he would have difficulty.

"When you have learnt how to be Chief, I will be pleased to sail with you," I said.

I made up my mind that if it got any worse, I would go to the Consul and tell him that I wanted to leave the ship. I was determined to stay as long as I could, for the sake of the money.

The more I thought, the more certain I was that I must be paid off in Trieste before the ship left. I did not want to sail on her any more and I was also dubious about her cargo. There was certainly something funny going on. One of the greasers had jumped ship, as he could not stick the Chief, and I felt it was only a matter of time before the rest of the engine room crew left, too. When I joined I had been told it was a quick three month voyage to Bombay and back. Now we were stuck in Trieste and there was talk of going to Australia.

I went to the garrison church on Easter Sunday, which was like a little bit of England, filled with quiet English people, mostly in the services. They wore their tidy Sunday clothes and didn't speak to one another, all separate and aloof. Afterwards I went to the hills and walked from village to village, silver saints' frescoes outside and chestnuts, all in leaf. From there I got the funicular back to the town. It was so lovely having my picnic lunch among the alpine flowers, bright blue hyacinths under the trees and along the roadside dark purple anemones. And acres of blossom, first plum, then almond and peach, then pear and finally wisteria and early vine leaves.

My departure when it came was rather a blow. On 28th April 1949 they told the two remaining greasers they were to pay off that day. Then they told me to pay off at 10 am, I received only £16 after they had deducted income tax and money drawn, so I reckoned my pay was only $42 a month. Also they gave me £15 for my fare home, which did not include a sleeper although it was a 36-hour journey, and £1 for food and subsistence along the route. I decided to go to Venice, and then St Raphael to catch a bus to Paris where I planned to meet Frances at the Hotel d'Albion. I packed all my things into two large zip bags and a flour sack and sent them registered to Victoria Station. There were new clothes and old clothes mixed up and I buried some cacti among the dirty boiler suits and uniform. When I got to St Raphael it poured with rain and was cold, and I was not feeling well and thought I had been poisoned by the bad food and water. However, I had a lovely time in Paris with Frances and it cleared away all the nastiness of my time on the *Lenamill*.

Tresco was becoming quite a port of call now for all our friends. Cherry was there on and off for June and July, and Jock Lane, Margaret Cecil's son, also made it his London headquarters. I enjoyed having the young people coming and going with their hordes of young friends, and later we had Caroline Hughes and her daughter from Virginia. I took them up to Edinburgh and managed to fit in a visit to Hamish Murray, to whom I gave some of the sugar I had been sent from Virginia for his jam making activities. Later in the year we also had the de Booy family staying.

On 11th August I was off again, sailing as Chief Engineer on the 1,550 ton *SS Elsie Beth* of the Storship Transport Ltd from Barry. We first sailed to Spain and then to Portugal for Cork. We were back in Hull at the end of September, and on 1st October went right up north sailing into the Norwegian fjords. The water was lovely and clear, the weather fine. Even as Chief Engineer there was a lot to do, and after our arrival at Trondheim there proved a great deal of work on the engines, so that I was able to get ashore for only 2 hours on Saturday afternoon. All the shops shut at 3 pm on Saturday and there was not much time for shopping. Besides which, all clothes and some food were on rations, so it was difficult to get anything. Trondheim was a bright, clean place with painted wooden houses and streets lined with chestnut trees beginning to turn gold. Everyone was blue-eyed and fair-haired like Vikings, and so friendly. Every evening I went to a cafe where I had cakes, coffee and sandwiches.

We sailed north for Archangel to load wood for Dublin, but later altered course for Onega in the White Sea, where I had been during the war. On Trafalgar Day I went ashore, through the great wood yard and down the long lanes between two wood piles.

Twenty minutes walk brought me to the port gate and the woman sentry, complete with rifle in a faded khaki uniform, with whom I exchanged friendly greetings. Through the workers settlement I walked and straight along the road to Onega, bounded by woods for 5 miles. There were banks of bracken and yellowing grass beside the road, and in the wide streets of Onega the poplar leaves were falling green and yellow, lying flat on the wooden pavements.

These wide, grass-grown streets which had been sandy in summer were now a morass of mud with ruts two feet deep. The quiet houses of silvered timber seemed to sleep in the autumn sun, their shining double windows catching the last faint rays. In the windows of each house was a matching set of embroidered white linen curtains. The houses were all built of round timber notched on the corners, the crevices between the logs neatly packed with spaghnum moss. Here and there I stopped to smile at girls piling wood, picturesque in printed cotton skirts, padded jackets and white handkerchiefs on their heads.

235

Past Lenin Square I wandered, where yellow coreopsis and orange marigolds seemed to brighten the grey, larger-than-life statue which dominated the garden with its pointed beard and cold cement eyes gazing into space.

I headed down towards the river and along the shopping street which lies parallel with it, shops with doors a few steps up off the wood pavement and small windows high from the ground. But there were no goods displayed, so from the outside one would not imagine the building to be a shop at all.

Inside there were rough wood counters holding a few rolls of cotton prints, some in flannelette or light wool and cotton. There were also oddments of shoes, felt boots, galoshes, a few enamel brooches and buckles, dark cotton stockings, scent and some reels of thread. The prices were enormous. There were about 10 roubles to the pound, a blouse was 175 roubles, a print frock about 300 roubles and felt boots 66 roubles.

I strolled down to the market. Playing on the grass outside the butcher shop was a blue kitten with deep orange eyes. It was very like Silver. I stroked it and a girl came up and said, "Merka Mesha."

The girl had recognised me and explained in sign language that this was the brother of Silver, and that she wanted to give me this kitten, too. A soldier who spoke some English explained how it could be tucked into my coat, but I said the weather was too bad in winter and that it might get hurt on the ship. He said, "Cats should be black, white or grey; that is the colour for good cats."

The girl insisted on giving me a medallion of Stalin, which I felt sure was a great treasure, so I gave her my new pair of leather gloves and a red art silk scarf I was wearing. She was delighted.

"Dosvidanya," I said, as I had a long way to walk back before it grew dark.

We were still in Onega by the end of October, when it grew bitterly cold and a few snowflakes tentatively fell. One day I walked out to the little village of wooden houses, Modva, bunches of red rowans hung outside the windows.

Through the village I walked to the forest where the rock outcropped a deep pink granite. Here the trees were all spruce with an undergrowth of cranberries and bilberries, leaves were turning crimson and still covered with deep red fruit. Grey lichens grew everywhere and fir cones scattered the ground. The further I walked the more silent it became. Already the red spaghnum moss was frozen stiff. So intense was the silence that I could hear a twig fall in the clear frosty air. As the light waned the cold increased.

I met the schoolmaster in a thick coat lined with yellow fox fur and black fur cap. He walked with me exchanging Russian words for English, juniper was ferros and spruce was yorker.

It was freezing up so fast that we only just got out of the river and through the White Sea. I got frostbite through going out with my gloves off. We stopped at Alesund in Norway which was much warmer, and were in Dublin by the first of December, where I had to leave the *Elsie Beth* as Mr Borries, the former Chief Engineer, had come back to take over. By now my poor hands were suffering considerably with frostbite and I was glad to get back to the cosy warmth of Tresco for our London Christmas.

I spent the first six months of 1950 really working at Tresco to get it right for all the visitors who had planned to stay with us. The Strawberry Room on the first floor was now completely finished with strawberry patterned curtains and bedcovers which we had made from the material I had brought from Philadelphia. The large spare room on the first floor was also finished, painted green with fern patterned chintzes and curtains, and we also finished the Long Room, as we called the big drawing room, with cream walls and blue patterned chintzes on the chairs.

By the end of June I was down at Cardiff working on the *SS Canford*, where I had been sent by the pools. It was just as well that I had been so busy on the house, because it became full in no time. Adrienne Smythe, Cherry and Jock Lane all stayed over the summer, and now there was Heather as well, and all their friends. Frances wrote me long accounts of the festivities, dances and parties, a reception at the Wallace Collection, and a ball at the Painted Hall at Greenwich. It was nice to think of all the young people enjoying the delights of our London home. I was meantime sitting on the *Canford* in Cardiff docks, repairing her engines. I was with the ship about five months and left on 13th November to come back to London for Christmas.

For Easter 1951 Frances and I planned to take Cherry and Heather south to Paris and Avignon. Cherry was now twenty one and in her last year at St Andrew's University. Heather was eighteen and studying cooking at Constance Spry's. Avignon was lovely, full of bright sunshine and early grape hyacinths. We took bus trips into the hills and to Arles and Tarascon. There was a rather superior English family staying in the same hotel with whom I had the greatest fun. Somehow they always seemed to be visiting the same tourist sites as us. I got into the habit of creeping up on them behind pillars or ruins, and saying in a sinister voice, "I am a Spanish gypsy, shall I tell your fortune?" They never knew whether it was a joke, or whether I really was a Spanish gypsy.

But I suppose there was quite a lot of truth in it, because we had hardly got back before I was away again, sailing as Chief Engineer on the SS *Theems* from London to Malta with a cargo of cement. We set sail into the teeth of a gale and had such bad weather in the Channel we had to take shelter at Portland. After this we had rough seas and strong winds right through the Bay, rolling and pitching all the way, and I had some trouble with the engines, but I managed to fix it. After Finisterre the wind abated and we had sun and clear green Atlantic sea, but that didn't last, and by 16th April we were in the midst of a howling south-easter, running for cover to Cadiz.

There was more trouble in Gibraltar when a gauge glass burst and I got cut in the neck and had to go to hospital to get it stitched.

I signed off on 28th April in Gibraltar, but the company asked me to stay on for a few days and put me up in a hotel. I travelled home by train through Italy and Jean came to meet me at Ventimiglia, where we stayed in a small hotel with a room facing the sea. There were fields of roses and carnations, orchards of lemons and oranges with fruit and blossom on the trees.

In July I went to Megginch for Cherry's graduation. The ceremony was in the university hall and she was capped by John Knox's cap. I thought how many Drummonds through the centuries had been capped in the same way. She wore a black gown with a crimson silk hood, and afterwards we all picnicked with several other young graduates on the sandy dunes of St Andrew amongst the wild yellow lupins blowing in the sea breeze.

On 24th October I was at sea again on another ship, the *Alpha Zambesa*, sailing as Second Engineer for Montreal. The ship was very light and rolled horribly. We had a stormy crossing with the Atlantic gales and the waves were higher than the ship. As we neared the St Lawrence we saw an iceberg drifting south. It was a very frightening looking thing, when you thought how much was beneath the water, and I thought of the Titanic.

In Montreal I had letters from Jean and Frances. Now it seemed Cherry was seeing more and more of one young man, Humphrey Evans. When she came up from Cambridge where she was studying for the Foreign Office exam, it was always he who brought her to Tresco. They passed on glowing reports of him and when I discharged from the *Alpha Zambeza*, Cherry brought him to Tresco and I cooked one of my special curries which I had learnt from the Lascar greasers. I was not surprised when John and

Violet telephoned on Christmas Day to say that Cherry and Humphrey were engaged. It seemed no time since all the excitement of their own wedding when I had been in India on the *Mulbera*. Once again a new chapter was opening in our family life.

A new chapter was also opening in my life. I was tired of sailing on small, dirty boats with often disagreeable Chiefs. I had decided to find a shore job, perhaps supervising the building of a ship. I was nearly 60 and it seemed the time had come to take things a bit easier. At least that was what I thought.

Chapter Sixteen
Tramping Round the World - 1952-54

The *Master Nikos* was being built by the Burntisland Shipbuilding Company for Mr Eustathiou of the Phocean Ship Agency for the Compagna de Navigacion Oriental de Panama. On February 11th 1952 I was appointed as resident engineer at a salary of £60 a month along with any hotel and travelling expenses I might incur while staying at Burntisland.

It was very cold when I arrived at Burntisland to join the 65 men already at the yard working on engine room flats, side bunkers and hold pillars, and welding under deck girders and stringers. Mr Eustathiou came by two days later to see how it was going and left apparently satisfied, requesting that I send him a weekly report.

I was soon into a cosy little routine. On arrival at the yard I went round the ship after which I sat in my office going over plans. I shared the office with the Super for the other ship in the yard, and the Lloyds and Board of Trade surveyors came in twice a week.

I had comfortable accommodation and the people were very kind however, I had come north in such a hurry that I had left everything behind, my little Italian book, midbrown shampoo, mouthwash tablets, diary, vests, knickers, my white mac and of course money, because until I was paid at the end of the month I was, as usual, lamentably short of cash.

I went to watch King George VI's funeral in the window of an electrical shop where there was a television. Quite a big crowd stood silently round, a Union Jack fluttering at half mast.

By the beginning of March I had to report that work on the boat was slowing down because not enough steel was being delivered. This became a constant problem and I had to chivvy them all the time. There were now 106 men employed on the boat.

I spent my weekends visiting Hamish in Edinburgh or at Megginch, immersed in the excitement over Cherry's wedding.

At the end of March I wrote to the company to ask if they would like me to stay on after the two months and they agreed. This was a great relief with all the money coming in, and I was delighted to be so near Megginch for the wedding.

The wedding was to be in the little Chapel in the garden. Violet had hired huge sheets of canvas that were suspended from the holly trees in the avenue outside to keep off the worst of the rain. We knew it was bound to rain and it did. Benches were placed up and down the avenue like the aisle of a church, but the service itself was to take place inside the chapel. There was not much room except for closest relations and I was horrified when I heard that they planned to leave Hamish Murray outside.

"That will never do" I said firmly, and dug my heels in. Luckily, Hamish never knew.

Mummy could not come up for the wedding, but she had seen Cherry fitted in her white satin wedding dress, embroidered with pearls and cherry blossom and everyone kept her in close touch with what was happening. Heather and April were both bridesmaids, along with Hugo's little daughter Sarah and one of the young Drummond-Hays; and there were four little pages. Cousin Albert Baillie, who had been coming to Megginch every summer since 1870, was to marry them. Megginch was ablaze with rhododendrons and lilacs, and late pink tulips were still flowering among blue forget-me-nots in the formal parterre in front. The whole Chapel was filled with lilies, narcissi and lilies of the valley.

I had determined that there should be rice to throw and every time I came for a weekend I brought a few pounds of rice with me which I hid carefully in the Rose Room wardrobe. On the day of the wedding I had forgotten all about it, but it was discovered by the ushers who were helping Humphrey to change. They showered it on each other and then ran throwing it out of the windows on to people below. In fact, if I had planned it myself it could not have been more successful.

In no time Cherry tossed her bouquet off the drawing room balcony and she and Humphrey drove off. I retrieved the bouquet and Frances and Jean took it down to London with them for Mummy to enjoy, where it eventually ended up on the altar of her church. The lovely day had come to an end and I was back at Burntisland, riveting the second deck, erecting the upper stern, dealing with my 70 journeymen, tradesmen and other workers, and writing my weekly report to Mr Eustathiou.

I spent more weekends with Hamish in Edinburgh now. At work, as the boat neared completion, I seemed to spend more and more time crawling about her from length to length. She was to be launched by Mrs Eustathiou on 19th September. Frances came, as did Hamish. He was so excited about the whole thing that he quite forgot to give me a bunch of white heather he had brought down especially, although he sent it on afterwards.

Now that I had really got into the swing of building boats, I felt that this was to be my future. My routine was comfortable and relatively easy, and I particularly enjoyed thinking of all the little details like extra port-holes and plumbing facilities. But it was not to be. Mr Eustathiou was certainly delighted with all I had done, in fact so delighted that he asked me to sail as Second Engineer on a 10,000 ton boat, the *SS Markab*, which would sail to Canada in October.

So I packed up all my things and joined the *Markab* sailing from Avonmouth by Bristol. It was cold and fairly rough going across the Atlantic and I had plenty to do on the ship. We sighted the coast of Canada on 23rd October and that night saw an iceberg at least 20 feet high, which meant another 160 feet below the water. I sketched it from my cabin, along with the banks of the St Lawrence as we steamed up to Montreal. The autumn colourings were wonderful, but there was already some snow on the distant hills.

We reached Montreal on the 29th and I was able to get ashore where I sent a few postcards and bought some magazines and knitting patterns for my sisters, but everything was very expensive and I had a great rush. We loaded with Canadian apples, Mackintosh Reds, and were soon sailing back down the St Lawrence, with geese and wild ducks quacking in the reeds beside us, and into the autumn gales of the Atlantic. I had thought we were making for Hamburg, but instead we went up the Wester to Bremen and after seeing the cargo safely unloaded I signed off there on 11th November, once more determined to have my Christmas at home with Mummy and my sisters and not be swept away in another lengthy voyage.

Christmas was a lovely time for us all, although by the end of it both Frances and I had heavy colds, hardly the thing to start off with on a long, taxing voyage. The *Markab* had now gone to Denmark, so on 31st January 1953 I set off by air to Copenhagen to join her. It was just as well I did leave by air as a storm blew up. High tides were running and the sea broke up the whole of the east coast, Canvey Island was submerged and nearly 300 people drowned. The Irish Mail boat from Stranraer to Belfast sank in the gale with over 100 lives lost.

On arrival at Copenhagen Airport I drove through the night streets to the ferry for Arhus. It was an all night crossing, but the weather was so bad that it was with much relief that I went to the Hotel Regina for a hot bath followed by coffee and six different kinds of bread before proceeding to the *Markab*. Here I was met by Captain Christensen, his wife and four-year-old Gaynor.

As a Chief, my cabin was quite luxurious, about 17 feet by 11, with two ports, a washbasin, glass-fronted bookcase, settee, steam heater, table, wardrobe and desk, and also an arm chair. Next door I had an office of my own with a settee and desk. The bathroom was down the alley, where I could also dry my clothes and washing.

We left Arhus for Copenhagen on 3rd February. I liked Copenhagen very much, a bright northern capital town with lovely shops and beautifully dressed windows. I concentrated on buying a whole china dinner service with pale flower patterns round the edge for Tresco use, which I arranged to be sent over by sea.

The sea between Copenhagen and Hamburg was frozen in vast stretches. It was a wonderful sight, all these blocks of ice like crazy paving stones and miles and miles of it. We went through the Kiel Canal and there was a real blizzard blowing. I could see the landing stage where people came to take the ferry; the porters carried the baggage on little sledges.

We reached Hamburg on 10th February and sailed again two days later, so there was no time to go ashore, or do anything other than work. It was bitterly cold. The Elbe was full of ice and the water was frozen far out to sea, but it was not as cold as Denmark.

We sailed into the Bay on the 15th, where the weather was mild and calm and we got to Gibraltar five days later, it was bright sun, but still cold. I went ashore to get all the stores, as there had not really been time in Hamburg. After I had been to the ship's chandlers and checked all the stores and had a cup of coffee with the agent, I had time to do my own shopping. The Bay looked so lovely with all the coloured reflections of the boats in the water and Spaniards selling baskets of oranges with leaves and blossom on them.

We sailed about 6 pm with a slight feeling of snow in the wind, and indeed we could see the Spanish hills quite white the next morning. We didn't see Malta as we passed there in the dark on the 22nd, but a delicious warm smell of flowers and orange blossom wafted aboard.

After Malta the weather became very rough and we had a tragedy with the ships' cats. One died having kittens and two had such terrible mange that they had to be put down. The Chief Steward who looked after them was very upset and so was Captain Christensen. It was so rough and cold that I had to have two blankets and two hot water bottles at night and we were still wearing blues. My Lascar crew were very sweet and one night the sarang, Faizullah, brought me a large plate of curry and rice they had made me as a treat at tea time. Not what I would have chosen for afternoon tea, but of course I had to eat it.

I was preparing for the excitement of going through the Suez Canal as Chief Engineer of a 10,000 ton boat, something I had wished for all my life. We entered the Canal about noon on Sunday 1st March and came out at Suez at 3.45 am the next day. It was cold at night and the sky was illuminated with a green sandy colour from the canal light attached to the ship at Port Said showing miles of white and yellow sand with the dark shadows of the tamarisk trees planted for their fibrous roots. On the left was nothing but desert, on the right the sweet water canal.

We had to tie up in the Canal for a short time as a small sail boat had sunk in the channel. The Captain sent me to the next ship astern, a Danish vessel, to get him a bottle of special Danish spirit and a loaf of black bread. I went in the light boat, rowing down the Canal in the dark. When I climbed aboard the Danish ship the Captain was surprised to see me, although he gave me the spirit and bread in exchange for a bottle of whisky. I was most afraid that I would drop it climbing up and down, but all went well and I got back on board safely.

At Djibouti, where we arrived on 7th March, I got news of Violet and John's Silver Wedding Party at Megginch and of how Frances had been busy painting nursery furniture for Cherry's new nursery in London. Djibouti was very hot and we bunkered 600 tons of oil. We had all been inoculated on arrival for yellow fever in a rough and ready fashion by a French Doctor.

"In a few days you will feel very ill," he said, "then you may take an aspirin." He was right!

Crossing the Indian Ocean we found a native sailing ship, bound from India for Zanzibar, which had run out of food and water. They lowered a boat and we gave them water and rice. They were right off course and seemed to be navigating on a very antique chart.

Going through the Straits of Malacca was hot and steamy, with wet clouds and little islands covered with palm trees. In the distance was Sumatra, a blue-grey coastline with palms. We reached the oil berth at Pulau Bukom, near Singapore, on 23rd March and were there only 52 hours, during which time I had to go on top of the oil tank to take the dip. It was very hot!

Through the coloured lights from Singapore we sailed up the coast until by Palm Sunday it began to cool down. When we passed Formosa on 26th March there was quite a roll.

At 2 am on Easter morning we shipped a very heavy sea aft. We were shipping seas fore and aft as we were very low in the water anyway. The door was open at the end of the alleyway, as the carpenter hadn't shut it, and the water rushed up and flooded all the rooms on that side, including mine. I was sound asleep at the time and was woken by the rushing of water. I flashed my torch and found my room flooded out. I managed to save my things and the log books as I plunged out of my bunk into the cold water. I didn't get turned in again till 3 am. In all I got about a dozen buckets of water out of my cabin.

When the boy called me at 7 am it was broad daylight and Fujiyama was visible with its white snow cap and there were lots of little Japanese fishing boats on what was now a calm sea. It was like a dream and I was told it was very lucky to see Mount Fuji so clear. We arrived at Yokohama where we lay inside the breakwater a long way from the shore in Tokyo Bay. They started discharging our cargo of soda into lighters and the pungent white dust wafted everywhere.

On going ashore I found letters from home and an invitation from Dorothy Britton to stay with her. I rushed and changed into my blue suit and arranged the work to be done in my absence before I went ashore in the launch and stepped on to Japanese soil for the first time.

There were a few high buildings, but mostly small Japanese houses and open fronted shops, which stayed open until midnight or later. Yokohama had suffered a great deal of bomb damage and so had been more or less rebuilt. Most of the men and about a quarter of the women wore western dress. I went by taxi to the new grand hotel, with soft carpets and Japanese cherry trees in coloured pots. Here I had tea and then telephoned the Brittons.

We drove through villages in the dark with red Japanese lanterns lit outside the shops. In the car lights I saw trees covered with cherry blossom and even bare branches on small trees and shop windows were decorated with paper cherry blossom. Their house was built in the Japanese style with plain wood ceilings, polished floors and big sliding windows. A wood fire burnt in the big living room and the Japanese housekeeper welcomed us with hot cocoa.

The next day we drove through small villages to see the cherry blossom. The trees were not in orchards but in groups or scattered along the roadside avenues. Although they did not have any leaves yet, they were covered in pale pink blossom with large, almost translucent flowers. Back for tea by the fire with green seaweed soup, white fish and strawberries and cream, before another night lulled by the breakers.

Next morning we drove to Tokyo, through villages with chow dogs stretching in the sunshine, children going to school with satchels on their backs, and cherry blossom everywhere.

We left Yokohama on 11th April at 6.30 pm and arrived at Dairen six days later, having run right up the Yellow Sea at the back of Korea. One plane came to look at us, otherwise nothing much happened. We had to stop outside the harbour for the usual 3 hour inspection, much on the same lines as in Russia only less stringent. We were only allowed five passes for the whole ship, which would not go far amongst 60. However, I still managed to get ashore a good deal.

While we were there a cable arrived to say that Cherry had had a baby boy just as the Dundee witch had foretold. I was delighted.

Dairen was quite a large town with factories surrounded by dry, bare hills. It had changed a good deal since I was there last in 1924. All the Chinese were now "workers" and wore blue cotton drill jackets and trousers with black western buttons instead of loops. The girls wore their hair in long plaits till they were married, when it was bobbed. No silk was worn, as it was all kept for army uniforms. As a result it was very expensive, about £1 a yard. The fancy silk in the shops was old stock and I thought possibly rotten. The whole town was full of Russian officers and their wives, and they, like the American troops in Japan, were buying up everything, silk, jewels, and china, and their wives were having dresses made in velvet and silk and halo hats of ruched velvet. I asked the foreman stevedore about a flower vase that I had bought which I thought had Pekinese dogs painted on it.

"Oh no," he replied, "not dogs, god animals. They are lucky—the god animal that makes you rich!"

On 9th May, the Seamen's Club invited us to see the May Day procession and a number of us went from the ship. It was a bright day with a pale blue sky, but not warm, so I put on my navy woollen suit and a grey shirt which I thought suitably neutral. After breakfast the lorry arrived and they put me in the front seat beside the driver and everyone else in the back. Off we went through the gate where we joined up with two other lorries covering other ships companies, one Danes, the other Swedes, to whom we were not allowed to speak. We were at the head of this rather comic little procession. The acacia trees were just beginning to put on leaf, and there were occasional splashes of cherry blossom and the vivid pink of a double peach. There were a lot of people in the streets, all wearing something fresh and new, and bunting was hanging from the trees. The principal buildings were draped in scarlet folds adorned with huge pictures of the two Chinese leaders. They told us to shout "kung ho", which they said meant "very good" in Chinese, although of course this could have meant anything.

When we got to the central square where the procession was assembling, there were lots of cars decorated in the same manner as the Lord

Mayor's Show. They suggested I should go on top of the lorry to see better, so I scrambled out of the window and climbed up.

Then we started to move again and drove to another viewpoint, with me sitting on the roof of our lorry heading our procession rather like a Sacred Animal. We drove along the streets where the Japanese used to live. There were still remains of trees in china pots struggling to flower in untended conditions, cherry trees in the gardens and iris coming up, but all looked dirty and unkempt. We waved to the people in the streets as we passed and shouted "kung ho!" as we had been told. When we stopped to view the procession we were each given a large bottle of lemonade.

First in the procession came large silk flags, translucent in the brisk wind. Then came pictures of the world's Communist leaders, after which followed the officers of the new Chinese Navy in white uniforms, the sailors in striped vests and sailor collars. Then more bands and then the women's detachment of the Navy. Then still more bands and the Army in silk khaki. Behind the military procession were dancers in Chinese costumes beating drums as they danced. Each team was from a different village; some looked Tibetan. All the crowds got very excited when they heard the huge, barrel-shaped drums. Then came the workers, thousands of them, in blue drill with red banners.

When the workers began to pass they said we had seen enough and must go, so we drove through side streets, passing the end of the procession which consisted of housewives. We then drove to the Seamen's Club. Inside we sat in ginger-coloured leather chairs with velvet cushions. Cigarettes were handed round to everyone, but as I didn't smoke they gave me a Communist Shanghai paper.

We were later taken into the Club dining room where eight different dishes were laid out on round tables, strips of pork fat coated in sugar, strips of clear seaweed jelly, and a plate of goose liver pate and mushrooms finely cut. However, as soon as we started eating the head of the mission began a long speech in Chinese and then one in English about the Five Year Plan.

At last the speeches finished and we were able to eat. Our glasses were filled for toasts and at one stage they got excited and filled mine with beer, but I managed to get my tea back. There were more speeches and eventually they pressed me to make one. So most reluctantly I stood up and thanked them on behalf of the officers and men of the *Markab* for the delightful day they had given us.

It was while I was in Dairen that I realised I had no chance of getting home in time for the Coronation. They had originally told me the ship was going to load in Hamburg for Japan, discharge in Japan and then go to Dairen in the North of China to load again before returning to a continental port. However, it transpired that we were going to Constanta in Romania on the Black Sea to discharge our cargo of Indian corn. Later there was a rumour that we might go to Odessa in Russia and load grain, or salt, or iron for China, and go straight back there.

We sailed from Dairen on 12th May bound for Hong Kong. So many people came on board at Hong Kong with things to sell that it became quite like a fair. We only stayed long enough to bunker and then set off for Singapore where we arrived on 18th May, another short stop.

Here I heard all about Adam's christening, for the new baby was called Adam after my great-grandfather the Admiral. The christening had been in Megginch Chapel and I was wild to have missed it, and also to miss the Coronation for which I had seats. Everyone had seats on the Procession route it seemed; Jean and Frances were in the House of Lords stand, which they said was wonderful, and Cherry had a seat in the Abbey as Humphrey was a Gold Staff Officer. I listened to it all on the radio in the heat of the Indian Ocean as we were sailing west.

On 4th June we arrived at Djibouti. It was hot, so hot I could not breathe without the air seeming to burn my lungs. The sun burned down out of a blue, cloudless sky, turning the sea to silver; the glare was so bright that my eyes ached with the effort of seeing. We passed a big French ship with three funnels and every deck packed with foreign legionaries; the smell that emanated from her suggested that shipboard conditions were less than salutary. The quay was a burning desert of white dust with a few natives asleep, huddled in their ragged clothes under the narrow shade of various sheds. A few rowed out to the ship in wooden boats to try to sell dusty coloured handkerchiefs, lumps of white and red coral and large pink apricot lined shells.

Taking the dip on the oil tanks was almost too hot to bear and the metal burned under my feet. Every flying or crawling insect seemed to be abroad and they all bit savagely, apart from the millions of flies which stung without ceasing. There were a number of shops under pillared or arched arcades, dark and covered with dust. They were full of Foreign Legion, smart in their tropical kit, for the ship was sailing for Indo-China that night.

It never seemed to get less hot. In the evening I went with the Captain's party to the agents, a dirty place where everyone seemed to have prickly heat or sores. Later we went to a cafe by the shore where we had dinner and drank the Queen's health with the most unusual champagne. It was dark orange in colour and tasted of wood.

The next morning I got up early and walked over to the sea wall. Visible through the hot crystal blue water were the most beautiful fish, some striped like angel fish, some with rose markings and some iridescent like neon tetras. They had come in to feed in the shallow water before it got too hot later in the day.

We sailed at noon and arrived at Suez in the early hours of 11th June. It was dark, with a clear hot sky and millions of stars. We sailed into the Canal just before 9 am. All the flame of the forest trees were out in full scarlet blossom and on every twig was a flower, so bright in the white sunlight one could hardly look at it. Tree after tree we passed along the waterside at the entrance to the Canal. In the evening, darkness came suddenly and the stars shimmered from the depths of the sky. About 11 pm we glided out of the Canal and through Port Said without stopping. Every tree was a mass of brilliant red, floodlit by the street lights. It was a most beautiful sight, but over so soon as we passed into the blackness and away to sea, leaving a glittering ribbon of lights behind us.

I had a bad week going up through the Mediterranean with two big septic sores on my arm and one on my finger. I suspected the cause to be a leak of methylchloride gas from the fridge, which was next to my cabin, but the Captain did not agree.

We were headed for Constanta in Romania on the Black Sea and on 14th June passed through the Dardanelles and Gallipoli. As we came near I could see the lighthouse and behind it the War Memorial. Further along there was a huge graveyard on the side of the hill. They were awful cliffs and how anyone could have thought of landing there I could not imagine.

We didn't stop at Constantinople but went straight up to Constanta where we arrived early in the morning on 14th June. Constanta was built on the bay and at one time had been a lovely, fashionable place with a large white casino facing the sea, a sea more green than blue, with warm water lapping over sand and low rocks. The houses must have been nice when the city was a seaside resort, but now they bore the scars of wartime bombing.

It was a complicated business getting off the ship. First my name had to be submitted a day in advance, then the list had to be taken to the Head Police Officer. After this it was returned to the sentry at the bottom of the gangway who checked the list with my discharge book. Then I showed the police at the gate a card stamped with my departure time. Here I was shown into a small room where I was searched. The first day they gave me a good searching, but on the following days when I explained I had nothing and never took anything ashore, they often let me pass unsearched.

Coming back was a similar procedure. I showed them everything I had bought and told them the price I had paid and where I had bought it from.

We were there for three weeks and I spent every available moment ashore, each evening I went off, sometimes to the town, sometimes to the beach, sometimes to the country, and once to a cinema.

Constanta was planned along the sea with a main street, squares and parks. The long streets were lined with trees: mulberry; chestnut; acacia and maple. The market was laid out in the open on flat stone slab tables with heaps of peas, onions, carrots and sheaves of Madonna lilies. There were also bunches of herbs, tansy flowers and herb seeds in little dishes. In the streets I saw old women with handkerchiefs over their heads selling sunflower seeds which people ate like nuts.

There were few cars, except for the privileged, but many donkeys and cobs or ponies drawing wooden carts. One day I passed a group of gypsies on the road as I walked into the country. They had eight covered carts drawn by black long horned oxen. Each pair was led by a man and each cart was open in front, covered with canvas or matting and painted myrtle green picked out in yellow, or red picked out in green. The men wore high fur caps made of Persian lamb and wide cummerbunds of thin material pleated into folds.

There was very little in the shops in Constanta except for crowds of people and everything was very dear, even a small piece of bread cost nearly 7 shillings. The Romanians all seemed very thin, the only fat people were the Russians. In the country the villages were sun-baked with dry wild flowers. The grass was poor and the livestock I saw was very thin. Everywhere was covered in white dust. The few buses were even too crowded for me and seemed to run at no proper times.

On Midsummers Day in the market they were selling St John's wort and I bought a bit to keep witches away. I met an artist who painted enormous propaganda pictures of Stalin. "Once I was rich," he said, "but now I am poor," and he showed me his lunch which was the end of a bit of stale bread. I often used to drop in and see him in the evening and once I bought a little picture of wild roses from him. I gave him a No 8 sable brush and one or two paints I had and he was overjoyed. His paintbrushes were worn stubbles and his palette knife was an ordinary kitchen knife.

Two nights before we left my name was taken off the list by the Russians. The officials told me the ship had done it, not them, and I suspected the Second. He also told them I was not a Communist, which was a very dangerous thing to say, but they didn't believe him! When this didn't work he took my name off the list to stop me going ashore.

*At Foulden
during the
Second World
War*

*SS Bonita,
later attacked
by a German
bomber*

MERCHANT NAVY HONOURS

◆

M.B.E. FOR WOMAN ENGINEER

The King has given orders for the following appointments and awards:—

M.B.E.

Miss VICTORIA ALEXANDRINA DRUMMOND, second engineer.

The ship was attacked for 35 minutes by a bomber, when 400 miles from land, but by skilful handling many hits were avoided.

When the alarm was sounded Miss Drummond at once went below and took charge. The first salvo flung her against the levers and nearly stunned her. When everything had been done to increase the ship's speed she ordered the engine-room and stokehold staff out. After one attack the main injection pipe just above her head started a joint and scalding steam rushed out. She nursed this vital pipe through the explosion of each salvo, easing down when the noise of the aircraft told her that bombs were about to fall, and afterwards increasing steam.

Her conduct was an inspiration to the ship's company, and her devotion to duty prevented more serious damage to the vessel.

EVENING STANDARD—PAGE **3**

WEDNESDAY, OCTOBER 1, 1941

First Woman to Win Lloyd's War Medal

Miss Victoria Alexandrine Drummond, M.B.E., the only woman in England to hold the Board of Trade certificate as a qualified ship's engineer, has been awarded the Lloyd's War Medal, only presented for exceptional gallantry at sea in time of war, and never before in history won by a woman.

After receiving her MBE, outside Buckingham Palace, July 1941
(reproduced by permission of the Evening Standard)

In the engine room of the SS Eastern Med, 1948

*On board the
SS Elsie Beth
during a trip
to Russia*

*With the
Second and
Third
Engineers
from the SS
Elsie Beth*

In her cabin on board the SS Markab, 1953

The launch of the Master Nicos

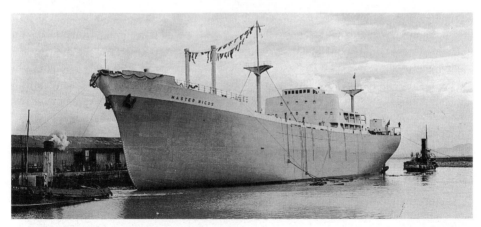

With her niece Cherry in 1957

On board the SS Shun Fung

With her Chinese crew

It was 3.30 am on 5th July and just getting light as we came in from the Black Sea to the Bosporus. The lights were beginning to twinkle out on shore and there was a spring smell in the air which came on the offshore wind. A crescent moon shone white in the lightening sky. We stopped for inspections and the day began to grow. First light was flooding the eastern sky in an ever deepening flush like the petals of a yellow tea rose, and the transparent mist hanging on hills and sea turned gold in the morning light. With the pilot now on board, we slipped through the Bosporus, every green ripple flushed with gold. Flocks of wild fowl rose and flew over the sea, making reflections in the calm water as the northern side of Istanbul came into full view, every house gilded in the morning light.

The ship glided on as the whole spectacle of domes and minarets of the magic city floated in a mist of gold. Brightly painted boats sailed past, cutting the water into hundreds of tiny ripples. Now we were heading away into the Sea of Marmara and the golden vision gradually faded and vanished from sight.

We stopped at Chios on 6th July to change an engineer. I sketched the city from across the water, houses and gardens with magenta bougainvillea splashed against walls, pink foothills and higher blue mountains, and a shimmering strip of beach. There was a domed mosque with a minaret and a Greek church with a cross on top. As the sun dropped like a stone behind the hills the little town came to life, fishing boats started out for the evening's fishing, nets piled on board, towing smaller boats with paraffin lamps. The stores were loaded aboard and we set off into the darkness for Turkey.

As far as I knew we were to be at Iskenderun until 30th July. We were to lie out for nine days, move in for six to load and then finish loading from barges. We were then to sail to Algiers before heading to America and back again to Europe by mid-September. I hoped to leave the ship and have a holiday abroad with my sisters, as I was getting very tired and my poisoned arm still felt weak.

Iskenderun was a lovely place and we lay out in a blue green bay with water so clear I could see down to the tiny fish swimming round. The town was built along the sea and there were palm trees along the beach. I sat in cafes with green chairs and clean tablecloths where I could have Turkish coffee with cold soda water made from a spring in the mountains.

In the mountains the pomegranates were in flower, with green fruit in the hedges and scarlet flowers. The goats and sheep were all fat and healthy looking. Pink oleanders grew along the dusty road and the trees cast a flickering shade on the whiteness. The women, some of whom still wore veils, always walked behind the men. I stopped a bus to get a lift and the driver would not take any fare. The Turkish people were all very friendly, great individuals and quite different from any other culture.

One Saturday I determined to go to Antioch. The agent said it was not safe and could only be visited with a permit from the police which luckily I managed to wangle. I got what they call a service taxi, which normally takes five people. There were four men and me, and I got the front seat . First we went through Iskenderun, then we began to mount the dry foot-hills with blue thistle flowers. There were wonderful views and peeps of the sea far below.

We arrived at Belen, a village in the hills built on two sides of a ravine with wonderful spring water. From here we drove up through villages with houses built of mud and round stones. The men we saw wore baggy trousers caught at the knee and sometimes red leather boots. The women wore loose cotton dresses with different types of veils draped about their heads. Everyone rode on donkeys with high saddles and packs, or Arab horses whose saddles were ornamented with brass and had bright blue beads on their harnesses. The road was good, but all twists and serpent turns, and unless you knew it well, you would be over the edge.

When we reached the summit we began to descend into a plain which stretched out below. The wind was as hot as a hair dryer. There were more blue thistles and clumps of pink oleanders, and when we came down to the plain there were herds of black goats and cows, and fields of long reeds with feathery tops used for house thatch. The river was predomi-nantly stones and there were fields of melons.

Antioch was quite a small place, built at the foot of a range of hills, and as we approached it I could see right up against the hills an early Chris-tian Church dating from 47AD.

Inside the church was dark and cool; pale light filtered in through the windows. The floor was rock, and there was a secret escape passage and a clear spring in the rock with maidenhair fern growing round. There was a stone altar and a niche which had held a statue of Our Lady. They had found a very ancient stone with carvings on it and said it was the oldest Christian church in the world.

Back in the town I saw a fight in the street, and a large crowd, so I went to the garage to get my seat in the returning taxi. This time there were only three passengers, so I had plenty of room. Away over the mountains we went, reaching Iskenderun that evening.

The next week I went back to Belen by bus, which took me direct. As I was walking through the winding streets over the cobbles where plants grew on the walls, I heard a voice calling, "Chief! Chief!" There was my friend the customs officer, with six of his friends, so I joined them and had fruit, Turkish coffee and black figs, so ripe you could see the red and white seeds under the cracking skin. They were also eating goulash and flat Turkish bread. The restaurant was built right up on the rock with the gorge below and there used to be an old castle underneath. After lunch the Customs Officer and the police showed me the great arches, which they said were 500 years old, and there were caves below that. Belen was on the road to Baghdad and the only road over the mountains went through the Pass of Belen, so it was a place of some importance.

Most nights I went ashore to sit in cafes or stroll down the streets of Iskenderun. One night I had been to the town to post my letters and on the way back was walking along a rather lonely stretch of road in the dark carrying my torch. As I crossed a bridge over a stream, I moved to pass a group of three men when one of them suddenly struck me.

I said in English, "Don't do that," and turned my torch on them.

My attacker made a signal to one of the other men who grabbed my arm and the group dragged me off the road on to a bit of waste ground. I struggled to get back on the road in pitch dark, but the man held me fast by the arm. I fought like a tiger and got him by the throat and nearly choked him, putting all my weight into the effort. He wrenched himself free and ran off.

The other two closed on me, but I knocked one down with a left and right. The other one snatched my torch and clipped me on the back of the head with it knocking me down. I was shouting all the time. One man put his hand over my mouth and I bit him as I kicked the other. We had a good rough and tumble before they tried to snatch my bag. They also tried to take my watch, scratching my arm. By this time a man who heard my shouts came running up from the beach and I ran, or rather floundered, in the darkness, through holes and prickly bushes and over iron railings in the direction of the road. My attackers ran after me, but I took my shoe off to hit them and they scurried off. I got on to the road and found the police box.

I was pretty knocked about; I had bruises on my arms where they grabbed me, my knuckles were swollen and my leg was black and blue from being kicked. There was also a large lump on the back of my head where I'd been hit with the torch.

I had also been having trouble with the Radio Officer who brought the letters aboard and I suspected that he was deliberately losing some of my letters by letting them drop in the sea. When I checked with my sisters there were several letters they had written to me at Constanta and at Singapore which had never arrived. I saw one in the water one night after he had returned to the ship and I was sure it was mine. I was also very worried as I was running out of shampoo and I was always hoping my sisters would send me a fresh supply. I had been away at sea for over six months.

As we were still at Iskenderun on Saturday 1st August I went on a trip to Harbia. I got a front seat in a car going to Antioch. Even the two weeks that had passed since I first went had made a difference to the country. The streams were dryer, the shrubs more covered in dust and spikes with bright orange berries like giant wild arums. There were still bright splashes of pomegranate flowers as we came down the other side of the mountain, but now the pomegranates were a deep yellow and nearly ripe. The fields of melons had all been gathered. Beyond Antioch the countryside changed to dry foothills backed by burning mountains and apricot trees. Suddenly we came to Harbia, a ravine with a crystal clear spring that rushed out of the mountain making everything green and fertile. Here was where the figs and maples grew. The water poured into a clear basin and I scrambled down the rocks and drank and drank.

The next day we left Iskenderun, where we had been for a whole month, and sailed for Mersin, arriving in the dark about midnight on 9th August. The lights were shining and glistening through the darkness and a hot sweet wind blew from shore.

Next morning the sea was dancing and glittering in the bright white sunlight, not the brilliant blues and greens of Iskenderun, but bright turquoise. The town was built in a rather rather helter skelter fashion and without much plan; the houses were mostly cream and white with thick Turkish tiled roofs.

On Tuesday 11th August I went ashore with the Captain. We walked up the landing stage, past the police into the baking square where various buses pulled up for Tarsus and Adana. In the agent's office we had cups of Turkish coffee and gazus, small bottles of ice-cold lemonade. Everyone was dripping hot and soon the men's shirts were soaked through. I watched them getting wetter and wetter.

When our business was finished I explored the gold shops crammed with bracelets, earrings and coins. There were also silk shops and open fronted stalls selling a bit of everything soap, beads, cotton, scent, writing paper, china and mounds of grapes, clear yellow and far sweeter than honey. For a shilling I got almost more than I could carry. They sold heaps of sweet, delicious green melons, too. Of course everything was covered with fine white dust, but they wiped it off when I bought them.

It was so hot I could hardly bear to look at the shops or drag my feet round the streets. The trouble was that the Captain had only arranged for the shore boat to operate between 8 am and 4 pm, the hottest time of all. If I wanted to go ashore in the evenings I had to pay for the boat myself which cost £2-10/- a time, and this was, of course, prohibitive.

Each day seemed hotter than the last and the wind was like a furnace. On the 13th when I was ashore I felt an earth tremor. I was walking in the street towards a shady garden with palm trees and tables when I felt a very funny feeling, as if the whole ground were being slowly lifted up and then slowly sinking again. I felt dizzy as if I had been whirled round suddenly. It only lasted a split second, although it seemed a lot longer. There was a heavy swell in the harbour for some days, and they said that at Iskenderun the ships had had to leave harbour and put to sea.

On Sunday 16th August the Captain took us all for a picnic in the life-boat. After going over to the landing stage for permission we hoisted our red sail and went 8 miles up the coast. We got to a reef of rocks and a sandy bay. It was burningly hot, even the slight breeze had dropped though there was still quite a swell.

We dropped anchor about 100 yards from the beach and they rigged up a raft with the oars and sail to transport the picnic ashore. Everyone had bathing suits except me, because I had packed in such a hurry when I flew out to Copenhagen that I hadn't brought one. So in my blue and white checked gingham dress, deck shoes and grey felt hat I just plunged over-board and swam ashore and was dry in about half an hour. The water was as warm as a bath. We made a tent with the oars and sail and ate lunch in the shade, hard-boiled eggs and chicken, salad and lemonade.

After lunch the Captain said there was a ruined castle somewhere near, so I started to walk to it up the rough road with cypress trees and bushes of myrtle in full flower. Suddenly, there rose in front of me a most mag-nificent colonnade with acanthus leaf capitals. Twenty two columns lay about in a scattered line, arranged in groups of three or four in a row, but of course many of them were smashed and lying among the myrtle bushes. I picked up a bit of marble but it was so hot that I had to drop it. While I gazed at all this, a man appeared carrying a gun and told me that this was all his land. So I walked along the road with him till we came to his farm. He picked me half a dozen bright green lemons which he insisted I take. He also wanted me to have some new laid eggs, but I could not carry any more, so I gave him some cigarettes as I knew he would not accept money. I walked back to the camp along the beach in and out of the water, picking up sponges and bits of seaweed. Then we packed up and swam back to the boat. It was lovely going back to the ship, not so burning with the sun setting, but still very hot, and we watched the pink hills deepen into blue and amethyst and then the dark came down just as we sailed back to Mersin and boarded the *Markab*.

My last Sunday in Turkey, 23rd August, I was lucky enough to get the boat ashore about half past ten and go for a long walk in the countryside.

I could hardly bear to sail away having been in Turkey nearly two months. However, that is the life of a sailor, and on the night of 26th August we sailed west down the Mediterranean towards Algiers.

We had a day's bad weather off the coast of Italy, but lovely weather going past Sicily. After we left Mersin the temperature dropped 20° from 100°F to 80°F and we all felt cold.

I was worried about Mummy who had broken her leg. She now kept almost entirely to her bed in Fleet and had a nurse and Lily who both fussed over her. I was also worried about money. All the trips ashore and the little cakes and things I had bought in Turkey had used up my dollar allowance, so now I would have nothing at all in America and all my clothes were beginning to wear out. I was trying to get my sisters to write to our cousin Jackie Cecil to lend me some dollars on arrival, but I didn't know yet if we would be going to Baltimore, Norfolk, or Newport News, or even New York, so it was difficult to make plans.

We came into Algiers on 3rd September and the sea and sky were a deep blue, but the colouring of the city was strangely different from Turkey, much harsher and stronger. We tied up alongside the quay and bunkered from a barge. When I got my letters I found that I had been given a Coronation medal. Thrilled, I rushed to write a letter of acknowledgement.

I had been to Algiers once in 1940, but this time was more brief, which was disappointing. After we finished bunkering, the oil manager took me for a run round the town in his car. I saw the mosque which a slave had built by himself, so the story goes, and had then been freed when he had finished it! Notre Dame d'Afrique was also pointed out to me, a church built in African style high on a hill to the northwest looking out to sea. The small streets winding up steep steps looked attractive as did the gardens with palms, aloes and scarlet hibiscus. I longed to explore, but the ship was due to sail at 3 pm.

We were out in the Atlantic on 13th September when we were told to expect a hurricane. For five days we waited and then it came. The day before had been terribly oppressive, like a hundred thunder storms in one. The night had been hot and very heavy, everything clammy and damp with rather a heavy roll. We battened everything down and locked up everything in the engine room. The Captain came round to see that all was tight.

Morning dawned grey, dark and overcast with a leaden sky and sea. The overpowering heaviness increased as the morning wore on. The sea was all rising in small waves and the crests did not blow off straight but rose right up and towered into columns of white spray, which shone against the dark sea and sky. Foam curled and streaked the sea in long straight lines and the oppressive feeling of something impending became intense.

At 12 noon after a busy morning in the engine room I changed into a white suit and went to the saloon for lunch. A few minutes later I got up and looked out of the port and said, "Look, the weather's changed, it's coming!"

The sea had straightened out and the visibility was almost obscured by a thick mist of flying spray. Hardly had I said this when a message came for the Captain to go to the bridge. As I went down to the engine room our speed was reduced and I told the Third who was on watch that it would not last long, but would be very bad while it did! I then changed into my boiler suit and stood by for emergency in the engine room and kept a look out on deck.

The engine room skylight had to be closed down entirely and I told the sarang to send the men up. It was a short job but by this time the wind was terrific and the spray blinding and drenching. I went up to encourage them but found I could hardly breathe in the gale. When the skylights were fixed I sent the men down to dry in the stokehold.

At 2 pm the hurricane was at its height. The whole of the sea was flattened by the strong wind as if it had been ironed out and the air was white with flying spray. No one could stand on deck, or come from aft to fore. I could only peep through the bending ports where no dead lights were fitted. I could not breathe and my ears felt the same as if I were at a very high altitude. Everything slid and banged. The noise of the wind was terrific and the decks were one mountain of water, great seas breaking fore and aft, whipped by blinding spray, the water roaring to dash out again through the scuppers. Water poured into the accommodation wherever there was a crack. The force and pressure of the waves were enormous.

It stopped with the same suddenness as it started and in a few minutes it was over, save for a heavy sea, and the sun came out. We had very little serious damage, but No 3 hatch cover was ripped to pieces as if by some awful giant.

At the height of the hurricane the wind was unmeasurable. The cargo, 9,000 tons of iron ore, was a bad one for this sort of thing, and if No 3 hatch cover had gone altogether it would have been a very dim lookout, for if the cargo had shifted it might have been a case of Davy Jones' Locker!

We arrived at Chesapeake Bay in the morning of September 23rd, having taken nearly 20 days to come from Algiers. A journey intended to take sixteen.

We stopped for inspection and quarantine. They had a form of questions to fill in, but I had no trouble; they just completed it for me and gave me a permit for a year. The Customs too searched very little. We had to go on to the boat deck for inspection. It took a long time though, and we didn't leave for Baltimore till 3 pm. We spent about 20 hours going up the wide river, and the shore in the distance looked grey and rather misty. When we arrived in Baltimore I had a busy day arranging for repairs to be done by a shore firm, the General Ship Repair Company: repairs done to the pipes, main ballast line fore, ballast pump to engine room bilge, main bilge line to the stokehold, and 37 tubes required renewing in the auxiliary condenser.

With all this I didn't get ashore till after 6 pm. I was worried by letters I had had from Jean and Frances saying that Mummy was not feeling well and her leg was hurting again, so I sent a cable home to find out. It took me nearly an hour to get back to the boat and I had to walk quite a way down a dark, lonely stretch of road which I didn't like, especially as Baltimore seemed a rough kind of place; I was very glad to get back on board by 11.30 pm!

I was working on repairs all Friday morning and we moved our berth even further away. Mr Mulvanney gave me a lift to the repair shop and afterwards ran me to near Harvard, but he said it was not safe to go along the dock road in the dark and he would meet me at the Western Union at 9.30 pm to take me back to the ship. Baltimore was a large city with soaring skyscrapers, but here and there little brick houses sandwiched in between, with white window surrounds and fan lights over the doors, fluted pillars and attractive ironwork. When I went to the central Post Office flocks of starlings were coming in to roost, just like in Trafalgar Square. As I was going back I heard a police car siren coming up, so I thought there must be some kind of a fight and hurried away. When I got back to the ship, I found that an escaped convict had been shot and killed at the cinema by two policemen who were trying to catch him.

We left Baltimore on 27th September all our repairs complete. Baltimore had not been a bit like I thought it was going to be.

I was angry as we left because the Captain had collected a cable for me from the agent's, carried it round all day in his pocket, and only gave it to me half an hour before sailing. The cable was from my sisters concerning Mummy's broken leg. When I received it I could do nothing, otherwise I really believe I would have given in my notice and left the ship there and then. I had been away at sea for eight months and it was too long. As soon as the ship got near a home port I determined to leave it. Shore jobs and short continental trips were what I would do now.

It was sleeting with rain and blowing hard when we arrived at the coal pier in Norfolk next morning. The rain was just whipping along the wooden pier, throwing up clouds of white spray. It looked a forsaken place and I could see nothing but fog and the outline of black coal chutes. As soon as I could, I got down the gangway and struggled along the pier where I phoned Julia Davies and Josephine Johnson who told me to come at once.

There were still some blooms on the pink crepe myrtles. I was so tired that once I arrived all I wanted to do was sleep.

Julia woke me at 3.30 pm to say they had telephoned from the ship and were bunkering at 5 pm, so I had to return.

There was a delay over bunkering as the barge broke down and I had to climb a long way down a very slippery ladder as she was a light ship. By the time I finished it was 10.45 pm, but I rang Julia just the same and within half an hour she was at the gate to pick me up.

I spent two nights with Julia and Josephine before they ran me back to the ship in the fog and rain, but I was able to bring them both on board and show them round. They had given me a lovely time and I think were quite pleased when people in the shops had recognised me from the picture in the *Virginian Pilot*. Cherry had written them a long letter all about the Coronation as seen from inside the Abbey and they loved that. So I said goodbye after such a happy time and at 4.40 pm we sailed down the Chesapeake in a red sunset to the open sea.

We sailed south to Trinidad and the weather was getting warmer all the time. I was very put out that the ship was not sailing straight back to a continental port from Norfolk, as we had originally been told, and instead going on to South America. I was desperate to get back and see for myself how ill Mummy was; soothing letters and cables didn't really fill in the whole picture. I also felt my clothes were getting shabby and worn out and I never seemed to have an opportunity to replace them. Besides I was finding it more and more difficult to get on with the Second Engineer who was nearly always rude and insolent to me and had gone for me several times. So I sent in my resignation saying that I wished to leave as soon as we reached a British or continental port as I felt I had been long enough at sea. I wrote a very nice letter with nothing controversial in it, as I still hoped to get another job from the shipbuilding company at Burntisland. I was not happy about the pay either. I was supposed to be paid £64 a month, although there was always difficulty about getting hold of it. I had heard from the Chief Steward that the Second was paid £100 a month and the other two £70 each.

Passing between rocky wooded islands and a coast thick with green foliage, steamy white clouds overhead piling into banks and floating away, we arrived at Trinidad on 8th October and dropped anchor about 4 miles out from Port-of-Spain. But there was little time to look at the distant view, as the Shell barge came alongside and I was very busy taking the dip. We were to bunker 900 tons. The foreman told me he was changing over ships at 1.30 pm and the launch was going to drop him and bring his relief back at 3 pm, so asked if I would like to run over to Port-of-Spain with him.

At 1.25 am the next morning we set off southwards for Buenos Aires. As we ran down to the Plata the weather was very hot. We were about 150 miles off shore, but when we passed the mouth of the Amazon I could smell the hot jungle in the air, flies and mosquitoes came on board, and the sea became stained with other colours. I felt more and more that I had been too long on the ship and hoped that I would be able to get home in time for Christmas.

On 14th October, my birthday, I was writing in my room having just come up from the engine room when the light went out. I went into the pantry to see what had happened to the fuses, and as I went to the fuse box the Second Engineer came from behind me and pushed me while screaming at me and using his customary bad language. He had the fuses in his hand, so had obviously just taken them out.

I went straight out of the pantry as I did not want to complicate matters by giving him the chance to strike me and straight to the Captain to report what had happened.

"I am trying to keep the peace," I said, "but as you know this has gone on the whole voyage. However, as it is only another two months I will stick it till I leave."

Later the sarang came to my room and told me the Second was going to do something to the fridge and wished me to take his watch. I knew that there was nothing wrong with the fridge and that it was only a frame-up as before in the Red Sea when I repeatedly took his watch, so I said, "No, I can't, I'm busy."

Five minutes later the Second came and tried to force his way into my room. He was in one of his tempers, so I shut the door. About 15 minutes or so later I had a note from the Captain suggesting that the Second Engineer should have relief, so I sent the Third Engineer down to relieve him.

Next day I was busy checking stores for the Argentine Manifest, which was an extensive one with every item listed. I was told by one of the men that the Second Engineer had fought the Captain on the boat deck and that the Captain had smashed a chair. I didn't think it could be true, but as I came up for lunch the Third Mate told me the Captain wanted to see me. I went as I was, in my boiler suit, and found them all there, the Captain, Chief Steward, Second and Third Engineers. The Chief Steward went out and the Chief Officer came in. Every word the Captain said to the Second was translated into Greek even though he could speak English perfectly well. The Captain said there had been a fight and he wished me to make a statement. I said I had been in the engine room store checking stores for the manifest and therefore knew nothing about it.

However, the Captain wished me to write and sign a statement, and I said, "If you wish me to make a statement, I will make it before the British Consul in Buenos Aires. I know nothing about the matter."

A statement was then read by the Second Engineer saying I had refused to take any watches and had pushed him out of my room and shut the door and a lot of other rubbish.

The Captain said it would be huge headlines in the papers.

I said, "If my name is mentioned I will haul them out for libel."

I think the Second had been trying to blackmail the Captain to give him extra money for running the fridge, which was his job, by threatening to disclose that the ship was loaded 2 feet above the marks, and trying to get rid of me at the same time.

It was all very unpleasant and I spent as much time as I could looking at the sea, which was wonderful, a deep lapis blue with purple shadows and rolling waves, flying fish skimming over the water and dashing through the foam. After we crossed the line we began to see sea birds and then the great albatross. Then there were large black birds with sooty plumage, birds with black and white marbled wings and huge gulls. The sea had been over 80°F all the way down from Trinidad, but on 25th October it suddenly dropped to 72°F and on the 27th it was 59°F. It changed colour to milky green as we entered the mouth of the Rio Plata on the morning of 28th October and there was a strong wind and a heavy sea. We could see blue hills on the starboard side and then we sighted Montevideo, the capital of Uruguay, at about 3 pm. The wind was quite cold by now.

We anchored just off Montevideo to wait for the tide as the channel was very shallow. The Plata was 42 miles wide here and I could imagine that I was in a great lake rather than a river as I could not see the shore on either side.

A ship had grounded in the channel ahead of us, so we had to wait until evening before proceeding to the discharging berth. Meantime we had the usual inspections and it was quite dark when we started up the river. We had 25 miles to go to Buenos Aires and it was a very long stand-by; we didn't get tied up until 1.30 am in the morning and I was not able to turn in before 3 am.

We were there a week and every evening I went ashore and wandered round the wide streets and beautiful buildings of this large city, the largest below the equator with a population of over 3 million. There were high white buildings and town houses sandwiched between blocks of workers' flats which absorbed all the light. The shops were wonderful, every street like Bond Street or the Rue de Rivoli, and filled with marvellous goods, dresses, furs, silver, watches. There were also many sweet shops piled high with every kind of sweet and also a great number of bijouterie shops.

I had several adventures while in Buenos Aires. One night there were so many people on the bus I could not see where to get off and got carried right past my stop. I got rather lost and was wandering down dark leafy streets looking for a bus to get me back when a man accosted me. I spoke firmly to him and walked briskly away, but I was very glad to see a bus passing and jumped quickly on it. Another night I felt a hand on my shoulder when I was on the dock going to the ship. I spoke firmly again and went on walking towards the ship. He followed me, but luckily the watchman sent him off.

We left on Saturday 7th November having half loaded with wheat. When it was light I saw we were passing through the Pampas, the cattle country, with waving grass, white clouds and herds of cattle, mostly Herefords and Redpolls though some Aberdeen-Angus and Friesians. The water had started to come down from the mountains of Brazil where the ice was melting and so the river was rising and cattle were being taken off the green islands to the shore. I saw one gaucho riding through flood water up to his saddle and when he got on to high ground he waved to the ship. We anchored off the port of Rosario. The next day there was a terrible thunderstorm, blue and green streaks of lightning and torrential rain.

On Wednesday 11th November the Captain said I could have a few days ashore to rest. This was a welcome surprise and at 7 pm that evening

Mr Jacobs, manager of the Anglo-Argentine Marine Engineering Company, came aboard and the Captain asked him to fix up a hotel for me, and at 7.30 pm the launch came back for me. It was quite a long way to the landing stage. Mr Jacobs was there to meet me with a car and he told me that in this country people just disappeared and were never heard of again.

After dropping a mess boy from a Swedish ship at the hospital, we went to the Savoy Hotel where he had booked me a room at 32 pesetas a day, about 16/-.

I really enjoyed my break in Rosario, the clean, cool bathroom all to myself and my leisurely breakfasts in the morning sunlight with fresh rolls, coffee and delicious jams. No one to come in and shout "Chief!" with news of some disaster. I enjoyed strolling through the streets, exploring the town and doing my shopping.

We had been a week in Rosario and it turned out we had nearly another fortnight there. On the evening of 16th November I was in town, but thought it was getting rather dark and perhaps another storm was brewing up, so I took a taxi back to the ship. The driver kept switching his lights on and off in a curious way and he refused to stop and let me ask the way, although I felt sure we were headed in the wrong direction. Finally, when we got to a lonely stretch of road he tried to hold me up for money. Luckily he had to stop the car to do this, so I got out. He tried to grab the money when I got out my purse, but I told him off firmly, gave him the fare and no more and he simply drove off. Luckily I was quite near the boat.

By Monday 23rd November I had finished all the repairs and there was no more work to do on the ship. We had to move up river on Tuesday to another berth to load maize from below a clay cliff with elevators on top. Bunches of bougainvillea and morning glory grew wild, making it quite pretty. The crew fished off the landing stage and caught large cat fish.

The next morning after a leisurely breakfast I went round to get my last minute purchases. There was a good artists' shop where I had decided to buy some paints for my sister Frances. I pointed to a tube of pink paint and asked the girl, "What is the colour of this paint?" as the label is so often different to what is inside. Instead of marking a little on a bit of paper, or letting me look at it she gave the end of the tube a little squeeze. It was pointing at me, however, and being a very hot day the tube went off like a rocket and spattered bright pink paint all over my face, my blue jacket, and my blue and white checked frock. I thought I must hold up the British habit of sangfroid, so I said calmly, "If it had been blue or white it would not have mattered."

But they all screamed and screeched, and the girl burst into tears. Eventually they took me out to the garden where there was a pump and a large scrubbing brush and they tried to scrub it off, but this only spread the paint and made it worse, besides making me soaking wet. When I left, bright pink and dripping, they offered to buy me a new dress but I assured them it would wash out back on the ship. So I walked back to the ship while everyone in the street turned and looked at me in horror; the Mate could not think what I had been doing. However, it did wash out and I was able to go back and tell them so that night.

On Saturday we were to sail at 11 am, but it was changed to 6 pm, so I had time to go ashore. I was just strolling back to the ship about 11 am when I found they had changed the time again and she was moving out. I just managed to make a jump for it, a real pier head jump and scrambled on board just as she was casting off. The ship was just moving berth, however, and we did not sail till midday on Sunday 29th November.

I felt quite sad to leave the shining white buildings of Rosario, the crimson flor de ceibos, and all the other flowering trees and oleanders as we glided down the coffee coloured Piranha in a cloud of mosquitoes.

We arrived at Buenos Aires on Monday 30th November. Most evenings I slipped out to the town centre, sending off Christmas cards, doing more shopping and eating light meals in cafes. There was always a change of plans as to when the ship would actually sail, but finally they said it would sail for sure on Saturday 5th December, so knowing that chances of getting time off are like quicksilver in your hand, I determined to go to La Plata.

The scent here was of honey, lemon and lime. Some of the avenues were lined with orange trees covered with oranges and some with jacarandas and acacias.

Everywhere in Argentina there were pictures of Eva Peron on buildings, stamps and monuments; people put bunches of flowers on the monuments and one man said to me, "She is in the moon, shining down on us."

There was the usual confusion about sailing on Saturday, but I still managed to dash ashore and stock up with fresh fruit for the long journey home before we finally sailed in the afternoon for Montevideo. The pilot nearly rammed the ship into the dock wall, we were heading fast in that direction and all the fishermen sitting in rows fishing wound their lines up in fright. However, the Captain saw what was happening and ordered full astern.

There was a strong wind when we sailed from Buenos Aires and the banks were so far away I could see nothing. We anchored for the night at midnight and continued at 9 am the following day. All day we ran down the wide river, until we arrived at the outer harbour of Montevideo.

Uruguay, they told me, means River of Birds and is an Indian name. They gave it this name because of the swans and flamingos that lived on the banks of the Uruguay River. It was sometimes called the Purple Land because of a fragrant purple flower that grows everywhere.

We arrived at St Vincente de Cabo Verde in the morning of the 23rd, and when I went out on deck there were the rock walls of the islands and we ran in between and anchored in the bay. I had two Christmas cables, one from Mummy and my sisters at Fleet, and one from all at Megginch. After I had read them I was back to work, busy with the oil barges and taking the dip. Shore boats were crowding round selling oranges, bananas, coconuts, pincushions made from seeds, boats made from horn, shells and very fine crocheted mats, I bought one in exchange for a pair of old shoes. All the crew were fishing, catching the most extraordinary looking fish, pink with gold spots, spikes, and bulging eyes, or silver and red.

On Christmas Eve after tea, the Captain, myself, the Chief Steward and the pantry boy all decorated the artificial green tree we had got in Buenos Aires with silver balls and spangles. By Christmas Day the ship had steadied up and we were able to hear the Queen give her Christmas broadcast. On 27th December we passed the Canaries and later Madeira just as the light was beginning to fade. And finally we reached Antwerp, where my long voyage at last came to an end.

Chapter Seventeen
"Dirty British Coaster..."- 1954-58

It was January 1954 when I got back from my voyage on the *Markab* and I made up my mind about two things, first I would have a long rest before returning to work and second I would not go to sea for such a long period of time again. Although if I didn't go to sea, I couldn't see how enough money could be made to keep everything going, even with Jean working at the British Council, Frances at the Admiralty and the money that Violet gave Mummy. There was more happy news at Megginch this year, as my middle niece Heather got engaged to Andrew Currey, who was in the Navy and whose father was Admiral commanding at Gibraltar. They were not to be married until August, so I decided that when I felt more rested there would be enough time to embark on a short voyage before the wedding.

I managed to get a job as Second Engineer on the *MV Lord Canning*, an 18,000 ton tanker which was running out to the Middle East to load oil and then back to Hamburg. I signed on at Tilbury on 18th May.

It was dark and blowing up a bit when we got to the ship. After climbing down into the launch, we pushed off for the *Lord Canning* which was lying a long way out, her lights dimly visible through the mist. I slept the first night in the owner's room as mine was not ready till next day. It was very hot with the heating full on and the ports screwed up.

Next day was all hurry, finishing up and preparing the ship for sea and inspection. We sailed on a cold dark night and there was a bit of a swell as we dropped the pilot at Dover. My room was one of the nicest I had ever had, dark walnut and mahogany, burnt orange carpet and curtains the same. It was 15 feet by 12 feet, with two ports, its own shower and wash basin, a bunk, settee, table, desk and two chairs. It was very comfortable.

As we neared the Iberian coast I could smell the strong spicy scent of herbs that always permeates the air there. We passed Gibraltar at 5 am in the morning in the dark and mist, and I sent a cable to the Admiral in passing:

"Best wishes from Heather's Aunt Victoria Drummond on *MV Lord Canning* passing Gibraltar Sunday 05.00. Outward bound but will be home for great event." I thought it rather well worded, but I got no answer and it cost me £1!

We passed Pantellaria on Tuesday 25th May, and then Malta the next day, and sighted Crete early on Friday. We arrived at Baniyas in Syria, about 100 miles north of Beirut, on Sunday 30th May where we tied up to a buoy 2 miles off shore, but that was as near as I got.

I could see the foothills, pale silvery green, occasional paintbrush strokes of cypress trees and the oil tanks shining silver like piles of pennies and, until overcome by the smell of oil fumes, there was a faint scent of flowers. The pipeline came 550 miles from near Abadan, it was 30 inches in diameter and discharged 1 million gallons of oil a year. The line ran under the sea for 2 miles and was connected up to flex hoses for filling the tankers. Pumping commenced at 10 am and continued for 12 hours. I was very busy with various engine room jobs which could not be done at sea. In the afternoon I had just changed for tea and sat on the deck for 5 minutes, looking at the lapping sea and the distant backdrop of mountains, when the Chief asked me to make out a complete store list in triplicate. So I went down to my cabin, turned on the light and thought I would go back on deck when I had finished, but by that time it was completely dark.

It was really an out and away job. They disconnected the pipeline at 10 pm and by 12.30 am we were sailing into the clear dark night. When we passed Cyprus next morning a swallow came on board, twittered a bit as if making up her mind which way to go, and headed off again towards Cyprus. Next day as we passed Crete the Arab crew brought me some flat crusty loaves they had baked and a little red pepper paste, so strong that a tiny bit burnt my mouth. June 2nd was the great Mohammedan feast day so I tried to get them some time off, which was not easy. They were very pleased and later brought me a bundle of fresh fruit they had somehow got on board at Baniyas, tiny green and yellow plums, little sweet apricots and two huge oranges.

Two days later the Captain told me we were to go to Finnart on Loch Long and not to Hamburg as I had been told. The weather continued beautiful, and as the sun set in a brilliant scarlet ball we could see the lights of Algiers twinkling bravely. Gibraltar looked steely and impregnable as we slipped into the Straits full of porpoises playing and diving round the ship. There were always lots of porpoises in the Straits of Gibraltar. The weather changed when we got into the bay and there was a great roll and we were shipping seas fore and aft. We finally reached Loch Long on 13th June where I paid off, as I did not think I could risk another voyage in case I did not get back in time for the wedding. I took a bus to Edinburgh where I saw Hamish again. It was over two years since we had met and he was just the same, making wry jokes and keeping me on my toes. "My old friend the stoker," he called me. I think he was as pleased to see me as I was to see him.

By 4th August, I was back at Megginch for Heather's wedding, Jean and Frances joined me later with new silk dresses they had bought in London. But of course I wore my uniform. It was a very nautical wedding with Andrew in the Navy, and all the bridesmaids wore flowing white organdie with sailor collars and carried anchors of flowers. My little great-nephew Adam was a page, wearing the tiniest sailor suit and only just able to toddle. I carried him down to the chapel and back, both of us in uniform. As the oldest and youngest sea-dogs present I thought it was appropriate.

I managed to get another short job in the autumn taking the *MV Dundalk Bay* from Poplar to Rotterdam as Second. I joined her on 25th October and worked hard getting everything shipshape. While I was there I read in the papers that my cousin Jackie Cecil had died. I was determined to get Frances to join me for a weekend's break when I paid off in Rotterdam as I knew how upset she would be. We sailed on 27th October and were anchored out in Rotterdam where I worked hard until the replacement Second arrived a week later. Frances joined me at the Central Hotel and we had a happy time together and went to see my old friends the de Booys.

It was when I came back in November that I had my accident. I was going down the Cut near Waterloo when a van suddenly mounted the pavement and knocked me over, cutting open my heel, bruising my leg and giving me a considerable shake-up. After I had been patched up, I was allowed home, but I stayed in bed for over two months and remained very shaken for a long time. In order to receive compensation for not working, I had the greatest difficulty proving that I had been earning between £64 and £70 a month, depending on the job. There was also the cost of nursing and the damage to my clothing. A pair of new nylon stockings which I had bought at the Army and Navy store for 8/11 and was wearing for the first time were a total loss. Eventually I had to sue Messrs Freeman, Hardy and Willis, and while I was waiting for the settlement, which took some time, I had to borrow money from my lawyer in order to keep abreast of the rent.

While I was convalescing, Cherry and Humphrey had a little daughter, Charlotte. Everyone was delighted, she was the fourteenth Charlotte in the family. This new arrival to the family had been preceeded by a great sadness, the death of Cousin Lucy Drummond-Hay. She had been a very special friend who always got me out of scrapes when I was small.

On 20th June I joined the *MV Blythe Trader* of the Moller Line at Hull. We were lying off the port and there was a great deal of work to do since one of the junior engineers on my watch had left and was not replaced. However, I took on an extra fireman to do the hardest work as otherwise it would have been impossible. But the work was extremely strenuous and I could only stick it because of the money, £81 a month. The crew were all Chinese and I had difficulty with them to begin with, but after I logged one I had less trouble.

I had thought we were going to New York, but to my surprise we ended up at Baltimore, where we arrived on 13th July, not a very auspicious date as it turned out. This coincided with a strike of the Baltimore tugs so we had to dock at the Oriole Ship Ceiling Pier where we were fitted out for grain. On Saturday we moved over to the Pennsylvania Railroad grain elevator without tugs and promptly rammed the pier, damaging three plates in the hull. This was not the fault of the engine room, I was glad to say, but the fact that ten of the Chinese crew from the engine room escaped probably was. Five were got back, the rest vanished into the interior of the States as illegal immigrants and the ship was fined $5,000 as a result. On Monday we had to move into the Bethlehem Quay Highway repair yard to get the plates mended and it was not till Friday that we were able to get back to the elevator to get the grain loaded. Unfortunately someone mixed wheat with the oats being loaded and the whole lot had to be sucked out again. Then we were constantly having to move out to let other ships in and all this with the temperatures soaring into the 90s, a very hot humid heat.

Baltimore was still the rather rough town that I had remembered from my voyage on the *Markab*. Some of the engineers were ashore in a beer garden when three youths came up to a respectable looking old lady holding a baby on her lap at the next table and snatched the baby from her, threw it into the back of their car and made off, kicking in the stomach a man who tried to stop them and pushing two women off the bumper.

With all these movements I never had time to get ashore properly, and although I rang Julia and Josephine in Norfolk I was never able to get away for long enough to see them. I also had the greatest difficulty in extricating any money from Captain Finlay, although I did manage to prise £5 out of him and went to Washington one evening and once to a place in the country called Frederick. We eventually left the States on 30th July, the day we should have been landing in Europe! I was up at 3.30 am to get her ready by 6 am and take her out. The Chief Engineer was very drunk the whole time and only made a very wobbly appearance when we were well down the river 5 hours later. We were headed for Antwerp or Rotterdam, no one seemed sure which, but I was determined to leave. We arrived at Antwerp on 10th August and I left the ship and signed off as I had heard she was going to Cuba for sugar and then through the Panama Canal to China and Japan. I did not regret leaving her.

Cherry and Humphrey had been to the Scottish Horse Dance at Blair and wrote to tell me about it. I thought of the time when I had been there when the eight pipers marched round the dining room table and I had danced every dance and wore a wreath of holly in my hair.

I could not help thinking of Hamish, he was a person who had never changed. Although his hair was now quite white he was still the dashing, good-looking man I first remembered. We still had our jokes and companionship together, and never a voyage did I start on but a letter arrived from him to wish me luck. I kept his photograph in my cabin and he had mine beside his bed.

In September Heather and Andrew had a son, Robert, and it was lovely to have another great-nephew. I only wished that so many of our older friends and relations were not dying off. In October my cousin Tommy Cecil died and now there was only Henny left of our four cousins we had played with at Didlington. The following month Cousin Albert Baillie died, but he was 91 and had lived long enough to enjoy the success of his autobiography *My First 80 Years*. I was still "resting", as the acting profession called it, at Tresco, but my leg was getting stronger all the time and I felt that by 1956 I would be fit enough to go to sea for longer periods. That November the Queen unveiled the Merchant Navy Memorial on Tower Hill. She said, "It is fitting that in this place, which for centuries has been at the very heart of the maritime life of our nation, there should stand this memorial which is indeed 'a token of all brave captains and all intrepid sailors and mates, and all that went down doing their duty.'" After the *Last Post* played by the Royal Marine Band, the hoarse voices of ships on the river sounded their tribute. I thought of so many of my shipmates, gone forever on the seas. It was a sad moment, but I knew they would be pleased to be remembered in this way.

After Christmas I felt a good deal better and I was ready to set off to sea again in January. This time I had a job as Chief Engineer for a Dutch company, Hoyman and Schurrmans, on their ship the *MV Rampart* which I was to join in Malta by flying from London on 9th January. After a brief stop in Rome, we eventually landed in Malta at 9 pm.

The agent Mr Sullivan and his wife came to meet me and drove me to my hotel in Selima. The weather that night was like a warm May evening.

My room was high and airy with yellow and white paving and a low bed with a blue cover. I had a theory that beds got lower and lower the further east one went, lower in Turkey, lower in Egypt until they finish as a palm mat on the floor in Japan.

No sooner had I closed my eyes, it seemed, than beams of sunlight filtered through the slats in the Venetian shutters. After ringing the agents and finding the ship might not be in till evening, I set out to explore my old haunts in Malta. Everything looked as if it had been washed in yellow ochre: the walls which divide the fields, the houses and the stones in the gardens. My impression was of wrought iron doorways, lanterns and window bars, splashes of magenta bougainvillea or Eton blue plumbago, glimpses of lemons with waxy blossoms among the green leaves and at the end of each street a flash of brilliant sea.

It was only a 15 minute bus ride to Valetta. Over the driver's seat was a little shrine with holy pictures, artificial flowers and a much needed St Christopher. Outside in the sunshine were donkeys loaded with country produce and some were hitched to carts. I passed the church of St John where a faint scent of incense drifted from the dark doors. Outside the silver gates hung the keys of various fortresses captured by the knights. The pillars inside were white up to the height that a man could reach and after that gilt up to the roof. The men who "reached" to steal the gold were Napoleon's troops.

Next morning after breakfast I signed on at the shipping office where I met Captain Angus and the old Chief.

"I wouldn't be you," he said to me rather cryptically as he left.

That night we sailed out from the Grand Harbour at Malta and I soon discovered what an awful sea boat she was. The Chief Steward, Vic Rogers, told me she had a jinx on her. I thought he was being foolish, although I did not feel satisfied with the thrust block and the day after leaving Malta I stopped and had a look at it. The last Chief had sold me a pup, for it must have been very hot and warped the metal the day before I joined. If I had known this I would have got it mended in Malta. However, I washed it out with oil and planned to get it done in Bordeaux.

As we passed Gibraltar the mate signalled with a lamp as quick as he could: *ADMIRAL CURREY, MOUNT GIB. BEST WISHES VICTORIA DRUMMOND C/E RAMPART.*

The Captain was on the bridge and I anxiously waited for a reply. I had begun to say rather weakly, "Perhaps they are at a bull fight in Spain," but

271

the Captain said, "They would surely be back by dark." Then the answer began to come through slowly and deliberately: *VICTORIA DRUMMMMOND, C/E RAMPART. THANKS VERY MUCH FOR MESSAGE SO SORRY NOT TO SEE YOU. CURREY.*

How nice of him, I thought, and my stock soared, as we sailed into the dark leaving the lights of Gib behind.

There was a bitterly cold wind and the lights of the villages on the banks of the Garonne shone out like cut diamonds as we passed in the moonless night. We tied up alongside the river quay at Bassens close to midnight about 12 miles from Bordeaux.

There was much to arrange and fix, particularly the repairs to the after shaft bearing and thrust block to be undertaken by STEMA, the Societe de Traveaux et d'Etudes Maritimes. The repairs took one day to complete, following which we commenced engine trials with the Lloyds Surveyor in attendance and by 9.30 had been issued with a seaworthy certificate. We then proceeded down the river, but I found I could not maintain the main engine lubricating oil pressure. I was on the main engine controls and asked the Second Engineer to inform the Captain that I must stop the main engines and I rang "Stop" on the telegraph.

The Captain replied, "You will have to carry on for a few minutes. We are in a dangerous position and might have a collision."

We carried on and the main bearing went. I rang "Stop" again and the Third Mate came to the engine room with a message from the Captain to say we had anchored. While I was waiting for the engine to cool off I looked for the cause and discovered that the oil in the main engine sump was at the same level as at time of sailing.

When the engine had cooled off sufficiently to open the crank case doors safely, I found the main bearing metal had overheated and run. I told the Captain what had happened and we had to go back to Bassens for further repairs. We were back from Sunday 22nd January to 3rd February. I was kept very busy as the French fitters worked from 7 am to 9 pm and I had to be there the whole time. They stopped from 12 pm to 2 pm for the long French dejeuner and if I had a quick lunch I could get off and walk ashore in that time.

One day I crossed the main road into the straggling village of Lormont with its grey stone houses and all the doors and windows painted grey also which gave an appearance of dilapidation. But not so the inhabitants who smiled on all sides; many of them were relations of the men who worked on the ship. Some of the women wore old fashioned sabots and I had noticed that some of the boys working in the engine room wore black painted wooden shoes. The old church stood at the top of the steep street with a carved doorway rather like a cross stitch pattern, and inside a faint scent of incense and a feeling of peace.

Everyone knew I was Chef de Machine on the British ship. I gave the men hot coffee and sandwiches every evening at 7.30 pm, a welcome break for them.

On 31st January I had a whole afternoon off and went to Bordeaux. The French workmen had worked splendidly and made a really good job of fitting the new main bearings which had been flown from Holland and refitting all the bottom ends and six new pads to the thrust block. The foreman came from Médoc and told me all about wine making and how claret was a corruption from the local name "clairet" which meant red wine. He bicycled over to his home on Sunday and brought me two bottles of Médoc from two small vineyards there, one white and one red.

I was quite sad to leave when we sailed for Bilbao on the early tide on 3rd February. We had snow and heavy seas and it took us a day. When I came out of the engine room and went on deck, instead of "sunny Spain", it all looked like a Christmas card. Everything was very pretty in the clear snow light, but it was cold! I had had a bad cold since the night the main bearing went and without heating in my room could not shake it off. I let the other engineers go ashore, trying to keep warm and catching up on my writing since the boat was such a bad sea boat that I could not write legibly at sea.

On 6th February, the work by the shore firm was finished and I went ashore. As I crossed the river to the new town I saw men dragging it for a body with a boat. They were watched by a large crowd which did not enliven the scene. All the shops and restaurants were shut and it was pouring with icy rain.

Next day we sailed into heavy grey seas and blowing snow flakes. We had only been going 24 hours when, without warning, the main circulating pump broke down. At 11.30 I heard a noise in the main engine and rang "Stop". After inspection I found the main sea water circulating pump had stripped some teeth on the gear wheels and had broken down. The last time this happened they couldn't make the repair and had to be towed in, I was told. However, I got the pump out and blanked off sea suction and got circulation through an independent pump. We worked all night at it and by a miracle the sea was as calm as a June night, but the moment we finished it began to blow again.

And it blew! cold snow, heavy seas and dark days. It was so bad we were only doing 3 knots and couldn't get out of the bay and make Ushant.

I said we were lucky not to be doing 3 knots astern. A huge tanker came out of the snow and tried for an hour to pass us, but even she was making heavy weather. We heard later that a coaster went down about 10 miles away, but all hands had been saved. Eventually we passed Ushant and the Channel Islands where we put in to Poole Harbour for shelter and to pump out the water. We were there for two days and it felt like heaven to rest up a bit.

However, on 14th February, we started off again through more blinding snow, up the Maas to Rotterdam. Great blocks of ice piled up at the mouth of the river which bumped and crunched against the ship's sides. The temperature was 5°F and all the ports in my room were covered with snow flowers and ferns. I turned in after taking all precautions against the engine freezing, but it was too cold to sleep so I made some hot milk and nutmeg.

The next morning we moved berth to Schiedam and there was quite a lot of work to get through. We got the pump ashore to the makers who said the breakdown was caused by the ball bearings giving out. The next day I went into Rotterdam to get some warm socks and some cough mixture. There was deep snow and it was a long way to walk; the wind was like scissors and knives.

Next day we sailed for London through an awful night of snow. I had three stand-bys on watch for snow blizzards. The snow was so thick I could see nothing, and I heard that two ships were in a collision somewhere off Harwich that night. We got across to the West India Dock, however, and the next day I paid off as my cough and cold were really awful and I felt very ill. They gave me a cup of hot tea at the Board of Trade while I was waiting and I coughed and spluttered and coughed and coughed. I could hardly wait to get back to Tresco and get into bed.

Whether the *Rampart* had been jinxed or not I could not say, but I heard from the Chief Steward that in Benghazi a wind had blown up so they couldn't leave the harbour. Then the Chief Engineer found oil leaking from the stern gland so they had to go into dry dock in Malta. Then the windlass would not work because of salt deposits and cables kept coming backwards and forwards to discharge the cargo or hold it back. Finally there was a fire in my old room which burnt the mattress to a cinder and ruined the deck and the chair. I felt I was lucky to have left.

When I got back I heard that Cousin Alice Drummond-Hay had died at the end of January, the eldest and most special of the four sisters. I had been thinking of her when we were in Malta, of all the games we had played, of how I looked forward to seeing her when I was at Burntisland, and how we had planned her London visits.

But nothing could spoil my delight in getting into a warm bed and staying there. Jean and Frances and Mrs Hanceri ran up and down stairs with trays and hot drinks and suddenly one day I felt well again, which I had thought I never could, and spring came. The snowdrops and early crocuses came out in the garden and the forsythia hedges began bursting into bud.

Andrew's ship, the *Mounts Bay*, went to South Africa and I took charge of seeing off Heather and little Robert who were sailing out to join him there. Being such an old sea dog myself, I soon saw about tipping stewards and seeing that her cabin was as it should be.

Money was still very tight, so on 5th April I packed my gear and travelled down to Sheerness to join the *Lord Canning* once more. It was cold with a sharp wind at Sheerness, and after calling at the shipping office I had a cup of coffee and met the Second Mate and the Third Engineer, who were also joining the ship. I scrambled down the steps which were slippery with seaweed and into a rather small, dirty launch with an open cabin. She was bobbing about in a heavy sea as we chugged away to another pier near the new oil refinery at Port Victoria, Isle of Grain.

There was a lot to do in the engine room as the No 1 piston was out with new rings being fitted top and bottom and the No 2 lines were leaking so the whole unit had to be changed. Instead of sailing on Saturday, we were not able to get away till Monday and the hours between were one mad rush. Two of the stewards had gone at Sheerness, but after some shuffling round we managed to get good replacements so my room was very clean and tidy. Although the weather remained obstinately cold my room was so warm that I kept very cosy. The water in the tap was so hot that I could fill my hot water bottle from it, a great change from the *Rampart*.

With so many engineers on board and a smooth trip, there was very little for me to do and I spent a lot of time in my comfortable room mending my stockings and blouses which I had felt too cold and ill to do on the last voyage. There was also some ornithological interest. In the Straits of Gibraltar a yellow wagtail came on board and spent about four days on the ship hopping happily about on deck. We passed Malta in the night and I could smell the land. The wagtail must have too, for it flew away. Near Crete a little brown bird about the size of a robin joined us. He drank fresh water from a tap that was leaking outside the galley door where it ran away down the deck. As we passed Cyprus on 20th April, a fly catcher with a brown and white spotted breast came on board, hopping about catching flies. The Fifth Engineer, asked me to come to his cabin where he showed me a quail he had found half dead on the deck and revived. He let it go as we passed near the coast. We were headed for Tripoli this time, half-way between Baniyas and Beirut, in Lebanon. As before, we were a long way out filling off a pipeline and there was no chance of going ashore. However, several small boats came out selling things and I was able to borrow some money to buy fruit and a string of wooden camels for Adam's birthday.

The Captain asked me how long I had sailed Second. "Second and *Chief*," I said, "for sixteen years."

We were only anchored off Tripoli for two days before we started back, passing Cyprus in the night. This time a yellow canary came on board and had a good drink from the tap.

On 24th April, after we passed Crete, I was on watch taking the temperature when I saw that the jacket and piston cooling water were rising. I dashed round to the sea valve and found it shut tight and I couldn't open it. I rushed to get a wheel spanner, rang the Chief Engineer and was just getting it open when the Chief came down. He was mad of course, but the temperature went down all right. As they were all right until 7.30 I could only imagine that someone had slipped down and shut it, thinking I wouldn't notice and that the job would be overheated. However, I had noticed. The donkeyman thought someone shut it because it was always kept open and regulated the water to the fresh water cooler.

On 25th April I saw a pair of turtle doves come on board for a rest. The decks had been painted but they were quite hard and dry. I gave the Bosun 15 gallons of red oxide out of the store, which was the quickest dry I could find, because of the birds. One of the firemen who had been painting the fore pump room had been knocked out by the fumes. It was a horrible place about 35 feet down a shaft by iron ladder to the pumps at the bottom. They had got him up, however, and I gave him some milk to drink to neutralise the fumes. Later the Chief Steward gave him some sal volatile and we put him on his bunk and covered him in blankets till he came round.

The rest of the voyage passed without incident and on 3rd May we took the pilot on board and went up the Scheldt to Antwerp. The next morning was calm and still with Dutch and Belgian barges gliding along past the mud flats, and here and there little villages with church spires surrounded by a cluster of houses and a foam of pink and white blossom. We were at the oil station, Berth 383, about 5 miles from the centre of Antwerp, and although the next day was Saturday I had to work till 4 pm. How lovely it was speeding along in a blue bus towards the town which I knew so well. All the trees were budding into full leaf and the chestnuts were covered with white candles.

However, after dropping the pilot at Flushing, there were two days of hell with everything battened down for the fog. The fumes were so bad I could scarcely breathe and I had pains between my joints because of them. It was such a relief to get ashore at Falmouth in the May sunshine and to breathe in the scent of the peach blossom and spring flowers to clear my lungs. Then we moved her into dry dock and I paid off on 12th May. She was now going to run between Africa and the Persian Gulf and everyone was very sorry that I was leaving.

In June I was in Scotland again, visiting Megginch. Best of all was a visit to Hamish at Blair. We sat by the fire and talked. I suppose one only gets a few such nice patches in life, otherwise this life would be heaven and then heaven would be no surprise. But I did wish Hamish wouldn't talk about dying. "I shall certainly be dead first," I told him.

By mid August I was away to sea again, this time as Chief Engineer on a small coaster, the *Concha*, lying at Cherbourg. I flew over from Eastleigh Airport on a wet blowy August day and into Cherbourg where the fruit trees were already covered with ripening apples and pears. I went down to the dry dock where quite the dirtiest and most ill kept ship I have ever joined was lying. The *Concha* was a very small, very dirty tramp.

I got my bags aboard and down to my room. The two blankets were very thin, the floor matting covered in coal dust and oil, the whole room dirty, neglected and begrimed. On this class of ship I kept my own fork, spoon, knife and mug. I took my mug to the galley for tea and a helping of Spanish rice or fish on the plate, which I ate sitting on a pile of rope in the sun, but as it did nothing but rain, I had to dodge into my room with the plate. I had a Second and Third Engineer and four men in the engine room.

On 24th August the Lloyd's Surveyor came and told me that my mother had died that morning. Of course I had known that it would happen but the shock was still terrible. She had been her usual self, had her breakfast and was reading the *Times* when she suddenly called "Nurse!" and slipped away in a matter of minutes. The company flew me back, and Jean, Frances and I travelled up to Megginch for the funeral. All was as she would have liked. Her coffin covered in Drummond tartan plaid with a wreath of holly and white lilies on it.

The Rev Fenwick Kirk, an old scholar from the Megginch Sunday school which she had so loved, came up from his parish church in Northumberland to take the service. The sun was shining, there were masses of flowers everywhere and we sang *Now the Day is Over*. John and Humphrey were the pall bearers and outside under the holly trees Sandy Redford, the blacksmith, played the pipes.

The day Mummy died the text in the *Times* was: "The Lord He it is that doth go before thee, he will not fail thee, neither forsake thee; fear not, neither be dismayed." She always read the texts first so it must have been the last thing that she read.

I thought of that often, as I went back to my ship; it was almost like a sign from Mummy herself. When I got back I cleaned out my room. I got a fireman up to help and we cleaned out all the dirt and rubbish and painted the cupboards so that they were clean enough to hang my clothes in. Every day I worked very hard, but in the evening I was able to run ashore into the attractive old world town. Everywhere I went and everything I saw reminded me of Mummy. She would have enjoyed the fisher folk with tanned faces wearing blue jerseys and mending nets, all the fisher boats marked CH for Cherbourg, the market with the fresh flowers from country gardens and the many cats and dogs of indeterminate breeds.

On 9th September there was a fight between the sailors and the Cook. It had started outside the galley and one sailor had thrown a plate at the Cook which had smashed on the stove. Then the knives came out. No one was hurt and I got hold of two of the knives, a carving knife and a bread knife, before any serious damage was done.

All this commotion meant there was no tea or coffee to be got in the galley the next morning, so I walked over the bridge and had a lovely cup of black coffee with plenty of sugar. It was too early for bread, but Madame suggested fetching some from the boulangerie, so I ran over and got some warm croissants which reminded me of Sunday breakfasts at Fleet when we went down to see Mummy. The rest of the day we were busy working on the ship and sailed early in the morning of the 10th September for Bordeaux.

I had asked the Captain for another 10 tons of bunkers as I thought if we had bad weather in the bay we would not have enough. The Captain said we could put in to St Nazaire if we ran short. However, the weather was so good, silvery and smooth with a fresh salt breeze, that I thought we would risk it, and we indeed arrived at Bordeaux with 6 tons in hand. By the time we tied up at Berth 12 amidst the wooden sleepers and pit props I had been on duty for 20 hours. However, rather than stay on the filthy boat I got a tram to the town where I sat in the Grand Hotel et Cafe de Bordeaux and drank orange juice and soda water. I found I could get a bath here, too, which was a delightful thought after washing in a bucket of cold water on board. There was a long dark walk past shore side cafes and wood piles to the ship after leaving the tram. Normally I would not have minded but I was a little nervous as I had had a spot of bother with a fireman earlier that day. I told him to get the ashes up and he threw a bucket of water over me. However, I told him I would log him three days pay and got him well beaten down.

The next day, Saturday 15th September, there were so many complaints about the filthy conditions on board that the British Consul and the Costa Rican Consul came down to inspect the ship. The Captain was ashore so they sent for me. The Consul seemed quite horrified about everything and asked me if I would like to pay off there.

I said, "No, I gave my word to the company I would go home with her, and I want to pull the job off and improve her."

Most evenings I managed to get ashore and have a bath. I would also look at shops or stroll in the gardens and sit drinking orange juice in cafes. I still didn't like the long dark road back to the docks, though I now knew the names of the dogs in the cafes and now that I called their names they stopped barking.

We sailed on Wednesday 19th September and after a rather trying voyage sailing through thick fog reached Hartlepool a week later. I still had a little more time on the boat to serve out my contract, so I gritted my teeth and stuck it. We sailed from Hartlepool on 29th September bound for South Shields which we left on 3rd October. While we were at sea the bearing bolts snapped and I had to lash up the broken parts. We eventually berthed after a lot of very complicated manoeuvring. In the end we crossed the Channel and arrived at Ghent two days later. From Ghent we went to Antwerp and in Antwerp at last I paid off. The first thing I did was to find my familiar hotel and have a bath.

After my return from sailing on the *Concha* I made a determined effort to get a proper Board of Trade Certificate as Chief Engineer. If I had this I would be able to command a much higher salary and sail on much better boats. I had my Board of Trade Second Certificate, I had a Panamanian Chief's Certificate and I had been sailing as Chief or Second for over sixteen years. Very often when I was sailing as Second I had had to take over from the Chief for one reason or another and run the engine room myself anyway. I had sat the examination 31 times and each time I had been failed, sometimes on one point, sometimes on another. Mr Martin of the Dundee

Technical College had told me long ago that my papers were as good as anyone else's and that the only reason I had failed was because they did not want to give a woman a Chief's Certificate. I wrote to the Board of Trade, to the Institute of Marine Engineers of which I was proud to be a member, to my local Member of Parliament and to Sir Winston Churchill. Some of them were sympathetic but it all boiled down to the opinion that I had to sit the exam again. I knew whatever I did they would fail me on my spelling, which was always rocky, if for nothing else. So I decided not to take the exam again.

By May 1957 I was once more scenting the sea in my nostrils and I got a job as Second of the *MV British Monarch* which I joined at London on 4th May. The accommodation was good but my room was very hot as the deck steam pipes ran along the deck just outside. I was a little worried about Hamish who had been ill when I joined the ship and I promised in my farewell note to send him a get well card from New York.

We left London in the morning on 6th May and were full away at sea the next morning. I was working 11 hours a day, blowing down the Scotch boiler, repairing the transfer pumps, cleaning the feed filters. The temperature was 92°F in the engine room.

At 8.32 am on the morning of 9th May I received a Marconigram from my sisters. It said simply: *H DIED TODAY LOVE J F.* It had been sent the day before. No wonder I was thinking of him so much.

When the Hedgehog died I had felt wild and desperate, not knowing where to turn. Now I felt only a deep and abiding sadness, too deep for sharp sorrow. I wondered if Hamish had always seen me as the girl with black hair and laughing eyes who wore a holly wreath at the ball at Blair and danced her slippers into holes. I never went to Scotland without seeing him, I never sailed without writing to him and he to me. I thought of my pride at having him with me for the launch of the *Master Nikos*, of weekends in Edinburgh, visits to Cuil-an-Duin, to Easter Moncreiffe and to Blair.

During the 11 hours working in the engine room and the stuffy hot night in my cabin as we crossed the Atlantic, I had plenty of time to think about Hamish. We arrived at New Orleans on 25th May at 10.55 am and were to leave again that night after filling up with oil. I was able to get off for 2 hours to go up to the town, and went with John Meigher, who was working as an AB. He had been a lieutenant in the Navy, but there had been some scandal or trouble and he had to leave. However, I found him very good company, though occasionally moody, and we shared many of the same tastes in books and art.

We were at Baton Rouge for two days and then headed down the Mississippi towards the Panama Canal. It took us six days through the Caribbean to Colon. We tied up alongside the oil berth at Christobal and bunkered on 4th June. I had hoped that perhaps here there might be letters for me with news about Hamish's funeral, some details to wrap around the bleak facts of loss. There were no letters. I thought of the last time we had gone through the Panama Canal in 1943 with guards on deck; how very different, although it had been as hot then as it was now. The engine room temperature never seemed to be less than 110°F.

From Panama on 6th June we were 31 days at sea to reach Japan. Two days after leaving Panama the diesel generator, which supplied light and power to the steering engine, broke a connecting rod. I was standing less than a yard from it at the time and I tried to get round to stop it when I heard the noise, but the connecting rod went right through the crank case and the bits flew in all directions at great force and a huge chunk of cast iron cut my foot deeply. They got me off to the Doctor at once and he tied up my foot, but I was off watches for a week.

That night we lost the Second Mate. He fell off the side of the ship when reading the log but no one noticed until breakfast the next morning. The Captain turned the ship around straight away and we went back over the course. At about 1.30 pm we picked him up, not one penny the worse. It was rather too exciting these past two days, but I couldn't help thinking how Hamish would have laughed.

On Saturday 15th June I started taking the morning watch again and by 30th June I was taking two watches, but my foot was still extremely painful. There was a lot of time to think when I was nursing my sore foot and I remembered what Hamish had written to me the year before when Mummy died, "I am sure the people we love who have died are never very far from us." During that long voyage across the Pacific I felt very close to Hamish.

On 7th July we arrived at Shimizu in Japan about 70 miles from Tokyo, and although there were no letters from home there were lots of letters from dear Alice and Dorothy Britton with all sorts of instructions as to how to get to them. Sunday evening about 6 pm I slipped ashore to telephone, the streets were filled with lanterns and lights, paper flowers, spangles and sequins all shining and sparkling in festoons as it was the festival of two stars that meet in the sky, the Love Festival. Alice and Dorothy were delighted at the idea of my joining them.

It was so lovely to get back into the cool bedroom at Hayama with the sound of the Pacific waves lapping on the beach. Alice took me to her doctor who X-rayed my foot and he said there was a crack in the bone which had mended and a dislocated small toe which was pulled crooked by a contracted tendon. He bandaged it up and suggested I should see another specialist the next day.

On Thursday morning 11th July, I was back on the *British Monarch* again feeling refreshed and different.

Now there were letters for me; everyone had written all the sad details about Hamish which I had so wanted to know. Jean and Frances had been to tea with Cousin Kitty Atholl, who told them she had been to see Hamish in Perth Infirmary. He had been getting better, but had written to tell her he would not go to the Caledonian Ball. She said "He seemed to be asleep and didn't talk to me at all, but he did talk to relations who came in the evening." It occurred to me that Hamish had been bored seeing Cousin Kitty sitting by his bed and merely shut his eyes so he didn't have to talk to her. He had a relapse that night and died early on Wednesday morning, 8th May. On Friday he was cremated and there was a small private funeral at St Bride's Church with two Atholl Highlander pipers.

On Saturday there was a memorial service in Dunkeld Cathedral. When we had that long talk about death I said to Hamish, "I could not bear to go to your funeral." Perhaps it was prophetic, but Hamish jokingly replied, "Funerals in Perthshire are like garden parties, there is so little entertainment that people look forward to them and talk all the time."

Cherry sent me the text from the *Times* on the day that he died: "God giveth to a man that is good in His sight wisdom, and knowledge, and joy...." It was something true to think about as we sailed for Fiji.

We arrived at Lautaka in Fiji on 29th July where we stayed for nine days loading sugar. It was surrounded by coral beaches and palms with tropical sunsets. The houses were thatched and built to withstand tropical storms while remaining cool inside. They were all built without hammers or nails and in each village the houses, or bures, were built of local material—bamboo, palm leaves and thatched with dry grass. We were there for just over a week, the place was charming and so were the Fijians.

We sailed from Suva on 8th August and after 20 days at sea, arrived alongside the sugar quay at Vancouver where we were to discharge. All the lights of Vancouver were shining over the water like coloured bars when we arrived. We were in port here for nearly two weeks, during which time I was very busy with repairs on deck, besides supervising the discharging of the sugar. Even so I managed to go ashore quite often and get up to the town centre and walk through the beautiful Stanley Park, full of golden willows drooping over the lake, and its collection of totem poles with fantastic Indian carvings on them.

I was ashore one day when the bridge of my plate broke. It was a moment of pure horror besides being very sore. I could hardly go back to the ship with gaps in my teeth. By luck I managed to find a good dentist who was able to restore my equanimity in addition to mending several holes in my own teeth which had been giving me toothache. There were a few days on board when I had to be very careful talking or smiling, but I think no one noticed and I was soon back to my old self again.

There were letters for me here, too. Jean and Frances were full of the busy time they had had all summer with their guests. April had been staying with them for three months, going to dances and parties almost every night, and there had been Violet and later Cherry and Humphrey with both children.

From Vancouver we sailed to New Westminster and then on to Victoria. Here I found an old cousin, Sophie Deane-Drummond, who was so old I had thought her dead. However, she wasn't and she entertained me royally and we drove into Thunderbird Park with more totem poles and out to Malahat Chalet where we had tea. Victoria was lovely and I enjoyed my four-day visit there, especially since I had overcome my teeth problem.

On 26th September we sailed 30 miles north to Cowichan Bay where we loaded timber. Then on Friday 4th October we left for the open sea. I thought a lot about Hamish and longed to get home. We came into Liverpool alongside Hornby Dock at 5.18 on Monday 11th November. The shore workers moved in, the shore donkeymen took over and on Tuesday 12th November I signed off the ship.

John Meagher signed off, too, and we had a vague plan to sail together again. He was staying with his brother-in-law at Wimbledon, although later he too often stayed at Tresco at weekends. I was passionate about opera, which unfortunately he did not like at all, otherwise he was a most agreeable companion. By the end of the year he had a job with the Edward VII Nautical School at Poplar. This did not last and by February 1958 he was sailing to Halifax and then Australia on the *Port Adelaide*.

I stayed at Tresco hibernating all winter and didn't think of returning to sea until 1st May 1958 when I answered an advertisement in the *Times* for a Chief Engineer for an old-fashioned motor yacht which was to sail from Southampton to Istanbul calling at all sorts of lovely places in the Mediterranean. She was called the *Adventuress* and belonged to Squadron Leader Williamson DFC. He, his wife and children had bought this large Edwardian yacht and were sailing her out as a sort of adventure with a crew of volunteers who were to pay their own way. I had somehow envisaged that I would have some kind of reimbursement although this was not the case. The *Adventuress* was in Camper Nicholson's Yard at Northiam, Southampton, and I had a nice room, but they seemed to work all hours, and besides there was a lot to do on the engine. The Squadron Leader gave a talk to the crew about diving and how fatal it was to drink any alcohol.

We sailed to Yarmouth on the Isle of Wight on 17th May where we anchored out about 7 pm in the evening. I got ashore for about an hour. It was a pretty place with wild flowers and yachts, and very quiet. We left the next day heading for the bay and Gibraltar, our first stop. We had a good roll going over and pitching, too. We had to stop on 19th May to clean the sea water cooling pipe and change the oil in the sumps and also to clean out the bilges. We stopped again to clean the bilges the next day and the *Port Victor* stopped and asked if we wanted assistance. This was after the Ailsa Craig generator gave out. However, I got it going again and off we went. The next day there was an oil pipe leak in the main engine which had to be mended and on 22nd May we were at last out of the bay.

We stopped to buy fish from a Spanish fishing boat near Finisterre and later a Spanish gun boat came after us and signalled to us to stop. They lowered a boat and went after the Spanish fishing boats too. I suppose they thought we had been smuggling something . Besides the crew and the Williamsons, there were their three children and Cadbury, a milk chocolate coloured dachshund on board. A lot of diving was going on from the ship every time we stopped, but not by me. The weather improved dramatically after the bay. On 23rd May we only had to stop once to repair a leaking plug on the main steam cooling line. We finally arrived at anchorage at Gibraltar at 5.24 am on the morning of Sunday 25th May. The Shell launch came out about taking bunkers and as luck would have it he was a Blue Funnel man, so he gave me a lift ashore. He told me all the small tramps were now laid up, or nearly all, and he thought it would break the small companies, leaving the big ones with a monopoly.

We were in Gib for three days and there were a lot of repairs and maintenance jobs to do. We were at anchor the whole time until our last day when we moved alongside Algeciras, a small Spanish town full of yellow and white houses with green shutters and ironwork grilles. We only stayed one day and then went out to take bunkers from the Shell oil vessel, and set off for Ibiza on 29th May. It took us two days to get there, an unspoilt pretty place with the houses rising sheer from the harbour, fishing boats and nets along the quay. And again marvellous wild flowers. We were there for four days until 4th June when we sailed for Palma, tying up that night.

We stayed in Palma for about a week and although I had quite a lot to do on the engine there was still time to wander off the boat and into the country, looking at wild flowers and buying fruit. Everyone on board was very pleasant to me, but I did find their somewhat lackadaisical timetable difficult to work with. I was up at 7 am every morning working on the engine and very often there was nothing to eat until after l0 am and one morning 11 am. Lunch was never until 3 pm, or sometimes later, and dinner any time between 10.30 pm and 11 pm, so although the food was good I was often too tired and hungry to eat it.

Mr Williamson said we were using too much oil and cut off half the supply to the main engines without telling me until afterwards what he had done.

I said, "Don't do it. If you do, you will run her out. She is an old engine and needs plenty of oil. There is too much risk. Just let us get to Malta first."

We had quite an argument, but as he was the owner, of course he won. It ended with me saying, "All right, but I am against it."

But I had the last word, or perhaps the *Adventuress* did, because at 11.30 pm on Friday 13th June she cracked her No 3 piston and we were adrift all Friday night. There was an awful lot of work and no proper tools. I worked all night.

Next day an engineer commander and pilot from *HMS Ark Royal* came on board by helicopter. Later, *HMS Scarborough* turned up and took the *Adventuress* in tow until 3.15 am the next morning when she dropped the tow off Pantellaria and we were again adrift in the Mediterranean. The next afternoon an Admiralty tug came and towed us from 3.30 pm to 6 pm. Every day a plane came and circled over us to see how we were getting on. I was working very hard indeed and as it was only for expenses I was beginning to feel hard done by.

Eventually, on 17th June I managed to get the old engine going again and we chugged into Malta. *HMS M162* came alongside and escorted us into the harbour where we remained at anchorage for five days. A port officer came on board to inspect the engine and on Friday we were moved by tug to a water berth. On Saturday they had a party on board for the RAF to thank the plane that came to look for us. I put on my one white suit and medal ribbons and looked quite smart.

On Sunday morning I found the Williamson family all having breakfast, but they said there was not enough for me, so I went ashore and had
a cup of coffee in a cafe before going to matins in the cathedral. I said
nothing but felt boiling with rage inside. After the service I intended to
meander about with my painting things, but had to be back on the ship at
2 pm for another 8 hours work. I thought with longing of Frances and
Jean who were staying in a seaside house at Elie with Humphrey and
Cherry, playing on the beach with Adam and Charlotte. I was also worried as I had had no letter since Sydney from John Meagher on the *Port
Adelaide* and did not know what had happened to him, although I wrote
to him faithfully.

I hoped that all the work I had put into the engine was going to get her
safely to Turkey where I was leaving the boat. We left Malta on the evening
of 23rd June and I had to stop and inspect the main engine to see that the
piston cooling system was working; the valves had to be taken out and
skimmed on the lathe, but in the end we made it to Melos, a beautiful
unspoilt Greek.

On the next voyage between Melos and Chios we were once more adrift.
The No 3 piston heated up this time, but I got everything going again and
we finally came alongside the quay after 9 pm on the evening of 1st July. I
sorted out the pistons when we were there and the voyage on 6th July
from Chios to Izmir was accomplished without disaster.

Here I left the *Adventuress* with few regrets. The Williamson family were
all charming, but like the Flopsy Bunnies, a little inclined to leave too much
to providence, and the poor old yacht required constant personal attendance and fiddling with her engine. Each time she had broken down I felt it
would surely be the final collapse. I then made a pleasant overland trip by
bus to Istanbul, seeing parts of Turkey which I had hitherto been unable
to take in. I spent a night in Istanbul, seeing the Blue Mosque, Santa Sofia,
the Golden Horn, palaces and boats and yet more mosques, and finally on
Sunday 13th July I came home via the Orient Express, another treat.

There was a letter from John Meagher at Izmir saying he had had a
little difficulty and had now left the *Port Adelaide*, but no word as to what
had happened. Later in August Mr Eldon Harris, the Mate, telephoned
me to say there had indeed been trouble over the deck boy and that John
Meagher had been sent to prison for a month in Port Patrick. I refused to
believe a word of it and wrote to John Meagher who was now returning to
the *Strathaird*, pressing him to come to Tresco for as long as he wished.

Chapter Eighteen
SS *Grelrosa* - 1958-60

After leaving the *Adventuress* in July 1958 I didn't go to sea again for over a year. Perhaps I felt that the *Adventuress* had been my swan song. Working all night, being towed by the Navy, found adrift by the *Ark Royal* in the Mediterranean, in a way I felt I was getting too old for all that. So many of my old friends had died. And new friends were not really satisfactory. I had nicknamed John Meagher the Monkey, which turned out rather apt for him. Like Kipling's Bandar-log he was always trying something new, never persevering, and when crossed in something he wanted, like a monkey, he could bite.

Life was not all bad though. Heather and Andrew came back from South Africa and had a little daughter, Arabella. April stayed often at Tresco, filling the house with her young friends. When I went north in the summer I stayed at Kilspindie with Cherry and Humphrey and took Adam and Charlotte to pick bunches of wild flowers which we had collected as children on those same hillsides. In the summer evenings I went fishing with Adam in the burn.

Perhaps it was just that an old sea dog is never happy too long on shore. She gets the whiff of the salt spray in her nostrils, she longs to be up and away again. At the end of July 1959 I joined the *Grelrosa*, a 10,000 ton boat belonging to the Jeb-Shun Shipping Company, as Chief Engineer. I walked down the garden path at Tresco past the brilliant blue morning glories twining through the soft blue of the lavender hedges to catch a taxi to Paddington where I exchanged the diesel fumes and crowds for the late summer country, where honeysuckle and wild flowers still grew in the hedgerows.

The ship was oil fired with three boilers and had been laid up for 18 months or possibly longer and everything needed doing. The Chinese crew were flying over from China next Thursday but I was the only engineer in charge, with four donkeymen and a foreman to help me. The union would not allow them to do any fitting so I had to do all of it. There was never time for lunch, so after my breakfast I would have a cup of tea and nothing more until I got back to the hotel at night.

By Monday, my room on board was ready and I moved in. That first evening on board I went ashore to see if I could find some supper and I found a cafe called the Moon and Sixpence. The Pole who ran it had known Hamish. He said, "I was thinking of Lord James this evening and then you came in."

All that week I was getting up steam and working on the engines and every evening I ran up to the Moon and Sixpence for supper. The shore donkeymen finished just as the Chinese crew arrived on Friday and one of them brought me a bunch of flowers; I was very touched. The Chinese seemed nice and I thought we were going to get on well. There had been some over-heating on Thursday and a nasty smell of burning, so I shut off and cleaned all the oil-burners and that did the trick. When he came on Saturday the Lloyds Surveyor said, "Your prompt action has saved serious damage." Later that day a policeman called to say that the residents were complaining about the smoke. I explained that the ship had been laid up for so long that it was impossible to raise steam without a little smoke; I was doing the best I could.

That evening, my last in Milford Haven, I went down to the Moon and Sixpence to say goodbye to the Pole. He said he would never forget Lord James and that when he first spoke to him he thought he was a Pole, too, because his Polish was so good. He insisted on giving me a huge box of chocolates "in memory of Lord James". I felt it was almost as if Hamish himself had been trying to get in touch with me at the beginning of my long voyage, as he always did.

We had to sail to Liverpool on Sunday 9th August otherwise we would have lost the charter. But what a rush it was! We stood-by at 6.44 pm on Sunday evening as the pilot guided us out of Milford Haven. Another pilot took us up the Mersey and we were finally tied up alongside the quay at Garston Dock at 5.06 am on Monday morning. There wasn't time to be tired, as there was the usual arrival bustle, the harbourmaster to see, the store lists to hand to the owner and a hundred and one other things to do. We were at the wharf where the Elder and Fyffe banana boats discharged and there were bananas lying everywhere, they were too ripe to ride in the heated railway vans so they were just allowed to rot.

Jean and Frances told me about the birth of Heather and Andrew's second son, Johnny. When I told my shipmates I only said "another little nephew", as I thought "great" was rather ageing.

We sailed to Bidston on 25th August where we were to load scrap; the noise and banging and whirling rust flakes were horrific and I had so much to do on the engine that I had to be on the ship all the time with it.

We left Bidston Dock just after 7 am on 16th September and moved out to the river. Birkenhead, Liverpool, the distant Liver Buildings and the cathedral on the hill all slipped past until we were out in the open sea. We lifted to the swell of Land's End on Thursday afternoon and by midnight had passed Ushant and were into the bay. Never have I seen the bay so charming as it was that September, satin smooth and lights of blue and copper. We passed Finisterre on Saturday and brightly coloured Spanish fishing boats bobbed on the water. About noon on Sunday we passed the Birlings, those terrible rocks which seem sinister even on a summer day, suddenly jutting up into the Atlantic. Down the coast of Portugal we went, in sight of the white villages and sandy beaches. The weather past Cape Trafalgar was grey and blowing with a heavy sea, but it calmed as we came into the Straits of Gibraltar and across the dark Mediterranean to Augusta just beyond Syracuse in Sicily, where we were to bunker.

We dropped anchor in the bay of the port, a pretty town rather spoiled by the new oil refinery built close to it, and bunkered from an oil tender. The agent asked me to come ashore with him, but of course I couldn't while we were bunkering and I had to be very careful we got the full amount of 843 long tons, so all I saw of Augusta were the white houses, the silvery olive trees and the dark green orange or lemon trees. As I sat in my room working out the averages, all the mates and sailors started chipping and banging just outside my room; the din was terrific. Nothing could be as noisy as when a good gang of enthusiastic chippers start removing rust from paint and paint from rust on rails and bulkheads.

We dropped anchor at Port Said and the long string of coloured lights glittered like a necklace of shining beads. Stand-by was at 2.15 am and I threw myself out of my bunk, slipped on my boiler suit and went out into the dark night lit only by the rim of the moon and the lights of Port Said. Though I have been in and out of Port Said in the dark and the light, on passenger liners, cargo tramps and tankers, I always had the same thrill. At night the dark waters of the harbour broke into a myriad lights as the ship cut her way through the reflections of the city. In the town many people wandered the streets; it was really the town where no one slept. Even in the middle of the night, as soon as the anchor chain rattled down, the ship was invaded by Arabs and Egyptians sailing up from nowhere in frail boats. They climbed up the ship's side with their bare brown toes or slippered feet and in a split second the hatches were turned into a bazaar with mounds of green peppers, melons and sweet grapes, bags of yellow leather smelling of goats, socks and shirts, music boxes, Turkish delight and dried fruit. As the sun rose and the street lights gradually went out, the bargaining reached its zenith. "Take it or leave it, there are plenty other ships," the merchants would say.

After Suez it got hotter and hotter and we saw droves of flying fish, sometimes as many as 50, skimming through the water. One landed on deck and died, so I scraped it out and stuffed it with paper soaked in varnish. A soft beige dove with bright red patches over its eyes boarded the ship in the Red Sea. The Captain fed it on bird seed and it stayed with us to Singapore, though when we were passing Ceylon it flew round the ship two or three times as if thinking of flying ashore. We used to call it The Passenger and it became quite tame. Then there was a big grey crane with a long bill. We put out buckets of water for him but he was very shy and sat on a lifeboat or on the rail. He had such a tired face and only stayed about three days. We passed two or three ships going the other way and they said he had flown to one of them. I hope he did.

The Malacca Straits were warm and steamy with round white clouds waiting to rain, and here and there strange round islands covered with green trees to the water's edge dotted the water. In the distance rose the blue misty hills of Sumatra, where there were wild elephants, so the Second told me. Sitting under the awning on deck with the pale stars moving in the sky, all I could hear was the even beat of the engines, the creaking sounds of a ship under way, the gentle wah wah of the water against the ship's side and occasionally the ship's bell.

After a few more days of steamy heat we could see Singapore in the distance. There was a new rule that as soon as a ship stopped bunkering she must sail, so I managed to negotiate with the Shell representative and we did not start bunkering till 10 am, which gave us 22 hours to go ashore and take a walk. No one had been ashore since leaving Birkenhead, so the whole crew was glad to get away for a bit and stretch their legs. I went down to the office in my white suit and arranged about the bunkering and then slipped off across the quay past some modern flats to a small village with shops selling everything for the ships that called. I got some soap powder, Lux and a fresh tin of chocolates. Everyone was always in a hurry at Pulau Bukom because ships were forever passing in and hurrying out which gave it a very restless feeling.

We sailed from Singapore on 25th October and by the 28th the sun set on the other side and we had turned the world. The Second always came out of the engine room for tea and, along with Charlie the number one fireman, we would have our breakfast on the deck together in the morning light when it was cool and clear. Sometimes Charlie told a story in Chinese but with so much mime and gesture that I could get the gist of it without the Second translating, mostly about his early apprenticeship and horror stories about cruel bosuns and over-crowded ships.

On the morning of 5th November I looked out of my port and saw the hills of Japan. We were passing the Island of Shikoku and we continued all day through the Kitak Straits passing Tokushima to port and Takayama to starboard as we headed towards Osaka. There were woods down to the sea, rocky islands with lighthouses and Japanese fishing boats. The woods got darker and the sun set with a liquid gold ripple and at 6.05 pm we dropped anchor in the deep water of Osaka Bay.

I worked until 2 am in the morning to get my abstracts and fuel accounts worked out, as I was determined to visit the Brittons if there was a chance and this looked like the only possible place. Finally I could keep awake no longer and dropped asleep. We were on stand-by at 6.53 am for moving into the inner harbour and were tied up to a buoy a long way from shore, though I could see the town and harbour in the distance. When the immigration people came they said the ships pass was only valid for Osaka and Kyoto and I could not go further. I was devastated! Captain Williams was going ashore so I wentwith him in the agent's boat. After customs we packed into a taxi and set off for Osaka, about half an hour's run. The streets were lined with cherry trees turning red and maidenhair fern trees a shower of gold. We had coffee in the agent's office and he phoned the immigration office for me, but they again said I could not travel ashore. I phoned Alice and Dorothy nonetheless and Dorothy said, "Oh do come, I am sure it will be all right."

What a rush it was! By the time we got back to the *Grelrosa* it was 2 pm. I bolted some lunch, grabbed some things and threw them into a bag with some brown sugar and Turkish delight I had bought as gifts. When I got to customs the official looked at my bag with deep suspicion but I said, "Washing," and opened it. Indeed everything was so jumbled in together it looked just like dirty washing, so he let me through. The agent tried the immigration office a final time, but they said no again. Moreover, if I were caught ashore I would not be allowed to land in Japan again and would be taken in chains to the ship, or put in prison. But I thought I couldn't care less and I would certainly chance it.

Safely on the train, I woke once in the night and could hear officials who had boarded the train asking about tickets. I could have sworn I heard the name Drummond, but there was no Drummond on the train, only a Miss Dodwell. For I was travelling under an alias.

I woke and dressed to rather a grey morning, rice drying in bundles on frames, persimmons gleaming gold on bare branches, splashes of maples in the woods, small farms and villages. In Yokohama Dorothy was waiting to meet me on the platform and she drove me to Hayama and the house on the beach. There was another warm welcome from Alice and Kaneko-san, the maid, and Terry, the bull terrier.

On Monday we made a splendid plan to go to Tokyo as Dorothy was lunching with Evelyn Waugh. While we were waiting at the train station we heard our names called on the loudspeaker: "Drummond and Britton!"

"Oh no," I thought, "they have discovered I have gone to Tokyo without a permit." And my heart sank.

But it was Kaneko-san who had had a call from the agents to say that the ship was sailing at 3 pm on Tuesday instead of Wednesday and had cleverly thought of contacting us at the station. If I had not known I would certainly have missed the ship.

We went on the Cherry Express and arrived in Kyoto that evening, then took a taxi to the Japanese Hotel Tawaraya. Next morning we drove through Kyoto and part of the old Palace Park and Nijo Castle, with its white walls and slate grey roof rising from the blue moat. I had a distant view of the Toji Temple, a five storey pagoda, before crossing the old bridge over the river Kamo on my way to the station for Osaka. An official looked at the label on my bag and merely said, "Very good hotel in Kyoto." With a struggle I got a launch and was back on the *Grelrosa* by 1 pm. I walked into the saloon and the Captain and Mate were very surprised to see me walking in as if nothing had happened.

Sailing out of port we saw the lights of Kobe as it got dark, sparkling out across the water. From Osaka to Hawata it was pilot water all the way, as it is Seto Naikai, the Inland Sea. This was a wandering stretch of water from 230 to 300 miles long and between 4 and 40 miles wide, stretching from Awaji Island to Shimonoseko on the west side and the Kommom Strait which comes between the mainland of Japan and the Island of Kyushu where we were going. The Inland Sea was most beautiful, dotted with green islands covered thick in trees.

It had been getting more and more smoggy as we approached the steel town of Yawata with all the furnaces and about 70 chimneys pouring out smoke continuously. There were about ten for the blast furnaces and they were very high, spewing forth pink smoke lit from the flames. We started discharging our cargo of scrap iron and metal at once into lighters and I had much to do as the ballast pump had to be overhauled and the fuel oil tanks sounded.

The next day I was able to get ashore by 4 pm to Tobata where I got lost twice. It was so dark, just red lanterns at the shop doors, and every turn seemed to end in the black waters of the bay. I was very thankful when a woman turned up and showed me the way to the sampan office.

It could be quite a rough passage out to the ship and as the cargo came out and the ship got lighter, the gangway became higher and higher; luckily the sampan man was always ready to help me. We were two weeks in all unloading cargo to lighters, 24 hours a day, at Yawata. During that time I got to know by sight one of the families who lived on the lighters. Every morning at 7 am the man would come out to check all the mooring ropes. The woman would come out next and always do the same household tasks in the same order. She would first bring in the coal and light the fire, I could see the smoke coming out of the chimney, then she would sweep out the deck cabin and bring out the dishes and chopsticks, and after she had washed her face and brushed her teeth in a little bowl of water, she washed the dishes in the same water. Later she would do her washing and hang it on a line. They often used to wave to me.

During the time we were there I managed to get away three times to see Hakata, which used to be called Fukuoka, where they made silk sashes.

On 18th November we were all taken to visit the steel works at Yakata, which were en fete. I never thought that any works could be made so pretty with strings of paper flags, stalls selling refreshments and toys for children. All the workers' families were enjoying the visit, but the fumes and smoke were awful.

I managed to walk up to the Castle of Kokura at sunset. The whole sky shone crimson in the still waters of the moat and Japanese firs cast dark shadows against the walls of the castle which gradually turned to deep rose. Inside it was rather bare and had been lived in by the same family for over 700 years until about 80 years ago.

We bunkered 598.32 tons on 24th November and I got soaked climbing over the slippery barges in the pouring rain. The two men Shell were also soaked, so I had them aboard to dry off and they dripped water all over my cabin. Later I visited them on board their vessel, but I had forgotten how small Japanese are and banged my head on the lintel above the door.

By 5 pm on 26th November we were lifting to the swell of the Pacific Ocean and as the sun went down over the grey hills of Japan, we sailed past Formosa and Hong Kong and on to Hainan Island where we arrived at Pasuo at midday on 5th December. We tied up alongside a long wharf with a couple of rather old-fashioned elevators and a conveyor belt for loading the brown iron ore. There was plenty of work, we had to pump out the ballast, pack the rudder gland and open up the main engine match box valve which had just started to knock. By the time this was finished the Captain had given out all the money, so I had to borrow $6 (about £1) from the Chief Steward.

It was 7 pm before the Second and I got ashore, a warm still night, intensely dark. I took my torch as the place was full of holes and rails and lumps of ore, and we went up the sandy beach past a large new building which was some kind of workers' club. It was filled with thin, tired people and dirty children, and the whole place smelt unpleasant. There were some propaganda pictures on the wall. One of the firemen joined us and we went into another building which had one room with low tables covered in books and books on shelves all round the room in yellow and white paper covers. A few people dressed in blue jeans and blue jackets were turning the pages listlessly. I imagined this to be some kind of lending library as people were continually carrying books in and out uninhibitedly.

We walked on in the dark past a pool of sewage at the side of the road before we reached a cinema built of wood and packed with Chinese people. Outside was a mass of people who could not get in and were trying to see the picture through the cracks in the wood. I wanted the fireman to go and see it, but he said, "No like," and screwed up his face. We moved on to a restaurant where there were cups and tea pots on the tables, but it was very dirty. Everything was in such a mess heaped up all over the floor, clothes and towels and bundles of cloth, and wooden tricycles for children, all of the poorest quality and all dirty. I met the ship's cook and the Chief Steward there and asked them if they were having something to eat, but they looked at the restaurant and the tea in a wooden tub, and rolled up their eyes saying, "Too dirty."

On 5th December we were due to sail at 6 am, then at 9 am, then at 11 am, but of course we didn't sail until the afternoon. After lunch I was sitting on deck waiting for stand-by and sketching the valve arrangement of the main engines in my notebook, when one of the yard guards pounced on me and snatched my notebook out of my hand. For some reason he thought I was sketching the quay and the ore elevators which could well have come out of the Ark. He rushed to one of the firemen who was sitting on the deck and held up the book, but the fireman just laughed, so then he rushed off to his commanding officer to show him the book, who of course just apologised to me and handed it back. The triviality and endless suspicion were very tiring.

We finally sailed away from the thick brown dust, the clanging conveyors and the half-finished buildings and headed north through the South China Sea. The next morning we saw 80 fishing junks, a lovely sight with their brown sails gilded by the rising sunlight and the blue hills behind. We passed Hong Kong for the third time and sailed away through the

Eastern China Sea to the Yellow Sea. By Sunday 13th December we had dropped anchor outside Dairen. The sky was cold and grey and there was a heavy roll and the sea temperature had dropped to 42°F.

The next day was bitterly cold and we moved from our anchorage to the discharging berth alongside the quay at Dairen. There were the usual formalities and the search, but everyone here seemed more friendly than in the south. The officials all wore fur caps and some had masks against the cold. I finally got ashore at 4.15 pm and remembered my way to the tram, where I was jammed between an old man with a bundle and black fur cap and a younger man with a fox fur cap and padded coat. There seemed to be many new buildings since I was here last in 1953 and more things to buy in the big department stores, but everything was also more expensive. It was so cold walking through the icy streets that I decided to go back to the ship. Half frozen, I was glad to struggle on board for a hot cup of cocoa in a very cold room with the wind coming in at every corner.

They were discharging iron ore by elevators and grabs which they loaded by hand in the holds. Although the winches were drained there was always a little ice in the pipes on deck which I had to thaw out with torches. I was very cold with the wind whistling round me as I held a paraffin torch on the pipes till the ice thawed. In the evening I went up to the Seaman's Club in a taxi with the Captain and Mate, which saved a long, cold walk, and bought myself a fur cap, for which I got a good discount. It was black corduroy with red fox, which I said was perhaps rabbit, but it cost only $6.80 compared to $10 or $12 outside. I also bought some lined leather gloves, as the wind whistled through my Japanese woollen ones. Afterwards I went to the shooting gallery where I treated some of the crew to shots.

On 19th December, the Seamans Club took us by bus to see a new ship that was being built. We were quite a large party from the ship and it was so bitterly cold it took my breath away. We were given musty, pale green tea to drink, but it was at least hot. We heard a long lecture and then were shown the model of the ship. Then we were taken through a very large machine shop and through the yard. There were 11,000 men and 3,000 women employed there. The new ship was to be 13,000 tons.

We left Dairen at 8 am on 21st December, an icy morning with a green arc of flickering lights in the sky, leaving behind the snow covered quays. We sailed for Taku-Bar, or rather the port for Taku-Bar which is called Hsin-Kang or *New Port*. The journey was only a few hours and we arrived the next afternoon and were at anchor off Taku-Bar in the yellow, ice cold water where we remained for ten days.

On Christmas morning I woke to the sea water washing against the ship's side and ice crackling on the iron deck as the red sun slowly rose. *Hark the Herald Angels* was on the radio from Australia and I thought of Fleet and our Christmases there with Mummy, and of the Sunday school children singing at Megginch so long ago by the great Christmas tree in the hall. We had drinks in the saloon with the Captain and the cook had made a large Christmas cake. After lunch the Second wrote very large in red in the engine room log book: *TODAY IS CHRISTMAS DAY.*

In the evening we all met again for one of the largest Christmas dinners I have ever eaten, fourteen courses. We ate our way solidly through it and finally the Captain toasted the Queen's health and thanked the cook. Later we listened to the Queen's speech.

On New Year's Day 1960 we went 10 miles in to the port, tied up to the buoys and loaded from lighters among the crunching ice. I longed to go ashore and perhaps visit Peking, where I had never been, as we were so near. We then heard we were to sail Sunday night, so there was no chance of doing it, so I planned to give a party at the Seaman's Club for some of my crew and their families instead.

We intended to start off at 4 pm and I went gaily and changed into my blue suit, and put on a brown corduroy jacket. It was so cold, however, that I also put on my flame jersey and blue knitted waistcoat, a brown scarf, my new gloves and fur cap, thick socks and my thickest lisle stockings. I couldn't get my shoes on over these so I had to wear my heavy engine room shoes. I was then ready to go down the gangway, but there was no gangway, only a very old ladder down the ship's side.

I went to the Mate and said, "I think it is dangerous to go ashore and come back in the dark with a ladder like that, as if any of the crew slipped and fell between the lighter and the ship's side they would go under the ice and no one could get them out."

"That's all the ladder you can get," he said rudely, "I can't put the gangway down."

I said, "Well, I am clear, but if there is an accident it's your fault."

And tossing my head I went off. But how was I to get down that ladder? It was very high right down on to the lighter and then there was a climb over to the big launch. My shoes were bad for climbing and I was numb with the cold. However, the crew held the ladder at the bottom for me and took my bag and gave me a hand. So I put a good face on it as if I couldn't care less and went down and over the lighter on to the launch.

It was an awful scramble getting ashore the other side, but they gave me a hand here, too. After this we had a long walk in the bitter wind. At last we reached the gate of the Seaman's Club just when I felt I could not go another step. It was a large, new building well back from the road, and when I got into the warm atmosphere out of that awful cold I felt faint and stupefied. However, I sat down on a chest and pulled round quietly.

We all sat down at a round table and had the most enormous meal with doughbuns, meat and mushrooms and every sort of thing. Afterwards I sat in a big comfortable room till it was time to go, when I got decked up in my warm things, and we set off on that very cold long walk, everyone clutching a small pink parcel from the shop. It was so cold I could hardly get my pass out of my bag and then the tide was out so there was a great drop down to the launch. However, the Second put a rather bent plank across the quay to the top deck of the launch and I walked over the dark water with the ice floating below; they all gave me a hand. We went out to the *Grelrosa* through the terrible cold of the floating ice, and then there was an awful climb on to the lighter as it swung and bobbed in the water with its deep open hatches, chains and ropes waiting to trip one up in the black darkness of the deck. Finally there was the climb up the ladder to the ship. It had one slipped rung and one rung missing altogether, so I could hardly stretch my numbed foot high enough to get the rung. They all helped me and held the ladder and my bag, but I was scared I would have a faint turn with the cold. Really with the lighter bobbing about it swung a lot and I could hardly reach up over the broken rung and my hands were so numb with the cold they could hardly hold the ice covered ropes. Despite all this I made it and found a lovely cup of hot chocolate waiting for me in my cabin.

We were due to sail on Sunday night, but of course it was Monday before we were away out of the cold Gulf of Chih-li to the Yellow Sea, with the temperature increasing and the sea becoming yellower and yellower the further south we went. On 7th January we took the pilot aboard to go up the river to Shanghai. I didn't turn in till 3 am and was up by 6 am for another stand-by as we proceeded up the river. It was a bright clear morning on deck and lots of river craft were plying up and down the waterfrom small boats with a family on board, to large sea-going junks with brown sails which carried stones, straw or vegetables. Up the river we went, past small houses, Holt's Wharf, and green fields and country stretching away to the south, past the Burr where the British Consulate was, with gardens looking over the river, big buildings, offices and banks.

We were at Shanghai from Thursday 7th January for five days, but had to shift from our first loading buoy to buoy 65 half way through, so there was a great deal of work. On arrival I had to arrange to make a sketch for a new exhaust pipe on the winch, but the agent was in such a rush they went off with it before I had checked that the sizes were right. Inspection and search had taken so long I didn't get lunch till late and then there was all the fuss about the new pipe. It was pretty on the river, but it had been a tiring trip and I was glad enough to turn in.

I awoke to thick fog and went ashore. The Second got me a tricycle and I went off to the Seaman's Club, which used to the Bank Managers' Club and so was filled with vestiges of grandeur. I showed my pass and went through the glass swing doors into the huge pillared hall and up a flight of steps leading to a very large dining room with an enormous long bar running the whole length of the room, which could easily seat 100 people. The room was panelled in mahogany and had an ornate plaster ceiling and a marvellous view. The Bank Managers must have done well, there were fine damask tablecloths and good cutlery. Later I walked through the gardens which were small but well laid out with fan palms, magnolia grandiflora and a pond surrounded by marigolds and roses. It was so lovely after the bitter cold of Dairen and Taku-Bar to see flowers still in bloom.

The next day I went to a big exhibition on engineering and textiles. As I was walking up the Nanking Road the Third Engineer came dashing up saying, "The ship's moving at 8 pm. The Second's ashore, the Fourth's on board and he sent a fireman to tell you and the fireman found me." So he and the fireman and the fitter had all been looking for me. Off we bolted in a taxi. However, the Captain told me we wouldn't be moving before midnight.

Next morning, 11th January, I was up at 5 am. We had the main engine warmed through by 7 am and were full ahead before midday, slipping down the Shanghai River to the sea. We steamed down the Yangtze past buildings and wharves, and big ocean-going ships of all nations. Nearer the mouth we came to the bigger country junks loaded with hay in bales, watchful eyes painted on the bows. Then we swept out of the yellow waters into the Yellow Sea and sailed away after six weeks in China. It was a heady feeling.

The weather became warmer and warmer and a lovely full moon rose at night. I spent every available moment working out my abstracts, for we were nearing the end of the voyage at Hong Kong.

On 14th January the boy came and told me we were passing the Needle Rock 40 miles from Hong Kong, and later that evening we made fast to a buoy. The lights of the city shimmered like a handful of jewels with the dark peak behind, sparkling through a fine white mist and reflecting in the waters of the bay. We had hardly got in before the press arrived and insisted on taking photographs of me for the morning papers. Then the wives of the Chinese crew came on board, so pretty in their Chinese dress. The home mail also arrived, I had had no letters since leaving Japan nearly three months ago.

Next morning I was up at dawn to finish my log abstract and add in the final figures. I could see it was to be a full day, and so it proved. The Second came over with me to Jeb-Shun's Shipping Office in the launch. The boat threaded its way among ships at anchor, past junks and all sorts of craft and finally through the congested sampans round the pier. We hurried up the slippery steps into crowds of milling people rushing this way and that, cars and rickshaws, fruit baskets, big straw hats, children, shops packed with goods; everything was brilliant, colourful and busy.

In the office I was congratulated on bringing the *Grelrosa* out and Mr Lam thanked me for my service. As we sipped jasmine tea, both he and his father pressed me to stay on another six months. Of course I had to get my permit to continue as Chief, so I dashed off to the shipping office to make the arrangements.

We returned to the ship with the directors and went through the store and repair lists, arranging to have the starboard boiler scaled and the soot blower repaired. Afterwards we trooped down to the engine room and Mr Lam went through everything, even under the boiler, so I was glad they were all chipped and red leaded underneath. They told me how clean the engine room was and how nice it looked, which was most gratifying, and again they pressed me to stay with them for another six months. Eventually I agreed to stay on another three and we all shook hands and they went off. I was very tired after all this but slipped ashore on a launch for a quick walk through the brilliant streets of Hong Kong.

Next morning I was again up at 5 am, checking my fuel account, as with so much money involved it was quite a responsibility. At the Marine Office I met Mr Barclay, the examiner, who said he had seen me in Hull on my way to Russia in the *Elsie Beth*. Finally I was taken to see the Principal who was also charming. "So you are Chief," he said, "and the little ship got here all right."

Our extensions secured, the Second and I went to be inoculated against cholera, and then later we all went for coffee and cakes. I sat at the head of the table surrounded by my Chinese engineers; I felt very proud.

At the Jeb-Shun Shipping Office, Mr Lam offered me a raise of £1.15 a week, though he said he could give me no more men in the engine room as I had asked. I went back to the Marine Office at 12 o'clock to sign articles, and here there was a delay as the Captain had sent no report of character.

"But we know you have a very good character," Mr Barclay said laughing, and stamped my book "VG VG!"

To complicate matters they had given me all my pay for the voyage to date the previous afternoon, and after paying my ship's account and some tips, there was still about £450. All the banks were shut by then and it was Saturday, so I was in rather a quandary. Luckily I went to Jardine's office and they kindly said they would transfer it to my bank in England.

We went to Mr Lam Senior's house for dinner. The Lam family gradually drifted in and Mr Lam arrived with his wife, who wore black silk with jade earrings, but I believe he had three wives and 23 children. His son Mr Andrew Lam had three wives, too, and many of them were here for dinner. In fact, except for me and the Captain, everyone else seemed to be related.

There was a large bowl in the middle of the table to which we helped ourselves with chopsticks and on the whole I managed fairly well. There were eight courses. The piece de resistance was a large rabbit mould made of cut chicken, beautifully shaped with even the rabbit's expression and sitting on a bed of lettuce which apparently the rabbit was nibbling. Mr Lam explained to me carefully that it was not a real rabbit, but meat cut and moulded like one. After dinner Mr Lam told us about his race horses and he said he had put on $15 and won $1000. His daughter replied, "Don't believe him, he always loses."

As we left Mr Lam came to the door and, patting me on the back, said "Well done." Why I didn't know, but I think it was for bringing the ship over.

Chapter Nineteen
SS Shantae - 1960

The old *SS Grelrosa* was now no more, but had emerged Phoenix-like as the *SS Shantae*. Nevertheless, underneath she was the same ship and I was still Chief Engineer on her.

I had been busy with repairs all morning but I managed to get ashore in the afternoon before we sailed. The crew were right when they told me in Liverpool, "You can get everything in Hong Kong and very cheap." The only thing which was difficult was finding a boat to take me back to the ship. Perhaps it was because of the wind and the swell and our buoy being such a long way out. Eventually I got one and we dashed over the dark waters; the tiny boy who was helping his father took an enormous boat hook to pull the launch alongside the *Shantae* and was nearly pulled overboard himself.

We sailed for Whampoa on 18th January, starting with steam on deck at 6.30 am and being full away just after 8 am. It was only a short run round the coast and we were soon going up the Pearl River in the Canton Delta, a wide river with a flow of water second only to the Yangtze, through green fields with distant hills. As we sailed up the river, the hills became nearer and the fields were dotted with fruit and crops. Whampoa was the port for Canton, 15 kilometres up the river, because the water was too shallow for big ships to proceed further.

The Second's mother-in-law lived in Canton and he said he wanted to see her and take her some frying oil. I wanted to see Canton too, so after a quick lunch we set off at 12.30 pm. It was quite a walk up the quay past heaps of sand, limestone chips, blocks of tin, and rolls and rolls of thick copper wire. Eventually we reached the bus station, which was a rather tumble down house with an old green bus outside, covered in dust, and just about to go.

The conductor was standing at the door blowing a whistle, but we managed to force our way in. A man gave up his seat to me and I squashed in beside a woman in black and a baby in a padded cover. We drove through lovely country before reaching the outskirts of Canton, which was a very large city.

There were lots of attractive old houses, but very little in the shops and all very expensive. I walked to the Intourist Hotel gardens, where I sat watching the ships. The Second joined me for dinner, by then it was 9 pm and quite dark, so we hailed a taxi to take us back to Whampoa.

On the deserted country road back to the port, we passed a horrible sight, a man strapped with chains, his hands tied behind his back, and chains round his legs and arms, and one round his neck. He was being driven along the road by a man walking behind him. The car lights lit him up and he turned his head and looked at us with such a terrible look of imploring fear on his bloodstained white face. His hands were bloodstained too. It made me angry not to know what it was about and to be unable to help him.

We could not speak or express our horror because of the driver, but later the Second told me that he must have been one of those who were against the government who had been caught and was being taken to a quiet spot where he would be murdered, unseen. It was a mystery of the dark, the beginning and end of a story which we would never know.

I did not go up to Canton again, although we did not leave for another five days. One day I went ashore and walked up a long straight road with pines and gums each side till I got to a small scattered village, strangely bereft of all the ducks and chickens which were such a feature of Chinese villages. I walked up towards the hills through red sandy soil, past a big hospital and a park surrounded by a lake with islands and bridges. It was all very ornamental and rather surprising to find in such a wild place, as if dropped from the moon. The distant hills were deep blue and white, black-veined butterflies skimmed over the fields. But, and there is always a serpent in any Garden of Eden, at about 4 pm they began to wheel out human manure in open wooden tubs. There was a little straw on top to prevent splashing, but the smell was awful! The tubs were filled from the public conveniences in the centre of each village, some of which were beautifully carved, but their purpose could not be disguised. It rather put me off eating vegetables.

Next day we moved out to the buoys in the middle of the Pearl River, a chocolate coloured estuary with a swift current; an apple core dropped into its waters sank instantly. The river people in the sampans seemed almost part of their boats as they handled them so expertly, men and women alike. Children scampered about the boats and gave a hand just as if on shore, though the very tiniest ones were tied with a piece of light cord as were the ginger cats.

28th January was the Chinese New Year, but my crew didn't know which year. For a long time they didn't seem certain as to which day it was either, but there was a three day holiday in Hong Kong and everything shut. Chinese New Year just seemed to be the last of a great vista of New Years stretching backwards perhaps four or five thousand years into the dimness of forgotten ages.

The Captain sent a wire to the agent saying NOT SUFFICIENT FOOD ON BOARD AND MINIMUM BUNKERS, but as it was the New Year he got no reply. We had a deck cargo of 500 drums of methylated spirit, about 100 tons, and rubber and carbide in the holds.

We had heavy monsoon weather, but then the sky cleared and the sea dropped. It was like an oven in my cabin and I had to shut all the ports. I thought it funny that only three weeks before it had been freezing and my room like an ice house. We passed the Manila Sea and the Philippines, and went between Borneo and Cochin China towards Singapore.

We anchored at Quarantine Station, Singapore, well beyond the Danger Buoy where we discharged rice and fireworks. Our deck cargo of 500 drums of methylated spirit from Whampoa was intended for discharge at Singapore, however, now we were told it had to be taken on to Penang. It was highly dangerous stuff. All day they worked cargo and the whole ship was swarming with coolies, who ate just outside my port, and the smell of their food was quite sickening. Mr Hervey Chia of the *Singapore Free Press* came out to interview me and take my photograph. He offered me a lift back in his boat, but I couldn't leave because there was only one engineer on board and all that dangerous cargo.

I had begun to worry about my eyesight, as I kept seeing black dots swimming up and down. My friend from Henry Waugh & Co, Mr Aucott, gave me the address of the best eye clinic in Singapore and lent me his car to get there, for which I was very grateful. Dr Lorimer, the opthamologist in the clinic, examined my eyes most carefully and said it was deranged pigment which caused the black dots, and they would soon drop down and float away.

After my appointment I went down to the quay where I had to wait an hour and a half for the boat. The Jeb-Shun boats were very lazy servicing the ship and they wouldn't let any other boats go, rather like a robin's territory. Then I was told, "The boat can't go, the boatman must rest."

I replied, "It's a motor boat and if he is too lazy to go himself, he should let one of the other boats go."

He went on and quite a crowd gathered.

"Are you a boatman?" I asked.

"No," he replied.

So I said firmly, "Well, clear out of it, it's nothing to do with you," and rather to my surprise he went and the crowd also dispersed.

I did find a boatman asleep in a matting hut, guarded by a huge dog which was all teeth and growls when I got near it, so there was nothing I could do. Eventually the police found a boat for me and a night shift foreman to take me out.

The next day my visit ashore was rather spoilt by the arrival of Mr Mackriell from the Australian Broadcasting Commission who wanted to do an interview with me. I told him I was just going ashore, but that I would do it if he took me ashore and gave me a drive round Singapore in his car. This he promised to do, so I gave him a 5 minute interview. We then went back to hear the playback at the studio, which was 3 miles out of Singapore. After we had heard it through he told me he was busy that afternoon and could not take me for the drive he had promised.

I said, "How am I to get back to town?"

He replied, "Oh take a taxi." By then it was getting on for 2 pm and I was tired, hot and hungry, and there was no offer from him for lunch or even a cup of coffee. When I asked how I was to pay for the taxi, he very grudgingly gave me $2 which barely covered it. Of course I should have demanded payment for the interview beforehand, which at least would not have left me out of pocket.

Later, I took a ride out to the Haw Par Gardens at Pasin Panjang, 7 miles west of Singapore. The taxi driver took me back by the Botanical Gardens, a cool and shady drive past the golf course and new housing estates.

On Monday 8th February, we shifted anchorage from the eastern anchorage at Singapore and steamed 10 miles west to the bunkering wharf at Pulau Bukom. Luckily I had changed into my clean white suit just before going to take the bunkers, because the oil representative and I met a friend of his, Captain Howell, driving a jeep.

The oil representative said, "Could you take the Chief round the Island?" and Captain Howell said he would be delighted.

So I set off with Captain Howell in his jeep. It seemed a long time since Halifax and that ill fated convoy which was cut to pieces in the full moon in 1940. There was a slight breeze and a marvellous sunset, and round the other side of the island we could see coral islands with palms and mango trees. Captain Howell said he sometimes went out in the launch to swim off the small islands. Pulau Bukom was free of mosquitoes, being sprayed with DDT three times a week, but the other islands all had mosquitoes. We drove past the splendid modern hospital and then down to the ferry to meet his wife who was coming back from work and bringing the children back from school.

The next morning I awoke to bright sunshine, distant blue hills and the funny little round islands of the Straits of Malacca. I had always wanted to see Malacca during the many times I had passed up and down the Straits and I wondered if would I have a chance to slip ashore and see it for myself.

This time I did. Mr Chua Bian Siew, the Foreman, took me ashore and to Stadt House which was now government offices but used to be the East India Company Offices, built by the Dutch. On top of the hill we visited the ruined church of St Paul with a wonderful view right across the sea, from where I could see the *Shantae* far out below. The grave stones had been inscribed in Dutch with the arms and armorial bearings. I felt sad for those buried here so far from their home and the tidy Dutch countryside.

Mr Siew and his brother then took me through the town and out into the country through coconut groves and sold me Malacca cane cut from a hanging creeper.

By 11 pm we were full away towards Port Swettenham where we arrived on the morning of Wednesday 10th February, a boiling hot morning, and dropped anchor after sailing 12 miles up river. I think Port Swettenham was one of the hottest places in the world and there was a shut-in feeling. The river was chocolate coloured and the banks were mostly mango swamps. The cargo workers who came on and worked all night said there were huge man-eating crocodiles in the swamps down the river. My room was like a furnace and the air wild with the buzzing of mosquitoes. I decided to try and go to Kuala Lumpur the next day, although I had little idea of where it was.

The boatman had a friend who drove me through the rubber country, miles and miles of rubber trees, each with its cut stems and small can for the rubber juice. We stopped at a rubber factory and walked to the sheds where the white soft rubber sheets were being passed through trays of running water. The rubber was solidified with acid and the crepe rubber was passed through spiky rollers which made the crepe effect. In another shed I saw big bales of rubber done up in canvas ready for shipment.

Kuala Lumpur seemed very large and nicely laid out with gardens and palm trees. We went to the Chinese Club where I found a tarantula when I went up to wash, so came down very quickly. Afterwards we drove through the Lake Gardens but we did not have time to stop. We had to race back to Port Swettenham so as not to miss the launch. I was delighted to have seen Kuala Lumpur.

Leaving behind the scent of tropical flowers and coconut palms, we were well out into the Straits of Malacca by breakfast time and into a rough sea and heavy swell, rain and thunder, with liquid ribbons of fire joining sky and sea. The rain was so blinding that we had constant stand-bys. With the rain the sea temperature dropped 4°to 82°F. On other ships I had used to catch the rain water and run it down to the tanks in the engine room, but there was no appliance on the *Shantae* to do this.

It took us about two days to come up the Straits of Malacca, past the rounded coral islands with their thick tropical vegetation and silver white beaches. We passed Singapore, seeing the lights in the distance, through the South China Sea and into the Gulf of Siam.

As we came nearer the land it became very hot and I could smell coconut groves and hot damp forests. Bright phosphorus lit the water as the ship passed through the blackness. It took us nearly 4 hours to come up the Chao Phya River, with all the lights of Bangkok dancing and sparkling in the distance. The air was filled with the hum of mosquitoes, so I got out my oil of citronella and sprinkled it about liberally, even though I had my ports screened and wire gauze frames fitted in.

Big lumps of water hyacinths were floating down the river, and shore boats had collected round the ship, slipping in between the lighters and the riverbank, dwellers were soon climbing over the lighters and up any rope they could find. They would catch a rope hanging over the side and climb up hand over hand with their feet going up the ship's side. They had a great assortment of fruit, green coconuts and pomelos, a green rather rough fruit.

At breakfast they all said they had been to Bangkok many times. "But today you must go and see it. You must see the Reclining Buddha, all shining gold, and the Golden Temple and the Royal Palace."

So I did. I took a motor tricycle which went at such a speed that we flew round corners almost on one wheel and jumped over road crossings past stagnant canals full of mosquitoes and pink lotus. At the Hotel Europe I booked the tour of the Royal Palace and the Temple of the Emerald Buddha with Mr Watsun Chiyawat, my guide. He wore a black cloth suit with white, stiff collared shirt and a black tie, so I was glad I was tidy in my blue dress and black coat. I was the only tourist and we had a lovely airy car with white covers on the seats. We entered the palace through a high gate called the Gate of Supreme Victory, a name which left nothing unsaid.

I was told that the gates were made so high to allow room for fully equipped elephants to pass them under in State processions.

The Temple of the Emerald Buddha was guarded by bronze lions. The outside walls were inlaid with flowers and patterns of blue and gold, and the temple was heavily carved and covered in brightest gold leaf. The hot air was filled with the sound of tinkling bells. I could not at first think where the sound was coming from till I looked up and saw the eaves of the temple hung with wind bells.

I slipped off my shoes and walked up the marble steps where inside I saw the Emerald Buddha sitting on a high, golden pedestal under a golden canopy.

Everything sparkled and danced with light, and looking at all the gold, I thought that here faith prevailed in the visible rather than the invisible, in the seen rather than the unseen. The Emerald Buddha was only 23 inches high, cut from one solid piece of green jasper jade. Though small, it was not insignificant and the green stone reflected clear green lights, dark and bright green always changing, and the golden vestments shone and sparkled. I felt as if I had entered a different dimension of time, a long way from bilges and back ends and the daily dirty routine of the engine room.

As we left the temple, Mr Watsun Chiyawat said, "I am Siamese, but I am a Christian of the Church of England." It seemed a curious anti-climax. By this time I was very tired and hot.

On the way back we passed the University, a modern hospital and several embassies, but the most memorable thing was the indescribable smell which rose from all the city canals. Mr Watsun Chiyawat said septic tanks for each house were a matter of personal choice; I felt sure no one had chosen. I was also sure that the contents of the septic tanks found their way into the waterways. Even the beautiful pink lotus with its blushing flowers rising above the waters could not compensate for the smell.

The mosquitoes, which had been biting on and off all day, skimming over shop floors and biting my legs and feet, now began their evening campaign in earnest.

The next day, 24th February, we were to have moved alongside at 6 am, but as usual this was first changed to 10 am, then postponed to 2 pm. Later we were told to have main steam up at 5 pm and finally we moved at 11 pm. If I had only known that we were not going to move all day, I could have gone off to the Floating Markets by motor launch. I could see from the amount of cargo lying on the side that they couldn't possibly finish loading from lighters. There was rice, cotton, charcoal, palmwood and flour; there was paper and palm oil, and all this only started loading at 1 am in the morning.

So my lovely return visit to Bangkok was off and instead I transferred oil from the centre deep tank to the port and starboard deep tanks so I could fill the centre tank from No. 3, as there was a suspected leak in the ballast line. I would have done more but had to be ready all the time for getting up steam. At about 4 pm they cancelled the order for steam at 5 pm and changed it to 11 pm.

From the deck of the *Shantae* I saw hundreds of big sweet buffalo nosing about on the quay waiting for the ship to come in to be loaded. Some of the country people had come down with them and there were children stroking them. Some of the buffalo looked very tired and were lying down along the quay.

I told the Mate, "There are far too many cattle to take. You must tell the agents you can't take so many."

He was a cruel man to contemplate taking so many livestock.

They started loading the buffalo in a box with a crane and the pigs in crates. I went for a walk along the shore in the boiling heat and looked at the little shops along the quay. When I returned it was bedlam; children kept slipping on board to pat them and it was amazingly hot. The smell of the buffaloes and pigs surrounded by swarms of flies passed description. We moved out slow ahead, while a sad, little group of children and drovers watched the buffaloes go. We slipped down the river to the sea, past all the small villages of the river dwellers and further back the farms in the tangle of trees which were the fruit orchards and waving coconut palms standing high above the rest, and on past the flat plain of rice country to the sea.

In all my years at sea, never had I seen anything like this stupid, greedy, landlubberly performance. The five lower holds had a full cargo of rice, firewood, paper, cotton, palm husks, charcoal, flour and palm oil, mixed up together just as it had come on the lighters; palm oil was packed on top of the cotton, firewood was stacked on the flour and paper and palm husks were shoved in between. And so they carried on.

I went to the Mate and told him, "Don't take so many cattle. If we run into bad weather, we won't be able to cope with so many, and it is against the Ministry regulations to sail with open holds. What's more is I don't like it, especially in the China Seas, where the weather changes so quick you wouldn't have time to batten down the hatches. And if you did you would kill all the cattle for want of air."

However the Mate replied, "Don't interfere with my cargo."

The buffaloes were very thirsty and they gave them no water till the next day. They were packed like herrings in two rows each side of the deck. There was a wooden railing on each side of the rows which made a narrow gangway, but one could hardly wedge through it as the wood bulged so much with the weight of the cattle which were tied to it by the driving rope in their nostrils, where in bad weather the only thing to hold them would be their nose. Then they were packed in the tween decks and in No 2 and No 4 upper holds. The whole deck was littered with straw, mountains of hay bales and also bananas; even the hospital was filled with bananas.

Then, as if 580 head of buffalo were not enough, there were over 500 head of pigs in crates on No 2 hatch and the poop. They were jammed up against the storm ports and I could hear their distant grunting and smell the strong pig smell. The crates were piled up, tiers high in the blazing sun and the buffaloes had no shade at all.

Before we got down the river, two buffaloes jumped over into the side. I saw one swimming and two boats from a little village got it and took it ashore. The other one I didn't see, but they said it swam ashore, too. They were so thirsty and longed for the water.

The next day we were well away down the Gulf of Siam in the South China Sea, with the burning sun beating down, turning the water into a silver glare. I could only manage to give water to the fourteen nearest animals, and that was difficult enough as there was so little room. They pressed so heavily on the wooden bars that they went over and nearly squashed me. They got so excited when they smelt the water, making no sound, only little soft squeaks. They got terribly thirsty and were only given water once a day in the morning. I gave mine water after lunch and at 6 pm. I got a bucket and carried it from the bathroom. Some drank very slowly, others wanted two buckets. Then I poured some water over their heads and washed their faces which they loved. Most of my fourteen lay down for the night when I always talked to them.

The whole ship became like a huge manure heap and the smell was awful, beyond all description. Everywhere was thick with black flies, and mosquitoes came out of the hay and bit like mad. I had bought some green cones which I burnt at night in the alleyway. The smell became so bad that I had to shut my port and leave the top light open. Then there were the mites and fleas which came off the animals and bit me. It was boiling hot and the sun beat down remorselessly through each hour of daylight. Even given good weather it would take us seven days to reach Hong Kong.

The deck scuppers became choked. They couldn't get between the buffaloes to clean the decks and the whole deck became a squelch of manure. I had been keeping a speed of 10 knots and we averaged 10 knots from Bangkok to Hong Kong. I did all I could to keep the speed up, but I had to be very careful not to have smoke because of the animals, also not to have any sparks because of the straw on the deck and bales of hay.

By 1st March we had been going for five days and I had her up to a speed of 11 knots; everything was going well. I had just finished checking over the bunkers and was going to make myself a cup of cold cocoa and have some fruit for my supper when I heard someone shout "Fire!"

Simultaneously the order for steam on the fore deck was given and I went to the engine room to see that the boiler water was all right when they opened the smothering steam from deck. I told the Fourth Engineer to watch the boiler water and put the extra feed on, as the water dropped at once. By this they maintained the water. I had the steam brought and slowed down the main engines a little to hold it, as the smothering steam requires so much steam and water. My department assumed fire stations.

I then went up on deck to see exactly where the fire was. I could see that the buffaloes knew there was fire as they were sniffing the air and their faces were frightened. They were moving about restlessly. I pushed my way through them and over the heaps of straw and saw the Captain who was calm and quick. He had had all the ventilator covers put on No 2 vents to lower hold where the fire was.

I asked, "Did you give the order to open smothering steam to No 2 Lower hold?" as I was afraid of a mistake and someone opening it to the Upper hold and tween decks where the cattle were.

The Captain said, "It is all right. The right valve has been opened. The fire is in No 2 lower hold."

I replied, "The smothering steam is taking an awful lot of water. I have had to put the main engines down a rev or two to hold the water."

I could not get to any of the fuel oil tank sounding pipes because of the mountains of hay and cattle so I returned to the engine room and felt the tanks from there. Luckily the oil had a flash point of 206°F and we had had 776 tons on board. The tanks were really converted bunkers as this ship was a coal burner at one time and I could feel them from the stokehold.

Because we had used steam to smother the fire, there was hardly enough water left for the boilers and cattle, and we were down to the engine room tanks.

"Chief, please give her as much speed as possible as the sooner we reach port the better," Captain Macfie wrote to me on 1st March.

I just managed to give her a bit more; it would have been easy if we had not been so short of water. By the afternoon of Wednesday 2nd March it was getting very hot and smoky. I had my carpet up on my desk to prevent it from trapping all the dirt being carried off the deck. In the night the cattle had got very restless, and the ones aft kept breaking loose and climbing on the after end of No 4 Hatch where there were about three wooden hatch boards across. It was so dangerous they could have fallen to the bottom of the upper hold and been hurt or gone over the side. The rails at the side were very weak and very low. One night I got the man who looks after the cargo to help me to get them back.

They thought the fire was spreading to other cargo and burning aft and the smell from the hold bilges where the cattle were was very strong . The Captain thought the fire was gaining and we were running out of water. My buffaloes were very thirsty that night.

To complicate things there was fog and we had a stand-by at 5.33 am in the morning. At 7.09 am the fog lifted and we took the pilot. The hills round Hong Kong were just visible in the grey morning. The buffaloes sniffed the cool and so did the poor pigs in the crates. The fire boat and the water boat came alongside and it was a welcome sight. The firemen started to tackle the fire right away and all the animals were discharged first. They slung them into lighters and I watched my adopted fourteen, they were very careful with them.

I asked an inspector what would happen to them and he said, "Oh, they are turned out on one of the islands; some go to the farmers and some to the butchers, but they have about three months first."

I was very tired, and I had a sort of gastritis and had been bitten all over by insects of various kinds. They pumped CO_2 into the holds to quench the fire and then opened the hatches and pumped in water. The Head Ministry man, Mr Woodward, sent for me. The bilges were by this time all choked up, and though the Mate had said nothing could be done, I took out the non-return valves and cleaned the line from the engine room.

The only people who were burnt by the fire were the cook and the saloon boys who went down before breakfast after the fire had started and were overcome by the fumes. The cook had his feet burnt by the hot deck and the two boys had a good dose of fumes.

I had to stay on the ship while they discharged the burnt cargo. They wanted to discharge all my oil into an oil barge, but I said not on a verbal instruction; I had to have it in writing from the Master.

The Mate said, "The barge is on its way now."

As luck would have it, the agent was on board, so I went to him and asked him about discharging the oil.

"Who gave you such an order?" he asked.

"The Mate." I replied.

He asked me if I thought it necessary.

"No, the flash point is 206°F, and the temperature now of the oil is under 100°F in the tanks."

The ship was bedlam with the smouldering cargo being discharged to lighters, the CO_2 and the smell of burning in the saloon. On top of this, the shore people had started what engine repairs they could, the winches were always breaking down, there was ballast to pump, and all the Hong Kong Chinese crew in the engine room wanted to go home. It was a very busy time indeed.

A little boy called Malli from one of the lighters came and helped me; he was about seven and he would hand me up spanners and help me to carry them back. It was Monday 7th March before I could dash ashore, and then only to the office to see about the men who were paying off. The fire had at last been extinguished, although it had taken the fire brigade five days to put it out. They gave me some money for carrying the buffaloes and I gave $10 dollars each to the engine crew and $30 to No 1.

It had been a bad week, especially the time at sea; somehow when I had looked at the picture of the fire at sea in the magic lanterns when I was a child, it never occurred to me that one day I too would be in just such a burning ship.

We spent another week in Hong Kong after that and I was able to get ashore quite a lot, away from the smell of the fire over the green blue water and all the sampans bumping against the landing jetties with a swash and gurgle of water.

On Friday I took the Second and his wife out to a restaurant in Kowloon and afterwards I walked along the road behind Des Voeux Road. It was rather dark so I walked on the road instead of the pavement, as I felt I was being followed. I looked behind but saw no one following me.

The next thing I knew a man had slipped two fingers under my watch strap and clawed it off, breaking the metal strap, and grabbed my bag at the same time. I hung on to my bag which I had under my left arm. The parcel was in my right hand. I tried to trip him with my foot and kicked out at him, but could not hit him as I was hanging on to my bag which had a lot of money in it as well as my passport. I couldn't get my right arm round to give him a good swipe as he was behind me. It all happened in a split second and he made off. I shouted to people to stop him, but of course they didn't. I ran after him down the street and over a turning but I lost him in the crowd. Not one person lifted hand or foot to stop him.

My wrist was dripping with blood where his nails and the metal strap had cut it quite deep. I asked someone where I could find a phone and he took me to a small cafe, where the people got through to the police for me. They said they would be round at once in a car.

In a few minutes an enormous Black Maria came and I climbed into it feeling just like a prisoner! They took me to the dock police and took down my statement.

Afterwards they took me again in the Black Maria to the Western Police Station where I saw the Head Inspector, who then got the Head of the CID and took another statement. He said it was very unusual for a European to be attacked in Hong Kong and felt it must have been a put up job. They brought me lots of photographs to identify but there was only one that was like my attacker; I said I didn't want anyone to go to prison, I only wanted my watch back.

I did get another watch before we left Hong Kong, but it was very expensive and not nearly so nice as the other one which I had had for twelve years. With my wrist bandaged up it was very rough taking the dip from the lighter and I could hardly hold on with my swollen hand.

We had Standby at 7.52 am on Tuesday 15th March and an hour later an object apparently touched along the ship's side, but although I examined the stern gland and shafting I found all satisfactory. No damage was reported to me, but as it was rough it was impossible to see the propellers properly. When we got out to sea, even though there was a bit of a swell and she was racing a bit, I thought, "We are losing some revs, she must have hit a blade."

On the morning of 19th March, we moved alongside the unpaved quay in Kalin Kan, thick with red brown dust from the ore elevators. There was quite a lot to do cleaning tubes and back ends, and also the propeller repair. We inspected the propeller from a raft and found a big bite out of tip and side. I thought the only thing to do was to straighten it as much as possible and then turn up the cracks to prevent it splitting further. The fitters said they could come back at 2 pm with the foreman, and then they said they would get their tools and return at midnight, as they had to go 12 miles to get them.

I went ashore just in my boiler suit, as it wasn't what I would have called a dressy place! When I showed my pass at the box on the quay I got permission to go on to the beach. It was very hot as I passed the few fishermen's huts, where they were mending boats over the rough ground and I walked along the white coral beach of the spit of land that ran out and formed the bay. Here I met the Second Mate and Sparks, and although I protested I was too dirty, they pressed me to walk with them. The Second Mate showed me the various plants growing in the gardens by the housesbananas, a special kind of Chinese root vegetable, Chinese cucumbers, gourds and tomatoes. All the various houses with craftsmen had signs outsidea fish for a fisherman, a straw hat for a hatmaker and a pair of scissors for a tailor.

The only trouble with Kalin Kan was the drainage. A deep concrete ditch ran alongside the street, into which everything went, and every afternoon this was ladled out into open buckets and carried two buckets at a time on a pole over the shoulder, slopping and splashing, and simply put on the vegetables and gardens. This I had found in all parts of China.

That night they worked to straighten out the propeller and seal up the cracks until 3 am in the morning. I could not help them as I had slipped going down the steep gangway, straight up and down, and when I grabbed the rope stanchion there was no knot on it and it came away in my hand. To save myself falling 30 feet I grabbed the one on the other side and knocked my thumb.

I found the next day that although there were many roads leading out of the one main street of Kalin Kan, on each and all of them was a large white board in English, Russian and Chinese saying *NO EXCURSIONS! NO PHOTOGRAPHING*! so I was not able to go up to the hills or along the beach, or to any of the other white sand beaches I could see so tantalisingly from the *Shantae*.

By 11.00 am on the morning of Monday 21st March we were full away and sailing northwards over the warm coral waters of the South China Sea, and as I looked back at the palms and the white coral beaches, I wondered if my foot marks were still on the shining sand.

It was calm and warm to begin with, but as we got into the Manila Sea, which was always rough, it turned to strong winds and heavy seas, so that instead of going to Hsin Kiang we had to go in to Tsingtao to discharge our iron ore. At sea it was very cold, but when we got inside it was much warmer with almost a spring feeling in the air. The only fine day at sea a little swallow came down the ventilator and a greaser caught it for me. I let it go and off it flew into the sunshine.

We arrived at Tsing Tao on 28th March, where we were for 5 days. Tsingtao used to be German due to some trading concession, and they must have put a lot of money into it as the building and lay-out of the town was unmistakably German.

By now my thumb was so sore that on 29th March the agent took me to the hospital, which was very dirty with people spitting into spittoons set on the floor. The doctor who examined my thumb said there was inflammation and it must be X-rayed. When the X-rays were developed the doctor said that I had chipped a piece of the bone. A small nurse with a very blunt needle pushed in an enormous dose of penicillin, sort of kill or cure, and the doctor gave me six glass tubes of red powder, which looked to me like red pepper; I think it was as he said it was very hot and I must drink wine with it and not water. Half a cup of wine mixed with half a tube of this stuff twice a day. I thought it safer not to and so I didn't.

After the usual series of false starts, we at length left at 1.37 am on the cold morning of 1st April, leaving the lights of Tsing Tao in the distance. It was only 385 miles to Chinwangtao and we anchored 3 miles off port, where we remained for a couple of days working on the deck steam main stop valve and renewing joints on the port boiler. On Tuesday we moved slowly in and were finished with engines at 8 pm , tied up alongside the berth.

I finally got ashore on 6th April and was determined to get up to see the Great Wall of China. I had asked the Second to find out about it from the Seaman's Club, but the man there said today was too cold and the wind was too strong, perhaps tomorrow.

The next day he came with a car at 9 am and off we set to the Great Wall. It was a long way, and took us about 5 hours. It was bigger than I had expected, made of huge blocks of stone, and stretched over the horizon until it was lost in the hills. It seemed such an achievement to build something like this which would last through generations and generations of people. Like the stars and the mountains and the sea, it was something stretched into infinity, even though it was made by man. It defined the edges of the civilised world and pushed out the barbarians. The Great Wall was a wonder and I think that was my main feeling about it—wonder.

We had three more days in Chinwangtao and left on 10th April for Hong Kong, the last leg of my voyage. I was very glad I had only signed on for another three months and not six, because it seemed a long time since I had left Tresco on that hot July morning. When we got back there was much to do with handing over the engines and mending the propeller. Then I signed off and Mr Lam said he hoped I would come back and sail again with the Jeb-Shun Shipping Company. I said I would, but not just yet, and finally I collected my luggage and headed for the airport and home.

Chapter Twenty
SS Shun Fung, the Following Breeze

Almost before the geese began to fly south, I began to get restless for the sea. Once more I had agreed to take a boat out to Japan for the Jeb -Shun Shipping Company.

"There's your tickets," they said, "and good luck."

Kennington Road was pouring with rain and quite dark as I went down the path to the taxi, loaded with my four zip bags and my shoulder bag. I did not know how long I should be away, nor how much I might need, so when I reached the KLM office in Sloane Street I was rather overloaded.

On the tarmac at Kristiansand, Norway, the air smelt clean, of pine and wild flowers, and walking over the short grass to the wooden air station I was greeted by a jolly Irish Captain and the agent.

"You are Miss Drummond. I am Captain Mahon of the *Shun Fung*. Is that all the gear you have? Come, let's get it in the car." He said it all in one breath, and in no time we were driving up hilly country roads bordered by pine trees and wild flowers.

The dry dock was cut from the rock and as we drove in I could see the ship. A large rather gaunt vessel, her hull green, her funnel yellow and her deck with trailing wire ropes. She looked a bit derelict. About 10,000 tons I reckoned.

After I was shown my accommodation, I slipped on a boiler suit and nipped down to the engine room for a good look round. They were raising steam on the main boilers; most of the repair work had been finished.

We shifted from dry dock at Bredal to the oil berth on 6th September. Even though I was very busy with the engines, I managed to get ashore in the evenings.

Taking the dip was awful, quite an acrobatic feat, as she was a light ship and very high out of the water. I had nearly 40 feet to go down a rope ladder, over the side on to the wharf. The oil tank was right up a steep hill, through iron doors and down a rock passage all crumbling and dripping. There was a gap all round the tank and a 50 feet drop down the side into darkness; with only my torch I was afraid of slipping and rolling off the curved top into nothingness. I was very glad to get out of that horrible place and felt quite dopey with the fumes. Then it was time to climb the 40 feet rope ladder and scramble over the rail at the top.

We sailed on the evening of 6th September and as the pine forests and rugged coast of Norway faded into the distance, the fragrant scent of the pines still drifted across to us in the off shore wind. Once more I was at sea again, bound for Otaru, on the northernmost island of Japan.

As the ship had been laid up for so long, we were constantly looking for trouble with the engines, but the only trouble on the first two days was the main valve joint on the starboard boiler. We came into Flushing at 10 am on 8th September, the countryside all green and wet with church spires in the distance. To take the dip this time I had a ladder put across from the deck to the oil station, on which I had to crawl on all fours, while it wobbled back and forwards. They certainly think out a variety of ways of getting ashore for the oil dip. We bunkered 324 tons and of course I had to retrace my wobbling bridge at the finish.

Later that day we left for Antwerp and glided up the Scheldt in the pitch dark with no sparkle of light from either bank. A cold breeze rippled the black water and there was a strong scent in the air of wet grass and rushes. Passing the docks lined with ships, the faint rattle of winches and thud of loading cargo drifted out to us on the night breeze.

At last we were off the wharf tied up alongside, lights glinting over the grey Belgian blocks as far as one could see. The Captain had come down from the bridge and said I could shut down on two boilers as we would be loading by shore cranes.

We were at Antwerp for just over a week while they loaded a full cargo of potash, which meant that white dust flew everywhere. I was very busy cleaning the fridge pipes which were full of rust flakes and the evaporator, I had stores to get, winches to pack, belts to fix on electric pumps, and in fact endless things to do. Many of the people on the docks were old friends I had known since the *Har Zion* in 1940—Paul Muller and Mr Lecocq, and Mr Menheer of Thomas Cook from even longer ago when I was on the *Mulbera*. I thought of the happy times I'd had when I was a carefree junior engineer and my sister Frances was a happy artist and everything was so cheap that money went round the world and back again.

The last few days were very busy finishing off all the work on the engines, and when I had a moment I had to stock up with all the little things I needed on a long voyage: note books and writing paper, soapflakes, biscuits and chocolate, and even a little red sedum in a pot. I wandered through the old streets, calling in at familiar cafes and restaurants, saying goodbye to Antwerp until next time.

We sailed down the river in the dark on Sunday 18th September, through the scent of the marshes. Soon we were lifting to the Channel and full

Twenty

away for Palermo. As we neared the Bay the weather deteriorated and we got in with a Gale Force 7. However, by the 21st it had improved and we were out at 8 pm. I was always glad to see the massive headland of Cape Finisterre, whether in daylight with its sharp cut shadows or in the dark. Wednesday was a clear night and I could see it in the distance, looming through the darkness with its tremendous white light flashing.

We entered the Straits of Gibraltar late on the 24th with Cape Trafalgar on one side and Cape Spartel on the other, flashing away into the darkness. It was Sunday morning when we passed Gibraltar, towering upwards into grey clouds, and so on we steamed into the Mediterranean towards Palermo.

Palermo looked lovely in the early morning light of September 28th just before the sun turned to gold. The blue hills unfolded from night shadows and I could see the far hillsides dotted with orange and lemon trees. The water of the bay turned ever deeper blue with the increasing light.

Next morning we were sailing through the Straits of Messina, with small puffs of white steam rising from the summit of Mount Etna. The morning sun grew hot and I could see the houses and orange trees clearly. So we sailed on through the Mediterranean, getting ever bluer, with the mountains of Crete just visible, and on to Port Said on 3rd October. There were quite a lot of ships lying off the port, but we were allowed in as we had to take water. We had missed the morning convoy so were going to go through in the evening.

The moment the anchor chain rattled out and the hook dropped into the soft sand clouding the water, the ship was invaded by Arabs and Gypsies from I don't know where. They swarmed on board while we were still gliding to our anchorage.

"I am your friend.... I know you.... Chief! Chief! Don't you remember me?....A friend of Jock Ferguson and George Robbie.... I know you many times...."

Dozens of scarlet fezzes bobbed round, dark grimy hands clasped mine. It was impossible to move. Shoes, model camels, bunches of grapes, oranges, socks, thermos flasks, tablecloths, real elephant ivory, sandalwood trays and boxes were all laid out on the hatch in a humming market which became shrieks and screams as excitement rose.

"You no find other place.... Real camel leather all made in Cairo.... Good...." And the vendor beat the bright yellow bag with his fists, which did little to improve the quality.

"Beautiful picture..." said another, pointing to the embossed camels and pyramids picked out in brightest blue.

Another seller rushed in between with a bottle of orange crush in one hand and a pair of slippers in the other.

So the screaming match continued, waxing more fierce and furious as midday and the long siesta approached. Suddenly, when the battle appeared lost, a bag, a couple of pairs of socks and a box of Turkish delight would be thrust in my hand.

"Take it, take it, you rob me. Me only poor man," they would say with mournful wails.

It was a clear night with a full moon and a cool breeze and stand-by went at 10.17 pm as we moved to take our station in the convoy, seventh from No 1. I was up all night of course and we took the stand-by in turns. I went on deck as dawn was breaking, casting a yellow light over the desert. I remembered those long ago days when I was black with coal dust, soaked through and too tired to take off my boiler suit, lying down and sleeping as I was. I remembered the old *Anchises* when the plates were so hot they burnt the soles of my shoes and I had to stand on pieces of wood. So often then and in the *Mulbera* with the Tiger I had thought, "Some day I shall go through the Canal as Chief." And now there were so many times that I had.

A great many alterations had been made to the Canal since I first sailed on it. The banks used to be sand right down to the water in places and tamarisk trees had been planted to keep the sand from slipping into the Canal. Now the banks were built up with stone walls nearly the entire length. It was also a lot wider now and we could get through in 18 hours or so instead of 24. The shortest time I have ever been through is 11 hours and the longest 28.

As we neared Suez a slight breeze rippled the Canal making the water like green silk. The pilot said, "You have kept perfect station, Chief, and been to the minute on every point." I felt rather pleased.

We spent five days sailing down the Red Sea to Aden and it was very hot, 114°F in the Engine Room, 120°F in the stokehold. Several parties of swallows came on board at night and trimmed round the open ports. One night a large number came and I put water out for them as usual, but they were fluttery and frightened as a large hawk had swooped at them and scared them. When they all left at daylight one little swallow was lying dead on the floor. The others circled round the port once or twice as if counting their number and wondering if he would come; then the leaders seemed to give the order to go and they were off, flying like the wind.

The Captain said a hawk got one forward. I used to clap my hands at the hawk and try to drive it off before they came in the evening. However, one night I saw the Chinese crew grouped round something aft and went to see what it was. I found they had trapped a large hawk somehow and had its feet tied with string and were tormenting it. The Fourth Engineer was with me, so I told him to get the hawk away from them and free it. Then I told them off and they were frightened. I walked off and left the Fourth to deal with them.

The next night a hawk came through my port and he perched on top of my door in the day room, so I left the door open with the curtain down and put a shallow dish of water for it, which it sipped in the early morning. I heard something at the first streaks of day and peering in saw the hawk flying out of the port. He perched a moment on the bridge rail, then circled the ship and was away.

We arrived at Aden early on 10th October and the agents and Shell representatives were on board at once. I set off in the Shell launch to take the dip before breakfast. There was a wonderful view of the harbour from the top of the silver oil tank. I went to the office and complained about the poor quality of the oil and they said they couldn't change it without authority from London, which would take 24 hours. I didn't believe it could take so long, even deferred rate, and thought they were shoving the bad stuff on to me. However, there was nothing they would do, so I started to head back to the ship. Suddenly there was a call at the office to say they'd had a blow back of oil on the deck, so of course I had to dash back at once. One of the Shell managers came with me, as they didn't know how bad it was. When we got back to the *Shun Fung* there was oil on the deck, but not very much. The Captain had just come on deck in his new white nylon shorts and shirt when it blew back and so was covered in oil which would not come out. I was so glad there was nothing worse wrong, and having bunkered 448 long tons I went back with the manager to take the dip.

It was a great rush, but we were full away by that afternoon, the barren rocks of Aden with their rugged peaks and sharp summits fading into the hot afternoon as we went down the Gulf of Aden for the 3,477 mile voyage to Singapore. Two days later we passed Socotra, a mysterious island, with strange plants and flowers, and trees like the Dragon's Blood tree which used to make a red dye for staining the poorer grades of mahogany. There were still some primitive people living here in caves, tending their flocks and herds, and making pottery. The peaks of Socotra were supposed to be the only mountains not covered by the Flood.

It took us sixteen days to get to Singapore, past the Maldive Islands, which we smelt but didn't sight, past the misty hills of Ceylon in the dark. Later we saw the lights of Colombo and the strong light flashing from

Cape Galle. I thought of Cousin Henry and his rather sad exile; how he loved Seggieden, the river slipping past, fishing and shooting, and his collection of bottled snakes he made to take "home". But he never went home, and died and was buried at Vraila. And all the many times I passed through there on the *Mulbera* he never came to see me.

By morning Ceylon and the shadows were left behind and we were dancing along over sunny blue water. On 23rd October we sighted the island of Sumatra and passed from the Indian Ocean and the Bay of Bengal into the Straits of Malacca. White steamy clouds hung over Sumatra, which was blue and mysterious like liquid sapphire. Towards evening it became a little cooler and I could see the distant coastline of dark green forest.

Then we passed the lights of Singapore spangled in a long multi-coloured line, over the dark waters, and as they faded to the darkness of tropical night I turned in.

The first few days were hot, sailing up the South China Sea, but the sea temperature soon dropped from 86°F to 75°F and by the time we arrived in Otaru, further north even than Vladivostock, it had dropped to 57°F. The Captain could have taken a route up by Borneo, west of the Philippines, but he thought it too dangerous with a loaded ship and the many coral reefs, so we went up by Borneo and Indo-China, past Hainan Island and through the Manila Sea which was always rough. When we tied up alongside at the discharging berth of Otaru on 11th November it was bitterly cold.

The next morning was bright and clear. We were discharging by winches, and despite all the work on them the two winters lying up in Norway had taken their toll. They were very old wartime winches, built in Canada and it was impossible to get spare parts for them. Suddenly the agent appeared to take me to Immigration. I went just as I was in my white boiler suit and patrol jacket and cap. I was terribly keen to go to Tokyo, but worried they would not give me a pass to go so far. There had been such trouble before when I had been so much nearer. The head Immigration official seemed very nice, and asked, "Why do you want to go to Tokyo?"

I showed him my telegram, and said, "To see my friends."

"You cannot get an extension on your pass to see friends," he said. "Is there anything else you wish to do, perhaps some business?"

"No," I said, "it was just to see my friends. What else can I say?"

So then he laughed and said, "No, you cannot go."

However, the agent added quickly, "The Chief Engineer must go to Yokohama on ship's business to look at the wood that the company is buying for shifting boards for the holds, and the Chief Engineer will have to arrange to fix it in the holds."

"Of course," said the Chief Immigration Officer, "that's different. I will extend your pass and grant permission for you to go to Yokohama via Tokyo to attend to the ship's business. You may go on Monday and return on Wednesday, but do not come to the office to report to me till Thursday morning."

I thanked him very much and the agent and I went out into the bright sunshine with the gold maidenhair fern fluttering down. I said to the Agent, "You must give me the address in Yokohama where I am to go and see the wood."

The Agent said, "There is no wood. But that is what you go to see, and the Immigration Officer has granted you the pass for it," and he laughed a great deal.

I was due to go the next day. That afternoon I wandered about the town and looked at tea sets. The people here were different to those in the south and the land was more rural. There was a lot of farm produce and salmon were caught round the coasts. There were also black bears in the forests. The agent told me that they used to be very quiet, but now they had turned savage and attacked people. There were many carved bears in the shops and I bought one. I also tried to find a pair of shoes, but they just looked at my feet and laughed, everyone had such tiny feet.

Monday 14th November was clear and I set off in my blue suit and blue beret in the car with the agent who took me to the bus and put me in a window seat with many instructions to the conductress to let me off at Sapporo, the capital town of Hokkaido. On the way we passed maidenhair fern trees bright with gold leaves and rowan trees turning scarlet with deep orange berries, scarlet maples, and larch a golden brown. Bunches of Indian corn and long white radishes hung under the eaves of the houses and the hills looked very volcanic. In Sapporo I found the JAL Bureau from where I could catch a bus to the airport.

Alice met me in Tokyo and drove me back to Hayam where, after dinner I fell asleep to the soft wash of the waves on the beach.

The next day happened to be the festival when the little Japanese girls were taken to the temples to be blessed. All the little girls aged between five and seven were dressed in their traditional costumes, bright kimonos with big bows at the back, in scarlets, blues and shining white. They wore Japanese shoes and had flowers in their hair and the kimonos were all worked in gold and silver thread, so that they looked like flocks of butterflies.

On Wednesday morning I said my goodbyes and we drove off to the station where we caught a train to Tokyo. After spending the morning touring, we met Dorothy at the Imperial Hotel for lunch. I was so sad to go after such a lovely time, and they even came out to the airport with me and sat talking while I waited for my plane.

By the time I returned to Otaru the winch parts had arrived and were fitted in the pouring rain. Mrs Matsuo of the repair company came to see it finished in her smart Japanese clothes, an umbrella held over her head by her fitter; she stood there till it was completed. I was soaked through going backwards and forwards. I had beaten her down in price for the work and made her take about 80,000 yen off the generator which was repaired badly, but she still brought me a lovely tea set and was all smiles and good wishes. After we had said goodbye she went off in the pouring rain.

By 6.42 am next morning we were full away south to Moji. I watched the coast line in the dawn, as the high blue mountains, deep green firs and yellow larches faded into the distance. I was really sorry to leave Otaru and the mysterious northerly island with its mountains and forests, hot springs and black bears.

On Saturday 26th November we bunkered from a barge and the oil ordered was far too heavy. It was bitterly cold and as we were a light ship they had to pump it up about 30 feet in a very heavy swell with scuds of snow turning to driving showers. It was cold on the barge and the bunkering pipe split when they got another pump to try and force the oil up; there was thick, black, gummy oil everywhere. So we didn't finish bunkering till early on Monday morning when we were away for Shanghai.

It seemed as if the Yangtze was really the busiest river in the world. There were so many junks, sea-going junks and coasting junks, fishing junks and numerous sampans with the whole family on board, chickens, plants, cats and dogs—which crowded the great yellow river with its strong current.

The charter party which had hired the boat to deliver rice and lorries to West Africa invited me to come with the Captain and his wife for a day and evening out. We were also meeting with Captain Duncan, master of the other ship bought by the company. In the Seaman's Club, where everyone remembered me, and I received quite an ovation. I also spent some time choosing some pink silk for the drawing room curtains at Tresco, which I had promised to bring back.

After some tea here we were rushed off to the Children's Palace. Our guides kept saying, "We must hurry, they are waiting."

I never thought it meant us, but when we arrived we found a large group of children all standing on the steps. When they saw us they rushed to meet us and four little girls took us each by the hand and led us through all the classrooms. I felt just like the Queen! We saw model building, photography, embroidery, singing, drawing and painting, and everywhere we went they all stood up and clapped.

My little girl was called Chieng Bei Ji and I promised to send her a postcard of London.

After all this we went to the Peace Hotel where the Charter Party gave a dinner for us. We had a private dining room and I sat between Miss Woo, and a man who spoke English well. There was shark's fin soup and egg soup, chicken and sweet and sour pork, and a pile of mandarin oranges for dessert.

We were there two more days loading the lorries and the bags of rice, and I went ashore once or twice, but the country villages and small curio shops had gone and now all was built up and different.

We sailed for Hong Kong on 3rd December and I had been on duty since 4 am warming through the engines. I saw a flock of white geese being herded along the swampy flats by a man holding a long rod with a rag at the end. They were so busy eating the grass they never even thought of jumping into the river and swimming away.

Each day we sailed south it got warmer, the sea became milky tea coloured, and we saw hundreds of junks with bright sails and eyes painted on their bows. The crew were getting excited at nearing their home port after such a long voyage. We had left Norway nearly two months ago. As we sighted the painted rock about 40 miles from Hong Kong excitement reached fever pitch. We arrived just after midnight on 7th December.

When I got up in the morning I felt too faint to eat breakfast or catch the 8.15 am boat. I told the Captain and he gave me sal volatile, and I turned in and slept till 2 am. I was just faint from exhaustion and tired out. Mr Barclay the surveyor came on board so I had a talk to him and he said to come to the office the next morning.

I signed off the next day, but by 9th December I had got my permit and signed on again, ready for another voyage. We had three more days in Hong Kong, during which time I was busy with repairs, arranging to get the pay for my last voyage back to London, posting letters and Christmas cards, stocking up with powder and soap, and a new pair of shoes, sending off china and frocks.

The next morning we were full away to Tsamkong, 264 miles down the coast, just on the borders of French Indo-China. I had been on the go all Monday and all Monday night, so on Tuesday when we got to sea I turned in for a good sleep in the afternoon. We went up a broad, shallow river with flat land on either side, and faint hills in the distance. Later in the afternoon we tied up alongside the loading wharf, where we were to load more sacks of rice.

We had trouble with the generators as they had not been properly repaired in Hong Kong and the people here did not have the materials to repair them. The only thing to do was to grind down the ridges and expand the ring myself. They were also chipping the dry tank top under the boiler and when finished, cleaned and red leaded it. I went ashore once or twice in the afternoons and evenings, and over to the Seaman's Club, but I did not stay out after dark, as they said it was not safe. On 17th December we moved out to anchorage so they could fumigate the whole ship to destroy the rice moth in the cargo, otherwise the caterpillars would have eaten all the rice to husks. They sent a launch for the crew to come ashore and the Captain and I were run up in the Humber to the Seaman's Hotel where I was shown a lovely suite for my stay on shore.

That evening I went back to the ship, which smelt strongly of gas, and brought up steam on all boilers. I was glad to be relieved at 8 am in the morning, and back to the Seaman's Club for breakfast, sitting in solitary state in my own dining room. Afterwards we were all taken off on a bus trip to a giant dam the government was constructing. It was 2,800 metres long and was to be finished by next year. They were making a vast number of salt pans and a new wharf so ships could come in and load salt. We all got out and watched them digging the earth and loading it into hand drawn wooden carts. Old, young and middle-aged were working without cessation.

"Look how clean they are!" exclaimed our guide with pride. "They can wear good clothes."

I had a suspicion that they were wearing their best clothes because of our visit.

The guide told me that these were the young people from the farms, who liked to come because they were paid and only worked 8 hours a day.

I do not know how many loads they carried, but I calculated roughly that they each walked 41 miles every day. Now and again loud speakers relayed messages to encourage the workers. "Hard work is good for you, one must work for China," they translated to me. Some of the workers looked very tired. I saw some of the men giving the old women a push up with their carts when they reached the short steep hill at the top of the dam.

We arrived at Pulau Bukom on Boxing Day and I was determined to stay at the oil berth as long as I could to give the crew a chance to walk along to the village; taking the oil by gravity made it much slower to bunker the 704 long tons. When I went to the office to finish the calculations, I told them that the oil was of very poor quality. They said we had been too long bunkering.

"That is how accidents happen," I said. "Too much hurry. Remember you are not making a present of the oil. We are paying for it."

I think I had the last word, so I went back to the ship and by 6.30 pm we were full away for Durban.

We brought in the New Year, 1961 by sixteen bells struck in the engine room and on deck. As we crossed the line we had the traditional ceremony of Neptune coming on board. I made Neptune, the Third Engineer, a crown of paper painted orange and a trident. Afterwards the Captain turned the hose on them. The Captain was very jolly and good at making things fun for them all.

On 6th January we passed Mauritius which we could just glimpse under steamy white clouds. We were too far off to see the Seychelles or the Cocos Islands, but on the 11th the Island of Reunion rose into sight. It passed swiftly turning into a deeper blue under the clouds which enfolded it, and so our old cargo boat chugged along, a tiny dot on the vast ocean. It would have been a quiet and peaceful time had it not been for the chipping. It was awful, just awful, and went on all morning and from 3 pm in the afternoon. It was like being in a tin biscuit box with someone banging on the lid. We had 23 days of it altogether and the noise was so great I could not hear the engine.

On 17th January we arrived at Durban. The bay looked lovely with the town spread round it, though there were many more high buildings since I was there last on the *Perseus* in 1943. We went through the narrow channel past the coaling wharf where we used to bunker coal; back then the noise and dirt had been awful. Now everything was very different and we glided up the channel to the oil bunkering wharf.

As we rounded the Cape the sea became bluer, the sun warmer. We sighted Table Mountain clearly outlined against a bright apricot dawn sky on 21st January and as we neared the equator it became hotter and hotter. After we crossed the line, we proceeded through the Gulf of Guinea, past the Slave Coast, the Gold Coast, the Ivory Coast and the Grain Coast.

Conakry, one square mile in size, was in French Guinea between Portuguese Guinea and Sierra Leone.

The Captain, who had never been there before, said that "surf days" were mentioned in the Charter.

"Look," he said, "work continues except on 'surf days'."

He took it to mean that we would have to lie off port and discharge cargo into canoes, which would be paddled to shore by the natives, wearing nothing but a string of beads round the neck. The rollers would carry the canoes high up on the shore and the natives would jump into the surf and pull them even higher up the beach and then carry the cargo on their backs. But on "surf days" when the rollers were too high, they would call a halt until the weather improved again.

"In fact," the Captain added, thinking of the beads, "I don't think this is a very suitable place to have brought you to, Miss Drummond."

The cook had been to Conakry as a boy and he confirmed this.

I said, "Could they have sent us to such a place? Ten thousand tons of rice in bags; we will be here about three months, or more, if there are many surf days!"

"The mosquitoes are so bad here that you cannot go ashore after dark," said the Captain, "and there is yellow fever also."

"How will they get the lorries ashore then?" I asked.

"Perhaps rafts," said the Captain, "if it is not a 'surf day'!"

Conakry was not an easy port to enter because of the coral reefs and shallow water. We arrived on 3rd February, a lovely morning with a glistening sea. Various canoes appeared as if from nowhere, very small, and paddled by hand. Their crews waved to us as we passed and I said to the Captain, "Ah, there are the canoes."

But no, they were just fishing boats. As I was wondering how they could land without turning over, I saw their fishing lines. We then anchored off a lovely coral island covered with palms while we waited for pilotage. All the next day the men fished over the side and caught a vast quantity of pink and blue fish. I offered a prize of a carton of cigarettes to the man who caught the most in an hour and they were all very happy. Afterwards the whole ship smelt of frying fish.

On Sunday morning the pilot suddenly appeared, and said we must come inside the breakwater straight away. I explained that this was not possible as she was a steam ship, not a diesel, and I had to get up steam first. However, at just past midday we had arrived and were tied up alongside a huge modern stone and concrete discharging wharf. Behind it a city stretched into the distance.

"What about the canoes and the surf days then?" I asked the Captain.

The next afternoon the Captain gave a large party to some Chinese Embassy officials and the chief people of the town to hand over the rice and the ten lorries. They had 24 people in the saloon, but I was not invited nor any of my people from the engine room.

I was very put out, so I said to the Captain, "After we have come from China without stopping, thanks to the work of the engine room crew, you are acting as if you had sailed the ship single-handed."

The Captain looked a bit sheepish, and so he should have.

It was blazing hot at Conakry with a damp heat like a moist stove, and we were unloading rice every day. I could only go ashore in the evenings when it was slightly cooler and even then it was very hot. Quite a lot of the men were sick and some knocked off. I thought it was from eating too many bananas. As they ripened so rapidly they didn't want to waste them and just gobbled them up, although a lot of the fruit was broken at the ends or split. It could also have been from the large bright blue crabs they got off the fishermen, which only last for an hour or so in that climate. I had a bit of malaria and took some quinine tablets, but as I never touched a banana or a crab, I survived all right. The Captain was most attentive at treating them and they all pulled round.

On 11th February a Russian delegate arrived in Conakry and I decided to go and have a look. As I was walking through the docks I saw one or two dock officials sitting in the shade and they asked me if I would like to see the arrival.

"Yes, very much indeed." I replied.

So I was assigned one of the lesser lights to accompany me, a very black, very tall man who spoke some English as well as French, and together we walked up the long mango avenue and right past the cathedral. My guide took me all the way to a splendid view point on the kerb, among the grandees of Conakry, and a church school of little girls in gingham frocks and amazing hair styles. Everyone had a picture of the Russian, a good-looking man, on a long stick to wave. It reminded me much of Hitler's visit to Vienna in 1937. There were dancers in the roadway, singing and dancing to tom-toms, dressed in brilliant colours, and the children near me each had an enamel plate with holes bored round with copper rings in, which they rattled as they sang in shrill little voices.

Then the great moment arrived and an enormously long pink car appeared. Next to the driver was a stout, hot elderly man with grey hair in a thick woollen suit and a stiff collar and tie, waving wildly from side to side. He was purple in the face and bore no resemblance to the good-looking young man on the flags. I only hoped he wouldn't die of heat stroke. On the back of the car was a large floral tribute, which looked exactly like a wreath. He gave me an exhausted grin as the car slowly passed, the crowd by now quite silent. After him came a big cavalcade of diplomatic cars with a very large Alsatian dog looking out of the window of the French one.

It was another week before they finished taking out the sacks of rice, there was some work to do with the engine, and I went ashore when the heat of the day had subsided a bit, buying pretty cottons in the market. When I got back to the quay there was the most enormous octopus lying dead with its terrible tentacles spread out, it must have weighed over two hundredweight.

The men at the dock gate were very polite and saluted me every time I came out, but there had been trouble with a few American sailors who had pulled down some of the flags. They were arrested and couldn't return to their ship. When the Consul came he could do nothing; and even worse, when the Admiral came down they wouldn't let him return to the ship either. There was a shouting match and finally the American Ambassador was sent for; he managed to get the Admiral out, but not the sailors who were put in prison.

We sailed from Conakry on 23rd February, leaving the lorries we had brought and the heaps of rice still standing on the wharf, as were a whole lot of lorries and cars which had come from Russia. I could not help thinking what would happen when the rains came in a few weeks time. So we passed out through the coral reef until Conakry was nothing but a blue haze in the distance.

We had good weather on our run to Casablanca, travelling along the coast. One evening some gold flies came aboard, with bright shiny wings as if of metallic gold. We anchored off the port at 8.15 pm on the evening of 7th March, a lovely evening with the lights of the port in the distance.

Here we stayed for two days, although I kept steam up on the main engines ready for a move. We couldn't manage much work, but skimmed and undercut the mica on the fridge motor commuter, renewed a length of pipe on the fire pump exhaust, and reconditioned the pinion gear on No 4 winch. It was very pleasant lying at anchor with the bright sun, blue sea and sky, and the distant outline of Casablanca shining in the sunlight. The last time I had been here was in 1940. We were the last ship to leave the port as they closed it after the fall of France. We had taken General Lord Dilhorne and Lord Villiers and all their staff to Gibraltar. We had painted our funnel red, put on all our lights and went round as a neutral.

We shifted anchorage on 9th March and five hours later we were along-side the discharging berth unloading our coffee. I was soon ashore, and I walked into the town, which was very much like the Arabian Nights, with copper and brass gleaming in the bazaar, palm trees against the sky, and the bright colours of all the goods, and hand woven blankets and little mats.

Next morning the Second Mate called me to come from breakfast, as there was a man on the quay selling oranges. He had a huge basket heaped up with beautiful large oranges, fresh from the trees, with dark shining leaves, which he was throwing up for us to catch and taste. I couldn't resist catching one to taste and it was just as sweet as it looked. So then I bought lots and filled the fruit basket in my room.

Later the Second and I went up with the Ship's Chandler in his car to get some nuts and bolts as we never had any spare when anything went. The store was enormous and quite empty, and I had the greatest difficulty in finding any bolts of the right diameter, and the ones they did have were far too expensive at 1/6 each, so the quantity I needed would have been prohibitive. We ended up in the bazaar where I began bargaining for a red leather note case.

"No, no," I said, "too much, too dear," and got into the taxi. They rushed after me screaming, waving their hands and thrust the case in the taxi window, eventually I got it at the price I had asked. The Second was amused and laughed, a thing he did not do very often.

We had stand-by at 8.32 pm and three hours later were again lifting to the Atlantic swell with the lights of Casablanca sparkling and twinkling astern. We passed Gibraltar in the night and by the morning we were leaving the Spanish hills. The weather was fine and cool, and after passing Algiers became warmer. At Palermo when I went up to take the dip, I found a telegram waiting for me: Cherry and Humphrey had a third child, to be called Humphrey. Confusing, I thought, to have two Humphreys in the same family, and not a name that shortens easily, but I was delighted to hear that all had gone well.

Next morning, St Patrick's Day, the chandler came early for me to take me to the dentist. The street we went to was dirty, as was the house, with washing hanging out from the upper floors. I climbed a dusty stair with peeling plaster and walked into a small dark room containing an old fashioned chair with all the stuffing coming out. The chandler offered to stay with me, but I said I thought I could manage, still imagining that the dentist was good. I sat in the chair and the dentist looked at my tooth. He told me to wait in a smaller even dirtier room without a window where some moaning peasants sat wrapped in black shawls. I had heard shrieks and screams as I came up the stairs, which was somewhat disconcerting. He called the waiting patients in and I heard more shrieks and screams, and a woman came out, supported by her friends, pouring with blood. Then an old dirty woman came out bearing a bowl with blood and teeth.

By this time I was thoroughly shaken and when I was called in he waved a pair of pincers at me and said the tooth was impossible to fill. At last I wisely fled, down the stairs and out into the sunlight and jumped into the waiting car. I said, "He wasn't very good; he only wanted to pull it out."

And the chandler smiled a knowing smile, and said "Now we will try and get my dentist, who is good." We drove to a nice part of the town with wide streets, and stopped by a large house with a garden and white railings. We went into a real dentist's surgery with a blue plush chair, shining chromium plate and a white coated assistant. He explained that the dental surgeon was ill in bed with a poisoned finger. However, the dentist, on being told of the situation, got out of bed, jumped into his car and drove round, all smiles. "For you I will do this," he said, and with most skilled remaining fingers completed the filling. I paid him and the parking fine which had been stuck on my car, so it was a rather expensive morning.

I just got back to the ship by 11.30 am and was told to raise steam on main engine for 12 pm and by 12.30 pm we were full away.

It was dark when we went through the Straits of Messina, and I stood on deck watching the lights and smelling the lemon blossom. We arrived at Port Said on 22nd March and were soon steaming into the anchorage, when I knew that scenes of bargaining would erupt on deck. I bought a beige suede bag and some new cotton socks for the men who had painted the top of the engine room, because they had only been able to work in socks due to the danger of slipping. I also bought postcards and some juicy oranges, but the screaming and bargaining made it very hard work. Finally, when it was quite dark they suddenly appeared with some enormous oranges which came, they said, from King Farouk's garden. Stolen, I supposed, and with many blessings they disappeared into the darkness again.

We were steaming No 2 place in convoy as a large ship in front of us had broken down; there were 26 ships behind. I only hoped we would be able to keep station as our bottom was so dirty after being so long in tropical waters, and also the generators were so worn that the canal light was a great strain on them.

I was up all night and had trouble keeping station, but somehow we managed. The boat men had rolled themselves in their blankets and were asleep on the hatch looking for all the world like mummies. And so the night wore on, with a chill breeze and then a faint sandy glow as dawn flushed primrose and we tied up at the Bitter Lakes. We were anchored in almost the exact spot where the Israelites had crossed the Red Sea and here they had dredged up parts of bridles, horses' bits, spear heads and parts of chariots.

The voyage over from Aden to Singapore was pleasant weather all the time. There was a huge Easter moon when we passed Socotra turning all to silver. On 3rd April, while I was having dinner the Fourth came for me to tell me that the main engine after bilge pump rod had snapped. I made a thorough check on main engine and air pump, and relieved load on the fore bilge pumps by putting the ballast pump on the bilges. I then told the Captain that I considered it safe to proceed to Singapore. The greaser Lancoy crushed his finger, having put his hand behind not realising the rod had snapped.

We ran for thirteen days with the bilge pump disconnected and on 16th April we approached Pulau Bukom, the oil installation island, for bunkering. While we were bunkering I made up my list and nipped down to the village to get all the things I could not get in Aden. The shore men came first of all and measured the rod to repair it and we worked on the engines.

The sea and sky were so bright that I could hardly look at them. We had a hard day's work anchored in that boiling heat, but in the evening we were off to Shanghai, a good voyage of eleven days, passing the Japanese islands in a sea mist.

During the time we were at Shanghai we were taken off to a banquet in the Peace Hotel by the charter party, who had hired two huge rooms for the occasion. I was really quite proficient by now with my chopsticks. We were there for the 1st May celebrations, when for one day in the year the whole of Shanghai is illuminated as it once used to be every night. We were not invited to see the parade, but in the evening were taken up to the Seaman's Club in a bus for a really marvellous circus performance by the steel workers, all amateurs, but very good. We had of course to wade through the usual Communist speeches first, which went on for hours, but then we had a post office telegraph boy jumping tables on a bicycle, juggling with hair brushes and cups and saucers and dancing with scarves and spinning umbrellas. Afterwards we drove back in our large bus through the lighted streets of Shanghai to the ship.

There was also much work to be done on the ship, and a great deal of hanging about waiting for them to shift berth. We finally sailed on 5th

May, heading south to Hong Kong. It was only about a four day run and we had good weather and no typhoons. When we got there, the super, Mr Chay, came to my room and pressed 1,000 Hong Kong dollars into my hand because they were so pleased with the voyage.

There was much to do the next day and I was seeing to the engines, and also arranging for my money and things to be sent home. We were to be in Hong Kong till 3rd June, and I had already decided that I should try and do some more voyages. The owners were charming and so was the Captain and I liked the crew. I was even fond of the old *Shun Fung*.

On 18th May I was ashore when a strong gusty wind blew up, but I thought it was just going to rain a bit. When I got back to the pier I found the wind was terrific. No boats were running. They just said, "Typhoon, typhoon! No more wallah wallahs go out."

It was a tearing wind by now and white seas were breaking under the slashing rain. I persuaded them to take me out to the ship as every minute it was getting worse. They brought in the largest boat from anchor and a man from the office came down with me. He and the boatman gave me a hand in, for one moment she was way down, and the next moment she was above my head. It was a wonder she was not smashed leaving the pier, but we got out all right. How we rolled and pitched! By now there were mountainous seas and tearing wind ripping up the canvas shelter screens. I was soaked through at once, and there was such a mist of flying spray and driving rain that I could hardly see a thing in the darkness.

It was a long way and even when we got near we could hardly see the ship. She was plunging about and the aluminium gangway ladder was flying backwards and forwards in the wind. I looked at it in horror, for the last steps of the gangway were very high.

However, the boatmen were wonderful and the quartermaster was splendid and came down the awful gangway which was flying out and then bashing against the ship's side. They could only bring the boat in for one split second, and in that second I had to judge the distance and jump as the boat was swept past on the crest of a wave. By now I was standing on the narrow deck, having crawled from the cabin. Hanging on for all I was worth, I held my breath as they brought the boat near the ladder with wonderful dexterity.

It was a good jump. I let go of the boat and the next thing I knew I was hanging on the drenched gangway rope and the wallah wallah was swept far down on the receding sea.

The quartermaster grabbed me and step by step we got up the gangway which swung right out away from the ship and then crashed against the side with a jolt that nearly threw me off. It was an awful night. I could see nothing but flying spray and the ship was so light she was bouncing about like a cork. I couldn't breathe with the strength of the wind.

We got through the night somehow, but when daylight came it was getting worse and not better. The Third Mate and I had breakfast together and, as I was the only senior officer on board, he asked me what he should do. I said, "I think you should check on the anchors and see we are holding and not dragging or we will be on Stonecutters. If they are dragging we will have to do something about it. And see the hatch covers are all hard down and the ports are all tight. Have any dead lights there are put up, because I think it is getting worse."

The Captain struggled back about 9 am with the Third who helped him get back by making a boat take them. The Captain was getting so desperate to get back he said he would buy the boat and take her out himself! They were soaked through.

It was getting worse and worse; ships were dragging their anchors and bearing down on us. The *Admiral Hardy* was dragging badly and the Captain called all hands to fix fenders to prevent her bashing our bows. It was certain now that she was going to bump us and her stern fouled our anchor chains, but the anchors held.

The Captain gave me the order to shut the watertight door in the engine room. Just in time, for there was a fearful crash and *Admiral Hardy*'s stern hit our bows and dented in three plates.

A ferry boat was rolling terribly and seemed quite helpless. All the ships at anchor seemed to be mixed up together, and the junks had all scudded for the typhoon shelter quite early. The ferry boat was banging about so much I thought she would turn turtle. She was trying to get up against another ship for shelter, but she didn't manage it and drifted away in the tearing waves and spray.

The wind suddenly dropped to a fresh breeze and the eye of the typhoon passed. The Captain pointed it out to me like a round hole in the sky with a light behind. The typhoon returned very briefly and violently from the other direction and then went. I was soaked through, bruised all over, very black, splashed all over with oil and very tired.

So ended Typhoon Alice and my second voyage on the *Shun Fung*.

Chapter Twenty One
Santa Granda, My Last Ship

I was to have one more voyage on the *Shun Fung* before I decided to leave. I had become increasingly unhappy, even though I was very fond of Captain Mahon and all my Chinese crew, I found the Mate quite impossible to work with. It wasn't only the question of leaving the ladder too high against the ship, of never putting on a gangway to accommodate anyone getting on or off, of overloading the cargo and being permanently rude and disagreeable, it was a combination off all these things. At any rate I had decided to go, so at the end of my third voyage I was busy throwing away and tearing up any non-essentials and making a complete clean set of my abstract copies.

We arrived back in Hong Kong on 1st November 1961 and were to pay off the next day. However, almost at once Mr Yann of the Shipping Managers Limited came aboard and asked me to join the *Santa Granda* of Hong Kong as Chief Engineer. She was coming from Japan and would be sailing again the day after she arrived. I said I would let him know if he returned in a little time, and I talked to the Second Engineer who was leaving with me; he very faithfully said he would go anywhere I went.

Mr Yann returned, and said, "You will get more money than you get here, about £50 a week." He asked me if I would sign on for six months. The ship was only coming to change the Chief and some of the crew.

I said, "The Second Engineer is leaving with me and I would like him to join the *Santa Granda.*"

He said, "We want to change the Second Engineer too, and you can have the Second, both you and the Second if you will only come."

I said I would, then Mr Chay of Q Lee came and said that the company would put me up at the Winner Hotel in North Point, Hong Kong, until I joined the ship the following week.

So that was all fixed. I was sorry I had to leave my garden behind but I gave my stones to the Second Mate and my plants to the Captain and the Quartermaster.

Then it was time to sign off. I was very sorry to leave the *Shun Fung*, the happiest ship till that awful Mate came. I said goodbye to the Captain who was very sad. My boy came ashore with me in the wallah wallah and wanted to leave the ship and come with me.

We sailed further and further from the ship, my friends still waving from the rail, over the blue water of Hong Kong Harbour till the *Shun Fung* was lost to view in the mass of ships at anchor. And I knew that I have left the best ship that I have ever had.

As I left Stonecutters from the Shun Fung my boy Tsu came to the door of the Marine Office.

"Take me with you, Chief, take me with you!" He was in tears.

I said, "Goodbye, Tsu, see you again. I hope to sail with you again some day."

He said, "Never another Chief the same, Chief very, very good," and he went off sadly waving and crying.

On Friday 10th November I collected all my baggage and after lunch went down to the Black Pier to begin another chapter in my life, leaving behind the flags and brightness of Hong Kong. I could hardly believe my eyes when I saw the *Santa Granda*, a 10,000 ton Liberty ship looking her age and red with rust from stem to stern without a scrap of paint on her. She looked dirty and rotten, which she proved to be. Even the two men from Mr Lee carrying my luggage looked at her in horror. "Is that the ship?!" they cried.

But there was no mistake. There she was with *Santa Granda* painted in large white letters on her bows and stern. She was hard to board and I could hardly get up the gangway as there were so many boats cluttered round her. I was met by an engineer off the *Shun Fung* who left a trip ago. He was pleased to see me and took me to the saloon where all was confusion as many of the new crew were signing on.

"When is she due for survey?" I asked Mr Yann.

"March," he replied.

"Will I be kept on for the survey or paid off?"

"Oh yes, yes," he said, "you will take her through the survey."

So on I signed.

Later I looked over the side and saw they were trying to pull my gear up by a cord as they could not get up the gangway for all the boats. I was afraid they would pull the rather weak handles off my bags, however, so I stopped that, cleared away the other boats and made them carry my gear up properly.

I was up by 6.30 am the next day getting things ready for the voyage—kerosene 16 imperial gallons, engine oil 736, DTE 184, diesel for galley 4.33 tons. The Second and I checked everything. It was a bright clear morning as we left Hong Kong, full away for sea passage to Pasuo, Hainan

Island, South China. The green hills around Hong Kong slipped away and we were soon lifting to a slight sea coloured by bunches of yellow seaweed which floated past.

The ship was very dirty and stuffy, as the crew seemed terrified of fresh air. At the Captain's service, the ports were always shut and the fans off; I preferred lots of fresh air, like on the *Shun Fung*. Although I only had to stick six months of this.

We arrived at No 1 Buoy Hainan Straits on Sunday 12th November and remained at anchor till the following morning, when we entered the Straits and proceeded to Pasuo.

Pasuo looked attractive from the sea, but I could not see the village, only blue grey hills rising behind a flat plain. The port had a breakwater on the south side for the fishing junks, and to the west there was one long wharf with a conveyor belt running from two elevators used for loading. Three ships could come alongside at once and one on the coal berth. Behind the elevators were heaps of ore divided into large pieces. A small railway ran behind these heaps and brought the ore from the mountains. On the south side of the small harbour there was a lighthouse and signal station and to the north a lovely white sand beach which ran right along the coast line, protected by an outer coral reef. It was bordered by low sand hills covered with thorny aloes and spiky prickly pears.

When we got alongside there were some small jobs to do, so I had no time to open up anything. I shut down the starboard boiler, but kept the port boiler in use. I also had a valve cover repainted and a socket soldered. After tea I went for a walk to the beach with the warm coral water breaking on the shore in tiny waves. The beach was strewn with white coral and many kinds of smallish shells. Feeling tired, I returned to the ship when it got dark.

Next morning I asked the Chief of the ship alongside about the boiler water treatment as ours was all at sixes and sevens and much of the equipment was missing. He came over in the afternoon and gave me advice and some litmus paper, but he was as shocked as I was at the condition of the engines. That was my last afternoon on the beach because the order for steam was at midnight, although the sailing time was put off and we had a long inspection and so didn't finally get away till 5.30 am after we had discharged the pilot and guard.

We were going to Tsingtao, we thought, and the weather was fine and clear until on the 21st November, when the order was changed to Shanghai. There was a moderate swell with drizzle and an overcast sky. The sea continued getting rougher and the boat rolled in the heavy swell. It began to abate on Saturday 25th November when we took the pilot and guard on board for Shanghai.

We had three days in Shanghai, unloading iron ore, and I felt pretty ill all the time. Both my hands were swollen with blood poisoning, my face and neck were breaking out in purplish spots, and a red line ran from my finger up my arm. No one on board seemed to have any clear idea of what to do, the medicines seemed stale and I heard that one man had died on the last trip. So I washed in Dettol, which luckily I had, restrained myself from scratching, used sulphur soap, put on face cream and drank lots of Enos. I went ashore on Sunday, which was fortunately a day of light duty after the late arrival, and did some shopping in the Seaman's Club and the Friendship Store, but this was curtailed by the ship being listed as a coastal trader and not a foreign going ship, so there was no longer a 60% reduction. My shopping was also curtailed by the Mate, who found me and tagged round with me. Although I did not like him, I determined not to fight with him and bore his presence as best I could, deciding to elude him next time I could get ashore.

On Monday when we inspected the starboard boiler we found a furnace row tube was leaking. It had been stoppered previously, but this leak would bring the brickwork down, so the boiler was blown down and the leaking tube stoppered and re-hardened up. After lunch I had to look at the fires being set away, but found all satisfactory. Next day, although my face and hands were still very painful, I did not feel cold, sick and shivery any more, so I hoped that the poison had stopped.

We slowly took 450 long tons of cold, thick oil from a barge. It took all day and we received 150 tons from the first barge, and 300 from the second. I even managed to dash ashore afterwards but it was a great rush to be back on board by 7.45 pm when in the event we did not have inspection till after 10 pm and then the long stand-by down the cold dark river to the sea, full away to Pasuo.

The journey from Shanghai to Pasuo took a week, and the fine weather soon changed, becoming overcast with drizzling rain and swell, and later on rough seas. We remained at anchor off Pasuo for just over a day until we moved in alongside. It was still blowing hard and white seas were breaking high on the coral reef, and the wind whirled the iron ore dust high into dark red clouds. Luckily I had got a screen door made for my room, which I could shut at night at sea, as it was too hot to shut the heavy door. Besides, with the heavy door shut, I could not hear the engines.

We had one full day at Pasuo loading iron ore and I had a lot of work on the engines before we set off on the 1,183 miles to Shanghai.

We had sea and swell and bright sunshine, so that I put my cactus plants out on deck for a little as the blue misty island of Hainan faded into the horizon. We had 559 long tons on board and there were four joints to renew on the deck steam line. After I had written the log and looked round the engine room to see all was right for the night, I turned in. It was after midnight and there was a strong wind holding us back and a night full of stars.

On the 9th the strong head wind was holding us back and we had only done 136 miles at 7.75 knots. Next day was not much better, 137 miles at 9.86 knots and a very high slip of 42%. It was no fun battling against the north east monsoon. There was water in No 1 hold bilge, which we pumped out port and starboard for about an hour and a half. I wondered where it had come from, perhaps it was the way the ship was lying. On Monday 11th December the wind was just as strong and we were heading right into it, the sea and swell remaining the same. We did 169 miles at 7.04 knots and had a slip of 49%. We pumped out the No 1 hold bilge for about an hour and three quarters, and I wondered again where the water was coming from. It seemed to be rising. By Tuesday things were looking up, it was fine and clear, the swell had abated and the head wind had dropped completely. What a difference the sunshine makes. She had steadied right up and I put my cactus cuttings out for an hour or two in the sunshine. We did 180 miles at 7.50 knots, but the slip was 26.2%. We now had to pump the No 1 hold bilge port and starboard continuously, but were holding the water. We had 645 miles to go to Shanghai. It seemed strange it should suddenly be so calm and sunny. It made me nervous, but perhaps we had run out of bad weather.

On 13th December we were pumping continuously, but still holding the water. It was cloudy and clear, but the head wind had returned with a moderate sea and swell. About 2 am the Captain asked me if I would come and have a look in No 1 hold. I slipped on my old boiler suit and shoes in a split second, took my torch and followed him down into the hold. We nipped down the ladder to the tween deck, climbed onto the deck and then slipped over the edge and slid down the mountain of iron ore to the bottom of the hold and scrambled to the starboard side, the mate following us. And there, in my first glance, I saw about ten frames adrift. The plate near the bulkhead was split a few inches on each side of the frame and the frames at that place were corroded right through at the bottom and broken completely across. The welding on the plates was holding but with the motion of the ship, the ship's plating was moving backwards and forwards with the unattached frames. I put my hand up and felt below the higher welded plate where the leverage was greater and the plate was warm. It was working backwards and forwards just below the weld, where the metal might crack right across any time. With the very heavy seas the whole plate would give way and with the inrush of water, No 1 bulkhead, which didn't look too good, would probably go as well. With the cargo of iron ore she would go down very quickly, maybe in only a few minutes, as once the plate went the rest would tear up with no fixed frames to support it.

I went scrambling over the ore and looked at the other frames and discovered that ten frames were gone at the bottom and the plates were working backwards and forwards, the welding on the top part of the frames holding to the plates. I had a look at the bulkhead and it didn't look at all good to me, very thin, and likely to buckle with any pressure.

"What do you think?" asked the Captain.

I said, "Make for the nearest port. Keep a double watch down here night and day, one at the top, one at the bottom, so that any change can be reported to you. Also try and shore up the frames alongside the crack so that they do not work the plate. I will try keeping the water down with the main engine pump as it is the best, but if there should be an inrush, no pump could hold it. We must remember we only see a few bad frames, but if they are all the same age, they may all be in a similar condition."

I gave one more look, felt the plate again, then scrambled up the great mountain of iron ore, a great lot of sand ore which would absorb water very quick. "This is like climbing up Glen Coe!" I said.

I thought the Mate was hopeless, he had no idea of the danger. The main thing was to keep the bilges down and keep the line clear and the pump pumping! The GS and ballast pumps were all patched, and there was a big hole in the ballast pump pipe with a clamp on it. How glad I was to have that good cement box put on in Pasuo on the main engine line. I hoped there were no more holes as the pipes were all rotten.

On 14th December we were still pumping out the No 1 hold bilges continuously, but there was a gale force head wind, rough sea and heavy swell. We had struggled on all through the afternoon and last night. She was by this time "rolling the milk out of the tea" and pitching heavily. Pale morning light showed a bleak storm tossed water world, dark white crested waves crashing on the ship with a thundering roar, the backlash of water hissing through the scuppers. Each time a heavy sea struck, the ship shuddered from stem to stern. I could hardly see for flying spray, and the moaning wind sounded like a thousand chained demons. As the morning dragged on the weather worsened. At noon we had only gone 96 miles with an average speed of 4 knots and a slip of 55.5%, our consumption being 27 tons and 359 miles to Shanghai. There was no sign of it letting up. At 4 pm, the Captain decided to change course and go about, making for Whampoa in South China, about 539 miles but with the wind behind us and a following sea. He put her about very quick and everything seemed to slide at once, then she seemed to right herself and we had the wind behind us. If the weather had changed to good we could have made Shanghai, but as it was the Captain did the only thing possible. And just in time, for before we went about the No 1 bulkhead had begun to buckle.

She was racing badly and we had no governor on the engine, which meant standing by the throttle all the time. But we had a following sea and we doubled our speed within minutes to 8 knots. We were keeping the incoming water down in the hold by continuous pumping and we were holding the level. But it was a near thing and we were jolly lucky to have come through so far.

However, so far, so good. It remained rough with a gale force northeast wind, but it was a following sea and we were making south for Whampoa. On the 14th we did 192 miles at 8 knots with only 20% slip and only 347 miles to go. By the 16th we had increased speed to 8.92 knots and had done another 214 miles since noon the day before.

On 17th December we sighted land and were arriving at Lafsami Pilot station at the mouth of the Pearl River. I was never more glad in my life to see a little twinkling point of light. Stand-by went at 4.15 am and we were at anchor awaiting the tide. It was so wonderful to have the pilot on board and be within sight of land with the sweet scent of wild flowers in the gentle breeze. We left anchorage and proceeded up river through flat green delta, fruit orchards and blue hills, till we finally arrived at Whampoa at 10.59 pm and tied up at berth alongside. I was never more glad in my life to have arrived at any port, so thankful, so very very thankful.

We were five days in port, discharging iron ore and doing what jobs on the engine could be done. I opened up the main condenser and air pump, brushed and cleaned the condenser tubes and inspected the king horn valves in the air pump. The port boiler was blown and the tubes and brickwork examined, and as we discharged cargo, we put in ballast. Various surveyors came on board to see the ship.

The Captain seemed pleased with me and said I did well.

The Mate said, "Oh, if the plate had gone I would have rigged a collision mat."

The Captain said, "You would have had time to do nothing, she would have gone very quick," and he said to me, "What do you think?"

I replied, "In a matter of minutes in that sea the whole side of No 1 would have gone."

The Captain said, "There wouldn't have been time to get a boat away."

The Mate replied, "But I would have rigged a collision mat, rolled up a tarpaulin."

"With the side of the ship gone?!" exclaimed the Captain.

On the 21st we had to shift ship. Various surveyors had been coming down to ask about the weather damage, and at one moment it looked as if they were not going to permit us to sail unless the repairs were done in Whampoa. However, they agreed to allow the ship to sail to Hong Kong, and gave permission for us to go the short way through the island passage which only takes 22 hours instead of 26. This showed how dangerous they considered the state of the ship!

We were due to sail at midnight, but we had a lot of trouble with the oil fuel solidifying in the pipes from the tank to the settling tank and could not get the settling tank pumped up. However, at last we got the discharge warmed up by bricking a joint and also by introducing a steam jet through a drain cock till the oil was fluid enough to pump.

After a final evening in the Seaman's Club we were all on board. Cargo finished at midnight, and after inspection stand-by went at 1.15 am for the long journey down the river, under a pale sky of faint stars. It was lovely going round the short way and arriving finished with engines on 23rd December after being up all night.

We spent Christmas Eve in Hong Kong and all was rush and bustle aboard the *Santa Granda*. The Supers had a quick look round everything on arrival and I had my lists all typed and ready, four copies for the engine room stores and four copies for repair work. It was a case of "No, no, next time, next time!" But I stuck out for the things that had to be done, they were jolly lucky to have the ship to repair at all as she very nearly sank!

I was busy pumping out the fore deck ballast, transferring fuel oil and draining the fresh water tanks. I also blew down the starboard boiler for cleaning.

Ashore everywhere was decorated with lights and Christmas trees. Shoppers crowded the streets, everyone carrying parcels and wishing each other Merry Christmas. There were carols over the radios and crowds of happy, bustling people packed the brightly lit shops.

It was still dark on Christmas Day when the watchman called me and I got aboard the wallah wallah, but day was dawning by the time we reached the Black Pier, with everyone still wishing each other Merry Christmas. I walked up to St John's Cathedral, decorated with dark green shrubs with holly-like berries. As the sun shone through the east window we sang *Hark the Herald Angels Sing* and *O Come All Ye Faithful*.

All that week we were busy on the engines and boilers, renewing the fireside tiles and working on the mountings. We also worked on the MP and LP impulse valves. On the 28th the Lloyds' Surveyor, Mr Manson, surveyed the starboard boiler. On the 29th we shifted ship from Yaumata to dry dock on Kowloon side. We were moved by tugs at 11.30 pm to the Cosmo dry dock where all the underwater fittings were to be replaced or repaired and the tail shaft drawn in. It was a small dock and could only just take a 10,000 ton ship.

As we stood checking the couplings at the end of the tunnel, Mr Manson asked me, "What is that ship's side valve for?"

I replied, "Oh, that is the anticipating valve for the governor, which we don't have."

The Super gave me such a look and said no more. There should always be a governor on a main engine, but this American type had been cut out and not replaced.

That night I did not get to bed till 2.30 am as they were working on the propeller and tail end shaft. The propeller was fitted but not hardened up to the old mark, so that meant drilling a new hole for the locking pin, coupling up the shafting, and packing the stern gland with turns of 1 $^1/_4$ inch lighthouse packing. I had to climb up the staging to see all was well, as some of this dry dock work wasn't too clever. So although I slipped ashore most days we were in dry dock I turned in early on New Year's Eve, but heard Jardine's gun booming out for 1962.

New Year's Day 1962 was bright and clear, everyone wishing each other a happy New Year. For me it was business as usual, however, and all the sea water connections between the ship's side valve, the circulating pump and the condenser were opened up and cleaned of shell. I found quite a large fish (dead, of course), 10 inches long, in the condenser. Later the saloon was decorated and we had another splendid dinner on board.

While we were in Hong Kong I heard very worrying news about Frances, who had to have an operation, but before we left I heard that she was better. So I got a boat at dawn on Sunday 7th, even though the gangway was now perpendicular, got to the Black Pier and went to the Cathedral to give thanks for her recovery. It was such a long way from Yaumata, almost as bad as Stonecutters, so I felt it in the nature of a penance. In the evening we all went ashore for the owners' dinner in the Metropole Hotel.

Before we sailed on 9th January Mr Manson came and floated the two safety valves on starboard boiler, steam and superheat. He brought an Australian Naval commander with him and another friend of his, asking me to give them tea while he surveyed No 2 tank. All the valves were more or less leaking on this ship and we could not get the heating coils blanked off properly because the boiler valve was leaking so badly and we could not shut it. So the tank was hot when he went in and he had a small burn on his wrist. I told the Captain it was too hot to survey and I couldn't get the coils blanked off because the boiler stop was leaking. As I was having tea with the Commander, Mr Manson came in spitting mad and just flew at me. The Commander was really horrified! Then Mr Manson flew up to the Captain's room, sweeping the Commander with him, and then I had to go up to see the Captain to have the surveyor's report. By then luckily Mr Manson had calmed down and came over and patted me on the back and apologised. Later he came down and said how sorry he was before he kissed my hand!

On 9th January we sailed for the bunkering berth at the Shell installation. We were alongside the oil wharf and I walked up to the oil tank and then climbed about 50 feet to the top of the tanks. They nearly twisted me out of 30 tons taking the dip, but I just caught it in time. I had to be very sharp. They apologised and said it was a slip on their part. No sooner had I got down to the ship than they cut the line again having only put in 34.63 tons! So I had to climb up to the top again for the third time. We then moved out to anchor and finished bunkering from a barge.

We sailed away on our passage to Pasuo that evening. The evening was warm and clear as the green hills round Hong Kong melted into the distance.

We remained at anchor in Pasuo for a week waiting to go alongside to load iron ore for the north. By 18th January we moved in alongside, but by the time inspection and tea were over it was too dark to go ashore. The next day it began to blow and there was no chance of going ashore, and for the next two or three days there were typhoon warnings, which was unusual for January. There were whirls of dust and sand everywhere, but the typhoon never materialised and by Sunday there was bright sunshine and it had all passed over. I went ashore to the white sandy beach with coral and shells which I picked up, and in the afternoon I strolled into the village where there had been a delivery of dried salt fish, a great excitement for the villagers as it was scooped from the dust into the shops for sale, and for the flies, too. The smell everywhere was very strong. Fish, fish, and more fish, and the country people piled it into their little wooden carts. Then there were the pigs, scrubbling and grubbing about in the dust, old pigs and pigs feeding young pigs dragging their stomachs along the ground, grey, black, pink and all colours.

I did some shopping and fixed up a car to take Captain Parr and his wife and little boy for a run, which we did on 2nd February. The air was thick and choking with discharging red iron ore dust, so it was nice to get out of it. We drove all through the town, and saw people pulling huge strings of heavily loaded hand carts and to the German style suburbs with red roofed houses, and a little bit into the country where seaweed was laid out to dry.

What a terrible rush it was leaving the next morning! We were to have left late on Saturday evening or early on Sunday morning but instead I was woken before dawn with orders that we were sailing, and steam had to be up for 9 am or sooner if possible! Of course I had the starboard boiler under steam for all purposes, and the port boiler kept handy at 100 lbs, so it was merely a matter to give the order to the Second to bring up the port boiler. I reckoned we needed an hour for inspection, and then 22 hours for warming through and taking them out. However, the Mate came flying along to say there was no ballast in her! Of course there wasn't, as I had had no order to pump ballast. The last of the cargo was out and there was no ballast in her at all.

I told the Mate, "I can't pump ballast without a written order from you or the Captain, and I have had no order at all."

Of course she was just like a cockle shell with all the cargo out, no ballast and only 318 tons of bunkers in her, so the Mate was mad. I said, "The Captain must know there's no ballast because of handling her." This made him madder!

However, I said I would start on the ballast as soon as possible, but must have enough steam for manoeuvring out of port. After inspection, the telegraph and steering test, we were full away and I managed to start pumping ballast. The Mate said he would have me up to the Captain, which he did. He tried to make it like a naval court martial. The steward came down and said the Captain wished to see me, so I got tidy and went up to his room. There was the Mate sitting all dressed up.

I said, "You wished to see me, sir?"

He said, "The Mate has reported to me that you wouldn't put in any ballast."

I said, "The Mate knows the reason why there was no ballast pumped. I never put ballast in or out without a written order signed by you or the Mate at sea or by the deck officer on duty in port. And I have never had a mistake in ballast. Ballast for 9 am was written on the Mate's chit and ballast takes about 8 hours to pump when light ship. It is usual to always run up ballast while cargo is discharged."

The Captain said, "We got out all right, Chief. You had a big rush to get her ready. Sorry about changing sailing time, but as you know it was the agents!"

We sailed up the river to Shanghai for bunkering, where we tied up at Buoy 32 and bunkered from a tanker. Fortunately, engineers were not allowed to go on board the bunkering tanker to take the dip, which is always such a scramble in the dark and cold. The oil was rather like warm axle grease and I wondered what it would look like when cold.

We left Buoy 32 on 5th February and were river steaming down the Yangtse. The guards all waved and saluted me as they boarded the pilot cutter, and as she dropped away astern they were still waving. I was always glad to get down the river with its heavy traffic of large and small water craft without a bump.

It was 6 pm when I went down to get my tea, having been on the go for 23 hours since we took the pilot on board. There were also clusters of junks ahead and a ferry, so after my watch and a last look round for the night at 2.30 am it was 30 hours non stop.

We had a good run to Pasuo with a slight wind and sea round the south of Hainan Island. We were there at anchor for two days, during which time I managed to do quite a lot of work and gave the port boiler a long blow and examined tubes and brickwork. It was very hard to fit work in at anchor off the China coast as they could suddenly tell us to move in, so every job had to be done quickly. On Tuesday 13th February we moved in alongside. The next morning it began to blow, and there was only a narrow 11-12 inch gangplank to cross the 15 feet gap between the ship's side and the quay. I told the Captain the men couldn't get ashore as the plank was very bad, so he made the Mate put up a proper gangway made with a rail. I think the men were doing this to get a good gangway for me, as there was a very heavy swell. They said "Chief go in, not come out, go under ship," and Number One said "Gangway very bad for men!" Of course the crew could climb and jump anywhere!

Just after midnight on February 17th we were away again bound for Shanghai and then Dairen. I had decided that after our return to Hong Kong I would leave the ship as she was very old and rotten.

We had a calm clear voyage for the first three days with moderate swell, but then there was a gale force wind and rough sea on 20th February, although not the typhoon season. On the 22nd there was occasional fog and I had to stop for 20 minutes as the Second came up to tell me there was a noise in MP. I came down and listened and decided either there was a slack nut or the washer was slack on the collar, so I told the Second to get the gear ready and turn out the men as we must stop. When I opened the cover, I found the slack washer and fixed it.

On the 23rd and we had to stop and anchor in thick fog from 5.45 am to 9.25 am. It was very cold and chilly and we were enclosed by a silent wall of fog, though we could hear the movement of unseen craft on the river and every so many minutes the banging of a tin plate on the fo'castle head to announce our existence. At 9.25 am the fog lifted with a bump and we could see quite a distance around. It had been a long cold stand-by and on the hop all the time, watching out for traffic on the river and popping down to the engine room. However, at long last we sighted the line of buildings of the famous Shanghai water front. I was delighted to be nearly there and see the Union Jack fluttering on the British Embassy flag staff, always a reassuring and refreshing sight. I really thought that the water front of Shanghai is one of the finest sights of the world.

During the five days in Shanghai, there was much to do on the engine. I checked the main engine bolts, cleaned the choked gauge glasses, and blew down the starboard boiler. I was also able to get ashore quite frequently, finish off all the shopping I had left undone, and do some more.

One day I went sightseeing with the Captain and the Third Mate. We went to an old house and lovely garden called Yeun Yen, opened for the first time that day. After walking through narrow streets and an irresistible market, we went through an old door into a wonderful garden with twisting paths, stone carvings and little humped bridges. The old house spread throughout the garden in Chinese style, ponds, canals and small waterfalls intersecting the greenery. There were deep red and blush camellias in full flower, orange marigolds, small dark purple iris and yellow jasmine as well as creamy apricot blossom buds.

On 27th February I got ready to bunker 450 long tons of very thick and heavy oil, like tunnel grease; I worked out that it was much better not to heat it too much. Luckily, we were bunkering from a barge, which saved me climbing aboard and the many goodbyes, they knew this was my last visit to Shanghai, in the way Chinese do.

We had stand-by at 11.47 am and so started gliding down the swift-flowing tea coloured river to the sea. Even at the night there was heavy traffic. At dawn we dropped the pilot and were full away to Pasuo. The weather was cloudy and clear with a following wind; we sailed down into the warmth and arrived at the anchorage off Pasuo at 12.30 pm on Monday 5th March.

We were due to sail again the next day but we did not sail till after midnight, bound for Dairen, 1,764 miles round Yu Lin Kiang.

The voyage was cloudy and clear with occasional rain and a moderate sea. All went well and I was able to make out my store lists for Hong Kong and keep my abstracts up to date. On Tuesday 13th March we arrived off Dairen in powdering snow showers and anchored off the port. There was just time to get breakfast before we moved in alongside. We were in a good berth, near the town, and after breakfast I shut down the starboard boiler and opened up the MP slide dome for examination. I found the new bush fitted in Pasuo in good condition. I also removed the forward telemotor guard and gear rack and examined the gearing, which was found to be worn out. And so it went on, when one thing was repaired something else went! I thought of nothing but how to patch up safely while running the engine room and writing lengthy abstracts from port to port! However, everyone was happy and I had a good hardworking crew.

We were in Dairen for over a week, so I had plenty time to go ashore, the gate was so near the ship and the new club store within walking distance. It was bitterly cold with light snow and I wore my black quilted jacket which was warm and lined, a thick scarf, cap and gloves.

On 14th March there was order to move ship from berth to berth, and I was hanging about all day waiting but we didn't have stand-by till 10.30pm and it was after midnight when I was able to turn in. The 10,000 tons of iron ore they were unloading were whirling round in red dust clouds in the icy air.

On 15th March I was due to go to the circus in the evening and was supposed to meet the Mate at the gate, but although I waited until I was nearly frozen, he never turned up, so they put me in a bus with a Greek crew, one of whom I had sailed with before. I had an awful idea that the circus might be in a tent like in the summer, but thank goodness it was in a comfortable theatre and I sat in the centre next to a Greek Captain from Kos who knew Captain Peters. The Mate came in halfway through rather the worse for wear and tried to push his way through to the middle of the row where I was sitting, but they kept him out. Later I shared a taxi with him, as I thought I should get back. He asked, "Who was that you picked up?"

I replied, "I am in the Merchant Navy and I don't pick up people. They were mutual friends of mine." This Mate was a great trial!

The next day a Chinese surveyor came about a winch which had been reported to him as not in good condition. Who had reported it I did not know, but I had my suspicions. It was so cold on deck and he gave the Second and me a lot of trouble. All the winches are old and worn and I had two fitters working on them nearly all the time at sea, and I had them watched in port when cargo was being worked. We intended to carry out the repairs in Hong Kong where we were going in a few days time, if the parts were obtainable, but the winch was safe for working cargo. So he was quite satisfied and we parted friends, but I thought it was a mean trick to stir up trouble for me, as it might have held up the cargo.

We finished unloading the cargo on 17th March, which was the end of Voyage 82, and then we re-loaded and Voyage 83 commenced. There was of course also continuous work and maintenance on the engines and organising the fuel. Loading was completed at 4 am and stand-by finally went at 8.35 am. Three miles out we dropped the pilot and guard and were full away to Hong Kong on the last lap, 1,236 miles to go.

On 25th March the Captain asked me up for a cola after Sunday inspection. I said I didn't see how we could get through a Lloyds' inspection as the ship was so rotten and carrying ore had strained her badly. It had been a difficult trip as far as the deck were concerned as the Captain had broken a bone in his foot falling down a hold looking at the cargo, which was the Mate's job. They sent for me when it happened; it was so swollen that I thought a bone must be broken. The Mate had done nothing but drink spirits and stick in stamps after the Captain was confined to his room.

The next day the Captain came down for a talk in my day room. He said we ought to reduce speed a bit so as to get in at a reasonable time, so I slipped down to the engine room and told the Second. When I came up the Captain told me he really couldn't keep the Mate, he would have to go.

I said, "You would really be better with a more experienced man, or a younger man who could get down the holds. A Captain shouldn't go down the holds when there's something wrong!"

He said, "Do you remember I had to get you to see the damage in No 1 hold as the Mate hadn't a clue what to do?"

"But he said he would make a collision mat!"

"With nothing to make it of and no time,", the Captain laughed.

I replied, "Well, I wouldn't say anything till we get in, as it may sort itself."

After the Captain left I had a long talk to the Second who wanted to leave with me. I advised him to stay on, but he wouldn't. The men wanted to leave, too, but I said they mustn't as everything was getting slack in shipping. We still didn't know what they were going to do about repairs.

On 27th March we arrived in Hong Kong, and after anchoring off Quarantine Station tied up to buoy No 13. Although all the owners came on board I could not find out what repairs were to be done, or how long we would stay in port, or when the survey would start. I handed in my typed work list and the store list for the owners and kept a copy of each for the new Chief. I told the Second to let all the men who lived in Hong Kong go ashore and keep the ones who lived further away on duty so they could go later. It was lovely coming into Hong Kong that morning with violet shadows chasing across the green hills in the sunshine.

Just as I was finishing up my writing, the Captain came in and said they were not having Lloyds and had changed their insurance to a French company, so they got out of the survey that way and avoided doing the repairs to make her safe and seaworthy. He also asked if I remembered the Mate saying anything about naval ships when we left Hong Kong last time.

"No...well, I do remember the Mate casually saying at lunch after we left Hong Kong that there were a lot of naval ships about that morning."

The Captain said, "That's what I remember, and I have told them that at the Marine Office who sent for me about this. It seems that some destroyers were leaving Hong Kong in formation when the Mate cut between them. They signalled and the mate answered, "*Santa Granda, Santa Granda,*" and so on, merely repeating the ship's name, as he can't read or send Morse. They had the whole report sent from the Navy and want to know if he has a captain's certificate. Apparently his certificate is not valid."

"Well, things *have* sorted themselves!" I said.

The Captain laughed. "Yes, now he goes on this!"

The next day the Second and I had a talk. He said, "They are not to do repairs, only very very little and no Lloyds. I may get money but if I am dead it is no use to me. I will leave with you."

I said, "But things are rather slack in shipping here. Perhaps another trip..."

"No, I will leave with you. No Chief, no ship," he replied.

On 30th March I told the Captain I would be paying off the next day. He seemed upset about my going. I said, "When I signed on they promised me that I would have six months to take her through the survey, so by rights I should have been on pay to the beginning of May."

I was very sorry to leave the Captain, but not to leave the ship, particularly as there was to be no survey, because I felt she was neither safe nor seaworthy. After this talk I dashed ashore to arrange for a boat to pick me up at 11.30 am the next morning and Mr Lee said he would send a man to come and collect my things. I also asked him to find a room for me in Hong Kong and bought several large canvas bags for packing my boiler suits and some odds and ends.

It took me all night to pack all my gear and to finish my abstracts and put in the last figures. My fuel and oil accounts and usable stores were all correct to a figure. By the time morning tea came in, my bags were packed and sitting ready in the day room and my figures were finished, neat and tidy on my desk. After breakfast I took them up to the Captain, and he said "I would like you to stay on just for a few days." But I was all packed and ready and thought it better to go.

The crew gave me a silver junk in a glass case and the carpenter made a strong box for it and packed it up firmly with engine room waste. The Third engineer, the crew and my boy saw me off to my boat and, with the Captain and his wife waving from the deck, I sailed away in the wallah wallah into the unknown, or at least to Hong Kong, which I knew quite well.

I stayed in Hong Kong until 11th April and then travelled to Britain by way of Japan, staying with my dear friends Alice and Dorothy Britton at Hayama before returning to Jean and Frances and the cats who were all waiting for me at Tresco. This had been my last voyage and the *Santa Granda* my last ship, but I did not know that then.

Epilogue

For the last 20 years of her life, Aunt Victoria spent her time at Tresco. The highlights of her life were when she went to the Institute of Marine Engineers for their annual meetings and once, unforgettably, for a whole conference. Even today there are people who remember the old lady who listened avidly to all the engineering lectures and took notes in an old exercise book. They did not know who she was and she did not know that one day there would be a room in that selfsame Institute named in her honour: the Victoria Drummond Room.

As she neared 90, her feet and legs gave so much trouble that she had great difficulty walking. Jean and Frances looked after her, running up and down the stairs as she demanded something from another part of the house.

My mother remembered sitting in the long room at Tresco, writing letters in the morning, and hearing the slow descent of Aunt Victoria from her top floor bedroom, sitting down and bumping with great difficulty step by step. Outside the door there would be a pause while she rose stiffly to her feet, grabbed her stick, pulled on her beret and slowly and breathlessly entered the room.

"Hullo, Violet," she would say breezily, "just got back from the docks—had to do a job there at 4 am this morning." As she painfully collapsed into her chair, my mother always pretended to believe her.

Most of the time, Aunt Victoria sat at her table looking out of her bedroom window framed by the changing lights of the lime tree in the garden: green with leaves in the spring; hung with scented blossom and buzzing bees in midsummer; golden in the autumn and in winter, bare against the frosty sky. So was Aunt Victoria herself surrounded with the bright reminders of her life and here it was that she wrote her life story.

In 1974 she fell out of bed, breaking her leg. Her sisters were unable to move her and she would not allow them to call a doctor. Finally, after three days they insisted and Aunt Victoria was taken to St Thomas's Hospital where her leg was put in plaster. But her mind had gone. She shouted at the nurses, at the doctors, and at her two faithful sisters, who come rain or snow and, burdened with her demands, walked from Kennington Road to the hospital twice a day. The result was that both sisters, devoted all their lives to Aunt Victoria, became ill and were admitted to the same hospital where they died within two days of each other.

Aunt Victoria survived. But the hospital could not keep her. She would not accept that her sisters were dead and kept calling and shouting for them, hitting out violently at the nurses with her stick.

After some difficulty, she was transferred to St George's Retreat in Kent, a large comfortable house set in beautiful grounds and run by nuns. Here she spent her last six years, gradually becoming more and more frail, more and more silent. Mrs Birdseye, the marvellous lady who had cleaned and kept house for the Aunts, visited her regularly every week. The rest of the family visited when they could. By now there were twelve great nieces and great nephews, but for them there were no stories of the seas, of bombs and shipwrecks, or even of the long ago home life in Scotland. Aunt Victoria sat silent, toothless, munching with pleasure at some soft-centred chocolate.

But yet there were gleams of light in the darkness. One of her own embroidered pictures of ships hung on the wall and occasionally her eyes would lift towards it as if wondering what cabin of what far ship she were now sailing in. Perhaps she wondered why in summer the strong scent of wallflower should drift through the open windows, and think she must be coming into harbour.

Sometimes we took down home movies and showed them to her. When she saw the oak tree outside the front door of Megginch ringed in daffodils, she suddenly said, "We always used to race up to it after church on Sunday."

The last time I saw her was a week before Christmas, 1980. We took down a fat branch of berried Megginch holly, which we stuck in a pot for a Christmas tree, hung with silver balls and glitters. Aunt Victoria looked at it, smiled and unexpectedly said, "Christmas."

Surely she was sitting there dreaming of Christmasses long past: Christmas in the South China Sea, the Christmas lights of Hong Kong, hot Christmasses so long ago in the *Anchises* under the Southern Cross stars, or even longer ago of Christmasses at Megginch, singing carols round the lighted Christmas tree in the hall, while Queen Victoria's god-daughter in her starched white dress and bronze shoes had worn the sparkling pendant given her by the great Queen. So, dreaming of Christmasses long gone, on Christmas Day 1980 Victoria Drummond was finally Finished with Engines. Or perhaps as her spirit left the land and floated out to the open sea, she was at last Full Away.

Voyages

1 *SS ANCHISES* Liverpool (25/08/22), Glasgow (26/08/22)

2 *SS ANCHISES* Glasgow (02/09/22), Las Palmas (15/09/22), Cape Town (30/09/22-01/10/22), Adelaide (19/10/22), Melbourne (21/10/22-26/10/22), Sydney (30/10/22-04/11/22), Brisbane (06/11/22-10/11/22), Sydney (12/11/22-20/11/22), Melbourne, Adelaide, Durban, Cape Town, Birkenhead (11/01/23)

3 *SS ANCHISES* Glasgow (02/02/23), Las Palmas, Cape Town (23/02/23-24/02/23), Adelaide (16/03/23), Melbourne (17/03/23), Sydney (23/03/23-01/04/23), Brisbane (03/04/23), Sydney, Hobart, Melbourne (19/04/23), Adelaide (23/04/23), Durban, Cape Town, Las Palmas, Liverpool (13/06/23)

4 *SS ANCHISES* Glasgow (30/06/23), Las Palmas (07/07/23), Cape Town (21/07/23), Adelaide (10/08/23), Melbourne, Sydney (20/08/23-25/08/23), Brisbane (27/08/23-02/09/23), Sydney (03/09/23), Melbourne (10/09/23-15/09/23), Adelaide (17/09/23), Durban, Cape Town, Las Palmas, Liverpool (10/11/23).

5 *SS ANCHISES* Glasgow (08/12/23), Las Palmas, Cape Town (28/12/23), Adelaide (17/01/24), Melbourne (21/01/24), Sydney (26/01/24), Brisbane, Sydney, Hobart, Melbourne, Adelaide, Albany, West Australia, Durban, Cape Town, Las Palmas, Liverpool (04/24)

6 *SS ANCHISES* Liverpool (10/05/24), Port Said (19/05/24), Suez, Singapore (07/06/24), Hong Kong (12/06/24), Shanghai, Taku-Bar (27/06/24), Chin-Wang-Tu, Dlaney, Tsing-Tao, Shanghai, Hong Kong, Singapore, Suez, Port Said, London (1924)

7 *TSS MULBERA* London (14/04/27), Marseille (21/04/27), Port Said (27/04/27), Suez, Port Sudan, Aden, Mombasa (13/05/27), Tanga (15/05/27), Zanzibar, Dar-es-Salaam, Beira (22/05/27), Dar-es-Salaam, Zanzibar, Mombasa, Aden (15/06/27), Port Sudan (19/06/27), Suez, Port Said, Malta, Marseille, Plymouth (06/07/27), London (08/07/27)

8 *TSS MULBERA* London (13/07/27), Middlesbrough, London (06/08/27-13/08/27), Port Said (23/08/27), Suez, Aden, Colombo (06/09/27), Madras (10/09/27), Calcutta (15/09/27-03/10/27), Madras (08/10/27), Colombo (13/10/27), Aden, Suez, Port Said, Malta, Marseille, Plymouth, London (11/11/27)

9 *TSS MULBERA* London (13/11/27), Antwerp, Middlesbrough (28/11/27), London (left 17/12/27), Malta (26/12/27), Port Said, Suez, Colombo (12/01/28), Madras (16/01/28), Calcutta (21/01/28/-07/02/28), Madras, Colombo, Aden, Suez, Port Said, Marseille, London, Dundee, Antwerp

10 *TSS MULBERA* London (21/04/28), Malta (28/04/28), Port Said (03/05/28), Suez,

Port Sudan, Aden (11/05/28), Colombo (18/05/28), Madras, Calcutta (10/06/28), Madras (14/06/28), Colombo, Aden, Suez, Port Said, Marseille, London, Hamburg, Antwerp, Middlesbrough

11 *TSS MULBERA* London (08/09/28), Malta, Port Said, Suez, Aden (25/09/28), Colombo (04/10/28), Madras (06/10/28), Calcutta (12/10/28), Madras (30/10/28), Colombo, Aden, Suez, Port Said, London (03/12/28), (left 04/12/28).

12 *SS HAR ZION* London (10/03/40-21/03/40), Gravesend, Antwerp (left 14/04/40), Gravesend (till 20/04/40), Lisbon, Gibraltar (02/05/40), Beirut (11/05/40), Haifa, Port Said, Alexandria, Marseille, Gibraltar, Casablanca, London (20/07/40).

13 *SS BONITA* Southampton (06/08/40), Fowey (left 23/08/40), BOMBING ATTACK IN ATLANTIC, Norfolk (08/09/40), Halifax, Newport (08/11/40).

14 *SS AVOCETA* Liverpool (mid February. Sailed as passenger), Lisbon (08/03/41).

15 *SS CZIKOS* Lisbon (08/03/41-22/03/41), Gibraltar, ATTACKED BY ENEMY PLANE, Moville (19/04/41-29/04/41), Ardrossan (29/04/41). Left (16/05/41)

16 *SS AUK* London (26/12/41), to south coast (28/12/41), Methil (03/01/42), Belfast (09/01/42), west coast of Scotland (left 04/03/42)

17 *SS MANCHESTER PORT* Manchester (02/04/42), Ellesmere Port (13/04/42), Eastham (20/04/42), left (21/04/42) in convoy to Quebec (06/05/42), Montreal (till 14/05/42), Three Rivers, Quebec (16/05/42-17/05/42), Halifax (20/05/42), bad convoy to Ellesmere Port (07/06/42).

18 *SS ELIZABETH LENSEN* London (22/07/42), Newcastle (28/07/42).

19 *SS DANAE II* Boston Lincs (31/08/42), North Shields (04/09/42), Methil (14/09/42), Aultbea, Northern Anchorage - sailed (16/09/42), arrived (18/09/42), sacked (22/09/42) and crew walked out.

20 *TSS PERSEUS* Liverpool (29/01/43), sailed (01/02/43), New York (19/02/43), Newport News (22/02/43-25/02/43), New York (26/02/43-09/03/43), Guantanamo Bay (16/03/43), Panama (21/03/43), Panama Canal, across Pacific, Sydney (23/04/43-10/05/43), Newcastle (10/05/43-12/05/43), Sydney (12/05/43-15/05/43), Melbourne (19/05/43-26/05/43), Fremantle (03/06/43-07/06/43), Durban (26/06/43-09/07/43), Cape Town (13/07/43-17/07/43), Freetown (03/08/43-14/08/43), Gibraltar (27/08/43-04/09/43), Liverpool (15/09/43).

21 MV *KARABAGH* Tilbury (06/04/44), Onega, Portsmouth (23/05/44).

22 MV *KARABAGH* Portsmouth (23/05/44), Isle of Wight, back and forth to Normandy (09/09/44).

23 *MV KARABAGH* Newport (16/04/45), Antwerp (06/05/45), Kiel, Grangemouth (signed off 18/06/45).

24 *MV KARABAGH* Grangemouth (18/06/45), Houston (07/45), Liverpool, Bouches du Rhone (breakdown so went to Port de Boux), Haifa, Port Said, Suez, Abadan, Liverpool (09/02/46). Laid off.

Superintending building ships in Dundee (04/46-07/46).

Relieving Cunard ships (05/09/46-14/01/47).
SS ST MARGARET
SS FORT SPOKANE
SS FORT CADOTTE
SS FORT SPOKANE
SS HILLCREST PARK
SS SIBLEY PARK
SS ROYAL EMBLEM.

25 *MV HICKORY MOUNT* Fowey (25/05/47), Philadelphia (06/47-06/09/47). Left by train to Halifax and sailed home as passenger on the AQUITANIA.

26 *MV BANCINU* Falmouth (03/01/48). Broke wrist and left (02/02/48).

27 *SS EASTERN MED* Plymouth (25/04/48), London (05/48), Famagusta. Left (02/06/48) and returned via south of France.

28 *SS ALBERTO GIANPAOLO* Malta (22/09/48-13/10/48), Sfax, Gibraltar, London (08/12/48).

29 *MV LENAMILL* London (20/02/49), Trieste (10/03/49-28/04/49). Came back by train via Venice, St Raphael and Paris.

30 *SS ELSIE BETH* London (11/08/49), Spain, Portugal, Hull (09/49-01/10/49), Onega (left end of October,1949), Alesund, Dublin (01/12/49).

31 *SS CANFORD* Cardiff (end of June, 1950), Sharpness, Leith, Cardiff (left 23/11/50).

32 *SS THEEMS* London (31/03/51), Cadiz, Gibraltar, Malta (signed off 28/04/51). Back through Italy and Ventimiglia.

33 *SS ALPHA ZAMBEZI* London (24/10/51), Montreal, Poplar (27/11/51).

Building the *SS MASTER NIKOS* at Burntisland (13/02/52-19/09/52).

34 *SS MARKAB* Avonmouth (10/10/52), Montreal (29/10/52), Bremen (11/11/52).

35 *SS MARKAB* Copenhagen (31/01/53), Aarhus (left 03/02/53), Copenhagen, Hamburg (10/02/53-12/02/53), Gibraltar (20/02/53), Port Said (01/03/53), Suez, Djibouti (08/03/53), Singapore (23/03/53), Yokohama (till 11/04/53), Dairen (17/04/53-12/05/53), Hong Kong, Singapore (18/05/53), Djibouti (04/06/53), Suez (11/06/53), Port Said, Constanta (14/06/53-05/07/53), Chios (06/06/53), Iskenderum (09/07/53-09/08/53), Mersin (left 26/08/53), Algiers (03/09/53), Baltimore (23/09/53-27/09/53), Norfolk (28/09/53-01/10/53), Trinidad (08/10/53), Montevideo (29/10/53), Buenos Aires (30/10/53-

07/11/53), Rosario (08/11/53-29/11/53), Buenos Aires (30/11/53-06/12/53), Montevideo, St Vincent de Cabo Verde (23/12/53-24/12/53), Antwerp (01/54).

36 *MV LORD CANNING* Tilbury (18/05/54), Baniyas (30/05/54-31/05/54), Finnart (13/06/54).

37 *MV BLYTHE TRADER* Hull (26/06/54), Baltimore (13/07/54-30/07/54), Antwerp (10/08/54). Signed off (26/08/55).

38 *MV DUNDALK BAY* Poplar (25/10/55), Rotterdam (paid off 04/11/55).

39 *MV RAMPART* Malta (09/01/56-11/01/56), Bassens (sailed 03/02/56), Bilbao (04/02/56-07/02/56), Poole Harbour (12/02/56-14/02/56), Rotterdam (15/02/56), Schiedam (16/02/56), London (20/02/56).

40 *MV LORD CANNING* Sheerness (05/04/56), Tripoli, Lebanon (21/04/56), Antwerp (05/05/56), Falmouth (paid off 12/05/56).

41 *SS CONCHA* Cherbourg (08/56-10/09/56), Bordeaux (14/09/56-19/09/56), Hartlepool (26/09/56-29/09/56), South Shields (sailed 03/10/56), Grimsby (06/10/56), Gent, Antwerp. Paid off.

42 *MV BRITISH MONARCH* London (04/05/57-06/05/57), New Orleans (25/05/57), Baton Rouge (26/05/57), Port Allen (28/05/57), Colon, Cristobal (04/06/57), across Pacific, Shimizu (07/07/57-14/07/57), Lautaka (29/07/57), Suva (left 08/08/57), Vancouver (28/08/57-09/09/57), New Westminster (left 13/09/57), Port Alberni (14/09/57-17/09/57), Chemainus (left 20/09/57), Vancouver (20/09/57-21/09/57), Victoria (21/09/57-26/09/57), Cowichan Bay (26/09/57-27/09/57), Port Alberni (27/09/57-04/10/57), Balboa (18/10/57), Liverpool (11/11/57). Signed off (12/11/57).

43 *MY ADVENTURESS* Southampton (01/05/58-17/05/58), Yarmouth (17/05/58-18/05/58), Gibraltar (25/05/58-28/05/58), Algeciras (28/05/58-29/05/58), Ibiza (31/05/58-04/06/58), Palma (04/06/58-11/06/58), Adrift (13/06/58), towed by Ark Royal and HMS Scarborough, Pantellaria, Malta (18/06/58-23/06/58), Melos (left 30/06/58), Chios (01/07/58), Izmir (left 06/07/58).

44 *SS GRELROSA* Cardiff (07/59-09/08/59), Garston, Liverpool, Bidston (25/08/59-16/09/59), Liverpool, Birkenhead, Augusta (20/09/59), Port Said (30/09/59), Suez, Aden (04/10/59), Pulau Bukon (23/10/59), Osaka (-5/11/59-09/11/59), Yawata (12/11/59-26/11/59), Pasuo (05/12/59), Dairen (13/12/59-21/12/59), Taku-Bar (22/12/59-04/01/60), Shanghai (07/01/60-11/01/60), Hong Kong (14/01/60). Signed off (16/01/60).

45 *SS GRELROSA/SS SHAN TAE* Hong Kong (17/01/60-18/01/60), Whampoa (left 26/01/60), Singapore (02/02/60-08/02/60), Pulau Bukom (08/02/60-09/02/60), Malacca (09/02/60), Port Swettenham (10/02/60-13/02/60), Penang (left 18/02/60), Bangkok (22/02/60-24/02/60), fire at sea, Hong Kong (03/03/60-15/03/60), Kalin Kan, Hainan Island (17/03/60-21/03/60), Tsingtao (28/03/60-01/04/60), Chinwangtow (05/04/60-10/04/60), Hong Kong (16/04/60). Paid off.

46 *SS SHUN FUNG* Kristiansand (03/09/60-07/09/60), Flushing (arrived and left 08/

09/60), Antwerp (08/09/60-18/09/60), Palermo (28/09/60-29/09/60), Port Said (03/10/60-04/10/60), Suez, Aden (arrived and left 10/10/60), Pulau Bukom (26/10/60-27/10/60), Otaru (11/11/60-23/11/60), Moji (27/11/60-28/11/60), Shanghai (30/11/60-04/12/60), Hong Kong (06/12/60).

47 *SS SHUN FUNG* Hong Kong (13/12/60), Tsamkong (14/12/60-22/12/60), Pulau Bukom (26/12/60-28/12/60), Durban (17/01/61-18/01/61), Conakry (03/02/61-24/02/61), Dakar (25/02/61-02/03/61), Casablanca (07/03/61-12/03/61), Palermo (16/03/61-18/03/61), Port Said, Suez (23/03/61), Aden (29/03/61-30/03/61), Pulau Bukom (16/04/61-17/04/61), Shanghai (28/04/61-05/05/61), Hong Kong (09/05/61-11/05/61), Swatow (12/05/61-14/05/61), Hong Kong (15/05/61).

48 *SS SHUN FUNG* Hong Kong (03/06/61), Hsinkiang (arrived 09/06/61), Tientsin and Peking (14/06/61-15/06/61), Hsinkiang (left 18/06/61), Dairen (19/06/61-14/08/61), Calcutta (19/08/61), tour to Benares, Delhi, Agra, Taj, Mahal, Fathabad, Jaipur, Delhi, Amber, Calcutta (21/08/61-28/08/61), Visakhapatnam (29/08/61-04/09/61), Pulau Bukom (11/09/61), Chung Jing (23/09/61-17/10/61), Tsingtao (21/10/61-23/10/61), Shanghai (26/10/61-29/10/61), Hong Kong (01/11/61).

49 *SS SANTAGRANDA* Hong Kong (10/11/61), Pasuo (14/11/61-16/11/61), Shanghai (25/11/61-28/11/61), Pasuo (05/12/61-08/12/61), Whampoa (17/12/61-22/12/61), Hong Kong (23/12/61-09/01/62), Pasuo (11/01/62-22/01/62), Tsingtao (01/02/62-03/02/62), Pasuo (13/02/62-17/02/62), Shanghai (23/02/62-27/02/62), Pasuo (05/03/62-06/03/62), Dairen (13/03/62-22/03/62), Hong Kong (27/03/62-30/03/62). FWE.